New Frontiers in Resilient Aging

Life-Strengths and Well-Being in Late Life

Edited by

Prem S. Fry, Ph.D.
Trinity Western University

and

Corey L. M. Keyes, Ph.D.
Emory University

10675413

CAMBRIDGE UNIVERSITY PRESS
Cambridge, New York, Melbourne, Madrid, Cape Town,
Singapore, São Paulo, Delhi, Mexico City

Cambridge University Press
The Edinburgh Building, Cambridge CB2 8RU, UK

Published in the United States of America by Cambridge University Press, New York

www.cambridge.org
Information on this title: www.cambridge.org/9781107412491

First published 2010
Reprinted 2011
First paperback edition 2012

A catalogue record for this publication is available from the British Library

Library of Congress Cataloguing in Publication Data
New frontiers in resilient aging : life-strengths and well-being in late
   life / [edited by] Prem S. Fry, Corey L. M. Keyes.
      p.   cm.
   Includes index.
   ISBN 978-0-521-50985-5 (hardback)
   1. Aging–Psychological aspects.   2. Cognition in old age.
   I. Fry, Prem S.   II. Keyes, Corey L. M.   III. Title.
   BF724.85.C64N494 2010
   155.67–dc22
   2010021485

ISBN 978-0-521-50985-5 Hardback
ISBN 978-1-107-41249-1 Paperback

1 5 MAR 2017

I warmly dedicate this volume to my family:
David and Shaun Fry, and Sheila Dua,
to the loving memory of my departed sisters
Bhag W. Malik, Shanta Khurana, Dorothy Lipp Harris,
and Santosh Dua,
and to the cherished memory of my parents
and parents-in-law
Kishni and Beharilal Dua and Ann and Johann J. Fry.

Their irrepressible spirit and their resilience have been truly inspirational

Prem S. Fry

Contents

Figures

Tables

Notes on contributors

RICHARD M. ALLMAN, M.D., is the director of the Birmingham/Atlanta VA Geriatric Research, Education and Clinical Center (GRECC) and is the Parrish Endowed Professor of Medicine at the University of Alabama at Birmingham (UAB). He serves as the director of the Center for Aging and the Division of Gerontology, Geriatrics, and Palliative Care at UAB. He also serves as Director of the Deep South Resource Center for Minority Aging Research. In addition, he serves as Co-Director of the John A. Hartford Foundation-funded Southeast Center of Excellence in Geriatric Medicine (SCEGM), a career development and training program for physicians at UAB and Emory University. Dr. Allman's research has been funded by the National Institute on Aging and focuses on understanding the causes of mobility loss and testing new ways of helping older adults maintain or enhance mobility. He also has a long-standing interest in age and ethnic disparities in health, and geriatric care quality improvement, especially as it relates to cardiovascular disease and preventive health services.

JACK J. BAUER, Ph.D., is Associate Professor of Psychology at the University of Dayton and holds the Roesch Chair in Social Sciences. His research addresses narrative self-identity and personality development from adolescence through old age. By integrating qualitative and quantitative methods, his research explores how people interpret and plan their lives in ways that foster happiness, meaning, maturity, and other facets of eudaimonic growth. He is an associate editor of the *Journal of Personality and Social Psychology* and serves on the editorial board of the *Journal of Research in Personality*. He is the co-editor of *Transcending Self-Interest: Psychological Explorations of the Quiet Ego* (2008). Before entering psychology he worked as a newspaper editor in northern Michigan.

C. S. BERGEMAN, Ph.D., is Professor of Psychology and Chair of the Department of Psychology at the University of Notre Dame. She is a lifespan developmental psychologist with research interests in resiliency and aging, behavioral genetics, and the theory–method interface. Her research focuses on investigating patterns of variability and change in physical and psychological health across the lifespan and identifying the genetic and environmental factors that may importantly influence that process.

AUBREY D. N. J. DE GREY, Ph.D., is a biomedical gerontologist based in Cambridge, UK, and is the Chairman and Chief Science Officer of the Methuselah Foundation, a 501(c)(3) non-profit charity dedicated to combating the aging process. He is also Editor-in-Chief of Rejuvenation Research, the world's highest-impact peer-reviewed journal focused on intervention in aging. His research interests encompass the causes of all the accumulating and eventually pathogenic molceular and cellular side-effects of metabolism ("damage") that constitute mammalian aging and the design of interventions to repair and/or obviate that damage. He has developed a possibly comprehensive plan for such repair, termed Strategies for Engineered Negligible Senescence (SENS), which breaks aging down into seven major classes of damage and identifies detailed approaches to addressing each one.

DOMINIQUE L. DEBATS, Ph.D., is a clinical psychologist who has steadfastly tried to integrate academic research and clinical practice. He formerly taught at Groningen University and has authored a series of articles and presentations at international conferences concerned with personal meaning and gerontological research. He is currently working in private practice and as an independent clinical researcher.

HOWARD S. FRIEDMAN, Ph.D., is Distinguished Professor of Psychology at the University of California in Riverside. Friedman is the recipient of the James McKeen Cattell Fellow Award from the Association for Psychological Science (APS) for outstanding career contributions, as well as the Outstanding Contributions to Health Psychology award from the American Psychological Association. His research is focused on psychosocial predictors and mediators of health and longevity. Friedman's recent edited book, *Foundations of Health Psychology* (2007) was named a *CHOICE Magazine* Outstanding Academic Title for 2007.

PREM S. FRY, Ph.D., is Research Professor in the Graduate Psychology Program of Trinity Western University in British Columbia, Canada. Previously she was Professor of Educational Psychology and Chair of the Learning, Development and Research Design Program at the University of Calgary, Alberta. Formerly a Fulbright Scholar, Woodrow Wilson Scholar, and a Killam Scholar, she is currently a fellow in various learned societies, including the Canadian Psychological Association, the American Psychological Association, the Association of Psychological Science, the Gerontological Society of America, and the British Psychological Society. She was recognized by Div. 17 of the American Psychological Association with an award for special research contribution. Her research area is predominantly the psychology of aging, where she has authored a number of research articles and books: *Depression, Stress and Adaptations in the Elderly*; *Psychological Perspectives of Helplessness and Control in the Elderly*; *Memory Enhancement Program Guide*. She is past Editor-in-Chief of *Canadian Journal of Behavioural Science* and of *Ageing International*. She has served on the Board of Directors of the Canadian Psychological Association and the Canadian Association on Gerontology. She is the recipient of several research grants from the Social Sciences and Humanities Research Council of Canada (SSHRC), and currently heads a funded project on "Resilient Aging."

KENNETH J. GERGEN, Ph.D., is a Senior Research Professor at Swarthmore College, and the President of the Board of the Taos Institute, a non-profit, educational organization linking social constructionist theory to societal practices. Among his major publications are *Realities and Relationships: Soundings in Social Construction*, *The Saturated Self*, *An Invitation to Social Construction*, now in its second edition, and *Relational Being: Beyond Self and Community*. For his various contributions, Gergen has received honors from around the world, including fellowships from the Guggenheim Foundation and the Alexander Humboldt Foundation, and honorary degrees in the USA, the Netherlands, and Greece.

MARY GERGEN, Ph.D., is Professor Emerita of Psychology and Women's Studies at Penn State University, Brandywine. She is also a founder and Board member of the Taos Institute. Among her major publications are *Feminist Thought and the Structure of Knowledge*, *Toward a New Psychology of Gender*, and *Feminist Reconstructions in Psychology, Narrative, Gender and Performance*. With her husband, Kenneth Gergen, she has written *Social Construction: Entering the Dialogue*. They edit the *Positive Aging Newsletter* (www.positiveaging.net), an online publication that provides conceptual, empirical, and practical resources for constructing a vision of aging as a period of unparalleled development.

CHRISTOPHER HERTZOG, Ph.D., is a Professor of Psychology at the Georgia Institute of Technology. He received his Ph.D. from the University of Southern California in 1979, where he studied adult development and aging under K. Warner Schaie. He was an assistant professor of Human Development at the Pennsylvania State University from 1981 to 1985 before moving to Georgia Tech. Hertzog has conducted many studies on individual differences in adult cognitive development. In addition to published longitudinal analysis of the Seattle Longitudinal Study data with Schaie, he has conducted longitudinal studies of cognitive aging with Hultsch and Dixon, using data from the Victoria Longitudinal Study. He has done extensive research on metacognition and aging, using questionnaire and experimental methods to evaluate what individuals believe about memory and aging and how they control and regulate their learning and acquisition of new information and skills.

RACHELLE HILL is a Ph.D. graduate student at the University of Minnesota. She works as a research assistant in the Flexible Work and Well-Being Center and is interested in time use as it intersects with work, family, and gender.

DANIELA S. JOPP, Ph.D., is Assistant Professor at the Department of Psychology at Fordham University, Bronx, NY. She received her Ph.D. in psychology from Free University of Berlin, Germany, where she studied under the mentorship of Margret M. and Paul B. Baltes. She also was a member of the Graduate Program "Psychiatry and Psychology of Aging: Psychological Potentials and Limits" at Free University of Berlin. Her research investigates determinants of successful development and aging, including personal resources, strategy use, and self-referent beliefs, with a special focus on resilience (i.e., maintenance of well-being, health, and cognitive functioning) in old and very old adults as well as centenarians.

MARGARET L. KERN is completing her doctoral dissertation at the University of California, Riverside. She received the Dean's Fellowship and Dean's Dissertation Fellowship awards at UCR to support her studies. Her research incorporates a lifespan perspective and advanced quantitative techniques (growth curve analyses, structural equation modeling, survival analyses, and meta-analyses) to explore predictors of older age health and longevity, patterns of adult physical activity, and the interaction of personality and social factors on activity and health across the lifespan.

EVA-MARIE KESSLER, Ph.D., is a lifespan developmental psychologist. She received her Ph.D. in psychology from Jacobs University Bremen in 2006. Afterwards she was a Postdoctoral Fellow at Jacobs before she became a Postdoctoral Researcher at Heidelberg University in 2008. Dr. Kessler is also receiving clinical training, with an emphasis on clinical gerontopsychology. Her research interests include emotional resilience in old age, intergenerational relations and media images of old age. In 2007, she was awarded the Margret-and-Paul-Baltes Dissertation Award of the German Psychological Association. Currently, she holds a Margarete von Wrangell-Habilitation Scholarship supported by the European Social Fund and by the Ministry for Science, Research, and Arts of Baden–Württemberg, Germany.

COREY L. M. KEYES, Ph.D., is Associate Professor in the Department of Sociology, Emory University, Atlanta, GA, and is currently a senior fellow at the Center for the Study of Law and Religion. He was a member of the MacArthur Foundation Research Network on Successful Midlife Development and contributed to the World Health Organization's publication on Mental Health Promotion Worldwide. Keyes has published over sixty articles and chapters and has co-edited five books, including *Well-Being: Positive Development Throughout the Life Course* and *Women and Depression: A Handbook for the Social, Behavioral, and Biomedical Sciences.*

MAURICE MACDONALD, Ph.D., is Professor of Human Development and Family Studies and an affiliate of the Gerontology Program at Iowa State University. He received a Ph.D. in economic demography from the University of Michigan. His research interests include family economics, lifespan development, and the economics of aging. He has been a co-investigator for major surveys on family and individual economic, social, and psychological development, including the Wisconsin Basic Needs Survey, the National Survey of Families and Households, the Wisconsin Longitudinal Study of Health and Aging, and currently the Georgia Centenarians Study.

JENNIFER MARGRETT, Ph.D., is Assistant Professor of Human Development and Family Studies and an affiliate of the Gerontology Program at Iowa State University. Her research program focuses on everyday cognition and functioning throughout adulthood, particularly as affected by contextual factors such as support from social partners.

PETER MARTIN, Ph.D., is director of the Gerontology Program and Professor in the Department of Human Development and Family

Studies at Iowa State University. He received a Ph.D. in Human Development and Family Studies from the Pennsylvania State University and a Doctor of Philosophy in Psychology from the University of Bonn, Germany. His research interests include personality, stress, coping, and well–being. For more than twenty years, Dr. Martin has been involved in studies on centenarians and longevity.

PHYLLIS MOEN, Ph.D., holds the McKnight Presidential Endowed Chair and is Professor of Sociology at the University of Minnesota. She founded the Bronfenbrenner Life Course Center at Cornell University and now co-directs the Flexible Work and Well-Being Center, part of a larger NIH-funded research network initiative. An underlying theme in her scholarship concerns the dynamic intersections between individual life paths and societal institutions. Dr. Moen has published many articles and books on social transformations in age, gender, work, retirement, and families. Her most recent books are *It's About Time: Couples and Careers* (2003) and *The Career Mystique: Cracks in the American Dream* (2005) with Patricia Roehling.

ANTHONY D. ONG, Ph.D., is Assistant Professor of Human Development at Cornell University and Director of the Resilience and Lifespan Development Laboratory. His research focuses on the socioemotional, cognitive, and cultural resources that people draw upon to adapt to stressful life circumstances as they age. A central goal is to understand how certain individuals show maintenance, recovery, or even improvements in adaptive outcomes despite the presence of challenge and adversity.

SUN W. PARK is currently a doctoral student in psychology at Northeastern University. He received an M.A. in psychology from the University of Dayton and a B.A. in philosophy from Yonsei University in Korea. His research focuses on motivations toward personal growth (self-improvement orientation) versus motivations toward merely positive self-evaluations (self-enhancement orientation) – and how these motivations relate to well-being and personality development. Specifically, he plans to investigate the roles of accurate versus over-rated self-perceptions in the two orientations.

LEONARD W. POON, Ph.D., is University of Georgia Distinguished Research Professor. He is also a Professor of Public Health and Psychology, Director of the Institute of Gerontology and Georgia Geriatric Education Center. He has been involved as the Principal Investigator of the Georgia Centenarian Study since 1988. His research interests include normative and pathological changes of cognition with age, clinical memory assessment especially for early stages of dementia, longevity, survival, and successful adaptation with aging.

JOHN W. ROWE, M.D., is a Professor in the Department of Health Policy and Management at the Columbia University Mailman School of Public Health. Previously, from 2000 to late 2006, Dr. Rowe served as Chairman and CEO of Aetna, Inc., and prior to his tenure at Aetna, he served as President and Chief Executive Officer of Mount Sinai NYU Health. Prior to the Mount Sinai–NYU Health merger, Dr. Rowe was President of the Mount Sinai Hospital and the Mount Sinai School of Medicine in New York City from 1988 to 1998. In addition to his tenure at Mount Sinai, Dr. Rowe was Professor of Medicine and the founding Director of the Division on Aging at the Harvard Medical School, as well as Chief of Gerontology at Boston's Beth Israel Hospital. He has authored over two hundred scientific publications, currently leads the MacArthur Foundation's Network on An Aging Society, and chairs the Institute of Medicine's Committee on the Future Health Care Workforce for Older Americans. Dr. Rowe was elected a fellow of the American Academy of Arts and Sciences, is a member of the Institute of Medicine of the National Academy of Arts and Sciences, serves on the Board of Trustees of the Rockefeller Foundation and is Chairman of the Board of Trustees at the Marine Biological Laboratory in Woods Hole, Massachusetts, and is a former member of the Medicare Payment Advisory Commission (MedPAC).

PATRICIA SAWYER, Ph.D., is Associate Professor of Medicine in the Social and Behavioral Sciences Section of the Division of Gerontology, Geriatrics, and Palliative Care at the University of Alabama at Birmingham. She also serves as Assistant Director of the Center for Aging and Director of UAB's Gerontology Education Program, and has been Co-Principal Investigator and Program Director for the NIA funded UAB Study of Aging, a longitudinal study of community–dwelling older adults. Her research interests include ethnic disparities in health, gerontology, and mobility in older adults.

URSULA M. STAUDINGER, Ph.D., is Professor of Psychology, Dean of the Jacobs Center on Lifelong Learning and Institutional Development and Vice President of the Jacobs University Bremen. Among her research interests are lifespan development of self and personality, the plasticity of aging, and adult development in the work context. Ursula M. Staudinger is Vice President of the National Academy of Sciences, Leopoldina, President of the German Psychological Association, a Fellow of the American Psychological Association, and a Member of the Heidelberg Academy of Sciences.

STEPHEN SWEET, Ph.D., is Associate Professor of Sociology at Ithaca College and was formerly the associate director of the Cornell Work and Family Careers Institute. He has published widely on work–family concerns and curriculum development. His most recent books are *Changing Contours of Work* (2008), *The Work and Family Handbook: Interdisciplinary Perspectives, Methods and Approaches* (2005), and *Data Analysis with SPSS: A First Course in Applied Statistics* (2008, 2003, 1998).

EDWARD TAUB, Ph.D., is University Professor in the Department of Psychology and Director of the CI Therapy Research Group and Taub Training Clinic at UAB. He received his doctoral degree from New York University in 1970. In his doctoral studies, he began an extended program of basic research on limb use after deafferentation in monkeys that overthrew Sherrington's reflex theory of motor control. At UAB, he directed the translation of this basic research into a family of behaviorally based rehabilitation treatments for enhancing recovery after brain injury known as CI therapy. At the same time, he, along with colleagues from Germany and elsewhere, made seminal contributions to the neuroscience literature overthrowing the view that the adult brain in humans is static. Dr. Taub's work has been recognized by six national society awards, including the Distinguished Scientific Award for the Applications of Psychology from the American Psychological Association and the William James Fellow Award from the American Psychological Society.

GITENDRA USWATTE, Ph.D., received his doctorate in clinical health psychology from the University of Alabama at Birmingham (UAB) in 2001 and is currently Associate Professor of Psychology and Associate Director of the CI Therapy Research Group there. He obtained his graduate training in the laboratory of Edward Taub, Ph.D., and has been active in the development and evaluation of Constraint-Induced Movement therapy, also known as CI therapy, since 1994. He was co-principal investigator of the UAB components of the EXCITE Trial, which is a multisite clinical trial of CI therapy for individuals with subacute stroke. Most recently, he has been awarded grants from NIDRR to test an expanded form of CI therapy for individuals with plegic hands and NIH to test and develop a method for administering CI therapy via telerehabilitation. In 2008, he was honored with the Mitchell Rosenthal Early Career Research Award from the Division of Rehabilitation Psychology in the American Psychological Association.

Foreword

John W. Rowe

Resilience, as defined by Fry and Keyes, the respected editors of this timely volume, "encompasses normal and exceptional development in the face of risk and adversity, recovery, plasticity and regenerative capacity and the ability to maintain function in the face of disability or physical disease." In short, the capacity to hang tough and bounce back when, inevitably, something bad happens.

Resilience is a hot topic. Interest is reflected by the rapidly growing multidisciplinary literature reviewed in this book's chapters, the attention this topic received in 2009 at the Keck Futures Initiative of the National Academy of Sciences, which was entitled "Future of the Human Healthspan" and in the theme of the 2008 annual meeting of the Gerontological Society of America, "Resilience in an Aging Society: Risks and Opportunities." In addition, interest in the capacity of individuals to respond to adversity is inevitably spiking as the current economic downturn poses major stress and dislocation for many.

Some of this current interest can be traced to the central importance of resilience in the interdisciplinary formulation of successful aging offered by the MacArthur Foundation Research Network on Successful Aging in the late 1980s and early 1990s. In that view, successful aging included three core elements: avoidance of disease and disability; maintenance of physical and cognitive function; and engagement in society. Resilience was seen as central to the first two elements and strengthened by the third.

As more and more scholars peel the onion of resilience, multiple dimensions are revealed. Thus, this volume includes scholarly summaries ranging across a wide variety of areas from social and behavioral issues to cognition, health status, and economic factors. As with Successful Aging, analysis of the core determinants of resilience repeatedly underscores the importance of mastery and self-esteem, social support, and the presence of meaningful roles for older persons, whether they are defined in the workforce or via civic engagement.

While the internal (person-specific) factors that influence resilience are being intensively studied, more attention can be productively applied to the external or societal factors. As the dramatic increases in active life-expectancy of the last century intersect with the aging of the baby boom generation, America is becoming an aging society. The core institutions of that society are not designed to effectively serve the demands that come with a dramatically and permanently altered age structure of our population.

If we are to emerge as a productive and equitable aging society we must recalibrate these key institutions, including the workforce, retirement, education, leisure, housing, transportation, and many others to serve better the needs of individuals. These societal elements are important determinants of the resilience of individuals in an aging society.

Time is short for the development of a proper infrastructure in time for the arrival of our aging society in 2030. We are well aware that societal lag, the resistance of society to evolve promptly in response to society's needs, will make this a difficult challenge.

It is important to understand that aging is a global rather than a domestic issue. Other developed countries, such as in Western Europe and Japan, have aged well ahead of the USA and have been implementing a variety of social policies for a couple of decades in order to cope with the challenges and opportunities they face. These countries have learned some valuable lessons from a variety of social 'experiments' and continue to evolve their approaches in attempts to enhance the resilience of their communities. In addition, these countries may offer valuable lessons for the USA. While differences in culture and the structure of many institutions, including the workforce, old age benefits, and health care, may limit the relevance of the experiences in these nations to our own situation, their experiences deserve careful study.

In recognition of the critical importance of these issues, the MacArthur Foundation has recently established a Research Network on an Aging Society to focus on the development of policies to deal with the challenges and opportunities that accompany the demographic transition in the USA and elsewhere. This volume will serve as an invaluable resource for the Network and other scholars as they engage the issue of resilience at the societal level.

Acknowledgments

The editors greatly appreciate the contribution of the authors of the chapters, and feel privileged to have worked closely with each one of them. All are extremely busy and committed individuals; we thank them for their cooperation in meeting deadlines for submission, and for so graciously making the suggested revisions.

Additionally, the editors are indebted to former Commissioning Editor Andrew Peart, and Editors Hetty Reid and Carrie Parkinson at Cambridge University Press, UK, for their confidence in this project, for their encouragement, and for much practical help and advice. The assistance of Sarah Price, Project Manager at Out of House Publishing Solutions Ltd, and Copy-Editor Alison Walker, was invaluable and much appreciated. Overall, it has been a privilege to publish this volume with Cambridge University Press.

Preparation of this volume was supported in part by a Standard Senior Scholars Research Grant (P. S. Fry, File No. 410–2004-0152) awarded to P. S. Fry by the Social Sciences and Humanities Research Council of Canada (SSHRC). Prem Fry extends her grateful thanks to Linda Lord for her secretarial assistance.

Introduction

Prem S. Fry and Corey L. M. Keyes

This volume addresses the topic of "new frontiers in resilient aging," which is of ever-increasing significance in current gerontological and geriatric discourse and research. The topic is not only very complex, but has enormous scope and breadth, encompassing a number of psychosocial and biological models of aging, theoretical formulations, definitions, and dimensions of resilience, and the core determinants of resilience that lay the foundations for discourse and research. Resilience as a psychological construct emerged from the study of children and youth at risk, and discourse on resilience, adaptation, and healthy longevity has focused mainly on younger adults, perhaps because of a misconception that resilience capacities diminish rapidly and perhaps irreversibly after young adulthood. Currently, increased life-expectancy without the compression of morbidity and vulnerability, together with the rising costs of healthcare, has highlighted the need for greater attention to the capacity for resilience throughout adulthood and in late life.

More recently, factors that influence resilience in later life are being studied more extensively. Within the last few years the theme of resilience in an aging society has been featured prominently in a number of national and international conferences and is the subject of intensive study in institutes of health sciences, mental health, and gerontology. This confluence of events suggests that the time is ripe to highlight some of the more recent and important research and writing on the topic of resilience in later life, and to bring the strands of this rapidly emerging scholarship together to showcase the movement toward promoting healthier aging.

This volume includes representative chapters of multidisciplinary discourse and research by a number of knowledgeable and highly respected scholars who have an active interest in studying the capacity of older adults to respond to and overcome adversity and age-related losses in affective, cognitive, and social domains of function. Resilience in human functioning is perhaps most remarkable when evident in the contexts of life challenges and adversity in old age. In this volume we have included scholarly contributions that address issues of cognitive, social, and emotional resilience, and seek to identify some of the core elements and determinants of resilience in the face of threatened or actual losses in cognition, health status, and well-being with increasing age. We present chapters that explore broad perspectives of resilience that take into account some of the interactive dynamics, processes, and mechanisms contributing to growth and positive change, and to thriving mental and physical health and function in late life, especially in the face of disability and physical decline. According to current theorizing, thriving health implies not merely the absence of disease, but rather older adults' intensive search for positive trajectories and sources of internal strengths, and older adults' conscious pursuit of ways to attain improved levels of emotional, social, and cognitive functioning. While the idea of resilience and the awareness of potentials for growth and thriving in old age is not new, the evidence for or against it is very limited. Past formulations of resilience in the context of aging have treated it primarily as adaptive and homeostatic, emphasizing the human ability to cope with and recover from age-related losses, but only to the extent of restoring equilibrium in behavioral, cognitive, and mental-emotional functioning. In the earlier definitions of resilience the focus has been more on "coping" and "adjusting" and less on enhancing the overall health and functioning of older adults. Observant readers of the chapters included in this volume will note the paradigm shift toward looking at resilience and aging from a somewhat more positive and broadened perspective that expands the conception of resilience as normal development in the face of adversity to include facets such as recovery, plasticity, regenerative capacity, maintenance of health function (e.g., mobility) in the face of disability or disease, and access to psychosocial and technological-ecological resources that may facilitate maintenance and improvement of physical and emotional health with age.

The volume includes chapters that expand on the multidimensional aspects of internal and external sources of life-strengths and the related psychosocial resources that are the springboards of resilience in later life. Together, the thirteen chapters in this volume reveal that, throughout adulthood, the capacity and potential for growth and new learning, positive emotions, thriving mental health and meaning in life, openness to experience, and expanded life-space add to the prospects for resilience as defined by maintenance and enhancement of functioning in later life.

The contributing authors in the volume are leading researchers from a variety of disciplines ranging from psychology (clinical, social-personality, psychology of aging, and health psychology), sociology, and biogerontology to advocacy proponents of quality of life and the human rights of older adults. The array of theoretical perspectives on resilient aging presented by the contributing authors is both exciting and challenging. This volume represents a small but important beginning of an attempt to synthesize the efforts of a few of the leading theorists, researchers and clinicians who have been working on the topic of resilient aging, each from their own perspective and from their own unique conceptual framework of what the construct of resilience means to them.

Although the authors themselves have included abstracts of their chapters, we take this opportunity to present an overview of the chapters to highlight aspects of each chapter that we consider to be of particular interest.

Chapter 1. (Fry and Debats) "Sources of human life-strengths, resilience, and health"

Based on an extensive review of the literature on aging, Fry and Debats present a conceptual framework and discourse on individuals' perceptions of their most valued sources of life-strengths from the psychological perspectives of existential-humanistic theory and social-cognitive theory. They examine elements that bridge across these two perspectives and identify sets of psychosocial resources that are seen to facilitate resilience from both perspectives, and are also valued within a broad historical-cultural framework. They discuss the powerful role of both self-efficacy and control beliefs (social-cognitive orientation) and the role of personal meaning for life and religious-spiritual beliefs (existential-humanistic orientation) in maintaining and enhancing resilient functioning. In their view, resilient aging implies that in addition to confronting challenges that are already occurring with advancing age, individuals need to make effective use of their existing cognitive competencies and decision-making skills to anticipate future challenges. Resilient aging implies the need for individuals to strike a healthy balance between accumulating and preserving valued sources of life-strengths and related psychosocial resources for the future, and using valuable resources to deal with important needs in the present. From the perspective of resilient aging, they conclude that identified sources of life-strengths are critical to the development and maintenance of older adults' identity, and that some individuals function more optimally than others because they successfully identify for themselves their most valued sources of life-strengths, their meaning for life, their beliefs about control and mastery, and because they are more proactive in selecting and mobilizing psychosocial resources consistent with their overall belief systems.

Chapter 2. (Bauer and Park) "Growth is not just for the young: growth narratives, eudaimonic resilience, and the aging self"

These authors coherently and diligently articulate a number of claims about resilience and the aging self. They integrate their own research data and reinterpret other published data to demonstrate the validity of their claims. As implicit in the title of the paper, Bauer and Park's major contention is that the slogan "growth is for the young, loss is for the old" ignores important empirical findings and oversimplifies and distorts the mindsets of older adults, and their personal concerns. They present convincing arguments to back up their claim that growth is a normative, often central concern in older adults' personal goals and that, like younger adults, older adults are at least as concerned with gain and growth as they are with loss. Older adults focus on growth not only in their personal goals but also in their autobiographical memories. Bauer and Park present a number of narratives from their research dialogues to distinguish between "growth" narratives and other narratives that focus on security, maintenance, and mere acquisition of pleasure in order to demonstrate that contrary to the common perception, growth is a prominent feature of the aging, narrative self. They conclude that older adults' heightened capacity for meaning-making, and possibly growth-oriented meaning-making, may well facilitate and enhance eudaimonic resilience that combines regulation of both affect and meaning, as contrasted with hedonistic resilience that involves the regulation of affect only.

Chapter 3. (de Grey) "Physical resilience and aging: correcting the Tithonus error and the crème brûlée error"

The author discusses the physiological basis for the confidence shared by many biogerontologists that the only way we will ever substantially extend the human lifespan is by extending people's healthy lifespan. de Grey directs attention to the "Tithonus error," which encapsulates the idea that combating aging will be done by developing ever-better geriatrics, capable of keeping people alive for longer and longer, but in a frail state. de Grey also directs attention to the "crème brûlée" error that encapsulates the idea that we can only avoid the miseries of premature death and extended frailty by avoiding many of the things that make life worth living. He points out that neither of these approaches to extending the lifespan is worthwhile and acceptable to biogerontologists. In de Grey's opinion, the best way to achieve a substantial extension of the life of a human body, in fully active, healthy, youthful condition, is to undertake periodic thorough repair of the cellular and molecular damage that occurs naturally with increasing age. Repair and maintenance at that level could probably be achieved using technologies already being developed on the basis of stem cells, tissue engineering, and gene therapy. From a general perspective, de Grey's ideas make perfect sense: organ transplants and joint replacements are by now common and generally accepted, so repair technologies operating at the more refined level of cells may become available before long. de Grey's views have important implications for the upkeep of resilience in that if it were not for the resistance of society to evolve more promptly in response to the needs of older adults, the interventions he suggests could alter the future lives of many individuals at risk for frailty.

Chapter 4. (Uswatte and Taub) "You can teach an old dog new tricks: harnessing neuroplasticity after brain injury in older adults"

The authors discuss the phenomenon of neuroplasticity after damage to the central nervous system (CNS), as demonstrated in animal and human experiments. Research on Constraint-Induced Movement therapy or CI therapy, which is a behaviorally based approach to physical rehabilitation, is the major focus of this chapter. This body of work, among other contributions, overthrows the reigning clinical wisdom that stroke survivors more than 1-year post-event can not benefit from additional physical rehabilitation. It also provides the first evidence that physical rehabilitation can produce large improvements in real-world arm function, and can change CNS organization and structure. It has been known for some time that parts of the brain can take over the function of damaged regions. This work shows how to encourage the reassignment process. The method involves considerable time and effort, but the results are remarkable, and hold great promise for further development. The results provide evidence for a neurophysiological basis for continued plasticity in behavior among older adults. The research findings are indeed most heartening and encouraging with respect to the prospects for interventions, mechanisms and processes now accessible for enhancing plasticity and increasing physical and perhaps emotional resilience as well.

Chapter 5. (Hertzog and Jopp) "Resilience in the face of cognitive aging: experience, adaptation, and compensation"

The authors articulate a lifespan developmental perspective on gains and losses in cognitive functioning during adulthood. Despite measurable age-related cognitive decline, older adults nevertheless function effectively in everyday life, and even in cognitively demanding situations. The authors contend that because individuals by and large grow and age in self-selected contexts, they can in later life successfully use expertise and knowledge, practiced routines of behavior, and reliance on sources of support in their environment to maximize their functional capacity. The major argument the authors present has vast appeal: while factors such as genetics and neuronal processes play a role in cognition, cognitive function also depends strongly on the person's efforts to maintain or enhance cognitive functioning. Failing memory can be corrected to some extent by learning techniques for remembering, and by using notes instead of relying on memory. Metacognitive self-regulation and an active lifestyle can be important means for older adults to preserve cognitive capacity and to effectively compensate for declines in cognitive mechanisms as they occur. Thus from Hertzog and Jopp's perspective, positive aging results in cognitive resilience, which helps in maintaining autonomy and effective functioning for extended periods. Attitudes, lifestyle practices, and cognition can in that sense work in a fruitful symbiosis. As Hertzog and Jopp so cogently conclude, practising self-regulation, and keeping mentally and physically active, will not only improve functioning but increase confidence and a sense of control, and thereby help to improve functioning further, toward the best that can be achieved with declines in cognitive mechanisms.

Chapter 6. (Kern and Friedman) "Why do some people thrive while others succumb to disease and stagnation? Personality, social relations, and resilience"

The authors present a discourse on the role that personality plays in resilience across the lifespan, and also with respect to its role in late life. The authors are to be commended on the wide scope of their investigation. Of immediate interest is their uniquely broadened concept of personality which according to them captures a combination of genetic, familial, social, and cultural elements. Another point of keen interest and of relevance is their concept of resilience which they define as a dynamic process that unfolds across the life-course and necessarily involves both the individual's trajectory and his or her current psychosocial context. In particular, the authors highlight findings from their work with the Terman Life Cycle Study, the longest longitudinal study conducted to date, to demonstrate how core aspects of the individuals' personalities impact on how resiliently and positively they react to life's challenges, and what core elements of personality contribute to an individual's resilient functioning. Against the background of their longitudinal findings the authors trace the links between personality and a number of life-span processes, including, for example, the links between personality and resilience and early life experiences, health, longevity, and social relations. They sum up their conclusions regarding the core elements of resilience by noting that resilience is not a personality trait but rather an emergent attribute – a quality that appears with the appropriate combination of predispositions, behaviors, and socio-environmental circumstances such as divorce, marital status, social interactions, and career success, to mention a few factors influencing resilient response. Further, psychological and physical resilience are not necessarily separate entities, but are often two sides of the same coin. As Kern and Friedman note, what differentiates individuals who thrive from those who succumb to disease and stagnation is not merely their toughness or ability to recover quickly from challenge or misfortune, but rather their flexibility and adaptability in reacting to stress.

Chapter 7. (Fry and Debats) "Psychosocial resources as predictors of resilience and healthy longevity of older widows"

In this chapter, Fry and Debats report the findings of their longitudinal study on predictors of longevity/mortality of older widows. The major hypothesis that guided the study is that following spousal loss the possession of certain psychosocial resources is a key protective factor helping to enhance stress resistance and thereby reduce the risk of mortality. Although a number of previous longitudinal studies of all-cause mortality among older adults have identified several socio-demographic factors, health status factors, and personality factors that have reduced or increased the risk of mortality, the links between resilience, longevity, and psychosocial resources have not been studied as extensively. In the research reported in this chapter, Fry and Debats view resilience to be a developmental process. The 6.5-year longitudinal study of 385 older widows assessed the influence of psychosocial resource factors on their resilience and healthy longevity. Study participants were assessed at baseline on predictor measures of psychosocial resources, health-related self-reports, and psychological traits of challenge, commitment, and control. A Cox regression analysis of predictor variables was used to examine the mortality risk related to baseline measures of psychosocial resources and psychological trait measures. Those widows who survived longer had higher scores on spiritual resources, and on resources of family stability, social engagement, and commitment to life tasks. In contrast, high scores on control and challenge traits had an unexpected negative effect on longevity. The findings confirm that psychosocial resource factors have a significant contribution to make to resilient functioning and longevity, and also that healthy aging and longevity are consequential outcomes that can serve as indicators of personal resilience.

Chapter 8. (Martin, MacDonald, Margrett, and Poon) "Resilience and longevity: expert survivorship of centenarians"

In this chapter the authors present their research findings on three important aspects of resilience (personality, intellectual functioning, and economic and social support resources) that may contribute to the expert survivorship or longevity of centenarians. The researchers seek to discover how people come to possess the resilience characteristics required to achieve very long life, whether they are inherent in the person from birth, or whether the person acquires them through life experiences, and through what psychosocial pathways resilient people become long-lived individuals. A further question is what heritable and environmental influences combine to inculcate resilience among the oldest-old. The study design is unique in that the authors take both a person-centered approach and a variable-centered approach to identifying the elements of resilience and the psychosocial resources that contribute to longevity. The findings the authors report are a synthesis, integration, and consolidation of the results derived from the perspective of three study models. In phase 1 the predictors in this model measure the direct and indirect impact of family longevity, environmental support, individual characteristics, coping abilities and styles, and nutrition on physical health, mental health, and life satisfaction. In phase 2 the question of interest is what specific resilience factors contribute to a continual survival that exceeds all normal expectations. Phase 3 is a population-based study examining both biomedical (genetics, neuropathology, blood chemistry, nutrition, health) and psychosocial elements (neuropsychology, adaptation, resources) that contribute to the exceptional longevity. Additionally, the study addresses psychosocial factors that contribute to differences in the mental health functioning, coping and adaptation of some centenarians compared to others living in similar contexts. Among the admirable features of the investigation are the ingenuity of its design, its broad scope, and its effectiveness in demonstrating that resilience is a developmental process, which can contribute to an exceptionally long period of survival.

Chapter 9. (Ong and Bergeman) "The socioemotional basis of resilience in later life"

In this chapter Ong and Bergeman describe select parts of their ongoing program of research studies on the nature of emotional resilience. Although their program of research involves multiple methods of data collection (i.e., longitudinal, diary, life-history interviews), in this chapter they highlight findings derived from the daily diary process component of their work, the primary goal of which is to investigate the daily context in which resilience arises in response to challenge. The authors' major contention is that the daily process approach has a distinct advantage over other approaches they have previously used in that it allows the researcher to conduct intensive, day-to-day monitoring of reported stresses. In addition to providing a framework in which to study inherently intra-individual (within-person) questions, diary methods allow individuals to report their behavior and experiences within a short time after they occurred, over the range of potentially stressful circumstances encountered in everyday life, thereby facilitating ecologically valid research. Using a daily process approach to data collection (i.e., diary methods) the authors examine how the nature of stressors, the social context, and the affective experiences of the individuals involved can affect the process of resilience in adulthood. They conclude from their series of daily process studies that positive emotions strengthen individuals' stress resistance, facilitate recovery from stress, and broaden individuals' attention and thinking. Their findings also provide the first concrete empirical evidence of the link between individuals' level of social connectedness and their biological resilience (i.e., diminished cardiovascular reactivity and more rapid recovery following negative emotional arousal) confirming that having quality social ties contributes to resilience in the face of life challenges. The results of their research on bereavement processes (indicating that the trajectory of emotion regulation following conjugal loss resembled a damped linear oscillator) provide researchers with initial empirical "guideposts" for understanding the process by which widows typically adjust to conjugal loss. Taken together, the authors' research findings add substantially to the generality of extant empirical work on positive emotions. A primary finding emerging from the research is that a significant proportion of older adults are somehow able to experience positive emotions, even in the midst of overwhelming loss. Despite variation in the types of stressors experienced, the results across multiple studies that the authors have conducted are remarkably consistent: positive emotions have demonstrably beneficial effects when present during times of stress.

Chapter 10. (Kessler and Staudinger) "Emotional resilience and beyond: a synthesis of findings from lifespan psychology and psychopathology"

The authors review and analyze empirical studies of emotional resilience, including several from their own extensive program of research. They looked for evidence of changes in emotional resilience with age, from the perspectives of normal successful aging as indicated by emotional well-being and emotional maturity, and from the psychopathological perspective as indicated by the frequency of depressive disorders. These are quantities rarely studied in combination, and give some illuminating new insights.

It is encouraging that the authors confirm that aging individuals typically have great emotional resilience; indeed emotional resilience tends to increase with age, except for a decline in very old age. The frequency of depressive disorders is largely constant with age until very old age, implying the ability of older adults to withstand effectively the losses and disabilities of aging, reaching the limits of their resilience only in very old age. Contrary to what older people might like to believe, emotional maturity ceases to increase beyond early adulthood, and even decreases in extreme old age. Emotional maturity, according to the authors, includes complexity of emotion-regulation, and is not the same as emotional resilience, though some researchers have not made a clear distinction. Older people who believe they are wiser now than when they were young may be disappointed to learn that a measure of personal wisdom shows no increase with age.

Positive and negative affect are often used as indicators of emotional resilience. The authors conclude that negative affect decreases with age, helping to maintain emotional resilience until advanced age, when negative affect increases. The results for positive affect are however mixed, possibly because little attention has been paid to the level of arousal. Overall, positive affect tends to decrease in advanced old age. It is noteworthy that the authors have devised ways of assessing several sub-categories of emotional state that have already helped to dissect components of emotional resilience which will give further insight into what is a very complex phenomenon. The thoughtful interpretations that the authors provide of their findings are very insightful.

The authors point out that information about the emotional resilience of the very old is scarce, although the number of very old people is increasing quite rapidly. Getting accurate information about the emotional state of very old people is challenging when they are somewhat disabled and/or cognitively impaired, yet such information is urgently needed so that such people can be assessed accurately and receive appropriate care.

Chapter 11. (Moen, Sweet, and Hill) "Risk, resilience, and life-course fit: older couples' encores following job loss"

In this chapter Moen, Sweet, and Hill examine conditions and processes that promote resilience in older couples who have been forced out of career jobs long before they expected to retire, or who are threatened with job loss. The research addresses a number of questions including: what specific factors may contribute to the resilience of men and women faced with the crisis of career job loss; what adaptive strategies they employ in order to combat the stress; and what changes, if any, are indicated in the capacities and ability of individuals to respond productively to the stressful challenge of job loss in the most vulnerable years of their lives. In order to inquire into the question of what "encores" the individuals are seeking in their future plans the researchers present a program of research that allows for a study of both the "ecology of life course" and "stress-resistance process." First, they describe the general theoretical model of risk, resilience, and life-course fit. Then drawing on qualitative data, they provide excerpts from interviews that give excellent insightful information about adaptive steps and strategies that the laid-off older couples are using or have used in order to protect their own and family members' physical and mental well-being, and to promote a resilient life-course fit. These adaptive strategies include the following: (a) changing the situation; (b) redefining the situation; (c) altering relationships; and (d) managing rising strains and tensions. Consistent with their hypotheses, the researchers identified three key resources conducive to the older couples' resilient encore of fit: *control* or mastery over one's life, *social connections* and support, and making a *meaningful contribution* (through paid work, civic engagement, or family work). These resources may be seen to be personal markers of their resilience under conditions of insecurity and job dislocation.

It is interesting to note that the questions that the researchers address in their chapter are most topical. It is clear that interest in the capacity of individuals to respond to an adversity of this nature has recently spiked as a consequence of the current economic downturn that has forced substantial numbers of older men and women out of work.

Chapter 12. (Sawyer and Allman) "Resilience in mobility in the context of chronic disease and aging: cross-sectional and prospective findings from the UAB Study of Aging"

In this chapter Sawyer and Allman present empirical findings from their cross-sectional and longitudinal studies and provide a renewed perspective on the meaning of life-space mobility. Their conceptual framework allows for an in-depth examination of factors that contribute to the maintenance and enhancement of life-space mobility among community-dwelling older adults. A major strength of their conceptual model is that it broadens the definition of life-space mobility to include a measure of how far, how often, and how independently older individuals move, or are able to move, in their geographically defined environments. The assessment of life-space mobility thereby provides not merely a measure of the mobility associated with physical disability but is a measure of mobility across the full continuum of function observed among community-dwelling older adults who may have differing levels of disability. Their procedure for assessing life-space mobility also reflects the level of the individual's participation in society, based on the degree to which movement within one's environment is required in order for the individual to engage in social activities. The study of life-space mobility also includes a study of the psychosocial and ecological factors that contribute to the long-term maintenance of older adults' participation in a number of social activities despite the presence of disability, age-associated physiological changes, disease, and chronic health conditions. In this sense, the measure of life-space mobility translates to a measure of older adults' perceived sense of independence in various domains of their functioning. In presenting their findings, Sawyer and Allman underscore the need for identifying and understanding the factors associated with the maintenance of mobility among community-dwelling older adults. They also ask for a fuller understanding of the mechanisms and resources, such as social and emotional support, economic support, and easy access to other psychosocial resources that may contribute to strengthening older adults' resilience in important functional domains. In their view, maintenance of mobility is an important component of quality of life. Thus identification of factors that contribute to resilience is an important consideration for future interventions that would further facilitate older adults' engagement in society. As Sawyer and Allman observe, multiple factors (other than performance) may be included in determining the scope of individual life-space, including environmental characteristics, socioeconomic and emotional resources.

Chapter 13. (K. Gergen and M. Gergen) "Positive aging: resilience and reconstruction"

Gergen and Gergen point out the many negative stereotypes of aging in Western society, and insist that is it not necessary, and indeed not desirable, for aging people to accept the typical view of aging as a time of deterioration and losses. They argue that during all stages of life one constructs one's own life-view, usually paying particular attention to the positive aspects. They encourage older people to continue the reconstruction and re-evaluation process in later life, and to consider the occurrence of potentially negative events such as loss of friends or increasing disability as providing the opportunity for a positive change by meeting a challenge. The ability to reinterpret events in this way increases one's capacity for resilient aging. The Gergens seem to have followed their own advice very successfully, and the tone of the chapter is uplifting. They follow their own suggestion that one should seek the counsel of other older people in learning how to see the positive side of negative events, and quote many inspiring examples of how some people can see the positive aspects of traumatic events, taken from participants in their workshops on positive aging.

Parallel paradigms

After reading the highlights of the various chapters included in this volume, the astute reader will notice that parallel paradigms have been developed by each author in isolation, and with little cross-referencing. We suggest that the diversity of ideas represented in the various chapters calls for rigorous debate and creative synthesis among the contributing authors themselves and among students, researchers, and practitioners, whose partnership is necessary for the further advancement of our knowledge of resilient aging. Although the idea of growth and thriving in old age is not new, and while some progress has been made in research and discourse to illuminate at least a few of the intricate and complex underlying processes in resilience and resilient functioning in later life, there are still numerous unresolved issues challenging researchers to move toward reaching consensus on the essential determinants. It is hoped that the readings in this volume will help to promote a somewhat clearer integration and consolidation of some of the elemental factors of resilience (risk factors, protective factors, preventive factors, enabling factors, and stimulating factors that are delineated in various chapters) and how these factors individually and collectively facilitate the attainment of optimal physical and mental health in the later years. Our hope is that this volume will stimulate further research and discourse to expand the horizons of our understanding of how greater numbers of individuals may live resilient, healthy, fulfilling, and longer lives.

1   Sources of human life-strengths, resilience, and health

Prem S. Fry and Dominique L. Debats

Abstract

The recent gerontological literature confirms that life-strengths are critical to the development of older adults' identity. Based on a review of the literature on aging, we present a conceptual framework and discourse on individuals' perceptions of their most valued sources of life-strengths from the psychological perspectives of existential-humanistic theory and social-cognitive theory. Viewed from an existential-humanistic perspective, individuals' major sources of life-strengths are rooted in individuals' definitions of personal meaning and purpose for life, in their religious faith and spiritual values and beliefs. From the perspective of social-cognitive theory, individuals' major sources of life-strengths derive largely from their self-efficacy and control beliefs. We examine elements that bridge across these two perspectives and we identify sets of psychosocial resources that are seen to facilitate resilience from both perspectives, and are also valued within a broad historical-cultural framework. We conclude that some individuals function more optimally than others because they have more successfully identified their most valued sources of life-strengths and psychosocial resources consistent with their belief system.

Introduction

What do we know about the sources of life-strengths that contribute to resilient aging and well-being of older adults? The answer is surprisingly little, compared with what we know about mental illness, dysfunction, and disorder in later adulthood. To date, the topic of human strengths and their determinants has been understudied. A lot is known about the genesis of depression, interpersonal stress, cognitive impairment, and physical decline in late-life functioning. Although we have some under-standing of the vulnerabilities that overtake us with advancing age and how individuals struggle to compensate for them, much remains to be learned about the origins and sources of life-strengths that nourish older adults' motivations and their striving for health, life satisfaction, and optimal functioning. Relatively little is known about the sources of life-strengths and the related psychosocial resources that nurture the capacity for human resilience, and that lead some older adults to continue to strive, thrive, and flourish in the face of numerous challenges, while others languish and become increasingly vulnerable to stress and at risk of declining mental health. Similarly, little is known about the social-historical and cultural influences on resilience that may account for some societies and cultures moving forward with impressive efficiency, empowerment, and influence.

Why study life-strengths?

The resurgence of interest in the positive psychology of aging (Seligman and Csikszentmihalyi, 2000) provides an impetus to consider what is known and conjectured about the sources of human life-strengths, especially as they apply to resilient aging. Gerontologists (e.g., Aspinwall and Staudinger 2003; Brandtstädter, Wentura, and Rothermund, 1999; Kivnick, 1998) concur that life-strengths are critical to the development of older adults' identity, and contribute significantly to their perceptions of empowerment and positive outlook. The recent gerontological literature accentuates the need to further explore sources of life-strengths.

In order to meet the newer challenges of aging in the *twenty-first* century, the present generation of older adults, more than previous generations, is striving to maximize internal and external resources and to explore new sources of life-strengths. What older adults are increasingly experiencing is the need to evaluate and take stock of their reservoir of social, emotional, and cognitive strengths that may assist them in facing present and future challenges, crises, and struggles. There is increasing evidence that older adults are more strongly motivated than ever before to transcend negative circumstances and to accentuate the positives in life and to age successfully. Growing numbers of older adults are engaged in evaluating their personal life-strengths in terms of personal assets, personal resources, and internal protective mechanisms that may help to keep them resilient in the face of stress and the threatened decline in physical and cognitive capacities (see Fry, 2000a, 2000b, 2001a, 2001b). Overall, the recent gerontological literature (e.g., Aspinwall and Staudinger, 2003; Keyes and Haidt, 2003; Kivnick, 1998; Seligman and Csikszentmihalyi, 2000; Smyer and Quall, 1999) draws specific attention to older adults' unexplored potential for strength and vitality and their search for expanding the self in order to turn adversity to advantage.

There is also the growing realization among older adults themselves that factors conducive to strengthening their internal resources are inextricably tied in with resources outside the person (e.g., social support resources and interpersonal network resources) and that the external resources are equally essential to the long-term maintenance of physical health and psychological well-being (Fernández-Ballesteros, 2003; Kivnick, 1998; Ryff and Singer, 2000). Thus throughout the body of the gerontological literature increasing attention is being given to identifying internal and external sources of life-strengths that contribute to older adults' enduring sense of well-being, vitality, and confidence, and their search for personal and social resources that may assist them in realizing their full potential, or alternatively enhancing their capacity to protect themselves against external threats to their well-being (M. M. Baltes, 1996).

The human resources that have been most widely studied as sources of human strength in Western societies are personality-based resources which include, for example, psychological resources related to control, self-esteem and goal pursuits, and dispositional traits such as self-confidence, determination, and mastery. In contrast, less attention has been given to how aging individuals' existential and humanistic concerns, desires, and needs contribute to their resilience, or lack thereof. Similarly, little attention has hitherto been given to key existential, social, environmental, and ecological resources that are of importance because of their potential to be developed into intervention programs to foster resilience.

Increasingly, it is recognized that there is a powerful ecological interplay between individuals' self-resources and the social environment as seen from the viewpoint of humanistic-existential theory, social-cognitive theory, and historical-cultural frameworks. As first posited by Kelly (1966), the ecological interplay involves the transfer and rotation of resources between persons and their settings. In other words, people's well-being is dependent not only on their own self-resources but also on their access to specific psychosocial resources valued within their ecological niche. According to Kelly (1966) and Sarason (1974), of intrinsic interest are those sources of life-strengths and related psychosocial resources that facilitate the following: (1) the individual's control or mastery of one's own life; (2) the individual's ability to acquire and maintain social relations and social connections, and to mobilize social support; and (3) the individual's ability to make a meaningful social contribution, whether it be through civic engagement, through work and professional commitment, or through volunteer pursuits within one's limited sphere of community or within a larger societal-cultural context.

Overview

In this chapter, we engage in discourse about real and perceived sources of human resilience and life-strengths, whether these emanate from ways of thinking derived from an existential-humanistic perspective, a social-cognitive perspective, or an historical-cultural perspective. First, from the perspectives of humanistic-existential theory and social-cognitive theory we identify in some detail sets of psychosocial resources and the related mechanisms and psychological processes at work within those frameworks. We also identify elements that bridge across these two perspectives in order to derive insights about other potential sources of human adaptation, resilience, and positive health that have not received attention so far. Subsequently, we consider the sources of life-strengths viewed from an historical-cultural perspective.

In our way of thinking, most individuals may, at some conscious or subconscious level, define for themselves their most valued sources of life-strengths. For some, the valued sources of life-strengths are grounded in their existential beliefs about their self-worth, their purpose and goals for life, and their intrinsic beliefs about the extent to which their lives are governed by Providence or other natural forces outside their control. Conversely, some individuals may define their most valued sources of life-strengths as residing within themselves and under their own control. Still others may define their sources of life-strengths as emanating both from forces within themselves and under their control, and also from forces outside themselves and not under their control. Individuals will then, consciously or subconsciously, seek to obtain psychological facilitation and psychosocial resources that cohere well with their belief systems. Our discourse is based on our personal stance that some people function more optimally than others because they have more successfully identified their major and most valued sources of life-strengths, and have accordingly mobilized a large and effective arsenal of life-strengthening resources consistent with their belief systems. Thus, in our discourse we attempt to draw attention to the link between individuals' capacity for resilient aging and their success in identifying the major sources of life-strengths, garnering a wide array of psychosocial resources, and making wise choices concerning the use of resources that will be most meaningful to them in meeting their present and future challenges. We propose that these various mechanisms and processes represent the "building blocks" that individuals gradually assemble to protect themselves against present and future stressful encounters.

Sources and determinants of life-strengths: understanding the construct

It is important at this point to provide a general definition of life-strengths. To avoid a definition of life-strengths that is not sufficiently encompassing, what is meant by human life-strengths, and the related sources of these life-strengths, must be further delineated to include those life-strengths that are understood by groups of people who share a set of common cultural, economic, and political traditions. Thus, for example, although individual autonomy, self-efficacy, and self-worth may not be dimensions of the life-strengths construct that are regarded to be a source of internal strength for all persons, in all situations and in all cultures, these characteristics and attributes are by and large highly valued by most people in a broad array of situations, in most democratic Western societies (Bandura, 1997; Hobfoll, 2002). In our examination of the sources of life-strengths and the internal and external resources emanating from humanistic-existential and social-cognitive perspectives or an historical-cultural framework, we consider largely those psychological perspectives of resilience and human strengths that are well accepted and valued within Western cultural traditions. We base the definition of life-strengths on the thinking proffered by Nesselroade (1991), who theorized that differences in older individuals' perceptions and determinants of their life-strengths are intrinsically linked with their individual life histories and current experiences. Individuals choose purposive action through which they hope their cognitive, affective, and physical strengths will translate into goals, aspirations, and visions for the future. Thus various psychosocial sources and resources that contribute to life-strengths may be understood, used and interpreted in diverse ways by different individuals in the context of their own experiences, roles, and functioning.

In arriving at broad definitions of strength-inducing resources, those proffered by Diener and colleagues (e.g., Diener and Fujita, 1995) have had an intrinsic appeal because the sources of life-strengths contributing to human well-being, as outlined by them, take into account sources of life-strengths both at the level of the individual, and at the level of the broader society. Their definition of strength-inducing elements includes objects, personal characteristics, conditions, or energies that are valued in their own right or that are valued because they are suggestive of ways and means by which individuals may achieve access to other sources of life-strengths that co-exist in the larger society.

For our present purposes, it is reasonable to define life-strengths as a constellation of both inner resources including skills, habits, personal, social, religious, and spiritual beliefs, values, goals, behaviors, commitments, and expert knowledge, as well as the ability and resourcefulness to draw on resources in the external environment (e.g., social support, social interaction and social engagement, social status and other economic and monetary assets) in order to adapt to changing circumstances. Thus the "life-strengths" construct is a multidimensional and multifaceted dynamic construct assumed to have a reciprocal relationship with a number of primary constructs delineated in the literature on self-efficacy, personal mastery, sense of control, emotional attention, and also with external sources (such as social supports and socioeconomic resources) that may impact positively on social, emotional, and intellectual well-being. Similarly there is a reciprocal relationship with a number of primary constructs delineated in the existential theory literature (such as religious and spiritual beliefs, values, goals, and relationship with ourselves and with others), which are viewed as having a positive impact on individuals' response to challenges and stressful encounters. From our perspective, the construct of life-strengths is strongly linked with the current construct of resilience and resilient aging which implies the individual's capacity to retain, sustain, and enhance an array of psychological resources. We argue that the individual's capacity to mobilize sources and resources of life-strengths will determine each individual's level of psychological well-being, mastery, and control in times of stress and adversity. Put differently, the concept of life-strengths implies the individual's capacity to "hang tough" by garnering psychological resources that protect against vulnerabilities that may be precursors of morbidity, depression, and emotional distress (Keyes, 2002).

Sources of life-strengths have thus far been divided into those that are distal or proximal to the self, internal or external, and psychological or biological. It is also important to describe the concept of life-strengths from various theoretical and psychological perspectives, for example, the existential-humanistic perspective or the social-cognitive behavioral perspective. Figure 1.1 is a schematic representation of the major sources of life-strengths from these perspectives. It presents three broad but somewhat overlapping theoretical frameworks within which life-strengths may be understood. The figure presents a conceptual framework incorporating only a small subset of potentially relevant psychological sources of life-strengths. The small subsets delineated in Figure 1.1 may be expanded to illustrate other sources of human life-strengths that contribute to vital personal dispositions, for example sense of coherence, optimism, and hope which in turn may lead to the avoidance of negative predispositions, for example, helplessness, anxiety, and morbidity that inevitably result in neglect of mental and physical health.

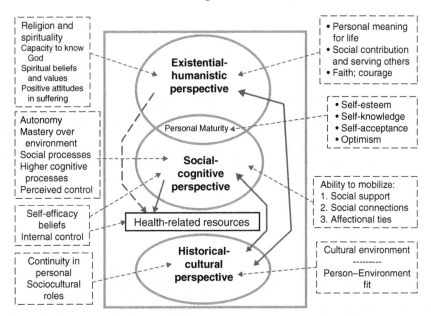

Figure 1.1. Schematic representation of the major sources of life-strengths from different theoretical perspectives.

The existential-humanistic theory framework and related sources of life-strengths

From the perspective of existential theory, individuals' appraisals of the sources of life-strengths will vary in terms of the personal maturity they perceive themselves to have achieved. In this context, personal maturity is assessed in terms of depth of personal meanings for life, purpose in life, and goals and aspirations for the future. The existential-humanistic theory framework argues that the search for new and emerging sources of life-strengths is continual throughout life, but greatly accelerated in late life as individuals move toward further seeking and redefining their meaning for life and achieving some measure of self-transcendence over the stress and pain of physical and emotional losses (Baumeister, 1991; Coward, 2000; Fry, 2000a, 2000b, 2000c, 2001a; Tornstam, 1997; Wong, 1998a, 1998b). Major sources of life-strengths that have been identified within the existential-humanistic framework include the following: (a) the quest for personal meaning; (b) the quest for spirituality and religious faith; and (c) the quest for personal growth, maturity, and self-knowledge. There is now a convergence of expert opinions that personal meaning is of foremost importance.

In what sense is meaning and purpose an imperative?

Baumeister (1991) conceptualized life-strengths as emerging from four different aspects of the need for meaning for life: purpose, value, efficacy, and self-worth. He postulated that older adults are likely to rate the significance of each factor differently, and to appraise each of these factors differentially in different contexts, as sources of personal strength. In the literature on creative aging, the search for higher levels of meaning and purpose for living reflects the individual's decreasing reliance on externals for definition of the self, and an increasing reliance on one's expanding sense of connectedness with one's present and future.

Wong (1998a, 1998b) defines personal meaning as an individually constructed cognitive system, which endows life with personal significance. Thus for Wong (1998a, 1998b), meaning for life is solely a personal matter and the determinants of meaning and purpose emanate from within the person. Along somewhat different lines, Dittmann-Kohli (1995) contends that the personal meaning system incorporates the cognitive and affective network containing person-directed and environment-directed motivational cognitions and understandings, such as goal concepts and behavior plans, conceptions of character, and competencies, and various kinds of standards and self-appraisals.

Klinger (1998) adds a new evolutionary dimension to the concept of personal meaning and how it contributes to human strength. He proposes that the search for meaning and purpose is rooted in biology to the extent that goal striving is a biological imperative for all humans. "The human brain cannot sustain purposeless living. It was not designed for that. Its systems are designed for purposive action, and when that is blocked, they deteriorate, and the emotional feedback from idling those systems signals extreme discomfort and motivates the search for renewed purpose and meaning" (Klinger, 1998, p. 33). It is human beings' cognitive and symbolic capacity that elevates the biological drive to the transcendent experience of higher purpose and meaning that comes also through interaction with other social systems, and results in affective richness. Thus the continual search for meaning and purpose serves as the largest source and reservoir for the emergence of life-strengths and becomes vitally linked to mental, physical, social, and biological health and wellness (Klinger, 1998).

Frankl (1963) observed in himself and others that meaning in life is important under all conditions, and that individuals suffer more when their search for meaning is lost, blocked, or destroyed. Deficits of purpose and meaning in life have been scientifically associated with psychopathologies such as depression and suicide (see, e.g., Heisel and Flett, 2004) and problems of adjustment to trauma (e.g., Thompson *et al.*, 2003). In this connection, Joske (1981) raised the question of what differentiates a meaningful from a meaningless life. He suggested four elements of meaninglessness, "worthlessness, pointlessness, triviality, and futility" (p. 252). It is important to note that the second element relates to having a purpose in life, and the fourth element relates to the realizability of meaning for life. The other two elements relate to the value of the goal and whether it is meritorious or not, and the degree of its importance. To conclude, a well-defined purpose for life serves as an antidote to meaninglessness, depression, and suffering (Johnson, 1959; Joske, 1981).

Along similar lines of thought, purpose for life (viewed more fully as the process of individual growth toward vocation) (Fowler 1981; Mahan 2004) serves as a major source of life-strengths at all stages of development. Two key developmental tasks for individuals, if they are to claim and pursue lives of purpose, are as follows: (a) to discern what are good, or useful, objectives in life; and (b) to successfully and ethically realize those ends in life. Both tasks are the underpinnings of human resilience and emotional and spiritual well-being. This point is particularly well articulated by Lucas (1998) that a well-defined meaning for life makes for successful coping even when the worst possible trauma or affliction strikes or even in the face of chronic and terminal illness. By saying "yes to life," even terminally ill people testify that life is unconditionally worth living; they inspire healthy people to face life's difficulties. "In what direction would a society of healthy people drift, if it were not for the sick, the old and the disabled, who caution the healthy to reflect on the true values of life" (Lucas, 1998, p. 315).

Thus from the perspective of most existentialist theorists, the personal meaning system is conceived as a cognitive map that orients the individual in steering through the life-course. Overall, this meaning system, as defined, is a significant and universal health-enhancing, dynamic system allowing individuals, irrespective of culture, to discover purpose and goals for their lives, whether these goals are described in terms of meeting basic needs, leisure activities, personal relationships, personal achievements, personal growth, social and political activism, altruism, religion, or legacy (Reker and Wong, 1988). In this sense, individuals at different ages and with varying levels of ability or disability may continue to explore a meaning and purpose for life both in constrained and limited social situations and structures, and in the wider context of their life and functioning. Contrary to stereotypic thinking, the reservoir of personal meaning for life seldom runs dry. Adults are continually rediscovering and redefining their selves in the context of their present experiences (Albert, 1977). In the context of aging, there is growing evidence to support the notion that not only do older adults have a remarkable degree of resilience and adaptive and transformational capacity for reorganizing and reinterpreting their various life experiences, but their search for a new or redefined self that provides positive information about the present self is continual, and is a major source of life-strengths and resilient functioning (Lawton *et al.*, 1999).

To conclude, the individual meaning systems that persons carve out for themselves may change from time to time and become restructured according to the changing context of their lives, but the personal meaning system invariably serves as a major source and protective resource for affective and cognitive growth, resilience, and life-strength throughout the lifespan.

Research to date is beginning to provide systematic evidence that the tendency for "wellness breakdown," involving stress-related degenerative diseases (e.g., cancer, heart disease, stroke), characteristic mental illnesses (e.g., anxiety, depression), and performance deteriorations (inability to concentrate, forgetfulness, preoccupation) (Maddi, 1998, p. 11) is more rapid for individuals who lack meaning and purposive action as a source of life-strengths. However, "wellness breakdown" is a considerably slower process, even in the case of chronically ill and terminally ill persons, when they have the supporting force of a special meaning and goal for life.

During the past two decades, a relatively large number of empirical studies have demonstrated that meaning in life and purpose and goals in life are important sources of internal life-strengths for increasing numbers of older adults, enhancing both physical well-being (e.g., Reker and Wong, 1984) and psychological well-being, (e.g., Baumeister and Leary, 1995; Fry, 2000a, 2001a), and promoting mental health resilience (Thompson *et al.*, 2003).

More recently, however, the argument is posited that a personal meaning for life, carved out of one's own life-experiences, may not always be an enduring source of life-strength; it needs to be complemented with a more universal source of life-strengths emanating from a higher power outside ourselves. Individuals are searching for a sense of coherence, hope, and significance to their existence from a worldview of Providence or divine force that enables them to transcend the banality of their everyday living (Antonovsky, 1998; Lucas, 1998). In short, individuals are turning to religion and spirituality in the quest for the ultimate meaning of human existence (Hart, 1977; Tillich, 1963), and for sustenance, comfort, and emotional resilience. In view of the importance of religion/spirituality in older adults' lives, and its linkage with mental health and well-being, the next section examines more closely a few critical aspects of how religion/ spirituality serves as a basis for emotional resilience and strength.

The uniqueness of religion as a life-enhancing and life-strengthening meaning system

It has been suggested that the construction of religious meaning systems, like other meaning systems (e.g., Higgins, 2000; Janoff-Bulman, 1992), is necessary for humans to function in the world. Epstein (1985), for example, explains that purpose-based meaning systems fulfill four basic motives; namely, to maintain (1) the stability and coherence of a personal conceptual system (while assimilating the data of experience); (2) a favorable balance of pleasure and pain over the foreseeable future; (3) a favorable balance of self-esteem; and (4) a favorable relationship with significant others (see Silberman, 2005a, p. 645). In this context, religion and religious beliefs serve as potent sources of life-strengths in that they influence the formation of goals for self-regulation, affect emotions, and influence behavior (e.g., Cohen and Rankin, 2004; Emmons, 1999; Pargament, 1997; Park and Folkman, 1997; see Silberman, 2004, for a review).

Religion as a meaning system is unique in that it centers on what is perceived to be the sacred (cf. Pargament's definition, 1997, p. 32). The sacred refers to concepts of higher powers, such as the divine, God, or the transcendent, which are considered holy and set apart from the ordinary. As such, they are perceived as worthy of veneration and respect, and can become a unique source of significance and personal strength in people's lives (Pargament, 1997). The connection to the sacred can be fully manifested in each of the components of the meaning system, namely, beliefs, contingencies, expectations, and goals, as well as in prescriptive postulates regarding emotions and actions (Silberman, 2003, 2004). As summarized by Silberman (2005a, 2005b), when religion is incorporated into the meaning system of a person, conceptions of the sacred are connected to beliefs about the nature of people, of the self, of this world, and of whatever may lie beyond it. Religious meaning systems often include beliefs regarding contingencies and outcome expectations. One common contingency is that righteous people should be rewarded for their good deeds. This contingency makes room for the emergence of faith, hope, and optimism for the present and future (Silberman, 2005a, 2005b). Such a system may include self-efficacy expectations regarding the ability of individuals to change themselves and the world around them, but not without the help of a "Sacred and Higher Power" (Silberman, 2004).

Religious belief and meaning systems basically encourage the ultimate motivation of connecting or adhering to the sacred. However, any goal, ranging from goals of benevolence, forgiveness, and altruism to goals of supremacy, could take on religious value by virtue of connection to the sacred (Silberman, 2005a, 2005b).

Although inspiration and direction for purpose come from both religious and secular sources, and conceptions of purpose in life are both religious and secular, recently religious and spiritual approaches to the nature and utility of purpose in life have received wider currency. In Warren's (2003) *The Purpose-Driven Life*, the religious conception of purpose in life is exemplified through the divine act of God's creation. For Warren, God created human beings with a fivefold purpose: worship, fellowship, discipleship, ministry, and mission. Each purpose reflects the knowledge that God created humans to experience his pleasure, become part of his family, serve humanity, and tell others about Christ. According to Warren, a purpose-driven life finds its origins and roots essentially in relation to the sacred. Thus meaning and purpose in life are seen and developed through the lens of the sacred.

In directing attention to the power of religion and religious beliefs in enhancing resilience and acceptance of life, expert opinion is that religious beliefs and religion as a meaning system may influence emotional resilience in several ways (see Pargament, 1997; Silberman, 2003, 2005a; Silberman, Higgins, and Dweck, 2001, for reviews). First, they may offer the opportunity to experience a uniquely powerful emotional experience of closeness to a powerful spiritual force. Second, they may impact emotions in positive and life-enhancing ways or directly proscribe or discourage certain negative emotions. For example, religious meaning systems can prescribe emotions such as joy while proscribing other emotions such as sadness or anger (Silberman, 2004, 2005a, 2005b) that are detrimental to well-being.

Religion as a source of meaning has been described as qualitatively unique in its ability to propose answers to life's deepest questions and thereby sustain individuals' will to live and thrive (Myers, 2000; Pargament, 1997). In this context, religion has been described as a powerful source of meaning under even the most testing circumstances, such as when stressful events cannot be repaired through problem-solving strategies. Religious beliefs seem to prevail in difficult circumstances when other basic personal beliefs (such as the belief in personal invulnerability, the perception of the world as meaningful and comprehensible, and the ability to view ourselves in a positive light) may be shattered or at least seriously questioned (Janoff-Bulman, 1992; Janoff-Bulman and Frieze, 1983). Religion and spirituality have a protective effect on health. They are life-enhancing in the sense that they provide resistance to stress under the most traumatic and tragic circumstances. When life seems capricious and uncontrollable because of tragic accident or illness, when individuals are overwhelmed by a sense of helplessness and hopelessness, religion may provide comfort and encouragement. When there is unendurable pain and grief, belief in a divine purpose makes it possible to endure the bad happenings (Koenig, Smiley, and Gonzales, 1988).

Going beyond, religion, as a meaning system that is centered on the sacred and the spiritual, is one of the few types of meaning systems that can meet the basic human need for self-transcendence (Sheldon and Kasser, 1995), a striving that has been described as instrumental for accomplishing other strivings and as having especially strong relations with well-being (Emmons, 1999). This characteristic is consistent with the view of religion or spirituality as being able to give unity to all other concerns (Tillich, 1957, 1963). Also, it serves as an integrating framework that can reduce the overall conflict within a person's goal system, and can foster coherence in personality (Emmons, 1999).

Religion and spirituality as overlapping sources of life-strengths

Pargament (1997) defines religion as "a search for significance in ways related to the sacred" (p. 32). This definition implies that religion is an active process, involved in directing a person's thinking and actions. In other words, it is proactive rather than reactive. People do not necessarily wait for stresses and difficulties to occur in their lives, before they acquire religious beliefs, but instead act to foster religious and spiritual belief systems, and related resources that sustain them on a regular basis and to which they have ready access when adversity strikes.

For many individuals the personal side of religiousness translates to spirituality and many characteristics common to religion generalize to spirituality (Hill *et al.*, 2000; Thoreson and Harris, 2002). Both religion and spirituality refer to the most animating or vital issues of life, providing a sense of purpose and meaning in life. Spiritual and religious experiences offer an awareness of inner peace, harmony, hopefulness, and compassion for others and both involve a personal transformation, an encounter with transcendence, or a search for ultimate truth (Seybold and Hill, 2001, p. 21).

The proposal for an integration of religious and spiritual approaches to the nature and utility of purpose in life has recently received increased attention in the literature on health, resilience, and personal well-being. In *The Psychology of Ultimate Concerns*, Emmons (1999) offers a scientifically grounded approach to spirituality that highlights the nature of purpose in life. Noteworthy is Emmon's concept of *spiritual intelligence* – a core component of the spiritual strivings – that consists of five personal capacities. Individuals can transcend immediate physical and material concerns, and they can experience states of heightened consciousness in relationship with the "Ultimate" through a connection with nature, life, work, humanity, or God. Individuals can also pursue virtuous behavior, and they can use spiritual resources for problem solving and coping. Notably, individuals can sanctify human relationships and social interaction with purpose, meaning, and value (Emmons, 1999).

Empirical research findings

The effects of religious beliefs and spirituality on the health and psychological well-being of persons in later adulthood are of current interest in research (Koenig, 2000; Krause *et al.*, 1999; McFadden, 1995; Schaie, Krause, and Booth, 2004). Most proponents concur that religious beliefs and spirituality seem uniquely able to promote purpose, value, and meaningfulness in older adults, by providing them with an overarching interpretive scheme for making sense of their lives, and a place to regularly meet with like-minded persons (Debats, Drost, and Hansen, 1995; Ellison, 1991; Ellison, Gay, and Glass, 1989). Religious belonging and religious meaning have both been cited for their benefit in areas of resilience, mental health, physical health (Ai *et al.*, 2000; Ainlay, Singleton, and Swigert, 1992; George, Ellison, and Larson, 2002; Lawler and Younger, 2002), and adaptation (Thompson *et al.*, 2003). There has been increasing suggestion that religiousness and religiosity (defined as adherence to a set of ideological beliefs, rituals, and practices that include involvement with other members of similar faith and spiritual sense) are closely related to positive and successful aging outcomes, particularly life satisfaction, and coping with stress and life-threatening illness (Pargament, 1997; Pargament *et al.*, 2001).

Recent innovative theoretical perspectives (e.g., Baumeister, 1991; Klinger, 1998) have stimulated considerable biopsychological (see Ryff and Singer, 1998, 2000) and neural research (e.g., Inzlicht *et al.*, 2009) linking the depth of individuals' understanding of their personal and religious meaning systems with increasing vitality, resilience, and health improvement and resistance to biological and physiological stress.

It is interesting to note that parallel to the emphasis that the psychology of aging has hitherto placed on individuals' socio-cognitive capacities and resources (e.g., personal attributes of self-determination, internal control, and mastery) as sources of life-strengths accounting for individuals' resilience, there is now emerging an alternate and compelling area of the study of aging that recognizes the importance of individuals as existential beings. As existential beings, individuals have existential beliefs about their self-worth, personal meaning, and purpose for life, and religious beliefs and spiritual values that serve as enduring sources of life-strengths. There has been an abundance of discourse and philosophical treatises on religion, spirituality and existential beliefs as contributing to human adaptation and human resilience for many centuries. However, it is only recently that these sources of human life-strengths are emerging as contenders for serious scientific consideration in the psychological literature.

In sum, the literature we have briefly sketched within the existential framework on the topic of meaning for life, purpose, and goals for living, and the influence of religiosity and spirituality, underscores their salubrious connection with psychological resilience and beneficial consequences for psychological health and successful aging outcomes. The overall implication is that all these factors serve as internal sources of strengths in the face of the challenges associated with advancing age.

The social-cognitive framework and related sources of life-strengths

A number of key resource theories which are offshoots of a broad social-cognitive conceptual framework have received widespread attention. Among these, theories proposed by Bandura (1982, 1989, 1997), Hobfoll and Leiberman (1987), Rosenberg (1965), Scheier and Carver (1985, 1992) and Seligman (1975), have received special recognition for proposing mechanisms that facilitate individuals' resilience and well-being. A similar framework proposed by Thoits (1994, 1995) has since emerged under the rubric of key management theories. Thoits (1994) theorized that individuals' human strength and resilience come from the knowledge that they possess a number of social and psychosocial resources, personality attributes, and traits that can be deployed under difficult circumstances and in response to stressors. These are further delineated under the rubric of control, self-efficacy, and self-esteem (see Figure 1.1).

Control and perceived self-efficacy as sources of human strength and resilience

Control

Control has been defined in a number of ways (see Skinner, 1996) but in the main it refers to the self as the agent of control. It reflects the extent to which individuals think that they have internal control and can take charge of what happens in their life, including the ability to bring about desired outcomes, such as protecting health and preventing disease, especially in later life (Rowe and Kahn, 1987).

Recent theorizing has broadened the outlook on internal control and is concerned with examining the impact of a generalized sense of control which includes both constructs of self-control and perceived control. These are dimensions that may be particularly relevant as an important component of long-term health and well-being of older individuals. From this perspective, a sense of internal control or perceived control is intimately related to a set of other multidimensional trait structures: (1) *individual and environmental mastery*, delineated as the extent to which one feels a sense of mastery over one's life, or the extent to which one feels capable of managing the external world to suit one's need (Pearlin and Schooler, 1978); (2) *autonomy*, which reflects a level of self-determination and independence (e.g., the extent to which one feels capable of acting on personal convictions even if they are not shared by others who may influence expectations of oneself or expectations of goal attainments); (3) *clear purpose in life*, reflecting a sense of directedness and aims and objectives for living; (4) *motivation for personal growth* as reflected in the feeling of a continuing motivation to grow and develop; and (5) *self-acceptance*, which implies a positive attitude toward oneself both with respect to the present self and one's past life (see Ryff, 1989; Ryff and Keyes, 1995). Thus the construct of internal control and perceived control has been broadened to include a set of trait structures and psychological resources which may individually or globally influence individuals' self-expectations, determination about goal pursuits, and aspirations about the future. Assessment of the five structures outlined above provides information about individuals' sense of effectiveness in dealing with the external world, their determination to succeed and their capacity for continual growth. Each is seen to be contributing to individuals' maintaining and sustaining emotional resilience.

Self-efficacy

The concept of self-efficacy as a stress management resource was originally proposed by Bandura (1989, 1997); it stresses the primacy of the human agency and the acquisition of empowerment through self-efficacy beliefs and beliefs about control. Those with a sense of self-efficacy are more likely to see themselves as having the ability to exercise successful influence over their environment and may strive harder toward the accomplishment of their goals. Within the framework of life-strengths and resilience models, it may be argued (Kivnick, 1998) that those who possess high levels of perceived self-efficacy are likely to hold the self-view that they are emotionally and physically strong, tough-minded, and capable of greater stress resistance. Self-efficacy was first seen as a self-view related to a specific challenge such as an encounter with a fiercely threatening or stressful situation. However, increasingly self-efficacy is now viewed as a generalized sense of self-competence related to positive physical and emotional well-being. In longitudinal prospective studies of stress resistance, a sense of self-efficacy is regarded to be a protective resource, providing robust stress resistance in the face of trauma or major tragedy (Bandura, 1997). Bandura's perspective embraces a broad ecological view of human growth which argues that individuals' strength and persistence in the face of challenges and adversity comes from their self-efficacy beliefs and positive perceptions of their own knowledge, competence, and expertise to resolve problems and dilemmas. In addition, those who possess high levels of self-efficacy might be more capable of selecting, altering, implementing, and mobilizing other psychosocial resources, such as cognitive competence, financial resources, familial/social support, and so on, to meet stressful environmental demands. A number of empirical studies in the aging literature show how self-efficacy beliefs are not only sound predictors of older adults' psychological well-being, but also provide the foundations for higher levels of life satisfaction and self-esteem (Fry, 2001b; McAvay, Seeman, and Rodin, 1996). They have also been linked in prospective studies with robust stress resistance in the face of minor distress, such as fears, anxiety, and loneliness (e.g., Fry, 2001b, 2003; Fry and Debats, 2002, 2006), and major tragedy (see Bonanno, 2004, 2005).

Self-efficacy, health and resilience

The emerging fields of health epidemiology and health psychology have provided further impetus to the study of social-cognitive management resources that are increasingly acknowledged to be related to illness prevention, health protection, and well-being. Currently self-efficacy beliefs, as a psychosocial resource component, are heavily implicated in social-cognitive models for health behavior. Perceived self-efficacy is seen to affect health habits and health outcomes both directly and indirectly through its impact on health goals, outcome expectations, and planned health-promoting behavior (Bandura, 2004). Self-efficacy beliefs are a focal determinant of health outcomes because self-efficacy beliefs affect health behaviors both directly and indirectly by their influence on other determinants of goals and aspirations for health standards. The stronger the perceived self-efficacy, the higher the goals people set for themselves in terms of positive health behaviors, and the firmer their commitment to the attainment of those behaviors (Bandura, 2004). Self-efficacy beliefs shape the health outcomes people expect their efforts to produce. Those with high self-efficacy beliefs expect to realize favorable outcomes. Those with low self-efficacy beliefs expect that their efforts will bring poor outcomes. According to Bandura (2004, p. 145), self-efficacy beliefs also determine how obstacles, impediments, and road blocks to the attainment of health outcomes will be viewed. People with low self-efficacy beliefs will be easily convinced that they do not have the personality make-up or the cognitive and emotional resilience to overcome health problems, and will be easily convinced of the futility of effort for even starting. By contrast, people with high self-efficacy beliefs will view impediments as a challenge, and are determined to surmount impediments by improving their self-management skills. They show emotional resilience and will continue to persevere in the face of health problems (Bandura, 2004). Thus from the perspective of social-cognitive theory, the practical stance is that programs of health management should be tailored to people's varying levels of self-efficacy. The notion of congruence, or fit, between one's existing level of self-efficacy and the level required to successfully conform to the expectations of health providers becomes the axiomatic principle. Along similar lines, in longitudinal analyses of community-based health campaigns, Rimal (2000, 2001) found that perceived self-efficacy governs whether individuals translate perceived health risks into a search for further self-knowledge, and whether they will translate their acquired knowledge into healthful behavioral practices. People's pre-existing self-efficacy beliefs that they are capable of exercising control will contribute considerably to their adoption of healthy habits (Maibach, Flora, and Nass, 1991).

To summarize, perceptions of internal control and self-efficacy control may function to promote resilience and health in a number of ways. First, control beliefs will influence individuals' decisions as to whether action will be taken to prevent or remedy health problems. Further, perceptions of control or self-efficacy may affect the extent to which individuals will gather health-related information, will interact actively with medical or health service providers, or comply with medical regimens. Second, internal control or the absence of control may affect physical and mental health through its impact on physiological functioning (Bandura, 2004). Thus for example, research by Rodin, Timko, and Harris (1985) indicated that catecholamines and corticosteroids increase when individuals are confronted with uncontrollable situations. An increase in these hormones has been linked with coronary disease resulting from elevated blood pressure and heart rate, elevation of blood lipids, and changes in the regulation of the metabolic system and in the suppression of the immune system (Yang and Glaser, 2000). By contrast, high internal control was associated with reduced perceptions of stress and lower mortality (Fry and Debats, 2006).

When is control no longer a source of life-strength?

First studied under the rubric of stress management resources, concepts of self-efficacy, internal control, and mastery have received the most attention for their potential contribution to human resilience and as sources of life-strengths. Outcomes of higher resource levels of control and mastery are favorable, and especially in high-stress circumstances, are related to better functioning, more active goal-directed behavior, and better psychological responsiveness (Hobfoll, 1998). Lately, however, people's characteristic degree of control has been examined on both ends of the continuum (Heckhausen and Schultz, 1995). Even though its potential as an important source of life-strength continues to be fully recognized, the negative end of this continuum is also receiving more attention in terms of the negative implications for resilient aging. At the basic level, it is noted that preference for control changes with age. Increasingly it is recognized that people differ in their desire for control and there are some conditions in advancing old age in which the perception of high level of control is more likely to induce stress as opposed to having a beneficial impact. Many older individuals may report a decrease in objective and subjective control, and although this loss of perceived control is associated with increasing vulnerability, the point to remember is that older individuals' desire for absolute control may also diminish with age, and hence there is little change in individuals' satisfaction with their level of control. Since the need to control is influenced by a number of other resources such as self-esteem, self-efficacy, and sense of self-worth (see Cozzarelli, 1993), older adults with a pre-existing sense of high self-efficacy and self-esteem may be more willing and capable of voluntary surrender of control, and may not perceive delegating control to others as threatening to their self-esteem. This raises the question of whether having too much of the resource of control can have a negative impact on health and longevity. For example, Janoff-Bulman and Brickman (1982) suggested that the tendency to take control or to need control can backfire in circumstances of extreme stress in which control is not possible. Following the death of a loved one, for example, a survivor's need for strong control and mastery may be an obstacle to accepting the death and returning to the task of living. Finally, there may be a threshold level for some psychosocial resources (including, for example, high self-efficacy beliefs, and high control needs) after which having the desire to possess higher levels of these internal resources is not advantageous to resilient functioning, but may stand in the way of individuals' maintenance of mental health. In this context, M. M. Baltes (1996) notes an important *adaptive function* that is served by voluntary surrender of control under circumstances of severe stress. She posits that in order that older adults be able to maintain autonomy and control in select and important domains of cognitive functioning, the effective exercise and use of dependency behavior in other less important domains is a robust *compensatory strategy*. By surrendering control and by invoking dependency and inviting the support of others, cognitive resources are freed up for use in other domains "selected" for personal efficacy and growth. Thus in circumstances in which control is not easily possible or feasible, there is the indication that the ability to relinquish control is adaptive (Janoff-Bulman and Brickman, 1982).

Another key resource that provides meaning for life and contributes substantially to perceptions of human strength and vitality is the degree of tenaciousness in goal pursuits (Brandtstädter and Renner, 1990). While the positive end of this continuum (which represents the personal trait of tenaciously pursuing behaviors that are goal-directed) is recognized for its value in emotional well-being and as a stimulating and motivating trait resource, more attention is now being given to the negative end of the continuum where it is clear that the tenacious pursuits of goals coupled with the potential for non-realization or non-accomplishment of those goals may lead to a loss of self-esteem, depression, and anxiety in older adults. Here again there is the indication that the ability to narrow the scope of goals to be attained such that they become more easily attainable, or even to abandon certain goals that expose them to risk of anxiety is adaptive (Janoff-Bulman, 1992; Janoff-Bulman and Frieze, 1983), and should be encouraged, especially in advanced old age.

Self-esteem

Another internal resource which has been less well studied, but may be of enduring interest because of its links to resilience, is self-esteem. People high in self-esteem may be less likely to interpret life's difficulties as a reflection or mark of their own lowered self-worth (Rosenberg, 1965). However, it is to be noted that the individual resource of self-esteem does not develop independently of other internal personal resources, for example self-efficacy, perceived control, and a sense of purpose and directedness. Self-esteem, like self-efficacy, has been found to be related to well-being and better stress resistance (Cohen and Edwards, 1989; Hobfoll and Leiberman, 1987; Hobfoll *et al.*, 1986). There is some recent evidence that high self-esteem is linked with better self-regulation and better coping with health problems (Holahan and Moos, 1991; Rini *et al.*, 1999), and greater dispositional optimism (Scheier and Carver, 1985, 1992). These findings concerning the positive influence of high levels of self-esteem, internal control, and tenacious goal pursuits converge neatly with the conception of individuals as *psychological activists* (Thoits, 1994) who shape their own destinies and who make tremendous gains in cognitive-emotional resilience by diligent efforts to protect high levels of self-esteem. While, on the one hand, we applaud the utility of an activist stance, we caution against an overemphasis on activist possibilities, especially in advanced old age. Against the potential strengths of the activist orientation to dealing with life's challenges, we juxtapose some of the negative indicators following from the constant struggle to maintain high levels of self-esteem. The continual struggle to keep the activist self and the related elevated levels of self-esteem and self-dependence in full motion in later life may have negative consequences, in that they may lead to rapid ego-depletion and a loss of other related life-strengthening dispositions, such as optimism, openness, and extraversion (Baumeister *et al.*, 1998; Baumeister, Heatherton, and Tice, 1993). On a precautionary note, it is suggested that beyond a certain point, an overemphasis on the activist possibilities is detrimental to stress resistance and resilient functioning.

Personality resources as important sources of life-strengths

While individual personality traits of conscientiousness, extraversion, openness, and agreeableness have been acknowledged as conducive to physical and emotional health and longevity both in meta-analysis studies (e.g., Kern and Friedman, 2008) and in longitudinal studies (e.g., Friedman, 2000; Fry and Debats, 2009; Martin, Friedman and Schwartz, 2007; Wilson *et al.*, 2004), increased attention is now being given to the usefulness of invoking *personality resource convoys* having what Hobfoll (2002) describes as *multiple and multi-pronged components*. Two principal resource theories of this variety, (1) *Dispositional Hardiness* and (2) *Sense of Coherence*, have been extensively examined in the psychological literature and merit further discussion because of their meaningfulness as social-cognitive sources of life-strengths that mesh well with the existential-humanistic needs of persons to grow, to transform and transcend. The first of these multi-pronged personality trait models is one that was proffered by Kobasa (Kobasa, 1979; Kobasa and Puccetti, 1983), who posited that one key way to characterize resilience is through the multi-pronged trait resource of *personality hardiness*. This trait theory originally had its theoretical basis in existential personality theory (Kobasa and Maddi, 1977; Maddi, 1987) and which was previously discussed under the rubric of existential courage (Tillich, 1952) and as a response to the existential notion of faith and optimism (see Evans, 1990, on Kierkegaard). Personality hardiness is identified by its three components: (a) *control* is the extent to which the individual perceives oneself as having influence over certain outcomes, especially when encountering life's trials and tribulations; (b) *challenge*, suggesting that life's problems represent challenges rather than threats; and (c) *sense of commitment to living and to life tasks* which helps to prevent one from becoming alienated from the self and the outside world.

The more recent concept of hardiness, as discussed by Maddi (1998), constitutes a significant cognitive concretization of the existential concept of courage which has now found a solid place in the scientific literature in personality theory and in the psychosocial literature on adaptation and resilience. It also continues to be viewed as an existential formulation that is helpful to individuals in dealing with the ontological anxiety arising from present tensions and tensions of choosing a meaningful future (Maddi, 1998).

Another family of personality-based life-enhancing resources which has been examined extensively for its salutogenesis orientation is the SOC (Sense of Coherence) theory developed by Antonovsky (1979, 1998). It has multiple dispositional components of commitment, control, and mastery, which collectively contribute to the individual's sense of coherence. SOC is a dispositional orientation composed of three subconstructs: *comprehensibility, manageability, and meaningfulness*. The comprehensibility component refers to making "cognitive sense" of the events in one's personal life, and the sense that one can usually predict one's future. Manageability refers to an individual's perception of having the personal and social resources to cope with the demands of life. Meaningfulness refers to the conviction that the demands of life are worthy of investment and commitment. According to Antonovsky (1979), meaningfulness is the most important component of SOC because it motivates individuals to make sense of their environment and empowers them to cope successfully. These notions have an existential flavor, and they differ from what is termed as "sense of control or self-efficacy" in the social-cognitive orientation. From an SOC perspective (Antonovsky, 1979), control might well exist in outside forces such as God, government, or destiny. When these divine or secular forces are viewed favorably they may be perceived as kindly and benevolent, so that persons with a high sense of coherence continue to see themselves as retaining a fair margin of control both in the practical and philosophical sense. Underpinnings of personal maturity as incorporated in the SOC model are consistent with the social-cognitive view that a sense of coherence serves as an integrating framework that can reduce the overall conflict within a person's goal system and can also foster coherence in personality and thereby become a major source of strength and resilience (Emmons, 1999; Sheldon and Kasser, 1995).

Although the Sense of Coherence model and the Hardiness model are each conceived in terms of three subconstructs, there is much overlapping among the tripartite concepts which cannot be measured separately. However, as a unitary concept having both social-cognitive and existential-humanistic underpinnings, there is good evidence for the relationship between sense of coherence (measured by Sense of Coherence scale) and emotional strength and stability, and psychological well-being (Kivimaki *et al.*, 2000; Smith and Meyers, 1998; Suominen *et al.*, 1999). Equally, good evidence has been found for hardiness being related to physical and psychological health and for its stress-moderating function (Kobasa and Puccetti, 1983). For example, the evidence was quite compelling for hardy individuals, compared with nonhardy, being physically sturdy, having lower blood pressure, heart rate, and skin conductance. This finding suggests that hardiness is related to the ability to withstand stress effectively and to have fewer negative health outcomes. In particular, the idea of the hardy personality may begin to explain why some individuals age more optimally and successfully than others (Magnani, 1990).

Taken as a whole, the review of the literature on successful aging within a social-cognitive framework draws attention to thematic strengths in old age as being directly linked to one's sense of coherence, positive perceptions of one's abilities and competencies, one's self-efficacy beliefs and convictions about control, autonomy, and independence. In the realm of stress resistance and health resilience, the most widely studied social-cognitive resources of control and self-regulation are seen to be agentic factors that are a robust source of personal strength and protective power, and contribute to resilience and positive health outcomes even in the face of significant challenge, adversity, and stressful circumstances (Davidson, Jackson, and Kalin, 2000).

Social resources as sources of life-strengths and resilience

Since the mid 1970s there has been an ongoing interest in social support as a key source of strength and emotional resilience that emerges from the social environment. The importance of social and community support to stress resistance was first stressed by Kelly (1966) and Sarason (1974), who conceived the notion that people's well-being was dependent on the social environment and on their access to social support within their ecological niche (Norris and Kaniasty, 1996). For Sarason, thematic strengths in functioning are directly linked to unique psychosocial and socioeconomic challenges that individuals encounter, and which are embedded in the changing social, economic, and political structures of Western society (Featherman, Smith, and Peterson, 1990; Rowe and Kahn, 1987), but these challenges cannot be easily met without social support and related social resources such as having close friends, and taking part in informal and formal support groups. There is evidence to support the view that when people have lost a psychological sense of easy access to community support and social reinforcement, they are more susceptible and vulnerable to the impact of stress (Caplan, 1974; Sarason, 1974). The dimension of social support, as viewed further by Garmezy (1985), includes familial and community support factors, and refers to affectional ties between family members that provide a cohesive family environment during times of stress, as well as supports that come from outside the family, including friends, community organizations, and socioeconomic support. Within a sociocultural framework, social support refers to the provision, access, and receipt of tangible and intangible goods, services, and benefits. Tangible help refers to more concrete forms of help such as care giving when a person is ill versus intangible help such as emotional support, advice, and consultation given to the person in times of stress as measured objectively, or as perceived by the individual with respect to the amount and quality of support (Bergeman and Wallace, 1999; Ong and Bergeman, 2004a, 2004b; Vaux, 1988). The latter type of social support as perceived by the individual is a buffer between the individual and stress encounters. According to Cohen (1988), social support, especially when it comes from people who are an integral part of the individual's sociocultural or socio-historical niche, can buffer the adverse effects of stress on older individuals in a number of ways. First, the social network provides stress-buffering information that helps an individual to reappraise the negative event more positively; second, social support can enhance an individual's sense of identity or self-esteem and thereby reinforce his or her coping abilities; third, social pressure, if coming from a supportive network of family, friends, and informal groups, may catalyze the individual's adoption of more effective problem-solving and coping behaviors; and fourth, support providers can make more tangible resources of support available to the individual (Bergeman and Wallace, 1999).

A review of the research on social support and its related health outcomes indicates that there is a consistent relationship between support
from family, friends and culturally like-minded social groups, and mental health and well-being (for reviews see George 1996; Shumaker and
Czajkowski, 1994), and there are direct links between affectional family ties and social support and effective neurophysiological function and
healthy survival (Seeman *et al.*, 1994). It should be noted that social support constitutes a major source of life-strengths because it represents not
one specific resource but a large *social convoy of resources* and a complex
family of social resources, including aspects of supportive interactions,
perceptions of being supported in concrete ways, and social interdependence (I. G. Sarason, Sarason, and Shearin, 1986). In particular, the presence of intimate others who can be confided in and whose caring has a
certain amount of constancy is the most significant support (I. G. Sarason
et al., 1987). Additionally, Ensel and Lin (1991) have posited that those
with strong social support networks are better guarded from stressful
encounters. Through the information and facilitation they receive from
the social support resource, individuals are more clearly positioned to
avoid stressful experiences. Overall, however, what is of importance is the
fact that providing social support is a developmental process, the need
for which begins or increases during times of stress (Barrera, 1986), but
it may not be valued or be influential across large horizons of time and
circumstances. Unfortunately, not all support is beneficial and there may
be liabilities associated with certain forms of support where the input of
the recipient is either not sought or not taken into account. Excessive
support can sometimes lower autonomy, self-reliance, or feelings of control, and may result in feelings of helplessness (Krause, 1990; Seligman,
1975). In this context, M. M. Baltes (1996) spoke of the importance of
the productive and creative use of social support, in ways that enhance
continued autonomy and are effective in that they satisfy the immediate
needs created by a particular stressor, such as when health problems
develop in older adults. Thus, in order for a support network to be effective, the members of the support group must have the ability, knowledge,
and motivation to act in a way that meets (but does not exceed) the person's support needs (Schulz and Rau, 1985), and at the same time provide enabling guidance for self-help, anticipatory plans for coping with
problems, and for mobilizing a wide array of social support resources.

To conclude, although loss of resources may be inevitable, especially
for older adults, possessing a wide array of social support and successfully mobilizing these resources becomes all the more critical in the later
years of life (Norris and Murrell, 1987). By garnering a wide array of
social support resources in the earlier years of life, individuals in later

years can be selective in their use, identifying, and calling upon social support resources that fit in best with their immediate needs (Cohen and Wills, 1985) and which fit the specific ecological demands inherent in the circumstances that confront these individuals (Lawton and Nahemow, 1973). Although having more resources is not always beneficial for the maintenance of emotional resilience, according to French, Rodgers, and Cobb (1974), it generally will increase the individual's likelihood of having available the particular resource that best fits the particular stressful situation.

Social interaction, social connectedness, and social well-being

Fitting well within the scope of the current psychosocial framework of social interaction systems assumed to enhance resilience are other models of stress resistance and resilience, such as the social convoy model (Antonucci, 2001) and the socioemotional selectivity theory model (Carstensen, 1992) suggesting that life-strengths in late life are frequently a culmination of strategic changes older adults are able to make in their social relationships with highly selected groups of people from whom they derive a basis for self-identity and social identity. There is evidence to show how close social relationships and family ties are a strong external source of strength. Not only do they serve to protect adults' social identity, but they are linked to beneficial health outcomes and maintenance of resilience (Ryff and Singer, 2000). Social well-being is also linked with emotional and instrumental support from external sources (Bergeman and Wallace, 1999; Ong and Bergeman, 2004a, 2004b) and at the same time is linked to the idea that social well-being develops out of a humanistic (altruistic) sense that adult lives are lived with other people, and often for other people and surrounding communities (Kaniasty and Norris, 1995; Sarason, 1974). In other words, a sense of social well-being comes out of the self-knowledge that one's life is useful and constructive for the collective good. Toward that end, and drawing from sociological theory, social well-being implies positive functioning through the lens of social contribution (Kaniasty and Norris, 1999). The suggestion is that individuals are challenged by social inequalities and social injustice to create lives in which they can and do engage in activities that provide something valuable to society (Kekes, 1995). To a certain extent this view corresponds to earlier models of personal growth developed by Buhler (1975) and humanistic psychologists (e.g., James Bugental, 1976; Viktor Frankl, 1963, 1973; Rollo May, 1953, 1967), who stressed the theme that personal growth comes from transcending the narrow confines of self-centered existence, and making a significant contribution to society, "to reach out beyond oneself and do things for others," and not for the purpose of self-actualization (Frankl, 1963, p. 9).

From the perspective of successful aging, there is also an increasing emphasis on older adults' motivation for "continuous growth in context" (see Baltes, 1987), and a continuous need to compensate for the loss of significant earlier social roles. Along similar dimensions, continuity theory has argued that some individuals are motivated to achieve maximum optimization in late-life functioning by selectively pursuing goals in late life that allow for executive control, autonomy, and the continuity of personal commitments and aspirations that were developed in earlier life stages (Atchley, 1999). Continuity theory (Atchley, 1989) rests on the assumption that individuals seek to maintain role stability throughout the life-course. The suggestion is that although the aging process may present an individual with changing social norms and expectations, and possible disruptions in the availability of social roles, older adults will attempt to preserve continuity of attitudes, dispositions, preferences, and behaviors throughout their life-course. Prior behaviors, roles, and attitudes form the most stable bases for self-identity in later life and provide a stable and secure base for making the transition from the midlife years to late-life functioning. Thus, continuity theory proposes that opportunities to resume or retrieve midlife roles and goals serve as a major source of life-strengths for individuals (Atchley, 1989).

Critics of continuity theory, however, suggest that achieving continuity of lifestyle and role stability is nearly impossible considering the inevitability of role loss through events such as retirement, death of loved ones, the emptying of the familial nest (Matras, 1990), and through marked socio-historical changes (Baltes, 1997). Proponents of successful aging (e.g., Baltes, 1997; Baltes and Baltes, 1990) while not disputing the significance of continuity in behavior, attitudes, and roles, also underscore the notion that continuity in life roles and life goals is not easily sustainable across time and cultures. Change is to be expected, and adjustment and adaptation to changing roles and changing cultural environments is fundamental to resilient functioning. The question arises as to whether the desire for continuity in role and activity adds to individuals' sense of coherence or whether the inability to maintain continuity leads to deterioration and negative consequences, when former roles and activities disappear in periods of rapid and critical loss of resources, or when the culture no longer supports individuals' ability to sustain former roles and goals (Kaniasty and Norris, 1993, 1999).

As an alternative to the continuity framework, Baltes and associates (Baltes, 1997; Baltes and Baltes, 1990) propose the SOC (Selection,

Optimization, and Compensation) model wherein they posit that throughout the lifespan there are *changing, cumulative, and discontinuous processes* involving the interplay of gains and losses in strengths and resources. In this context, continuity in roles and functions is less sustainable. The basic tenet of the SOC model is that individuals' paths through life are negotiated through three different, consciously engaged "life-management" strategies: selection, optimization, and compensation. Selection is about setting goals that adequately reflect the individual's current system of psychosocial resources and sources of support. Age-associated losses in biological potential or plasticity increase the pressure for selection. Optimization is about the acquisition and investment of goal-adequate means. Finally, compensation is about using new means and new resources when the old means to achieve an important goal are no longer available. Whereas selection and optimization are processes requiring individuals to make goal choices that best match their current resources and to strengthen and enhance existing resources to fit these goals, compensation involves an acceptance of their emotional, cognitive, and fiscal deficits and inadequacies, and requires concerted efforts to enhance or alter existing resources following loss of goal-relevant capacities. The SOC model outlines a dynamic and flexible process which allows individuals to retain or enhance resilient functioning by selecting goals, continuing with them, or modifying them if their personal and environmental resources are diminished and no longer support the pursuit of the earlier goals. Overall, the SOC model best integrates important components from the existential, social-cognitive, and psychosocial frameworks and achieves a substantial measure of compatibility among the different social and cultural frameworks that have proposed various components of human resilience and strengths.

In re-conceptualizing the notion of resilient aging and in identifying internal resources that serve as key sources of life-strengths, the important point to bear in mind is that trait resources (such as self-esteem, optimism, or hardiness) and social-cognitive competencies, such as superior cognitive skills, are not independent of one another. Indeed there is evidence that self-esteem, optimism, and sense of control are more or less exchangeable resources and that when one of these is high, the others also tend to be high (Cozzarelli, 1993). To the extent that these sources of strength and revitalization and related psychosocial resources overlap and interact with one another, it is tempting to consider that one individual human resource may act in concert or tandem with other social resources to create a viable social "convoy" of resources that co-exist in the individual personality structure and contribute to resilience in a lasting way (Rini *et al.*, 1999). For example, the presence of one confidant who is a source of comfort and strength may also remind an individual of other existing cognitive assets such as job status and educational attainment. If the key ego-strengthening and strength-providing dispositional traits, cognitive skills, and competencies are linked with one another, then positive adaptation and resilience become more easily attainable because of the interaction among the self-management resources and social resources. Thus when threatened with the loss of an individual resource, competency, or skill (e.g., hearing loss or disability, or financial loss), individuals do not necessarily fall victim to depression, anxiety, or wellness breakdown because other available internal resources such as self-esteem, optimism, or sense of challenge, or other social resources that protect individual resources, may come into play to enhance resilience and emotional strength (Cozzarelli, 1993).

Resilient aging implies individuals making timely and wise choices about allocation and investment of resources. Resilient aging also implies that individuals are proactive with respect to deciding what psychosocial resources need to be conserved for the future. There is evidence to suggest that cognitive skills diminish with aging (Salthouse, 1991). This suggests that in addition to confronting challenges that are already occurring with advancing age, individuals need to make effective use of their existing cognitive competencies and decision-making skills to anticipate and foresee areas that are likely to be sources of future challenges, so as to insure that appropriate resources are available for use when needed (Aspinwall and Taylor, 1997).

Resilient aging implies the need for individuals to strike a balance between accumulating and preserving psychosocial resources for the future, and using valued resources to deal with present needs. An over-emphasis on anticipating future needs and conserving resources for future use may result in missed opportunities for deploying valuable resources that are necessary for maintaining optimal well-being in the present, for example allowing time for leisure activities, and strengthening social and family ties. Individuals' decisions to avoid or confront the challenges of later life may very well depend on which sources of life-strengths in the total constellation of internal and external resources they are considering, and how one or other source of life-strength coheres with other sources in the total constellation (Hobfoll, 2002).

Historical-cultural perspective on adaptation and resilience

The emergent literature on resilience underscores the notion that the ability of individuals to adjust successfully can and should be defined not only in terms of the person–environment fit (French et al., 1974;

Kahana, Kahana, and Riley, 1988) but also in terms of the sociocultural fit (Baltes, 1997; Riley, Kahn, and Foner, 1994; Shweder, 1991; Triandis, 1994). Here the major innovation proposed is that personal and psychosocial resources possessed by individuals are invaluable sources of stress resistance to the extent that they fit cultural-environmental demands. Against this theoretical background there has been a push to support a conception of sources and resources of life-strengths in which resources are largely socioculturally framed rather than individualistic, and so there is the possibility of a better fit among individuals who share a common historical-cultural niche.

Baltes (1997) in particular has argued that current psychological formulations on how older adults can be assisted in acquisition, protection, and maintenance of their emotional and psychosocial resources have ignored cultural and historical contexts. P. B. Baltes (1997) and associates draw attention to the fact that culture-based sources of support and psychosocial and material resources are required at ever-increasing levels to ensure that culturally based material and psychological resources are not lagging behind at a time when increasing numbers of individuals across cultures are struggling to progress from merely surviving towards, at least, moderate thriving. The general expectation among most theorists working in the domain of stress resistance, resilience, and mental well-being has been that social values, psychosocial resources, and ecological resources that fit in one culture will generalize to other cultures and times. In other words, in Western societies the common assumption is that sources of life-strengths and the related psychosocial resources that are recognized to be contributing to maximum adjustment, adaptation, and resilient functioning among individuals are constant across cultures. Increasingly, however, the notion of cultural efficiency/inefficiency is gaining currency; it is being recognized that programs based on strength and resilience models of control, mastery, and autonomy, while highly valued in Western societies, are seldom efficient or effective in other cultural contexts because related biological, technological, and psychosocial resources required by individuals to function at expected levels of efficacy and control are frequently not available (Baltes, 1997; Riley *et al.*, 1994; Shweder, 1991). For example, in impoverished societies (e.g., with limited shelter and food resources), undernourishment, and reduced physical strength alone may interfere with people's attainment of intrinsic aspirations such as building a sense of competence, autonomy, and relatedness (Deci and Ryan, 2000). Similarly, loss of certain personal resources in certain cultures, for example, job loss, loss of social ties, may make the pursuit of self-directed and self-generated activities increasingly difficult in those settings. This may subsequently deplete emotional resilience on a permanent basis in those cultural environments (Baumeister *et al.*, 1998; Karuza, Rabinowitz, and Zevon, 1986).

It is now recognized that the principle of cultural efficiency/inefficiency is axiomatic, in that certain psychosocial resources, for example, shelter, transportation, food, and employment, which are recognized to be essential sources of resilience in all cultures and across time horizons, should be readily available. The question arises as to whether nations and cultures with greater resources have a moral responsibility to provide and protect these resources in other nations and cultures when resource loss has occurred or is threatened. Particularly because the impact of life-strength supports and deficits in psychosocial resources is long term, and those lacking in resources and sources of social support may develop intractable problems that deteriorate their physical health and well-being (Holahan *et al.*, 1999), promptness, and efficiency in responding to others' need for support and resources are vital. Instead of blaming victims who lack or who have lost basic sources of strengths and basic resources, it is suggested that those with stronger psychosocial, cultural, and economic resource reservoirs be more efficient in responding promptly to the demands posed by stressful circumstances in those other cultures (Baumeister *et al.*, 1998; Janoff-Bulman and Frieze, 1983; Karuza *et al.*, 1986).

According to Cole (1996), there is historical constancy in the notion that harm is to be expected when individuals are either inappropriately taking responsibility and blame for problems beyond their control, or if they are expected to maintain a level of control beyond their limits of functioning. Gerontologists and psychologists (e.g., Baltes, 1997; Cole, 1996; Manton and Vaupel, 1995) remind us that our entry into the new millennium and increased globalization is bringing with it the recognition that culture and history play an important role in determining the kinds of psychosocial and material resources we will need in adapting and adjusting in a rapidly changing world society, and what types of personal skills, personal attributes, cognitive competencies, social supports, and psychosocial and material resources will be valued. While specific cultures have each individually defined for themselves what sources of human influence and levels of physical and personal attainments are valuable resources and sources of life-strength and are therefore to be encouraged and applauded, broad culture – which according to Baltes (1997) refers to "the entirety of psychological, social, material, and symbolic (knowledge-based) resources that humans have generated over the millennia" (p. 368) – has lagged behind in defining basic resources and supports that are essential to resilient functioning and well-being from the perspective of a world society. From an historical-cultural perspective, sources and resources that are assumed to facilitate resilient functioning can be and will be effective only to the extent that they cohere with the demands and values of the culture, and are also deeply valued in the culture (Baltes, 1997; Schwartz, 1992; Shweder, 1991). As an example, while financial and material resources, including social status and influential job status, may be important and long-term sources of life-strengths in certain modern cultures, by contrast the preservation of family stability and honor, and veneration of the elders constitutes a highly valued resource in other cultural contexts, for example in Japan (Fukuyama, 1995; Takahashi, 1990). Thus personal values of protecting family honor and the practice of related religious and other rituals to protect family honor have been robust sources of strength in times of adversity among the Japanese, in part because their very possession is valued in the culture, and, in part, because they invoke other community values of family-groundedness, social cooperation, collective coping, and collective success, as distinct from individual success and independence that are more highly valued in Western societies (Fukuyama, 1989, 1995, 2001; Schwartz and Bilsky, 1990; Triandis, 1995). This line of thought suggests that while many personal resources such as self-efficacy beliefs, internal control, and perceived mastery are more typical sources of life-strengths that have been viewed in the Western world as buffers against stress, the indisputable fact remains that these capacities for internal control and mastery become diminished with advancing age; sadly these capacities diminish more rapidly with aging in certain cultural settings because they are not valued in the culture. Furthermore, if the capacities for independence, internal control, and mastery are kept in constant use despite the lack of social support or cultural value, they may deplete plasticity and reserve capacity even more rapidly (Baumeister *et al.*, 1998). Thus, when viewed historically, the skills, resources, and plasticity and resilience of individuals are, in part, a reflection of historical-cultural context (Baltes, 1997; Bandura, 1997).

Although we may not be able to predict what psychosocial resources or sources of resilience and support will universally and globally contribute to human energy, vitality, and optimal aging in future time frames, we must bear in mind that those psychosocial resources known to protect resilience in the individualistic cultures in the West may have to converge with more traditional and communal cultures, requiring perhaps a gradual de-emphasis on internal resources of control, autonomy, independence, and environmental mastery and a corresponding increase of emphasis on resources involving reciprocity, social interaction, interdependence, social involvement, and social contribution.

In short, we are reminded that with our entry into the new millennium and with increased globalization while some psychosocial resources (e.g., food supply, shelter, transportation, social interaction) may remain robust resources across cultures and history, and continue to promote plasticity and resilience in the affective, cognitive, and biological domains, certain other vitalizing resources (e.g., high levels of independence and autonomy, desire for individual material wealth, and social success) may become less relevant to optimal human functioning, and may need to be re-assessed in the context of major socio-historical change. Clearly, our whole conceptualization of what resources contribute to human life-strengths in a global society may need a major re-examination leading to a re-evaluation of the relative importance of different sources of life-strength.

Conclusions

In this chapter we have presented a general discourse on sources of human life-strengths and the psychosocial resources that support them. In Figure 1.1 we present a conceptual framework and schematic representation of diverse perspectives on sources of life-strengths. These different lines of inquiry into the sources of human life-strengths (embedded in existential, social-cognitive, sociocultural, and socio-historical traditions) provide important pieces of the larger puzzle as to the diversity of sources of strengths that may be accessed by older adults, and how these are linked to psychological health and to the maintenance of resilience and hardiness in the face of adversity and challenge. There is agreement that while each framework we have considered in our discourse emphasizes a different set of factors contributing to resilient aging, together they provide a network of structures and pathways for the emergence of life-strengths that contribute to optimal resilience.

Drawing from prior theoretical and philosophical formulations of existential and humanistic theory (see Figure 1.1), we conclude that meaning and purpose in life, religious, moral, and spiritual beliefs, and a relationship with the sacred are not only contributors to, but in fact defining features of, positive mental health and critical determinants of ego-strengths, and tenacious pursuit of life and human resilience.

We also examined sources of human resilience and sources of life-strengths from the perspective of social-cognitive theory (see Figure 1.1) in relationship to internal and external psychosocial resource structures such as internal control, autonomy, and self-efficacy beliefs that operate in concert with cognized goals, outcome expectations, and perceived mastery over environmental obstacles (Bandura, 1982, 1989, 1997). We discussed the extent to which they are valuable facilitators in the regulation of human motivation, action, well-being, and optimal mental health. We also considered the implications of these concepts within an historical-cultural framework (see Figure 1.1). In sum, our discussion of these perspectives converges toward a central thesis that has both an existential flavor and respects the tenets of social-cognitive theory, through the lens of historical-cultural change. To be lived well, life must have purpose embodied in activity and pursuits that give dignity and meaning to daily life, goals that are valuable to oneself and also valued in the culture for their social contribution, social involvements that allow for the realization of individuals' potential, and the growth of a benevolent and caring society in which individuality finds its meaning in the context of community (see Frankl, 1973; Ryff and Singer, 1998b, 2000; Tornstam, 1997; Yalom, 1980).

We conclude with the proposition that sources of life-strengths emanating from existential-humanistic perspectives, social-cognitive perspectives, or historical-cultural perspectives all operate in concert to contribute to human plasticity, reserve capacity, and resilience. Resilient functioning implies each individual's ultimate freedom to take charge, to strive, to thrive, and live a healthy life by invoking whatever sources of life-strengths or human resources they possess and value, and that are appropriate to their needs. Experience confirms that individuals are inherently resilient and will use whatever management or adaptive resources they have, whether these are derived from a sense of personal control, efficacy, and mastery, or from personal or religious faith, or faith in the goodness of humanity or Providence, to overcome life's problems, and to seek solutions to the dilemmas that face them (see Bonanno, 2004, 2005).

In the final analysis, resilient aging involves a continual process of restructuring through which older individuals select their highest priority meanings for life, their highest goals and activities, and implement their most highly valued abilities and competencies to attain desired goals, and also to compensate for lost or diminished capacities.

Acknowledgment

Preparation of this chapter was facilitated in part by a 2004–2005 internal research grant from Trinity Western University to P. S. Fry.

REFERENCES

Ai, A. L., Dunkle, R. E., Peterson, C., and Bolling, S. F. (2000). Spiritual well-being, private prayer, and adjustment of older cardiac patients. In J. A.

Thoreson (ed.), *Perspectives on spiritual well-being and aging.* Springfield, IL: Charles C. Thomas.

Ainlay, S. C., Singleton, R., and Swigert, V. L. (1992). Aging and religious participation: Reconsidering the effects of health. *Journal for the Scientific Study of Religion,* 31, 175–188.

Albert, S. (1977). Temporal comparison theory. *Psychological Review,* 84, 485–503.

Antonovsky, A. (1979). *Health, stress, and coping.* San Francisco, CA: Jossey-Bass.

(1998). The sense of coherence: An historical and future perspective. In H. I. McCubbin, E. A. Thompson, A. I. Thompson, and J. E. Fromer (eds.), *Stress, coping and health in families: Sense of coherence and resiliency* (pp. 3–20).Thousand Oaks, CA: Sage Publications.

Antonucci, T. C. (2001). Social relations: an examination of social networks, social support and sense of control. In J. E. Birren and K. W. Schaie (eds.), *Handbook of the psychology of aging* (5th edn., pp. 427–453). San Diego, CA: Academic Press.

Aspinwall, L. G., and Staudinger, U. M. (2003) (eds.). *A psychology of human strengths: Fundamental questions and future directions for a positive psychology.* Washington, DC: American Psychological Association.

Aspinwall, L. G., and Taylor, S. E. (1997). A stitch in time: Self regulation and proactive coping. *Psychological Bulletin,* 121, 417–436.

Atchley, R. C. (1989). A continuity theory of normal aging. *The Gerontologist,* 29, 183–190.

(1999). *Continuity and adaptation in aging.* Baltimore, MD: Johns Hopkins University Press.

Baltes, M. M. (1996). *The many faces of dependency in old age.* New York: Cambridge University Press.

Baltes, M. M., and Baltes, P. B. (1990). Psychological perspectives on successful aging: The model of selective optimization with compensation. In P. B. Baltes and M. M. Baltes (eds.), *Successful aging: Perspectives from the behavioral sciences* (pp. 1–34). New York: Cambridge University Press.

Baltes, P. B. (1987). Theoretical propositions of lifespan developmental psychology: On the dynamics between growth and decline. *Developmental Psychology,* 23, 611–626.

(1997). On the incomplete architecture of human ontogeny: Selection, optimization, and compensation as foundation of development theory. *American Psychologist,* 52, 366–380.

Bandura, A. (1982). Self-efficacy mechanism in human agency. *American Psychologist,* 37, 122–147.

(1989). Human agency in social cognitive theory. *American Psychologist,* 44, 1175–1184.

(1997). *Self efficacy: The exercise of control.* New York: Freeman.

(2004). Health promotion by social cognitive means, *Health Education and Behavior,* 31, 143–164.

Barrera, M. (1986). Distinctions between social support concepts, measures, and models. *American Journal of Community Psychology,* 14, 413–445.

Baumeister, R. F. (1991). *Meanings in life.* New York: The Guilford Press.

Baumeister, R. F., Bratslavsky, E., Muraven, M., and Tice, D. (1998). Ego depletion: Is the active self a limited resource? *Journal of Personality and Social Psychology,* 74, 1252–1265.

Baumeister, R. F., Heatherton, T. F., and Tice, D. M. (1993). When ego threats lead to self-regulation failure: Negative consequences of high self-esteem. *Journal of Personality and Social Psychology,* 64, 141–156.

Baumeister, R. F., and Leary, M. R. (1995). The need to belong: Desire for interpersonal attachments as a fundamental human motivation. *Psychological Bulletin,* 117, 497–529.

Bergeman, C. S., and Wallace, K. A. (1999) Resiliency in later life. In T. L. Whitman, T. V. Merluzzi, and R. D. White (eds.) *Life-span perspectives on health and illness.* (pp. 207–225). Hillsdale, NJ: Erlbaum.

Bonanno, G. A. (2004). Loss, trauma, and human resilience: Have we under-estimated the human capacity to thrive after extremely aversive events? *American Psychologist,* 59, 20–28.

(2005). Clarifying and extending the construct of adult resilience. *American Psychologist,* 60, 265–267.

Brandtstädter, J., and Renner, G. (1990). Tenacious goal pursuit and flexible goal adjustment: Explication and age-related analysis of assimilative and accommodative strategies of coping. *Psychology and Aging,* 5, 58–67.

Brandtstädter, J., Wentura, D., and Rothermund, K. (1999). Intentional self-development through adulthood and later life: Tenacious pursuit and flexible adjustment of goals. In J. Brandtstädter, and R. M. Lerner (eds.) *Action and self-development: theory and research through the life-span* (pp. 373–400). Thousand Oaks, CA: Sage.

Bugental, J. F. T. (1976). *The search for existential identity.* San Francisco, CA: Jossey-Bass.

Buhler, C. (1975). *The role of values in personality development and for psychother-apy.* Stuttgart, Germany: Klett.

Caplan, G. (1974). *Support systems and community mental health.* New York: Behavioral Publications.

Carstensen, L. L. (1992). Social and emotional patterns in adulthood: Support for socioemotional selectivity theory. *Psychology and Aging,* 7, 331–338.

Cohen, A. B., and Rankin, A. (2004). Religion and the morality of positive mentality. *Basic and Applied Social Psychology,* 26(1), 45–57.

Cohen, S. (1988). Psychosocial models of the role of social support in the eti-ology of physical disease. *Health Psychology,* 7, 269–297.

Cohen, S., and Edwards, J. R. (1989). Personality characteristics as moder-ators of the relationship between stress and disorder. In R. W. J. Neufeld (ed.), *Advances in the investigations of psychological stress* (pp. 235–283). New York: Wiley.

Cohen, S., and Wills, T. A. (1985). Stress, social support, and the buffering hypothesis. *Psychological Bulletin,* 98, 310–357.

Cole, M. (1996). Interacting minds in a lifespan perspective: A cultural/his-torical approach to cultural and cognitive development. In P. B. Baltes and U. M. Staudinger (eds.), *Interactive minds: Life-span perspectives on the social foundation of cognition* (pp. 59–87). New York: Cambridge University Press.

Coward, D. D. (2000). Making meaning within the experience of life threatening illness. In G. Reker and K. K. Chamberlain (eds.), *Existential meaning: Optimizing human development across the life span* (pp. 157–170). Thousand Oaks, CA: Sage.

Cozzarelli, C. (1993). Personality and self-efficacy as predictors of coping with abortion. *Journal of Personality and Social Psychology*, 65, 124–126.

Davidson, R. J., Jackson, D. C., and Kalin, N. H. (2000). Emotion, plasticity, context, and regulation. *Psychological Bulletin*, 126, 891–909.

Debats, D. L., Drost, J., and Hansen, P. (1995). Experiences of meaning in life: A combined qualitative and quantitative approach. *British Journal of Psychology*, 86, 359–375.

Deci, E. L., and Ryan, R. M. (2000). The "what" and "why" of goal pursuits: Human needs and the self-determination of behavior. *Psychological Inquiry*, 11, 227–268.

Diener, E., and Fujita, F. (1995). Resources, personal strivings, and subjective well-being: A nomothetic and idiographic approach. *Journal of Personality and Social Psychology*, 68, 926–935.

Dittmann-Kohli, F. (1995) *Personal meaning systems: Age differences in adult development and aging.* Göttingen, Germany: Hogrefe.

Ellison, C. G. (1991). Religious involvement and subjective well-being. *Journal of Health and Social Behavior*, 32, 80–99.

Ellison, C. G., Gay, D. A., and Glass, T. A. (1989). Does religious commitment contribute to individual life satisfaction? *Social Forces*, 68, 100–123.

Emmons, R. A. (1999). *The psychology of ultimate concerns.* New York: The Guilford Press.

Ensel, W. M., and Lin, N. (1991). The life stress paradigm and psychological distress. *Journal of Health and Social Behavior*, 32, 321–341.

Epstein, S. (1985). The implications of cognitive-experiential self theory for research in social psychology and personality. *Journal of the Theory of Social Behavior*, 15(3), 283–310.

Evans, C. S. (1990). *Søren Kierkegaard's Christian psychology: Insights for counselling and pastoral care.* Grand Rapids, MI: Zondervan.

Featherman, D. L., Smith J., and Peterson, J. G. (1990). Successful aging in a post-retired society. In P. B. Baltes and M. M. Baltes (eds.), *Successful aging: Perspectives from the behavioral sciences* (pp. 50–93). New York, NY: Cambridge University Press.

Fernández-Ballesteros, R. (2003), Light and dark in the psychology of human strengths: The example of psychogerontology. In L. G. Aspinwall, and U. M. Staudinger (eds.). *A psychology of human strengths: Fundamental questions and future directions for a positive psychology* (pp. 131–148). Washington, DC: American Psychological Association.

Fowler, J. W. (1981). *Stages of faith: The psychology of human development and the quest for meaning.* San Francisco, CA: Harper & Row.

Frankl, V. E. (1963). *Man's search for meaning.* Boston, MA: Beacon Press. (1973). *The doctor and the soul* (2nd edn.). New York: Vintage.

Friedman, H. S. (2000). Long-term relations of personality and health: Dynamisms, mechanisms, tropisms. *Journal of Personality*, 68, 1089–1108.

French, J. R. P., Jr., Rodgers, W. L., and Cobb, S. (1974). Adjustment as person-environment fit. In B. V. Coelho, D. A. Hamburg, and J. E. Adams (eds.), *Coping and adaptation* (pp. 316–333). New York: Basic Books.

Fry, P. S. (2000a). Religious involvement, spirituality and personal meaning for life: Existential predictors of psychological well-being in community-residing and institutional care elders. *Aging and Mental Health: An International Journal*, 4, 375–387.

(2000b). Introduction and Guest Editorial for special issue on "Aging and Quality of Life (QOL): The continuing search for quality of life indicators". *International Journal of Aging and Human Development*, 50(4), 245–261.

(2000c). Whose quality of life is it any way? Why not ask seniors to tell us about it? *International Journal of Aging and Human Development*, 50(4), 361–383.

(2001a). The unique contribution of existential factors to the prediction of psychological well-being following spousal loss. *The Gerontologist*, 41, 69–81.

(2001b). Protecting the quality of life of older adults. *Geriatric Times* 2(4), 19–24.

(2003). Perceived self-efficacy domains as predictors of fear of the unknown and fear of dying among older adults. *Psychology and Aging*, 18, 474–486.

Fry, P. S., and Debats, D. L. (2002). Self-efficacy domains as predictors of loneliness and psychological distress in late life. *International Journal of Aging and Human Development*, 55(3), 233–269.

(2006). Sources of life-strengths as predictors of mortality and survivorship in late life. *International Journal of Aging and Human Development*, 62(4), 303–334.

(2009). Perfectionism and the five-factor personality traits as predictors of mortality in older adults. *Journal of Health Psychology*, 14(4), 507–518.

Fukuyama, F. (1989). The end of history? *The National Interest*, 16, 3–18.

(1995). *Trust: The social virtues and the creation of prosperity*. New York: Free Press.

(2001). Social capital, civil society, and development. *Third World Quarterly*, 22(1), 7–20.

Garmezy, N. (1985). Stress resistant children: The search for protective factors. In J. Stevensen (ed.), *Recent research in developmental psychopathology* (pp. 213–233). Oxford: Pergamon Press.

George, L. K. (1996). Social factors and illness. In R. H. Binstock, L. K. George, V. W. Marshall, G. C. Myers, and J. H. Schulz (eds.), *Handbook of aging and the social sciences* (4th edn., pp. 229–252). San Diego, CA: Academic Press.

George, L. K., Ellison, C. G., and Larson, D. B. (2002). Explaining the relationships between religious involvement and health. *Psychological Inquiry*, 13, 190–200.

Hart, H. (1977). Anthropology: Some questions and remarks. In A. E. De Graaff (Ed.), *Views of man in psychology in a Christian perspective. Some readings* (pp. 69–77). Toronto: Association for the Advancement of Christian Scholarship.

Heckhausen, H., and Schulz, R. (1995). A lifespan theory of control. *Psychological Review*, 102, 284–304.

Heisel, M. J., and Flett, G. L. (2004). Purpose in life, satisfaction with life, and suicide ideation in a clinical sample. *Journal of Psychopathology and Behavioral Assessment*, 26, 127–135.

Higgins, E. T. (2000). Social cognition: Learning about what matters in the social world. *European Journal of Social Psychology*, 30, 3–39.

Hill, P. C., Pargament, K. I., Hood, R. W., McCullough, M. E., Swyers, J. P., Larson, D. B., and Zinnbauer, B. J. (2000). Conceptualizing religion and spirituality: Points of commonality, points of departure. *Journal for the Theory of Social Behaviour*, 30, 51–77.

Hobfoll, S. E. (1998). *Stress, culture, and community: The psychology and philosophy of stress*. New York: Plenum.

(2002). Social and psychological resources and adaptation. *Review of General Psychology*, 6(4), 307–324.

Hobfoll, S. E., and Leiberman, J. (1987). Personality and social resources in immediate and continued stress-resistance among women. *Journal of Personality and Social Psychology*, 52, 18–26.

Hobfoll, S. E., Nadler, A., and Leiberman, J. (1986). Satisfaction with social support during crisis: Intimacy and self esteem as critical determinants. *Journal of Personality and Social Psychology*, 51, 296–304.

Holahan, C. J., and Moos, R. H. (1991). Life stressors, personal and social resources and depression: A four-year structural model. *Journal of Abnormal Psychology*, 100, 31–38.

Holahan, C. J., Moos, R. H., Holahan, C. K., and Cronkite, R. C. (1999). Resource loss, resource gain, and depressive symptoms: A 10-year model. *Journal of Personality and Social Psychology*, 77, 620–629.

Inzlicht, M., McGregor, I., Hirsh, J. B., and Nash, K. (2009). Neural markers of religious conviction. *Psychological Science*, 20, 385–392.

Janoff-Bulman, R. (1992). *Shattered assumptions: Towards a new psychology of trauma*. New York: Free Press.

Janoff-Bulman, R., and Brickman, P. (1982). Expectations and what people learn from failure. In N. T. Feathers (Ed.), *Expectations and actions: Expectancy-value models in psychology* (pp. 207–237). Hillsdale, NJ: Erlbaum.

Janoff-Bulman, R., and Frieze, I. H. (eds.) (1983). Reactions to victimization. *Journal of Social Issues*, 39(2), 1–17.

Johnson, P. E. (1959). *Psychology of religion*. Nashville, TN: Abingdon Press.

Joske, W. D. (1981). Philosophy and meaning of life. In E. D. Klemke (ed.), *The meaning of life* (pp. 248–261). New York: Oxford University Press.

Kahana, E., Kahana, B., and Riley, K. (1988). Person-environment transactions relevant to control and helplessness in institutional settings. In P. S. Fry (ed.), *Psychological perspectives of helplessness and control in the elderly* (pp. 121–154). Amsterdam: North Holland Publishers.

Kaniasty, K., and Norris, F. (1993). A test of the social support deterioration model in the context of natural disaster. *Journal of Personality and Social Psychology*, 64, 395–408.

(1995). In search of altruistic community: Patterns of social support mobilization following Hurricane Hugo. *American Journal of Community Psychology*, 23, 447–477.

(1999). The experience of disaster: Individuals and communities sharing trauma. In R. Gist and B. Lubin (eds.), *Response to disaster: Psychosocial, ecological, and community approaches* (pp. 25–61). Washington, DC: Taylor & Francis.

Karuza, J., Rabinowitz, V. C., and Zevon, M. A. (1986). Implications of control and responsibility on helping the aged. In M. M. Baltes and P. B. Baltes (eds.), *The psychology of control and aging* (pp. 373–396). Hillsdale, NJ: Erlbaum.

Kekes, J. (1995). *Moral wisdom and good lives*. Ithaca, NY: Cornell University Press.

Kelly, J. G. (1966). Ecological constraints on mental health services. *American Psychologist*, 21, 535–539.

Kern, M. L, and Friedman, H. S. (2008). Do conscientious individuals live longer? A quantitative review. *Health Psychology*, 27(5), 505–512.

Keyes, C. L. M. (2002). The mental health continuum: From languishing to flourishing in life. *Journal of Health and Social Behavior*, 43, 207–222.

Keyes, C. L. M., and Haidt, J. (2003). *Flourishing: Positive psychology and the life well-lived*. Washington DC: American Psychological Association.

Kivimaki, M., Feldt, T., Vahtera, J., and Nurmi, J. E. (2000). Sense of coherence and health: Evidence from two cross-lagged longitudinal samples. *Social Science and Medicine*, 50, 583–597.

Kivnick, H. Q. (1998). Through the life cycle: Psychological thoughts on old age. In G. H. Pollock and S. J. Greenspan (eds.) *The course of life*, vol. VII. Madison, CT: International Universities Press.

Klinger, E. (1998). The search for meaning in evolutionary perspective and its clinical implications. In P. T. P. Wong and P. S. Fry (eds.), *The human quest for meaning: A handbook of psychological research and clinical applications* (pp. 2–50). Mahwah, NJ: Erlbaum

Kobasa, S. C. (1979). Stressful life events, personality, and health: An inquiry into hardiness. *Journal of Personality and Social Psychology*, 37, 1–11.

Kobasa, S. C. and Maddi, S. R. (1977), Existential personality theory. In R. Corsini (ed.), *Current personality theories* (pp. 243–276) Itasca, IL: Peacock.

Kobasa, S. C., and Puccetti, M. C. (1983). Personality and social resources in stress resistance. *Journal of Personality and Social Psychology*, 45, 839–850.

Koenig, H. G. (2000). Religion, well-being and health in the elderly: The scientific evidence for an association. In J. A. Thorson (ed.), *Perspectives on spiritual well-being and aging* (pp. 84–97). Springfield, IL: Charles C. Thomas.

Koenig, H. G., Smiley, M., and Gonzales, J. A. P. (1988). *Religion, health and aging: A review and theoretical integration*. Westport, CT: Greenwood Press.

Krause, N. (1990). Perceived health problems, formal/informal support, and life satisfaction among older adults. *Journal of Gerontology*, 45, S193–205.

Krause, N., Ingersoll-Dayton, B., Ellison, C. G., and Wulff, K. M. (1999). Aging, religious doubt, and psychological well-being. *The Gerontologist*, 39, 525–533.

Lawler, K. A. and Younger, J. W. (2002). Theobiology: An analysis of spirituality, cardiovascular responses, stress, mood, and physical health. *Journal of Religion and Health*, 41, 347–362.

Lawton, M. P., Moss, M., Hoffman, C., Grant, R., Ten Have, T. and Kleban, M. H. (1999). Health, valuation of life, and the wish to live. *The Gerontologist*, 39, 406–416.

Lawton, M. P., and Nahemow, L. (1973). Ecology and the aging process. In C. Eisdorfer and M. P. Lawton (eds.), *The psychology of adult development and aging* (pp. 619–674). Washington, DC: American Psychological Association.

Lucas, E. (1998). The meaning of life and the goals for life for chronically elderly people. In P. T. P. Wong and P. S. Fry (eds.), *The human quest for meaning: A handbook of psychological research and clinical applications* (pp. 307–316). Mahwah, NJ: Erlbaum.

Maddi, S. R. (1987). Hardiness training at Illinois Bell Telephone. In J. Opatz (ed.), *Health promotion evaluation* (pp. 101–115). Stephens Point, WI: National Wellness Institute.

(1998). Creating meaning through making decisions. In P. T. P. Wong and P. S. Fry (eds.), *The human quest for meaning: A handbook of psychological research and clinical applications* (pp. 3–26). Mahwah, NJ: Erlbaum.

Magnani, L. E. (1990). Hardiness, self-perceived health, and activity among independently functioning older adults. *Scholarly Inquiry for Nursing Practice: An International Journal*, 4, 171–184.

Mahan, B. J. (2004). *Forgetting ourselves on purpose: Vocation and the ethics of ambition*. San Francisco, CA: Jossey-Bass.

Maibach, E., Flora, J., and Nass, C. (1991). Changes in self-efficacy and health behavior in response to a minimal contact community health campaign. *Health Communication*, 3, 1–15.

Manton, K. G., and Vaupel, J. W. (1995). Survival after the age of 80 in the United States, Sweden, France, England and Japan. *New England Journal of Medicine*, 333, 1232–1235.

Martin, L. R., Friedman, H. S., and Schwartz, J. E. (2007). Personality and mortality risk across the lifespan: The importance of conscientiousness as a biopsychosocial attribute. *Health Psychology*, 26, 428–436.

Matras, J. (1990). *Dependency, obligations, entitlements: A new sociology of aging, the life course, and the elderly*. Englewood Cliffs, NJ: Prentice Hall.

May, R. (1953). *Man's search for himself*. New York: Norton.

(1967). *Psychology and the human dilemma*. New York: Van Nostrand.

McAvay, G. J., Seeman, T. E., and Rodin, J. (1996). A longitudinal study of change in domain-specific self-efficacy among older adults. *Journal of Gerontology: Psychological Sciences*, 51B, 243–253.

McFadden, S. H. (1995). Religion and well-being in aging persons in an aging society. *Journal of Social Issues,* 51, 161–175.

Myers, D. G. (2000). The funds, friends, and faith of happy people. *American Psychologist,* 55(1), 56–67.

Nesselroade, J. R., (1991). Interindividual differences in intraindividual change. In L. M. Collins and J. J. Horn (eds.), *Best methods for analysis of change: Recent advances, unanswered questions, future directions* (pp. 92–105). Washington, DC: American Psychological Association.

Norris, F. H., and Kaniasty, K. (1996). Received and perceived social support in times of stress: A test of the social support deterioration deterrence model. *Journal of Personality and Social Psychology,* 71, 498–511.

Norris, F., and Murrell, S. (1987). The transitory impact of life event stress on psychological symptoms in older adults. *Journal of Health and Social Behavior,* 28, 197–211.

Ong, A. D., and Bergeman, C. S. (2004a). Resilience and adaptation to stress in later life: Empirical perspectives and conceptual implications. *Ageing International,* 29, 219–246.

(2004b). The complexity of emotion in later life. *Journal of Gerontology: Psychological Sciences,* 59B(3), 117–122.

Pargament, K. I. (1997). *The psychology of religion and coping.* New York: The Guilford Press.

Pargament, K. I., Koenig, H. G., Tarakeswar, N., and Hahn, J. (2001). Religious struggle as a predictor of mortality among medically ill elderly patients: A two year study. *Archives of Internal Medicine,* 161, 1881–1885.

Park, C. L., and Folkman, S. (1997). Meaning in the context of stress and coping. *Review of General Psychology,* 1(2), 115–144.

Pearlin, L., and Schooler, C. (1978). The structure of coping. *Journal of Health and Social Behavior,* 19, 2–21.

Reker, G. T., and Wong, P. T. P. (1988). Aging as an individual process: Toward a theory of personal meaning. In J. E. Birren and V. L. Bengston (eds.), *Emergent theories of aging* (pp. 214–246). New York: Springer.

(1984). Psychological and physical well-being in the elderly: The Perceived Well-Being Scale. *Canadian Journal on Aging,* 3, 23–32.

Riley, M. W., Kahn, R. L., and Foner, A. (1994). *Age and structural lag: Society's failure to provide meaningful opportunities in work, family, and leisure.* New York: Wiley.

Rimal, R. N., (2000). Closing the knowledge-behavior gap in health promotion: The mediating role of self-efficacy. *Health Communication,* 12, 219–237.

(2001). Perceived risk and self-efficacy as motivators: Understanding individuals' long-term use of health information. *Journal of Communication,* 8, 633–654.

Rini, C. K., Dunkel-Schetter, C., Wadhwa, P. D., and Sandman, C. A. (1999). Psychological adaptation and birth outcomes: The role of personal resources, stress, and sociocultural context in pregnancy. *Health Psychology,* 18, 333–345.

Rodin, J., Timko, C., and Harris, S. (1985). The construct of control. In C. Eisdorfer, M. P. Lawton, and G. L. Maddox (eds.), *Annual review of gerontology and geriatrics*, vol. V (pp. 3–35). New York: Springer.

Rosenberg, M. (1965). *Society and adolescent self image*. Princeton, NJ: Princeton University Press.

Rowe, J., and Kahn, R. (1987). Human aging: Usual and successful. *Science*, 237, 142–149.

Ryff, C. D. (1989). Happiness is everything, or is it? Explorations on the meaning of psychological well-being. *Journal of Personality and Social Psychology*, 57, 1069–1081.

Ryff, C. D., and Keyes, C. L. M. (1995). The structure of psychological well-being revisited. *Journal of Personality and Social Psychology*, 69, 719–729.

Ryff, C. D., and Singer, B. (1998a). The role of purpose in life and personal growth in positive human health. In P. T. P. Wong and P. S. Fry (eds.), *The human quest for meaning: A handbook of psychological research and clinical applications* (pp. 213–235). Mahwah, NJ: Erlbaum.

(1998b) The contours of positive mental health. *Psychological Inquiry*, 9, 1–28.

(2000). Interpersonal flourishing: A positive health agenda for the new millennium. *Personality and Social Psychology Review*, 4(1), 30–44.

Salthouse, T. A. (1991). *Theoretical perspectives on cognitive aging*. Hillsdale, NJ: Erlbaum.

Sarason, I. G., Sarason, B. R., and Shearin, E. N. (1986). Social support as an individual difference variable: Its stability, origins, and relational aspects. *Journal of Personality and Social Psychology*, 51, 845–855.

Sarason, I. G., Sarason, B. R., Shearin, E. N., and Pierce, G. R. (1987). A brief measure of social support: Practical and theoretical implications. *Journal of Social and Personal Relationships*, 4, 497–510.

Sarason, S. B. (1974). *The psychological sense of community: Prospects for a community psychology*. San Francisco, CA: Jossey-Bass.

Schaie, K. W., Krause, N., and Booth, A. (eds.) (2004). *Religious influences on health and wellbeing in the elderly*. New York: Springer.

Scheier, M. F., and Carver, C. S. (1985). Optimism, coping and health: Assessment and implications of generalized outcome expectancies. *Health Psychology*, 4, 219–247.

(1992). Effects of optimism on psychology and physical well-being: Theoretical overview and empirical update. *Cognitive Therapy and Research*, 16, 201–228.

Schulz, R., and Rau, M. T. (1985). Social support through the life course. In S. Cohen and S. L. Syme (eds.), *Social support and health* (pp. 129–149). Orlando, FL: Wiley.

Schwartz, S. H. (1992). Universals in the content and structure of values: Theory and empirical tests in 20 countries. In M. Zanna (ed.), *Advances in experimental social psychology*, vol. XXV (pp. 1–65). New York: Academic Press.

Schwartz, S. H, and Bilsky, W. (1990). Toward a theory of the universal content and structure of values: Extensions and cross-cultural replications. *Journal of Personality and Social Psychology*, 58, 878–891.

Seeman, T. E., Berkman, L. F., Blazer, D., and Rowe, J. W. (1994). Social ties and support and neuroendocrine function. The MacArthur studies of successful aging. *Annals of Behavior Medicine*, 16, 95–108.

Seligman, M. E. P. (1975). *Helplessness*. San Francisco, CA: Freeman.

Seligman, M. E. P., and Csikszentmihalyi, M. (2000). Positive psychology. *American Psychologist*, 55, 5–14.

Seybold, K. S., and Hill, P. C. (2001). The role of religion and spirituality in mental and physical health. *Current Directions in Psychological Science*, 10(1), 21–24.

Sheldon, K. M., and Kasser, T. (1995). Coherence and congruence: Two aspects of personality integration. *Journal of Personality and Social Psychology*, 68, 531–543.

Shumaker, S. A., and Czajkowski, S. M. (1994). *Social support and cardiovascular disease*. New York: Plenum Press.

Shweder, R. A. (1991). *Thinking through cultures*. Cambridge, MA: Harvard University Press.

Silberman, I. (2003). Spiritual role modeling: The teaching of meaning systems. *The International Journal for the Psychology of Religion*, 13(3), 175–195.

(2004). Religion as a meaning system: Implications for pastoral care and guidance. In D. Herl and M. L. Berman (eds.), *Building bridges over troubled waters: Enhancing pastoral care and guidance* (pp. 51–67). Lima, OH: Wyndham Hall Press.

(2005a). Religion as a meaning-system: Implications for individual and societal wellbeing. *Psychology of Religion Newsletter: American Psychological Association Division 36*, 30(2), 1–9.

(2005b). Religious violence, terrorism and peace: A meaning system analysis. In R. F. Paloutzian and C. L. Park (eds.), *Handbook of the psychology of religion and spirituality* (pp. 524–549). New York: The Guilford Press.

Silberman, I., Higgins, E. T., and Dweck, C. S. (2001). *Religion and wellbeing: World beliefs as mediators*. Paper presented at the 109th Annual Convention of the American Psychological Association. San Francisco, CA.

Skinner, E. A. (1996). A guide to constructs of control. *Journal of Personality and Social Psychology*, 71, 549–570.

Smith, T. L., and Meyers, L. S. (1998). The sense of coherence: Its relationship to personality, stress, and health measures. *Journal of Social Behavior and Personality*, 12, 513–526.

Smyer, M., and Quall, S. H. (1999). *Mental health and aging*. Williston, VT: Blackwell.

Suominen, S., Blomberg, H., Helenius, H., and Koskenvuo, M. (1999). Sense of coherence and health – Does the association depend on resistance resources? A study of 3115 adults in Finland. *Psychology and Health*, 14, 937–948.

Takahashi, K. (1990). Affective relationships and their lifelong development. In P. B. Baltes, D. L. Featherman and R. M. Lerner (eds.), *Life-span development and behaviour*, vol. X (pp. 1–27). Hillsdale, NJ: Erlbaum.

Thoits, P. (1994). Stressors and problem-solving: The individual as psychological activist. *Journal of Health and Social Behavior*, 35, 143–160.

Thoits, P. A. (1995). Stress, coping, and social support processes: Where are we? What next? [Extra issue]. *Journal of Health and Social Behavior*, 53–79.

Thompson, N. J., Coker, J., Krause, J. S., and Henry, E. (2003). Purpose in life as a mediator of adjustment after spinal cord injury. *Rehabilitation Psychology*, 48, 100–108.

Thoresen, C. E., and Harris, A. H. S. (2002). Spirituality and health: What's the evidence and what's needed? *Annals of Behavioral Medicine*, 24, 3–13

Tillich, P. (1952). *The courage to be*. Newhaven, CT: Yale University Press.

(1957). *Dynamics of faith*. New York: Harper & Row.

(1963). *Morality and Beyond*. New York: Harper & Row.

Tornstam, L. (1997). Life crises and gerotranscendence. *Journal of Aging and Identity*, 2, 111–113.

Triandis, H. C. (1994). *Culture and social behavior*. New York: McGraw-Hill.

(1995). *Individualism and collectivism*. Boulder, CO: Westview Press.

Vaux, A. (1988). *Social support: Theory, research and intervention*. New York: Praeger

Warren, R. (2003). *The purpose-driven life: What on Earth am I here for?* Grand Rapids, MI: Zondervan.

Wilson, R. S., Mendes de Leon, C. F., Bienias, J. L., Evans, D. A., and Bennett, D. A. (2004). Personality and mortality in old age. *Journal of Gerontology: Psychological Sciences*, 59B, 110–116.

Wong, P. T. P. (1998a). Spirituality, meaning, and successful aging. In P. T. P. Wong and P. S. Fry (eds.), *The human quest for meaning: A handbook of psychological research and clinical applications* (pp. 359–394). Mahwah, NJ: Erlbaum.

(1998b). Meaning-centered counseling In P. T. P. Wong and P. S. Fry (eds.), *The human quest for meaning: A handbook of psychological research and clinical applications* (pp. 395–435). Mahwah, NJ: Erlbaum.

Yalom, I. D. (1980). *Existential psychotherapy*. New York: Basic Books.

Yang, E., and Glaser, R. (2000). Stress induced immunomodulation: Impact on immune defenses against infectious disease. *Biomedicine & Pharmacotherapy*, 54, 245–250.

2 Growth is not just for the young: growth narratives, eudaimonic resilience, and the aging self

Jack J. Bauer and Sun W. Park

Abstract

In this chapter we present the case that growth is a central concern in older adults' self-identity, facilitating dispositional well-being and resilience in older adulthood. Contrary to the view that "growth is for the young and loss is for the old," research on personal goals and memories demonstrates that older adults are at least as concerned with gain and growth as they are with loss. As for personal memories, we turn to quantitative research on narrative self-identity. Growth-oriented narratives are common in older adulthood. They predict well-being, differentiate hedonic from eudaimonic well-being, and differentiate two forms of eudaimonic well-being. Finally, we present a framework for studying resilience: hedonic resilience involves affect regulation in the wake of loss or potential trauma, whereas eudaimonic resilience includes affect regulation but additionally considers meaning regulation.

Introduction

Psychological resilience in old age, like in any period of adulthood, is intimately tied to self-identity. Some forms of self-identity are more likely than others to facilitate resilience across the lifespan (Greve and Staudinger, 2006). For example, growth-oriented identities are more likely than others to precede increases in meaning-making and adaptation (e.g., Adler, 2009; Bauer and McAdams, in press; King and Smith, 2004; Pals, 2006b). In this chapter we argue that a growth orientation in one's self-identity serves as a central feature of the aging self and in doing so facilitates resilience. We make three claims about resilience and the aging self. First, *growth is a normative, often central concern in older adults' personal goals.* Contrary to the common view that "growth is for the young and decline is for the old," we provide evidence from goals research to show that the concept of growth serves as a prominent source of meaning in the lives of older adults, even amid escalating concerns about loss. Second, *growth is a prominent feature of the aging, narrative self.* Older adults focus on growth not only in their personal goals but also in their autobiographical memories. By interpreting themselves as having grown in their narratives of the personal past, adults of all ages construct a personally meaningful self-identity. Quantitative measures of growth narratives have established ties to meaning, happiness, and adjustment – a connection that may be especially strong for older adults. Third, *hedonic resilience can be distinguished from eudaimonic resilience, which has implications for resilient aging.* We first provide a perspective on eudaimonic well-being that includes hedonic well-being (affect) as well as concerns for meaning and growth. We then propose that hedonic resilience involves the regulation of affect, whereas eudaimonic resilience combines affect regulation and meaning regulation. Older adults' heightened capacity for meaning-making, and possibly growth-oriented meaning-making, may well facilitate eudaimonic resilience, as suggested by quantitative, narrative research. A conceptual overview of the chapter appears in Figure 2.1.

Theoretical/conceptual bases

We first establish that older adults are very much concerned with the idea of growth. We then describe how people use the idea of growth as a theme in their life narratives – something older adults are especially good at doing. Finally, we examine research on eudaimonia and its relation to growth narratives. This section is an attempt to lay an empirically based foundation for the study of eudaimonic resilience.

Who says growth is just for the young? Not the data

Personal losses naturally accumulate, at an accelerated pace, with age. Physical abilities, friends and family, peak income, some psychological abilities, and more tend to fade away in one way or another in older adulthood. Adults of all ages have been shown to believe that such a portrait accurately depicts the aging process (Heckhausen, Dixon, and Baltes, 1989). In response to all this loss, older adults shift their personal priorities and goals to accommodate and deal with these losses (Ebner, Freund, and Baltes, 2006; Freund and Riediger, 2006; Greve and Staudinger, 2006; Heckhausen, 1997; Ogilvie, Rose, and Heppen, 2001). This shift in priorities amounts to an increasing number of goals oriented toward maintenance and prevention with age as well as a decreasing number of gain-oriented goals, all of which is consonant with the Selection, Optimization, and Compensation (SOC) model of lifespan development (Freund and Baltes, 1998). These findings have

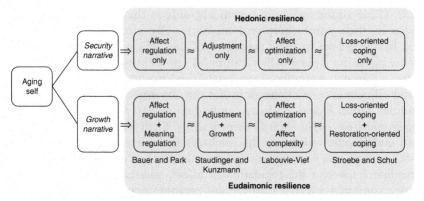

Figure 2.1. Conceptualizations of the aging, narrative self in relation to hedonic and eudaimonic resilience. When the aging self is narrated in terms of security, that self is focused on maintenance, recovery to baseline, or the acquisition of mere pleasure, which are characteristics of hedonic resilience. When the aging self is narrated in terms of growth, that self is focused on concerns of not only maintenance and affect regulation but also on personal meaning-making and prosocial development – a combination that is characteristic of eudaimonic resilience. Growth narratives interpret the individual's life as involving progressive, prosocial development of both the past (autobiographical memories) and the future (personal goals). The aging self may be especially prone toward growth narratives – despite the mounting losses that come with age – as the older adult increasingly recognizes the finitude of time and increasingly places meaning on psychosocial life instead of extrinsically meaningful concerns. Not only do older adults' goals seem as least as likely to focus on gains as on losses, but older adults also seem especially capable of interpreting themselves as having grown in the past.

been replicated with different methods, and we take no issue with this research to this point. However, we do take issue with a message that is typically extracted from the data – that older adults focus primarily on loss, maintenance, and prevention but not on growth. We view this as a misrepresentation of the data's fuller story.

The gain orientation of older adults

The reporting of this research, particularly in discussion sections, overwhelmingly emphasizes only one of two important findings on aging and gain-versus-loss orientations in personal goals. The finding that gets more attention involves two shifts in adulthood: older adults

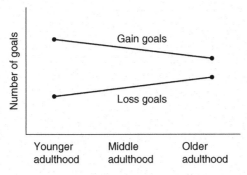

Figure 2.2. Growth – or at least gain – is not just for the young. This figure approximates the findings across several studies reported in Ebner *et al.* (2006), Heckhausen (1997), and Ogilvie *et al.* (2001). Over the course of adulthood, gain orientation decreases and loss orientation increases, but gain continues to be an important concern in older adulthood – at least as much of a concern as loss. In some studies older adults emphasize significantly more gain goals than loss goals, whereas in other studies older adults report gain and loss goals equally. Thus older adults are at least as concerned with making gains as with preventing losses.

focus less on gain-oriented goals than younger adults do, and older adults focus more on loss-oriented goals than younger adults do. The published interpretations of these findings often mistake these shifts to mean that older adults do not focus on growth. The problem with this interpretation – in addition to the fact that "gain" is not necessarily the same as "growth" (see below) – is that this interpretation does not consider the other important finding that comes from the same data: despite these two shifts, older adults still have as many gains goals as loss goals. In other words, older adults' focus on gain goals may have decreased since young adulthood, and their focus on loss goals may have increased since young adulthood, but they started off in young adulthood having a great deal more gain goals than loss goals. Even after "decreasing" in their gain orientation and "increasing" in their loss orientation, older adults are still placing at least as much emphasis on gain as on loss (see Figure 2.2). (We use quotation marks around "decreasing" and "increasing" because all these findings come from cross-sectional studies, so interpretations of individual development are made tentatively and only after careful consideration of generation effects, as these studies point out.)

Perhaps the clearest depiction of this finding appears in Heckhausen's (1997) study of 510 younger, middle, and older adults' goals, where older adults report almost twice as many gain-oriented than loss-oriented goals. The article reports neither exact means of gain and loss goals at each period nor whether the gain-versus-loss means at any one age period were significant. However, a graph on p. 180 portrays the following mean levels of gain and loss goals reported for a total of five goals measured per person. Older adults had a nearly 2:1 gain–loss ratio for their goals (means of approximately 3.0 gain goals to approximately 1.6 loss goals, judging from the graph), whereas younger adults had upwards of a 4:1 ratio found in young adulthood (approximately 3.9 gain goals to 1.1 loss goals). Thus, even though this ratio was significantly different – suggesting a "decline" in gain goals and an "increase" in loss goals (quotes to note the study was cross-sectional, not longitudinal) – the clear majority of older adults' goals in this study still dealt with concerns for gains rather than losses.

Similarly, in two more studies, Ogilvie *et al.* (2001) measured four kinds of goals – acquire (gain), keep (maintain), cure (recovery), and prevent goals – of adolescents, midlife adults, and older adults. Acquire goals comprised older adults' highest percentage of goals (51 percent and 46 percent in the two studies). These percentages of acquire goals were statistically the same for midlife adults but were significantly lower than for adolescents (71 percent in both studies). Keep goals were more common for the older group than the other two groups (20 percent and 29 percent for older adults; 9 percent and 8 percent for midlife adults; 1 percent and 4 percent for adolescents). However, cure goals were more common for midlife adults, and then in only one of the studies (28 percent and 19 percent for midlife adults; 17 percent and 14 percent for older adults; 19 percent and 19 percent for adolescents), suggesting perhaps that in midlife, problems are still thought to be correctible whereas in older adulthood the focus is less on corrective measures and more on maintaining what strengths one has.

In a third set of studies, Ebner *et al.* (2006) found similar results. In the first study, older adults placed as much importance on gain goals as on maintenance and loss goals. Means for gain, maintenance, and loss goals for older adults were not reported, so in the words of the authors (p. 668), "older adults rated their goals to similar degrees as being oriented toward growth, maintenance, and loss prevention." In the second study, "younger and older adults did not differ regarding their orientation toward growth" (p. 671). With this finding, we only wish to note that older adults do in fact place importance on growth in their lives.

These three sets of studies (Ebner *et al.*, 2006; Heckhausen, 1997; Ogilvie *et al.*, 2001) are similar in two ways. Older adults had generally fewer (or the same number of) gain goals and generally more loss goals than did younger adults. However, this does not mean that older adults had fewer gain goals than loss goals *per se*; indeed they tended to have at least as many gain goals as they did loss goals. The continued (albeit diminished) focus on gain goals is important as a starting point for studying the self-identity and subjective experience of older adults. Despite the mounting losses and depleting resources that come with age, older adults seem to place at least as much personal importance on gain as they do on loss. Thus the idea that "growth is for the young, loss is for the old" ignores important empirical findings and oversimplifies the mindsets of older adults' personal concerns.

Toward a fuller model of the aging self: perspectives on growth

The presentation so far just scratches the surface of the role of growth in older adults' capacity for resilience.

Growth versus gain The studies on gain goals presented earlier focus exclusively on people's subjective focus on gains versus losses, or else on gains versus maintenance and prevention/recovery. However, published reports on gain goals frequently use the word *growth* to interpret and summarize the findings. We wish to note that, whereas growth is a form of gain, growth has specific meanings that involve not merely "moving in a positive direction" or "boosting affect." Growth can refer to a progressive, prosocial form of gain. Whereas a gain goal might involve accumulating more wealth or achieving higher status, a growth goal might involve deepening one's relationships or improving personal skills that are personally meaningful (Bauer and McAdams, 2004a; Kasser and Ryan, 1993).

Growth as a value Gain goals may concern any desired good, hedonic or eudaimonic. A common view of gains and losses in older adulthood is couched in mechanistic or economic terms: older adults' "resources" are depleted and require more "investment" (e.g., Freund and Riediger, 2006). Without dismissing an economic metaphor outright, we counter that implications of rational self-interest and balance-sheet analysis are not apt metaphors for how people plan and evaluate their lives. To start, not all personal resources are valued personally on the same scale (see Sheldon and Elliot, 1998). What matters is the way in which individuals *identify* with those resources (e.g., the relatively intrinsic versus extrinsic or hedonic versus eudaimonic value placed on a goal; Bauer, McAdams, and Pals, 2008). With this in mind we call for a fuller, less mechanistic portrait of the aging self – one that includes the processes by which older adults create meaning in life. In this chapter we focus on the process of associating the concept of growth with their lives in the past, present, and future. Still, it is important to note that, even when just looking at the numbers of gain versus loss goals, older adults seem to be at least as concerned with gains as they are with losses.

Growth as an orientation of self-identity   Brief descriptions of goals may reflect self-identity by revealing personal values, but this is a step shy of knowing how the person integrates life events into a coherent and meaningful identity (McAdams and Pals, 2006). Indeed older adults may be especially prone toward getting meaning in life from narrative descriptions of their personal memories: not only is life review important at this time of life (Staudinger, 2001), but older adults also seem to have a heightened capacity to make meaning out of their personal experiences (Pasupathi, 2001).

Growth versus security in the narrative identity of older adults

Personal memories (in addition to goals) play an important role in the construction of a growth-oriented self-identity in older adulthood. Life review – largely a narrative endeavor in creating meaning in autobiographical memories – is itself a central concern for older adults (Erikson, 1968; Staudinger, 2001). Indeed, most of the research on narrative meaning-making in adulthood focuses not on goals but on memories (Bluck and Habermas, 2001; McAdams, 2008; McLean, Pasupathi, and Pals, 2007; Pasupathi, 2001; Singer, 2004; Staudinger, 2001). Furthermore, as adults experience major life changes, such as the loss of loved ones and personal resources, the sense of personal continuity is threatened. Resilience is facilitated by the capacity to make sense of the loss by constructing a sense of continuity, connection, and purpose in one's personal narratives and life story (Bauer and Bonanno, 2001a; McAdams, 1993; Pasupathi, Weeks, and Rice, 2006).

Themes of growth and personal meaning-making in life narratives constitute a central feature of meaning-making in older adults' lives (e.g., Ardelt, 2008; Bauer, McAdams, and Sakaeda, 2005b; Carstensen, Isaacowitz, and Charles, 1999; Gluck *et al.*, 2005). In this section we describe growth narratives, which are contrasted with narratives that focus on security, maintenance, and the merely acquisition of pleasure. We claim that older adults (like younger adults) commonly use the concept of growth to endow their self-identity with meaning.

Growth narratives

A growth narrative is a personal story that frequently emphasizes some form of progressive development (Bauer *et al.*, 2008). A growth narrative emphasizes developing, learning, exploring, expanding, deepening, or strengthening in a prosocial domain of one's life. A growth narrative can be contrasted with a security narrative. A security narrative emphasizes safety, preserving, conserving, protecting, maintaining, or defending the self. The following two excerpts come from narratives about a high point in life (Bauer *et al.*, 2005b):

- "I was by the lake at night ... I was able to formulate all my values and beliefs into one comprehensive system ... At that moment I understood and more importantly felt my relationship with the rest of the living world."
- "My daughter's bar mitzvah ... our whole family was very proud of her ... the months of preparing for the event were very strenuous both emotionally and financially. It is certainly a big relief that it is over."

The first excerpt uses growth themes. It involves an improved conceptual understanding of one's life as well as an improved felt experience of it, both as an individual and in relation to others. The second excerpt does not portray progress or improvement; indeed it emphasizes escape and mere recovery to baseline. These excerpts illustrate the difference between a growth orientation and a safety or security orientation in interpreting life events (Maslow, 1968).

Growth may be found in the structure (i.e., integrative complexity) or content (e.g., narrative themes) of a narrative. The present chapter focuses primarily on themes of growth. Life stories, like stories generally, have themes that give the story a sense of coherence and a specific value orientation (McAdams, 2008). The two most common narrative themes deal with power or achievement on one hand and love or intimacy on the other – or more broadly, agency and communion. Here we argue that life stories with themes of growth hold particular promise for facilitating resilience. Like themes of agency and communion, growth themes are not found in every narrative.

Also like other themes, growth themes can serve as a source of continuity among the myriad autobiographical memories that constitute a life story (Bauer *et al.*, 2008; Bluck, 2003). In other words, growth themes in personal narratives often involve growth that has happened already but that continues to serve as an important source of meaning in the present. The more a person's life story uses the concept of growth to give meaning to various life episodes (e.g., high points in life, low points, turning points), the more growth-oriented that person's self-identity is. A life story that consistently emphasizes growth has been called a growth story (Bauer *et al.*, 2008).

Two kinds of growth themes   Two general kinds of growth themes have been studied routinely: experiential (or social-emotional) and cognitive (or social-cognitive) growth themes. Experiential growth themes involve intrinsically motivated, humanistic concerns, such as the importance of doing personally meaningful activities, cultivating personally meaningful relationships, and contributing to the development of society and future generations (Deci and Ryan, 2000; Kasser and Ryan, 1993). Experiential growth themes emphasize a deepening or strengthening in the felt experience of one's psychosocial life, but *not* necessarily with an emphasis on gaining a deeper *conceptual* understanding of it. In contrast, cognitive growth themes emphasize the importance of differentiating and integrating new conceptual perspectives on the self and others. Cognitive growth themes focus on the personal value of differentiating and integrating perspectives on the self and others. Examples of cognitive growth themes in personal memories include accommodation in meaningful life events (King and Noelle, 2005; King *et al.*, 2000), causal connections between life events and one's broader concept of self (Pals, 2006a), and various forms of gaining insights, learning lessons, exploring new perspectives, integrative memories, and wisdom (Bauer and McAdams, 2004b; Bauer *et al.*, 2005b; Blagov and Singer, 2004; Bluck and Gluck, 2004; McLean *et al.*, 2007; Pals, 2006a). Narratives of personal goals, particularly major life goals, also have themes of cognitive growth, measured as goal complexity (McAdams, Ruetzel, and Foley, 1986), elaboration of possible selves (King and Smith, 2004), and exploratory goals (Bauer and McAdams, 2004a). Any one narrative may have themes of both experiential and cognitive growth, and indeed the two correlate moderately (Bauer *et al.*, 2008). However, experiential growth themes are much more common than cognitive growth themes (in Japan as well as in the USA; Kamide and Daibo, 2008). Furthermore, narrative themes of experiential and cognitive growth differentiate happiness and psychosocial maturity, as discussed later.

Examples of cognitive and experiential growth narratives   It is easy to oversimplify what growth narratives are. A growth narrative is not simply a rosy view of life, not merely a narrative emphasizing positive affect. A growth narrative emphasizes change – and progressive change at that. In older adults, the concept of growth may well involve concerns for loss, but the thrust of the narrative is on growth. For example, a narrative about a peak experience, from a study of life stories (Bauer *et al.*, 2005b):

I was about 55–56 years old. My granddaughter Mandy (note: name changed) was at my house. She was approx. 3 yr. old. We were lying on my bed and she had asked me to "nice" her – translation: gently scratching her back. I suddenly felt this incredible love for her and almost simultaneously I felt a surge of deep pain and sadness and I became conscious, I feel, for the first time, that the price of loving so completely, so unconditionally is that the other side is that I would feel excruciating pain if she were to die or be separated from me forever. This event is significant because I felt so alive – so capable of being loving without consciousness about acceptance/nonacceptance and other self-centered thoughts. The awareness of the other side of connection is loss – and I know this – have felt this since, and the knowing has greatly enhanced my life – much more freely able to love and to understand why I have been so fearful of this kind of loving in the past.

This narrative was coded as expressing both cognitive and experiential growth. Cognitively, the narrative revolves around an insight. The narrative explicitly states a newer, more adaptive, psychosocially more mature awareness of herself and of love. Experientially, the narrative explicitly describes a deepened sense of being alive, loving generally, and loving her granddaughter in particular. The narrative describes a peak experience that happened approximately 10 years ago (in midlife), but the growth-oriented meaning of the memory continues to provide meaning in old age. Interestingly, this narrative integrates growth and loss, such that the newfound awareness of loss allowed for a more mature perspective. We note that this new awareness (of loss) is portrayed in the narrative as a form of growth.

As another example, a narrative of a turning point in life, from the same study:

It is my 40th birthday, and I am with some friends playing bridge. I look outside and it is too beautiful a day for one to be inside playing cards. I leave early and get out our old bicycle and go for a ride. This is the beginning of my cycling, a hobby which takes me all over the country. I make a conscious decision to begin to do things I want to do with my life. I don't want to play the role of lady any more. I don't want to dress in good clothes and go to a lot of charity organization meetings. I wanted to break free of doing things with my life that I felt I should be doing and do things with my life that I wanted to do. This even marked the beginning of the end of my pretending I was something or someone I really wasn't comfortable being.

This narrative also revolves around a life insight. It conveys cognitive growth through the "conscious decision" to take a path of experiential growth, which takes the form of leading a more intrinsically motivated life rather than a life that is dictated by social convention. The narrative, also about a memory in midlife, continues more than 20 years later to be a self-defining moment (Blagov and Singer, 2004).

A growth-oriented, aging self? On the prevalence of growth in older adults' narratives

We do not claim that older adults' life stories are more growth-oriented than younger adults' life stories. Some empirical studies support this claim, while others do not. However, research has demonstrated that the growth story is alive and well in older adulthood, playing an important role in well-being and resilience. Pasupathi and Mansour (2006) found that aging adults are prone toward focusing on personal meaning-making as a way to organize self-identity. Socioemotional selectivity theory claims that older adults are especially prone toward identifying with goals with emotional and personally meaningful social implications (Carstensen *et al.*, 1999). In the studies that follow (as with all the narrative studies presented in this chapter, unless otherwise noted), narratives were coded quantitatively for expressing greater or lesser degrees of particular kinds of growth.

In a cross-sectional study of adults' life stories, older adults were significantly more likely to construct growth memories (Bauer *et al.*, 2005b) than were younger adults. Participants were instructed to write narratives of high points in life, low points, and turning points – approximately one page for each. An analysis of these data not reported in Bauer *et al.* (2005b) revealed that 61 percent of the older (over age 60) adults' narratives made reference to either cognitive or experiential growth (or both), whereas only 36 percent of the younger adults' narratives did so (those under age 45). Similar emphases on growth were found in participants' narratives of their major life goals – even more noteworthy given that these were "long-term" goals, not the medium-term goals that are typically studied in goal research (Bauer and McAdams, 2004a). In other words, despite the assumed losses that mount with age, these older adults were more likely than younger adults to have growth narratives. While the experiential-growth focus corresponds to socioemotional selectivity theory (Carstensen *et al.*, 1999), the increased emphasis on cognitive growth narratives seems to run counter to that theory, which predicts a decrease in knowledge-focus. However, the cognitive growth narratives here largely emphasize a growth in the knowledge of one's life. The broader issue seems to be an increasing focus on intrinsically motivating or humanistic concerns – rather than extrinsically motivating or materialistic or status-oriented concerns – with age.

Two more studies revealed that the personal narratives of middle-aged and older adults contained more autobiographical reasoning (i.e., explicit connections tying the event to one's broader understanding of self) than did the narratives of younger adults (Pasupathi and Mansour, 2006).

In a narrative study of personal events that participants thought to deal with wisdom, three forms of wisdom narratives were identified: giving empathy and support, self-determination and control, and knowledge and flexibility (Gluck *et al.*, 2005). Of the three, knowledge and flexibility dealt most squarely with the theme of growth; the others dealt squarely with themes of communion and agency, respectively. Whereas empathy-and-support narratives were more common in adolescence than older adulthood, knowledge-and-flexibility narratives were more common in older adulthood than younger adulthood – again suggesting that older adults do emphasize the role of growth in their lives. In another study of wisdom narratives, older adults were more than three times more likely than college students to emphasize the importance of learning life lessons from the event, though older adults were about one-third less likely than younger adults to do so (Bluck and Gluck, 2004).

A narrative study of reminiscence demonstrated that growth-oriented narrative memories were more common than loss-oriented narrative memories (Wong and Watt, 1991). A purely qualitative narrative study (the studies above involved the quantification of narratives) found that narratives of stroke victims frequently emphasized growth and exploration in the future (Faircloth *et al.*, 2004). Such narratives were ones that emphasized an interpretation of the stroke as a "wake-up call" and plans to gain new experiences that one had always wanted but never pursued.

Overall this sampling of studies shows that older adults, despite the onslaught of losses that come with aging, commonly think about their lives – in the past as well as in the future – in terms of growth. This is consonant with the research presented earlier on gain and loss goals and sets the stage for demonstrating how older adults' use of growth narratives in their self-identity relates to well-being.

Eudaimonia, aging, and growth narratives

Eventually we wish to demonstrate that growth narratives may facilitate a particular kind of resilience that involves the reconstruction of meaning in addition to the restoration of affect – what we propose to be "eudaimonic resilience." But first we must establish that eudamonia and growth narratives have a connection. In this section we review research on eudaimonia, particularly in older adulthood. We also aim to demonstrate that older adults with growth narratives tend to report a happier, more meaningful life and are likely candidates for resilience.

Eudaimonia (or as it is more commonly studied in psychology, eudaimonic well-being) is often contrasted with hedonic well-being. Hedonic well-being emphasizes maximizing pleasure and minimizing pain. It deals with how good one feels about one's life. Eudaimonia also deals with pleasure and how good one feels about one's life, but additionally involves an explicit concern for meaning-making and growth. For example, a measure of hedonic well-being or happiness, might simply ask participants to rate on a Likert-type scale how happy they are. A measure of eudaimonic well-being might ask questions about happiness, but also specifically about particular sources of meaning in life (e.g., personal growth, purpose in life; Ryff and Singer, 1998) or ask short, open-ended questions to assess the psychosocial maturity of the responses. Psychological research has historically studied happiness in its more hedonic forms, notably in terms of positive and negative emotionality and global life satisfaction (Ryan and Deci, 2001). However, the study of eudaimonic well-being has become increasingly valued, as evidenced by recent, special issues in the *Journal of Happiness Studies* (Deci and Ryan, 2008) and the *Journal of Positive Psychology* (Kashdan, Biswas-Diener, and King, 2008). As the research on eudaimonic well-being mounts, so do definitions of it.

Eudaimonia as meaningfulness

Some researchers study eudaimonic well-being as meaningfulness, that is, as a subjective sense of satisfaction with various sources of meaning in one's life. For example, a commonly used measure of eudaimonic well-being, psychological well-being (Ryff and Keyes, 1995), asks participants essentially to rate how much they have six qualities in their lives: autonomy, environmental mastery, personal growth, positive relationships with others, purpose in life, and self-acceptance. This measure is framed explicitly in eudaimonic theory and has been shown to be distinct from – while still related to – measures of hedonic well-being (Ryff and Singer, 1998). For example, experiential growth themes correspond more closely to eudaimonic-as-meaningfulness well-being than to hedonic well-being (Bauer *et al.*, 2005b).

Different dimensions of eudaimonic well-being appear to have quite different, even opposite, trajectories across adulthood (some of which differ for males and females; Ryff and Singer, 2008): in general, self-acceptance, environmental mastery, and positive relationships appear to increase by later adulthood, or at least remain constant. In notable contrast, personal growth (i.e., satisfaction with one's personal growth) and purpose in life appear to decline for older adults. However, we find the same kind of pattern here as in the gain-goal research: this research clearly shows that older adults score the personal-growth dimension of well-being *most highly* among the six dimensions. So despite the fact that levels of personal-growth well-being decline from younger to older adulthood, those levels start off so much higher than the levels of the other dimensions that they can continue to retain their strength in older adulthood, relative to other dimensions. In other words, personal growth is a keystone of older adults' well-being.

As suggested by numerous researchers of eudaimonic well-being, a focus on intrinsically motivating activities is essential to eudaimonic well-being (e.g., Bauer *et al.*, 2008; Ryan, Huta, and Deci, 2008; Waterman, Schwartz, and Conti, 2008). One study found that older adults' personal reasons for listening to music differentiated hedonic and eudaimonic well-being (Laukka, 2007). Listening to music for the purpose of emotion regulation correlated more strongly with measures of hedonic well-being (positive and negative affect). In contrast, listening to music for the purpose of enjoyment (an intrinsic motivation; Deci and Ryan, 2000) correlated more strongly with various dimensions of eudaimonic well-being (Ryff's measure) – and correlated with positive but not negative affect.

Eudamonia as happiness plus psychosocial maturity

Other researchers study eudaimonia as the combination of hedonic well-being plus psychosocial maturity, where maturity involves heightened levels of integrative complexity in meaning-making (e.g., Bauer *et al.*, 2005b; King and Noelle, 2005; Pals, 2006a). Loevinger's (1976) measure of ego development serves as perhaps the most comprehensive measure of psychosocial maturity, charting levels of complexity and integration by which people think about the self and others. However, ego development is not typically considered to be a facet of well-being, which is typically defined strictly in terms of affect (even in the case of eudaimonia as meaningfulness). Indeed, measures of ego development tend not to correlate with measures of hedonic well-being in adulthood (e.g., Bauer and McAdams, 2004a, 2004b; Helson and Roberts, 1994; King and Noelle, 2005; King and Raspin, 2004). In other words, people who think complexly about their psychosocial lives seem about as likely to be happy as unhappy. Furthermore, experiential and cognitive growth themes map differentially onto well-being and psychosocial maturity (Bauer and

McAdams, 2004a, 2004b, 2009; Bauer *et al.*, 2005b; King and Noelle, 2005; King and Raspin, 2004; King and Smith, 2004; King *et al.*, 2000; Pals, 2006b). Experiential growth themes correlate predominantly with well-being but not maturity. In contrast, cognitive growth themes correlate predominantly with maturity but not well-being. Thus, researchers who take the happiness-plus-maturity perspective claim that eudaimonic well-being involves two distinct qualities in life – *how good one feels* about one's life as well as *how integratively one thinks* about one's life.

Research has shown that older adults have at least as high – if not higher – levels of hedonic well-being and desirable emotionality as younger adults do (Mroczek, 2001). As for psychosocial maturity, older adults show heightened capacities to create an integrated sense of meaning in life (Pasupathi, 2001). However, old age may well involve a decrease in the differentiation or complexity of that integration of self-identity from the peak levels in midlife (Labouvie-Vief, 2003). Some of this decrease may come from decreased activity levels, which correlate with lessened complexity of self-identity, as well as from a lesser tendency to focus on negative affect (Labouvie-Vief, 2003). Some research on Loevinger's (1976) ego development also shows a decline of *peak levels of* psychosocial maturity in old age (Pfaffenberger, 2005). However, a normative decline in peak levels of maturity or integrative complexity does not mean that older adults have bottomed out in these categories. Furthermore, some research shows increases. For example, in further analyses of data presented earlier (Bauer and McAdams, 2004a; Bauer *et al.*, 2005b), older adults had higher levels of ego development than younger adults – and the same levels as those of midlife adults.

Older adults' heightened capacity for meaning-making (Pasupathi, 2001) suggests a heightened capacity for integration. We argue that older adults may simply be better at stating their highly integrated meanings in life more simply – such that measures of differentiation simply do not capture the differentiation that at one time was more conscious but with age and experience became more automatic. In other words, measures of integrative complexity do not measure exformation – the information behind the information, that is, the information that is not presently referenced but that the individual did grapple with earlier in the process of arriving at more simple, elegant, and integrative meanings (Norretranders, 1991). Perhaps older adults' lower scores of measures of complexity reflect their heightened capacity, gained over years of experience, to integrate the subtler complexities of life.

Finally, even if psychosocial maturity does on average decline in adulthood, it is important to consider whether older adults were still *personally concerned* with the integrative complexity of meaning-making.

Narrative data suggest they are concerned with it. In further analyses of data reported above (Bauer and McAdams, 2004a; Bauer et al., 2005b), older adults were approximately twice as likely as younger adults to use themes of *cognitive* growth in their personal narratives. In other words, older adults were more likely to emphasize – subjectively, *thematically* – the importance of conceptual integration (which is different than having narratives that are *structurally* more complex).

Growth narratives, eudaimonic personality development, and aging

Eudaimonic well-being can fluctuate across adulthood (Ryff and Singer, 2008). So can hedonic well-being, even if it tends toward a baseline (Diener, Lucas, and Scollon, 2006). Psychosocial maturity can increase as well as decrease across adulthood (Helson and Roberts, 1994; Labouvie-Vief, 2003). An increase in eudaimonia over time – most fully evidenced by simultaneous increases in hedonic well-being and psychosocial maturity – has been called "eudaimonic personality development" or "eudaimonic growth" (Bauer, 2008; Bauer and McAdams, in press). Research is showing a tie between growth narratives (as well as other growth orientations) and eudamonic personality development. In the following studies (unless otherwise noted), quantitative measures of narratives were compared to quantitative measures of resilience, maturity, and happiness.

Drawing from the Mills Longitudinal Study, women at the age of 52 wrote narratives about a difficult life event (Pals, 2006b). Narratives that emphasized coherent positive resolution (which falls under the category of experiential growth) predicted increased ego resiliency from the ages of 21 to 61. Narratives that emphasized exploratory narrative processing (i.e., cognitive growth) not only predicted psychosocial maturity at the age of 62 but also mediated the relation between the trait of coping openness at the age of 21 and maturity at the age of 62. Furthermore, themes of positive self-transformation (a combination of cognitive and experiential growth) predicted high levels of both maturity and happiness.

In a two-year longitudinal study, divorced women (mean age of 54 years, SD = 9 years) provided narratives of their lost (pre-divorce, retrospectively) and found (present) best possible selves (King and Raspin, 2004). Highly elaborated found possible selves (a form of cognitive growth narratives) correlated with psychosocial maturity both concurrently and two years later, but not with increases in maturity over that time. Highly elaborated lost possible selves did predict increases in maturity for participants whose divorce had occurred further in the past.

In cross-sectional research on growth memories and growth goals (Bauer and McAdams, 2004a; Bauer *et al.*, 2005b), participants' age correlated with well-being, such that older adults reported higher levels of both happiness and eudaimonia-as-meaningfulness than younger adults did. However, experiential growth memories and growth goals mediated the relation between age and life satisfaction. Similarly, older adults were marginally more likely to score higher on psychosocial maturity, but this age–maturity relation was mediated by cognitive growth goals. In other words, older adults had higher levels of eudaimonia, but this was explained by the fact that older people were more likely to have eudaimonic growth narratives.

In another study reported above, growth-oriented narratives also corresponded to psychological and physical health in older adulthood (Wong and Watt, 1991). The integrative and instrumental styles emphasized linking one's past, present, and anticipated future. However, the integrative style was more growth-oriented, focusing on increased self-understanding and personal meaning-making, whereas the instrumental style focused on more hedonic forms of coping and successful recovery.

Related, non-narrative studies also demonstrate the presence of growth in adulthood and its tie to well-being. In a study of non-narrative growth goals in adulthood, growth goals mediated the relation between age and well-being (Sheldon and Kasser, 2001). In the Terman study, participants rated whether they were living up to their abilities. Those who showed an increase in this self-assessment between the ages of 48 and 85 – that is, people who by the age of 85 had grown in their beliefs of their own self-actualization – also reported higher levels of health well-being compared with people who showed decreases in this self-assessment (Holahan, 2003).

Erikson's (1968) final stage of psychosocial development, ego integrity versus despair, involves a growth orientation in several respects, not the least of which is that ego integrity is facilitated by a sense of generative self-transcendence in midlife. Ego integrity involves the acceptance and integration of one's life as a whole, as it unfolded over time, both good and bad. A story of such an acceptance and integration is likely to involve a movement from at one time not accepting (or even recognizing) certain, undesirable, or unknown aspects of oneself to at a later time developing the capacity and wisdom to accept and integrate them. An aging self of such integration and growth holds great promise for resilience.

Some evidence, though with young adults, suggests that growth narratives can predict eudaimonic personality development in the strong sense, that is, increases in both happiness and maturity. The combination of experiential and cognitive growth in narratives has predicted simultaneous increases in both well-being and maturity three years later (Bauer and McAdams, in press).

In all, these studies suggest that growth narratives facilitate eudaimonic personality development and resilience, notably in older adulthood. Only one of these studies addressed resilience directly, but psychosocial maturity is known to facilitate adjustment during difficult times (Bursik, 1991). Furthermore, eudaimonia is viewed an enduring, adaptive form of well-being, at least compared with hedonic happiness, suggesting that eudaimonia serves a buffer against difficult times. It also seems that the relation between a growth orientation and eudaimonia is especially strong after the age of 60 (Bauer and McAdams, 2004a; Bauer *et al.*, 2005b; King and Raspin, 2004; Pals, 2006b; Sheldon and Kasser, 2001). Given that older adults have been shown to have higher capacities for narrative integration and meaning-making as well as levels of happiness and maturity (Mroczek, 2001; Pasupathi, 2001), it seems that older adults are more likely to experience eudaimonia than younger adults.

Discussion: the study of eudaimonic resilience

We now wish to integrate the previous sections by proposing a framework for studying resilience that is based on eudaimonia. Briefly, hedonic resilience is a process that, following a potential trauma or loss, involves a quick rebound or maintenance of affective balance (as in Bonanno, 2004). Eudaimonic resilience is a process that involves the qualities of hedonic resilience but additionally includes the quick rebound, maintenance, or growth of personal meaning in one's self-identity. In other words, hedonic resilience involves affect regulation, whereas eudaimonic resilience involves both affect and meaning regulation. A growth-oriented self-identity is a likely candidate of individual differences to predict eudaimonic resilience (see Figure 2.1).

First, is there really a difference?

Discussions of resilience generally involve the regulation of both affect and meaning (Greve and Staudinger, 2006): it would be hard to imagine people being resilient if they could make no sense of a loss or potential trauma. So it might appear that hedonic resilience implicitly demands meaning regulation, and thus eudaimonic resilience. However, theories and measures differ in terms of the emphasis placed on the role of affect regulation versus meaning regulation. For example, approach-versus-avoidance theories (see below), which tend to be more hedonic, focus less on *how* people subjectively construct meaning after a difficult event, focusing more on merely *whether* they do. Other theories elaborate on the structure and/or content of meaning-making after a difficult event.

As for measurement, researchers may assess merely whether a person has returned to affective balance or may assess adaptation by considering specific forms of meaning-making. When hedonic resilience ensues, chances are that a certain degree of meaningfulness emerges (i.e., eudaimonic resilience) as well, regardless of whether meaningfulness was assessed. For example, in the wake of a significant loss, the individual person is likely to sense that a significant source of meaning has been lost; this is what makes the loss *feel* like a loss. Thus measures of hedonic resilience may depend on an underlying eudaimonic resilience that is implicit and simply not measured. What matters for the distinction between hedonic resilience and the "meaningfulness" definition of eudaimonic resilience, then, is whether the researcher (or anyone thinking about) the person in question is explicitly considering a return to baseline levels of both affect and meaningfulness (e.g., Neimeyer, 2001).

We view eudaimonic resilience as a framework for thinking about and conducting research on adaptation that attends more to the individual's self-identity and development, which includes affect regulation – rather than attending to affect alone. The findings on eudaimonia presented earlier suggest that eudaimonic resilience serves as an important resource for adults as they age. If, as stated earlier, older adults are more prone toward eudaimonia than younger adults, then older adults are more likely to exhibit eudaimonic resilience. But eudaimonic resilience is at this point a proposition. Below we outline a framework for studying eudaimonic resilience.

The dual process of eudaimonic resilience and related models of adaptation

Eudaimonic resilience can be framed as a dual-process model of adaptation. On the one hand is affect regulation, and on the other is meaning regulation. Affect regulation involves the capacity to regulate positive and negative emotionality, notably the hedonic concerns of approaching pleasure and avoiding or escaping pain. Meaning regulation involves the capacity to focus on, construct, and reconstruct meaning in one's life – that is, one's self-identity. For example, meaning regulation in the wake of a loss might involve a shift or increase in the importance (i.e., meaning) of an interpersonal relationship, thereby keeping one's sense of meaningfulness afloat (and possibly turning into a new, enduring, or otherwise heightened form of meaning in life – as in posttraumatic growth; Calhoun and Tedeschi, 2001).

Whereas hedonic resilience involves merely a concern for affect regulation, eudaimonic resilience involves concerns for both affect regulation and meaning regulation. Meaning regulation can facilitate affect regulation after a difficult life event (Bursik, 1991), just as affect regulation (e.g., impulse control) can facilitate meaning regulation (e.g., as psychosocial maturity and perspective-taking; Loevinger, 1976). However, as noted earlier, measures of affect and conceptual meaning-making tend not to correlate. Thus eudaimonic resilience incorporates two processes of adaptation. This dual-process model of resilience is related to other dual-process models that focus on affect and meaning-making in self-identity development (Bauer *et al.*, 2008; Labouvie-Vief, 2003; Staudinger and Kunzmann, 2005). Each model approaches health from a more eudaimonic than merely hedonic perspective, such that the two processes of affect and meaning-making are both essential to healthy adaptation (see Figure 1.1).

Adjustment and growth
Staudinger and Kunzmann's (2005) model of positive adult personality development distinguishes adjustment processes from growth processes. Adjustment processes, which are largely avoidance oriented and hedonic (i.e., they aim to escape pain) would be necessary for resilience or recovery and are most likely primary to growth processes. Growth processes are largely approach oriented and emphasize social-cognitive meaning-making. As described earlier, growth processes are largely a matter of individual differences in motivation and self-identity, expressed explicitly in people's descriptions of their goals (e.g., Bauer and McAdams, 2004a; Sheldon and Houser-Marko, 2001). "Optimal development" in Staudinger's and Kunzmann's model involves both adjustment and growth. As such, hedonic resilience maps onto Staudinger's and Kunzmann's adjustment component only, whereas eudaimonic resilience involves both adjustment and growth.

Affect optimization and affect complexity
In another dual-process model, Labouvie-Vief (2003) distinguishes affect optimization from affect complexity. Affect optimization deals with emotional adjustment and the capacity to maintain and enhance levels of hedonic well-being. Affect complexity deals with cognitive-affective growth, including the ability and willingness to understand, differentiate, and integrate emotional experiences – including their psychosocial dynamics, causes, and consequences – into one's self-understanding. Whereas hedonic resilience maps onto Labouvie-Vief's affect optimization, eudaimonic resilience involves both affect optimization and affect complexity.

Loss-oriented and restoration-oriented coping

In a third dual-process model with eudaimonic concerns, Stroebe and Schut (2001) present a model of adaptation via meaning-making. After a significant loss in life, the individual's attention and actions oscillate between loss-oriented coping and restoration-oriented coping. Loss-oriented coping focuses on making sense of the loss, whereas restoration-oriented coping (which might sound avoidance-oriented and hedonic at first) focuses on the reconstruction of a new, personally meaningful understanding of the self after the loss. Whereas hedonic resilience maps onto Stroebe's and Schut's loss-oriented coping, eudaimonic resilience involves both loss-oriented and restoration-oriented coping. As demonstrated in research on goals, older adults appear to have a balanced focus on recovery and growth (e.g., Ebner *et al.*, 2006), suggesting that older adults are likely to be engaging in both forms of coping.

Contrast: dual-process models of hedonic resilience

Other dual-process models of adaptation focus not on affect and meaning but on approach and avoidance motivations. Brandtstädter, Wentura, and Rothermund (1999) outline a model with one process for counteracting losses and another process for preference adjustment. Counteracting losses involves making changes in actions and priorities in life that minimize the losses associated with aging. In contrast, though working in conjunction, preference adjustment involves setting new goals to attain and new understandings of self-identity, but these new understandings are largely measured in terms of positives and negatives, gains and losses. This model is consonant with the SOC model of aging, where growth is defined explicitly as gains, which may merely mean an increase in positive affect or a decrease in negative affect. While these models offer an important portrait of the affective and approach-avoidance orientations of older adulthood, they tend not to address value-based meaning-making in self-identity, adjustment, and resilience.

Growth narratives and eudaimonic resilience

Resilience versus recovery: the role of individual differences

Resilience is commonly associated with recovery in that they both involve dealing with difficult life events, but they are not the same thing (Bonanno, 2004). The difference is largely a matter of the degree and the endurance of psychological disruptions: resilience involves milder, relatively shorter periods of disruption than does recovery. Bonanno frames the difference between resilience and recovery in terms of personality, citing the adaptive benefits of individual differences in characteristics such as hardiness and positive emotionality. In a prospective, longitudinal study, people who showed resilience entered an interpersonal loss with more adaptive characteristics (Bonanno *et al.*, 2002). Also, more resilient individuals interpret the events surrounding a loss in a more adaptive manner. For example, resilient individuals showed an "optimal balance" of mostly positive yet some negative self-evaluations in their personal narratives (Bauer and Bonanno, 2001a). In contrast, those who had exclusively positive self-evaluations adapted as poorly as those who had many negative self-evaluations, suggesting an inability to incorporate the loss – much less learn from it – in their life story. In addition, more resilient individuals showed a capacity to exercise relatively more behavioral than characterological self-blame, to integrate important events surrounding the loss with their broader self-identity, and to express a greater degree of self-efficacy (Bauer and Bonanno, 2001b, 2001c). Thus it seems that resilience (and adjustment more generally) is tied to individual differences in growth-salient interpretations of their lives.

Recovery versus growth: focusing on the past versus the future
Recovery generally involves returning to baseline, re-establishing equilibrium, and "bouncing back" (Bonanno, 2004; Davidson and Roe, 2007). Thus recovery emphasizes an escape or avoidance orientation. Merely ending the pain is enough for the person. What happens in the future, after the cessation of pain, is not of primary concern. In contrast, a growth focus is primarily concerned with what happens in the future, after the pain has ceased and even in the meantime. A growth orientation allows the person to interpret the adversity from a future-oriented perspective. For example, a desire to "get better" is found in both recovery and growth orientations. However, "getting better" is the endpoint for the recovery focus, whereas "getting better" is merely part of the process for the growth/approach focus. Similarly, a focus on prevention emphasizes avoidance, albeit avoidance with foresight. A focus on prevention is largely a focus on avoiding having to escape. Even maintenance involves a focus on maintaining the past more so than on possibilities for the future. A narrative study of adults' decisions to make major life changes distinguished the crystallization of desire from the crystallization of discontent (Bauer, McAdams, and Sakaeda, 2005a). Almost all decisions involved making a change from an undesirable life circumstance. A crystallization of desire was defined as a decision that was made primarily because one wanted to move toward a desired future. A crystallization of discontent was defined as a decision that was made primarily because one wanted to escape an undesirable past and present (i.e., to recover; Baumeister, 1994). Participants who expressed a crystallization

of desire had higher levels of well-being (hedonic and eudaimonic) than did participants who expressed a crystallization of discontent – even when controlling for how well the transition turned out. Overall, a growth-oriented self-identity is more likely than a recovery-oriented self-identity to facilitate eudaimonic resilience.

Questioning the need for considering eudaimonic resilience

Is hedonic resilience not enough?

Eudaimonic resilience may well be a luxury when one is faced with trauma, severe illness, or interpersonal loss. Even if one lacks a recovery of meaningfulness in life, having one's emotions stabilized is certainly desirable. We are certainly not making an argument against hedonic resilience as a human good! Again, hedonic satisfaction is an essential part of eudamonic well-being and resilience. We are merely stating that there is more to managing life's difficulties than stabilizing one's emotions. This becomes an important measurement issue when considering the specific course of resilience of the individual person.

Posttraumatic growth? Not necessarily

At first glance, our description of eudaimonic resilience might sound like posttraumatic growth (Calhoun and Tedeschi, 2001). However, posttraumatic growth deals with only growth and therefore does not correspond to all facets of eudaimonic resilience, namely the recovery or maintenance of past levels of eudaimonic well-being. Plus, posttraumatic growth corresponds primarily to the facet of eudaimonic resilience that deals with the growth of *meaningfulness* ("I feel my relationships are stronger") but not necessarily to eudaimonic resilience as growth in psychosocial maturity. However, the growth element of eudaimonic resilience may involve primary characteristics of posttraumatic growth, such as the subjective sense of a strengthened sense of self, the subjective sense of strengthened relationships, and the subjective sense of a strengthened philosophy of life (Calhoun and Tedeschi, 2001). To the degree that eudaimonic resilience and posttraumatic growth overlap, recent critiques of posttraumatic growth raise important empirical questions and limitations for eudaimonic resilience. For example, a meta-analysis shows that the effects of posttraumatic growth might not be as strong as they appear in individual reports (Helgeson, Reynolds, and Tomich, 2006), though a close examination of the meta-analytic methods suggests that aggregated variables were couched in predominantly hedonic, not eudaimonic, terms (namely "benefit-finding"). As a possible underlying determinant of posttraumatic growth, which is primarily a retrospective, self-report variable, self-enhancement and other "positive illusions" may be driving people's perception of growth (Westphal and Bonanno, 2007). Still, subjective appraisals of one's life – illusory or not – are important predictors of behavior, well-being, and resilience (Bonanno, 2004; Wirtz *et al.*, 2003). Thus it remains noteworthy that people who adapt well to life's difficulties have been found to talk spontaneously about their lives in terms of integrated meaning-making and growth, as discussed earlier. In other words, growth is a prominent feature of the self-identity of those who adapt well to setbacks in life.

Is this not too simplistic? Dismissing the Pollyanna problem
The presence of growth – assessed subjectively or objectively – does not simply erase the negative feelings that follow the trauma or loss. The growth merely helps the individual to adapt, perhaps by focusing the individual's attention on something specific and desired to live for, rather than on the pain from which one wants to escape. A subjective focus on growth does not mean that the individual does not acknowledge the immense difficulties of trauma, loss, or aging. Furthermore, it is likely that eudaimonic resilience is not a matter of oversimplifying one's life, self-enhancement, or ignoring one's own anxieties (as in repressive coping; Bonanno, 2004) – even though these tactics do correlate with adaptation and well-being. Indeed, people with a high degree of growth motivation are more likely to acknowledge the negatives in their lives than people with low growth motivation (Park, Bauer, and Arbuckle, 2009). People – perhaps especially older adults – with a growth orientation are precisely the people (1) who directly deal with life's difficulties maturely and (2) who achieve affective balance sooner (Bauer and Bonanno, 2001a). The narrative that we presented earlier (the one that turned the awareness of loss into a life insight) exemplified this sort of integrative complexity. A personal focus on growth merely means that growth is perceived as a notable object of self-identification. Such a view of self is likely to facilitate eudaimonic resilience.

Conclusions

In this chapter we argue that growth is a central concern in older adults' self-identity and that growth narratives facilitate (or are at least indicative of) a eudaimonic form of resilience, particularly in older adulthood. First, we reinterpret published data to show that older adults are at least as concerned with gains as with losses in their personal goals. We then provide evidence that older adults are particularly prone toward constructing growth narratives in their life stories. In other words, despite the mounting losses in their lives, older adults persist in using the concept of growth to make sense of and plan their lives – noting that growth here comes in the form of not only goals but also personal memories in which one perceives personal growth. When it comes to well-being, older adults may have an age-related advantage by virtue of the fact that older adults are more prone than younger adults to define themselves in terms of intrinsically motivated, humanistic concerns – rather than extrinsically motivated, materialistic or status-minded concerns. Furthermore, a greater prevalence of growth narratives in older adults' life stories help explain the relation between age and well-being – an important fact, given that levels of well-being serve as a key source of resilience. Because a growth-oriented aging self sounds intuitively contrary to many people, we note first that an aging, narrative self – like narrative identity at any point in adulthood – is predominantly focused on stories of the past. So a growth-oriented, aging self is one that perceives growth in one's past. Having said that, we also wish to keep in mind that older adults' goals for the future are also weighted at least as much toward gains as losses. Finally, we outline a framework for studying eudaimonic resilience following loss or potential trauma. Whereas hedonic resilience involves merely affect regulation, eudaimonic resilience involves a dual process of affect regulation and meaning regulation. We pay particular attention to the psychological models that researchers use; a purely hedonic orientation necessarily ignores an analysis of the myriad ways that meaning-making and growth might facilitate resilience and longer-term forms of adaptation. We suggest that a growth orientation in the aging self, measured with narratives or otherwise, is a likely facilitator – or at least predictor – of eudaimonic resilience.

REFERENCES

Adler, J. (2009). In treatment: The healing power of agency in narratives of psychotherapy. Paper presented at the Society for Personality and Social Psychology Annual Convention. Tampa, FL.

Ardelt, M. (2008). Self-development through selflessness: the paradoxical process of growing wiser. In H. A. Wayment and J. J. Bauer (eds.), *Transcending self-interest: Psychological explorations of the quiet ego* (pp. 221–233). Washington, DC: American Psychological Association.

Bauer, J. J. (2008). How the ego quiets as it grows: Ego development, growth stories, and eudaimonic personality development. In H. A. Wayment and J. J. Bauer (eds.), *Transcending self-interest: psychological explorations of the quiet ego* (pp. 199–210). Washington, DC: American Psychological Association.

Bauer, J. J., & Bonanno, G. A. (2001a). Continuity amid discontinuity: Bridging one's past and present in stories of conjugal bereavement. *Narrative Inquiry*, 11, 123–158.

(2001b). Doing and being well (for the most part): Adaptive patterns of narrative self-evaluation during bereavement. *Journal of Personality*, 69, 451–482.

(2001c). I can, I do, I am: The narrative differentiation of self-efficacy and other self-evaluations while adapting to bereavement. *Journal of Research in Personality*, 35, 424–448.

Bauer, J. J., and McAdams, D. P. (2004a). Growth goals, maturity, and well-being. *Developmental Psychology*, 40, 114–127.

(2004b). Personal growth in adults' stories of life transitions. *Journal of Personality*, 72, 573–602.

(in press). *Growth goals and eudaimonic growth*. *Developmental Psychology*.

Bauer, J. J., McAdams, D. P., and Pals, J. L. (2008). Narrative identity and eudaimonic well-being. *Journal of Happiness Studies*, 9, 81–104.

Bauer, J. J., McAdams, D. P., and Sakaeda, A. R. (2005a). Crystallization of desire and crystallization of discontent in narratives of life-changing decisions. *Journal of Personality*, 73, 1181–1213.

(2005b). Interpreting the good life: Growth memories in the lives of mature, happy people. *Journal of Personality and Social Psychology*, 88, 203–217.

Baumeister, R. F. (1994). The crystallization of discontent in the process of major life changes. In T. F. Heatherton and J. L. Weinnerger (eds.), *Can personality change?* (pp. 281–297). Washington, DC: American Psychological Association.

Blagov, P. S., and Singer, J. A. (2004). Four dimentions of self-defining memories (specificity, meaning, content, and affect) and their relationships to self-restraint, distress, and repressive defensiveness. *Journal of Personality*, 72, 481–511.

Bluck, S. (2003). Autobiographical memory: Exploring its functions in everyday life. *Memory*, 11, 113–123.

Bluck, S., and Gluck, J. (2004). Making things better and learning a lesson: Experiencing wisdom across the lifespan. *Journal of Personality*, 72, 543–572.

Bluck, S., and Habermas, T. (2001). Extending the study of autobiographical memory: Thinking back about life across the life span. *Review of General Psychology*, 5, 135–147.

Bonanno, G. A. (2004). Loss, trauma, and human resilience: Have we underestimated the human capacity to thrive after extremely aversive events? *American Psychologist*, 59, 20–28.

Bonanno, G. A., Wortman, C. B., Lehman, D. R., et al. (2002). Resilience to loss and chronic grief: A prospective study from preloss to 18-months postloss. *Journal of Personality and Social Psychology*, 83, 1150–1164.

Brandtstädter, J., Wentura, D., and Rothermund, K. (1999). Intentional self-development through adulthood and late life: Tenacious pursuit and flexible adjustment of goals. In J. Brandtstädter and R. M. Lerner (eds.), *Action and self-development: Theory and research through the life span* (pp. 373–400). Thousand Oaks, CA: Sage.

Bursik, K. (1991). Adaptation to divorce and ego development in adult women. *Journal of Personality and Social Psychology*, 60, 300–306.

Calhoun, L. G., and Tedeschi, R. G. (2001). Posttraumatic growth: The positive lessons of loss. In R. A. Neimeyer (ed.), *Meaning reconstruction and the experience of loss* (pp. 157–172). Washington, DC: American Psychological Association.

Carstensen, L. L., Isaacowitz, D. M., and Charles, S. T. (1999). Taking time seriously: A theory of socioemotional selectivity. *American Psychologist*, 54, 165–181.

Davidson, L., and Roe, D. (2007). Recovery from versus recovery in serious mental illness: One strategy for lessening confusion plaguing recovery. *Journal of Mental Health*, 16, 459–470.

Deci, E. L., and Ryan, R. M. (2000). The what and why of goal pursuits: Human needs and the self-determination of behavior. *Psychological Inquiry*, 11, 227–268.

   (2008). Hedonia, eudaimonia, and well-being: An introduction. *Journal of Happiness Studies*, 9, 1–11.

Diener, E., Lucas, R. E., and Scollon, C. N. (2006). Beyond the hedonic treadmill: Revising the adaptation theory of well-being. *American Psychologist*, 61, 305–314,

Ebner, N. C., Freund, A. M., Baltes, P. B. (2006). Developmental changes in personal goal orientation from young to late adulthood: From striving for gains to maintenance and prevention of losses. *Psychology and Aging*, 21, 664–678.

Erikson, E. H. (1968). *Identity: Youth and crisis*. New York: Norton.

Faircloth, C. A., Rittman, M., Boylstein, C., Young, M. E., and van Puymbroeck, M. (2004). Energizing the ordinary: Biographical work and the future in stroke recovery narratives. *Journal of Aging Studies*, 18, 399–413.

Freund, A. M., and Baltes, P. B. (1998). Selection, optimization, and compensation as strategies of life management: Correlations with subjective indicators of successful aging. *Psychology and Aging*, 13, 531–543.

Freund, A. M., and Riediger, M. (2006). Goals as building blocks of personality and development in adulthood. In D. K. Mroczek and T. D. Little (eds.), *Handbook of personality development* (pp. 353–372). Mahwah, NJ: Erlbaum.

Gluck, J., Bluck, S., Baron, J., and McAdams, D. P. (2005). The wisdom of experience: Autobiographical narratives across adulthood. *International Journal of Behavioral Development*, 29, 197–208.

Greve, W., and Staudinger, U. M. (2006). Resilience in later adulthood and old age: Resources and potentials for successful aging. In D. Cicchetti and D. J. Cohen (eds.), *Developmental psychopathology*, Vol.III: *Risk, disorder, and adaptation* (2nd edn.), (pp. 796–840). Hoboken, NJ: Wiley.

Heckhausen, J. (1997). Developmental regulation across adulthood: Primary and secondary control of age-related challenges. *Developmental Psychology*, 33, 176–187.

Heckhausen, J., Dixon, R. A., and Baltes, P. B. (1989). Gains and losses in development throughout adulthood as perceived by different adult age groups. *Developmental Psychology*, 25, 109–121.

Helgeson, V. S., Reynolds, K. A., and Tomich, P. L. (2006). A meta-analytic review of benefit finding and growth. *Journal of Consulting and Clinical Psychology*, 74, 797–816.

Helson, R., and Roberts, B. W. (1994). Ego development and personality change in adulthood. *Journal of Personality and Social Psychology*, 66, 911–920.

Holahan, C. K. (2003). Stability and change in positive self-appraisal from mid-life to later aging. *International Journal of Aging and Human Development*, 56, 247–267.

Kamide, H., and Daibo, I. (2008). Autobiographical memories and a good life: Eudaimonic and hedonic well-being of Japanese students. Unpublished manuscript.

Kashdan, T. B., Biswas-Diener, R., and King, L. A. (2008). Reconsidering happiness: The costs of distinguishing between hedonics and eudaimonia. *Journal of Positive Psychology*, 3, 219–233.

Kasser, T., and Ryan, R. M. (1993). A dark side of the American dream: Correlates of financial success as a central life aspiration. *Journal of Personality and Social Psychology*, 65, 410–422.

King, L. A., and Noelle, S. S. (2005). Happy, mature, and gay: Intimacy, power, and difficult times in coming out stories. *Journal of Research in Personality*, 39, 278–298.

King, L. A., and Raspin, C. (2004). Lost and found possible selves, subjective well-being, and ego development in divorced women. *Journal of Personality*, 72, 603–632.

King, L. A., Scollon, C. K., Ramsey, C., and Williams, T. (2000). Stories of life transition: Subjective well-being and ego development in parents of children with Down Syndrome. *Journal of Research in Personality*, 34, 509–536.

King, L. A., and Smith, N. G. (2004). Gay and straight possible selves: Goals, identity, subjective well-being, and personality development. *Journal of Personality*, 72, 967–994.

Labouvie-Vief, G. (2003). Dynamic integration: Affect, cognition, and the self in adulthood. *Current Directions in Psychological Science*, 12, 201–206.

Laukka, P. (2007). Uses of music and psychological well-being among the elderly. *Journal of Happiness Studies*, 8, 215–241.

Loevinger, J. (1976). *Ego development*. San Francisco, CA: Jossey-Bass.

Maslow, A. H. (1968). *Toward a psychology of being*. New York: Van Nostrand Reinhold.

McAdams, D. P. (1993). *The stories we live by*. New York: Guilford.
  (2008). Personal narratives and the life story. In O. P. John, R. R. Robins, and L. O. Pervin (eds.), *Handbook of personality*, 3rd edn. (pp. 241–261). New York: Guilford.

McAdams, D. P., and Pals, J. L. (2006). A new big five: Fundamental principles for an integrative science of personality. *American Psychologist*, 61, 204–217.

McAdams, D. P., Reutzel, K., and Foley, J. M. (1986). Complexity and generativity at mid-life: Relations among social motives, ego development, and adults' plans for the future. *Journal of Personality and Social Psychology*, **50**, 800–807.

McLean, K. C., Pasupathi, M., and Pals, J. L. (2007). Selves creating stories creating selves: A process model of self-development. *Personality and Social Psychology Review*, 11, 262–278.

Mroczek, D. K. (2001). Age and emotion in adulthood. *Current directions in psychological science*, 10, 87–90.

Neimeyer, R. A. (ed.) (2001). *Meaning reconstruction and the experience of loss.* Washington, DC: American Psychological Association.

Norretranders, T. (1991). *The user illusion: Cutting consciousness down to size.* New York: Penguin.

Ogilvie, D. M., Rose, K. M., and Heppen, J. B. (2001). A comparison of personal project motives in three age groups. *Basic and Applied Social Psychology*, 23, 207–215.

Pals, J. L. (2006a). Constructing the "springboard effect": Causal connections, self-making, and growth within the life story. In McAdams, D. P., Josselson, R., and Leibich, A. (eds.), *Identity and story: Creating self in narrative* (pp. 175–199). Washington, DC: American Psychological Association.

(2006b). Narrative identity processing of difficult life experiences: Pathways of personality development and positive self-transformation in adulthood. *Journal of Personality*, 74, 1079–1109.

Park, S. W., Bauer, J. J., and Arbuckle, N. B. (2009). Growth motivation attenuates the self-serving attribution. *Journal of Research in Personality*, 43, 914–917.

Pasupathi, M. (2001). The social construction of the personal past and its implications for adult development. *Psychological Bulletin*, 127, 651–672.

Pasupathi, M. and Mansour, E. (2006). Adult age differences in autobiographical reasoning in narratives. *Developmental Psychology*, 42, 798–808.

Pasupathi, M., Weeks, T., and Rice, C. (2006). Reflecting on life: Remembering as a major process in adult development. *Journal of Language and Social Psychology*, 25, 244–263.

Pfaffenberger, A. H. (2005). Optimal adult development: An inquiry into the dynamics of growth. *Journal of Humanistic Psychology*, 45, 279–301.

Ryan, R. M., and Deci, E. L. (2001). On happiness and human potentials: A review of research on hedonic and eudaimonic well-being. *Annual Review of Psychology*, 52, 141–166.

Ryan, R. M., Huta, V., and Deci, E. L. (2008). Living well: A self-determination theory perspective on eudaimonia. *Journal of Happiness Studies*, 9, 139–170.

Ryff, C. D., and Keyes, C. L. M. (1995). The structure of psychological well-being revisited. *Journal of Personality and Social Psychology*, 69, 719–727.

Ryff, C. D., and Singer, B. (1998). The contours of positive human health. *Psychological Inquiry*, 9, 1–28.

(2008). Know thyself and become what you are: A eudaimonic approach to psychological well-being. *Journal of Happiness Studies*, 9, 13–39.

Sheldon, K. M., and Elliot, A. J. (1998). Not all personal goals are personal: Comparing autonomous and controlled reasons for goals as predictors of effort and attainment. *Personality and Social Psychology Bulletin*, 24, 546–557.

Sheldon, K. M., and Houser-Marko, L. (2001). Self-concordance, goal attainment, and the pursuit of happiness: Can there be an upward spiral? *Journal of Personality and Social Psychology*, 80, 152–165.

Sheldon, K. M., and Kasser, T. (2001). Getting older, getting better? Personal strivings and psychosocial maturity across the life-span. *Developmental Psychology*, 34, 491–501.

Singer, J. A. (2004). Narrative identity and meaning-making across the adult lifespan: An introduction. *Journal of Personality*, 72, 437–460.

Staudinger, U. M. (2001). Life reflection: A social-cognitive analysis of life review. *Review of General Psychology*, 5, 148–160.

Staudinger, U. M., and Kunzmann, U. (2005). Positive adult personality development: Adjustment and/or growth? *European Psychologist*, 10, 320–329.

Stroebe, M. S., and Schut, H. (2001). Meaning making in the dual process model of coping with bereavement. In R. A. Neimeyer (ed.), *Meaning reconstruction and the experience of loss* (pp. 55–73). Washington, DC: American Psychological Association.

Waterman, A. S., Schwartz, S. J., and Conti, R. (2008). The implications of two conceptions of happiness (hedonic enjoyment and eudaimonia) for the understanding of intrinsic motivation. *Journal of Happiness Studies*, 9, 41–79.

Westphal, M., and Bonanno, G. A. (2007). Posttraumatic growth and resilience to trauma: Different sides of the same coin or different coins? *Applied Psychology: An International Review*, 56, 417–427.

Wirtz, D., Kruger, J., Scollon, C. N., and Diener, E. (2003). What to do on spring break? The role of predicted, on-line, and remembered experience in future choice. *Psychological Science*, 14, 520–524.

Wong, P. T. P., and Watt, L. M. (1991). What types of reminiscence are associated with successful aging? *Psychology and Aging*, 6, 272–279.

3 Physical resilience and aging: correcting the Tithonus error and the crème brûlée error

Aubrey D. N. J. de Grey

Abstract

One of the most persistent misconceptions surrounding the prospect of combating aging – so persistent, in fact, that it has acquired a name, "the Tithonus error" – is that successful anti-aging interventions would postpone death but would not postpone the decline in health and vigor that characterizes later life. The psychological reasons for why so many people have for so long remained deaf to gerontologists' incessant and vocal correction of this error are complex and have been addressed in my previous work. Here I discuss the physiological basis for the confidence, shared by all biologists of aging, that the only way we will ever substantially extend the human lifespan is by extending people's healthy lifespan, rather than by keeping people alive in a frail state. I then discuss what these physiological realities tell us about which approaches to combating aging are the most promising, and why they are likely to lead to the substantial (and, eventually, dramatic) postponement of what is now humanity's number one killer.

Introduction: the Tithonus error and the pro-aging trance

Ill health is risky

That is really the beginning and end of what I need to communicate in this section. It certainly does not seem particularly controversial. But, in practice, a phenomenal amount of effort has been expended in both asserting and resisting this simple truth. Rejection of it has even infiltrated the world of popular music, perhaps most prominently in the case of the one-hit wonders Hedgehoppers Anonymous, whose "It's good news week," despite appearing in the supposedly optimistic 1960s, featured the following immortal (so to speak) lyrics:

> It's good news week,
> Someone's found a way to give

The rotting dead a will to live,
Go on and never die.

As the popularity of this song exemplifies, a huge proportion of society insists on exhibiting extraordinarily strenuous resistance toward being educated that a substantial extension of life is not going to occur except by keeping people healthy. The contrary presumption – that the only way we will extend lifespan is by keeping people alive in a frail state – is so ubiquitous that it has earned a specific name in the literature of social gerontology, namely "the Tithonus error." It is one of the more aggressive expressions of what I have termed "the pro-aging trance" – a state of denial in which people find it easier to suspend their normal respect for expert opinion (and, indeed, commonsense) than to embrace the distress that attends accepting that a future development that they desperately wish for may not occur in time for them. Pretending that they do not, in fact, wish for this development at all is the path of least (albeit still considerable) resistance.

Why pessimism matters: the yin-yang of desirability and feasibility

Historically, most biogerontologists have in my view been unduly detached from the public debate concerning the importance of their work. In a nutshell, there has been a tendency to feel that science can and should proceed in a sociological vacuum, furthering our understanding of things whether or not the general public understand why this is a good use of resources, because by and large the general public will not be able to understand that. This is clearly an oversimplification, not least because of the impact of public opinion on public funding. But in the case of postponing aging, it is a particularly severe oversimplification.

The distinguishing feature of aging that is most relevant here is the irrationality that pervades so many people's thinking about it. This essay will address only one or two manifestations of that irrationality, but it is much broader. In essence, extraordinary numbers of otherwise thoughtful people are willing to hold, simultaneously, the following two positions:

- I refuse to engage in meaningful debate about the feasibility of radically postponing aging, because it is obviously a bad idea even if we could do it.
- I refuse to engage in meaningful debate about the desirability of radically postponing aging, because it is obviously never going to be possible.

I doubt that I need elaborate – except in one regard. Until rather recently, the latter position above was actually quite defensible. Specialists had yet to devise a remotely detailed plan for seriously going after aging, and without such a plan it was altogether reasonable for non-specialists to presume that implementation of some such hypothetical future plan was so far off as to be best presumed fictitious.

This, however, is no longer so. As I have described in various past publications (e.g., de Grey, 2005b; de Grey *et al.*, 2002), it is now possible to envisage a panel of interventions, most of them falling within the broad category of regenerative medicine, that would jointly address the entirety of aging. These therapies will not resemble classical geriatric medicine, which combats individual pathologies of late life. Rather, they will target the causes of those pathologies, the life-long accumulating "damage" at the molecular and cellular level that our metabolism happily tolerates for a few decades but to which it eventually succumbs. It is therefore imperative to abandon the fatalism that has pervaded our thinking about aging since the dawn of time, and to address head-on the question of whether aging is or is not a good thing. And that means revisiting the simplistic assumptions that we have felt able to accept so uncritically hitherto.

Lest readers fear that I am pulling the wool over their eyes, I will elaborate a little on the nature of these regenerative interventions. They consist in restoring the molecular and/or cellular composition of one or another organ or tissue.

In the case of cells, this means either replacing cells that are not automatically replaced by the division of other cells – this is what stem cell therapy is, of course – or removing supernumerary cells that arise either from excessive cell division (cancer) or inadequate cell death (which is a major component of the aging of the immune system). Cancer is the hardest part of aging to address, since it has natural selection at its disposal, but a wide variety of creative methods are now on the horizon. Killing cells that have forgotten how to kill themselves is much easier, and various methods involving either vaccination or gene therapy are under development.

At the molecular level, restoring structure mostly means eliminating "garbage" – molecules generated as normal byproducts of metabolic processes, but then, for whatever reason, not broken down or excreted. Such molecules accumulate, initially harmlessly, but eventually to the detriment of metabolism. When such molecules accumulate outside the cell, such as the famous amyloid plaques in Alzheimer's disease, it may be enough to use vaccination techniques to cause immune cells to engulf them, because the intracellular degradation machinery is much more powerful than its extracellular counterpart. Material so refractory that it accumulates even inside the cell can be eliminated by using either gene therapy or enzyme therapy to introduce non-human enzymes that can break things down that we cannot; these can often be found quite easily in bacteria. Two other types of molecular restoration are also needed that do not consist of breaking things down. One is the cleavage of spontaneously generated chemical bonds between proteins that cause the structures they comprise to become less elastic, such as in the walls of major arteries. Drugs capable of selectively breaking these bonds are already under development. The other is the accumulation of mutations in the mitochondria, the cell's "powerhouse": these will probably be very hard to repair, but they can be obviated by gene therapy to introduce suitably modified copies of the mitochondrial genome into the nucleus. Again, progress in achieving this (albeit only in mice, so far) is highly encouraging.

For a detailed discussion of all these technologies and more, the reader is referred to de Grey and Rae (2007).

The pro-aging trance: a summary

I have dwelt at some length, in various prior publications (de Grey, 2004a, 2004b, 2004c, 2004d, 2005c, 2006c, 2007a, 2007b, 2007c) on the psychological basis for the pro-aging trance. Therefore, I will not elaborate at length on it here; I will focus instead on the biological basis for biogerontologists' absolute confidence that being frail not only is risky but always will be. In doing so, I will try to resolve some of the confusion that has resulted from the well-meaning but perhaps naive efforts of many biogerontologists to oversimplify this issue. However, before doing so it may be worth just briefly outlining why I am a good deal more charitable to those who sincerely defend aging than one might expect a leading opponent of aging to be.

Why the Tithonus error is an error: the irrevocable association between health and life

The foremost reason, in my view, why confusion exists regarding the linkage between aging and death is that it has become very popular for biogerontologists to stress that aging is not a disease. Whether aging is in fact a disease is actually not the issue here, not least because the answer to that question is mainly a question of terminology, dependent on how one chooses to define the word "disease," a matter on which there is a spectrum of opinion. No – the issue is what the separation between aging and disease in the minds of biogerontologists' audience leads that audience to assume. Most unfortunately, it leads them to assume a great deal that is not correct, and biogerontologists evidently fail to realize this – or, at least, to act on such realization by correcting those errors (de Grey, 2005a).

First of all, people know that diseases kill people, so the first thing they think when told that aging is not a disease is that aging does not kill people. This is illogical, of course – the valid syllogism is in the opposite direction. That is, that if aging does not kill people and diseases do, then aging is not a disease. (And yes, clearly that would also be incorrect because not all diseases actually kill people – but I digress.) But logic is not most people's strong point, so this error is hardly surprising. And its consequences in terms of what people care about are rather profound. First of all, there is the tendency to react by deprioritizing doing anything about aging, because by saying that it is not within a category that is agreed to be important and not at the same time saying why it is important anyway, one inevitably diminishes its perceived importance. But second, and even more disastrous, such statements greatly reinforce the Tithonus error, by implying that any success in postponing aging would not postpone disease.

Now, in fairness to those of my biogerontologist colleagues who have committed (and continue to commit) this rhetorical error, I must at once acknowledge that there is one way in which they do indeed attempt to undo the damage that it causes. The standard follow-up to "aging is not a disease" is "but it's still important because it increases people's *susceptibility* to disease." This surely sounds reasonable. Unfortunately, it is way off target. First of all, it is biologically incorrect: while some diseases are indeed independent of aging but made more lethal by aging, most of the diseases that predominantly afflict the elderly do so because they are intrinsic manifestations of the later stages of aging. And second, it is ineffective in correcting people's misinterpretation of the original "aging is not a disease" platitude, because people know that frailty – those aspects of age-related ill health that are not classified as particular diseases – is miserable too, indeed arguably just as unattractive as long-lasting disease. In other words, the link between aging and susceptibility to disease does not correct the Tithonus error – it still leaves people thinking that the postponement of aging will lead to people spending longer than they do today in an unenviable state of health before they die.

Does this follow? No, it does not logically follow, but the pro-aging trance – the desire of so many people to find ways to pretend that the postponement of aging would be a bad idea – means that if there exists *any* interpretation of expert pronouncements that can be used in defence of the Tithonus error, it will be the preferred interpretation. And in this case, there is a clear such interpretation, because frailty is not addressed in those pronouncements. Victims of the pro-aging trance are allowed to presume that, even if postponing aging will postpone age-related diseases (by postponing susceptibility to them), it will not postpone frailty, and thus that ill health not defined in terms of disease will be extended. Furthermore, since people know that most age-related diseases generally kill people within a few years of becoming prejudicial to quality of life, whereas frailty typically does not, the prospect of postponing aging and disease without postponing frailty can easily be concluded to be even worse than the prospect of postponing aging without postponing disease.

Biogerontologists will retort that this is all nonsense, talking in circles – but that is precisely my point. That is what the pro-aging trance makes people do. Biogerontologists do not, by and large, suffer from the pro-aging trance, and that is clearly a good thing in many ways; but it has the severe drawback of limiting biogerontologists' ability to anticipate how their words will be received by those who do.

The fact is that biogerontologists have brought this on themselves by talking in just as indefensible circles as their audience do. In explaining why this is so, I come back to a statement I made without elaboration a few paragraphs ago: "most of the diseases that predominantly afflict the elderly do so because they are manifestations of the later stages of aging." Once this is understood, and especially once it is generalized in two important ways, the opening statement of this section becomes indisputable.

The first generalization concerns the age-related diseases that are not manifestations of the later stages of aging. They are age related because they are diseases to which, as I mentioned earlier, the elderly are progressively more susceptible by virtue of frailty. The second generalization concerns frailty itself, and here we can be succinct: frailty is another thing that predominantly afflicts the elderly by virtue of being a manifestation of the later stages of aging. Thus, a version of the previous statement that takes these two generalizations into account is straightforward: "age-related ill health is the set of manifestations of the later stages of aging." Note the absence of any reference to disease.

Once health and aging are linked in this all-embracing way, all the confusions deriving from biogerontologists' ill-considered reference to "disease" instantly and automatically evaporate. Age-related diseases differ from frailty not in any biological respect, but in a medical respect, namely that we have not considered the components of frailty to be sufficiently important to get around to giving them names. That really is the only difference. And once we absorb that, the unavoidable, immediate question arises: what can aging possibly be *except* the process that leads to age-related ill health? There is no answer: that is exactly what aging is. So the final step is as follows: can the postponement of aging possibly extend the period of ill health at the end of life? And again, the answer is clear: no it cannot, because the postponement of aging is nothing more or less than the postponement of age-related ill health.

Why have biogerontologists so bizarrely avoided this approach to justifying their existence? The answer is very clear, boring, and saddening: they have done so because the alternative of contrasting aging with disease was seen to be expedient, and has indeed borne some fruit, in terms of funding. The National Institute on Aging would probably not have been founded were it not for this rhetoric. Unfortunately, even that does not justify this error, because that success was a miserably isolated one: ever since, biogerontologists have vocally and correctly complained that their field has received a pitifully small fraction of the funding that its potential for the improvement of human health merits, and their complaints have fallen on ears thoroughly deafened by their suggestion that aging is not a disease. My unequivocal conclusion is that biogerontology has shot itself spectacularly in the foot over a period of decades by departing from both biological reality and the mindset of its audience in its description of its purpose.

This section has summarized my view of the main problems that faced biogerontology until about 1980 and the reasons why those problems arose. Since that date, you might be hoping that things have improved. Unfortunately, the opposite has occurred: the above situation has persisted, and it has been exacerbated by a new and equally severe problem that is just as much the fault of biogerontologists as the earlier ones were. It is the topic of the next section.

Compression of morbidity: when you are in a hole, stop digging

First of all, let me provide a definition: morbidity is, simply, age-related ill health.

In July 1980, the Stanford geriatrician James Fries published an article in the *New England Journal of Medicine* that has exerted more influence over biogerontological self-promotion than perhaps any other (Fries, 1980). Its impact has been so immense that I feel justified in reproducing its abstract here. (As will become apparent, I also have other reasons for doing so.) The abstract reads as follows:

The average length of life has risen from 47 to 73 years in this century, but the maximum lifespan has not increased. Therefore, survival curves have assumed an ever more rectangular form. Eighty per cent of the years of life lost to non-traumatic, premature death have been eliminated, and most premature deaths are now due to the chronic diseases of the later years. Present data allow calculation of the ideal average lifespan, approximately 85 years. Chronic illness may presumably be postponed by changes in life style, and it has been shown that the physiologic and psychologic markers of aging may be modified. Thus, the average age at first infirmity can be raised, thereby making the morbidity curve more rectangular. Extension of adult vigor far into a fixed lifespan compresses the period of senescence near the end of life. Health-research strategies to improve the quality of life require careful study of the variability of the phenomena of aging and how they may be modified.

In order to explain the importance of this article I can begin by highlighting two extracts from the abstract: "Chronic illness may presumably be postponed ... and it has been shown that the physiologic and psychologic markers of aging may be modified" and "Extension of adult vigor far into a fixed lifespan compresses the period of senescence near the end of life." Taken together and in isolation from the rest of the abstract, these statements add up to a hugely seductive message for biogerontologists: not only would the postponement of aging not lead to an extension of the period that the average person suffers morbidity (i.e., the scenario foreseen in the Tithonus error), it might well lead to a compression of that period. As such, it might be so strong a refutation of the Tithonus error that the public – and, perhaps more directly importantly, policy-makers – might finally understand what the postponement of aging is actually all about, namely the extension of *healthy* life.

So seductive was this message, in fact, that biogerontologists the world over have run with this message as if there were no tomorrow (de Grey, 2006a, 2006b). Which is rather a shame, because it has made the actual persuasiveness of their case even weaker than it already was.

The abstract reproduced above, though merely 166 words long, encapsulates all the ways in which this response to Fries' paper was so catastrophic. They are as follows:

1. The rectangularization (assumption of an ever more rectangular form) of survival curves is equated with the rectangularization of what Fries terms the "morbidity curve." (A survival curve is simply a graph showing what proportion of a given population survives to each age. Thus, the survival curve of a population all of whom died at exactly the same age would be precisely rectangular, and that of a population who mostly die within a reasonably narrow age range, such as Westerners today, is more nearly rectangular than that of a

population with high early mortality, such as prehistoric humans.) The term "morbidity curve" is not defined, but the natural definition is easy to give: it is the counterpart of the survival curve in which age at death is replaced by age at descent into morbidity. However, this definition reveals that Fries's inference is illogical. He notes that the survival curve has *already* become highly rectangular, but he says nothing about what has happened to the morbidity curve: rather, he discusses what might happen to morbidity in the *future*. He gives no reason whatsoever to suppose that future postponement of morbidity would do either of the things he assumes it will do, namely (a) further rectangularize morbidity and (b) postpone morbidity without equally postponing death.

2. Actually, the maximum lifespan had increased rather a lot in the century leading up to Fries' paper, albeit certainly less than mean lifespan. Some demographers like to define "maximum lifespan" as the world record longevity; others prefer the age to which some small proportion (often 10 percent) of the world's, or the developed world's, population live – but by any measure, there had been a rise of at least a decade between the mid 1800s (when some nations began to keep adequate records) and 1980 (Los Angeles Gerontology Research Group, 2006)

3. Even if the pre-1980 increase in maximum lifespan is considered too small to matter, there is no biological or biomedical sense in presuming that it will stay that way – nor, in particular, in presuming that it will be unaffected by future postponements of morbidity. The presumption of a "fixed lifespan" is just that, a presumption, based solely on the failure of medicine *thus far* to impact aging very much. As such, Fries's prediction of a compression of morbidity is contingent on the (clearly very uncertain) continued failure of future medicine to do what medicine thus far has not done.

4. Most important of all, Fries highlights *lifestyle* changes as the main route towards further postponement of morbidity. He qualifies his assertion that this will work, to be sure, by the word "presumably" – but the critical point is that he does *not* presume, nor even speculate, that progress in combating aging will have this effect.

None of these features dissuaded the biogerontology establishment from leaping on Fries' paper as their perceived route to salvation. The fact that it has, instead, merely cemented the indefensibility of their previous rhetoric needs no further elaboration: it is hardly worth mentioning that when an argument is ineffective, an intensification of that exact same argument is awfully likely to be even more ineffective. In the past year or two, that is, a full quarter-century later, signs are emerging that this lesson is slowly being learned (Olshansky *et al.*, 2007) – but I will remain cautious regarding this development until it is much more secure than it is so far.

Both the Tithonus error and the compression-of-morbidity error are long standing and have been the subject of extensive previous discussions in the academic literature. I now wish to explore an error that has been rather less thoroughly covered, such that I have the opportunity to name it myself.

The crème brûlée error

Despite the spectacularly retrograde steps that the biogerontology community has so far taken in its attempts to dispel the Tithonus error, I am optimistic that we will eventually do so. Even once we definitively consign this misconception to history, however, the pro-aging trance will continue to drive people towards other errors concerning what life would be like if truly effective therapies against aging emerged. Perhaps the most insidious, which I here term the "crème brûlée error," is that expressed by the poet and undertaker (yes, you read that correctly) Thomas Lynch in a documentary about my work broadcast in 2006 (Sykes and Ogden, 2006): "Living 1,000 years and never having a crème brûlée strikes me as a waste of time."

Lynch has previously made clear his opposition to anti-aging research (Lynch, 1999); however, his original complaint was the altogether more absurd idea that success would not bring us happiness because, as with the advent of unlimited availability of food, it would promote gluttony – in this case, greed for more and more life.

His concern quoted above is, in essence, the reverse of this. He plucks out of the air the assumption that if we do indeed develop therapies that extend healthy life, they will require us to adhere to a lifestyle regime so onerous that the diminished quality of this life would outweigh its increased quantity.

The origin of this misconception is easy to locate: it is simply the fact that a long life has historically been associated, in anecdote if not in fact, with an ascetic lifestyle. Indeed, though there are certainly many exceptions, this association may well be accurate more often than not. But what is the evidence that the same would be true of future therapies?

It is reasonable to retort that the onus is on me to explain why the same would *not* be true, since precedent can legitimately be viewed as defining the null hypothesis when other things are equal. Thus, I will do exactly that. In doing so I will start by reminding you that the body is a machine, albeit an astronomically complex one, and by exploring how we keep simple, man-made machines in full working order longer than average. As an example, I will discuss cars.

Some cars are *built* to last much longer than the average. Land Rovers, for example, feature such accoutrements as a corrosion-resistant chassis, extra-tough tyres, and so on. Three noted gerontologists recently built on the implicit presumption that this is the only way that cars last unusually long: they wrote a tongue-in-cheek article in *Scientific American* suggesting a variety of design improvements to the human body that would increase its "warranty period" (Olshansky, Carnes, and Butler, 2001).

Luckily, their implicit presumption is not correct – at least, not if the analogy with man-made machines is accepted. As we all know, there are some cars on the road that are well over a hundred years old: they regularly take part in rallies, unambiguously demonstrating their road-worthiness. Moreover, it would not be correct to jeer at such examples on the basis that their top speed can, at least for a few hundred yards, be bettered by top-class sprinters: the correct comparison is not with con-temporary cars but with these same cars at the time they were built. And there is no doubt that they perform every bit as well as when they rolled off the production line, insofar as there were production lines back then. These are cars that are *maintained* to last.

"Aha," you may now be thinking, "but that's precisely Lynch's point, isn't it? Vintage cars don't age, no, but that's only because they don't get out much: their lives are miserably circumscribed, consisting of a day or two per year on the open road and the other 364 in a garage." And if vin-tage cars were the end of my line of reasoning, you would be right. But they are not.

The cars that make my point (and break Lynch's) are those that main-tain full function for unusually long, as a result of thorough maintenance and repair, *despite being just as frequently and fully active as any young car.* There are certainly plenty of 50-year-old Volkswagen Beetles, Citroen 2CVs, and Morris Minors driving around the roads of the USA, France, and the UK, respectively – indeed, probably just as many as there are 50-year-old Land Rovers. These cars are positive proof that, at least for simple man-made machines, maintenance really works. One does not have to choose between exceptional construction and exceptional inactivity in order to give such machines exceptional healthy longevity. Averagely constructed cars with at least average activity can have excep-tional healthy longevity, if they receive exceptionally comprehensive maintenance.

It remains for me, therefore, only to convince you that the analogy between cars and human bodies is valid. Is there, possibly, some feature of the human body that makes it more than just a machine, and thereby makes it less amenable to maintenance than the cars that give us such cause for hope? Luckily, though I have been presenting this analogy to audiences of all flavours for several years now, no one has come up with such a feature. In particular, the possession by living organisms of a massive arsenal of inbuilt, automatic repair-and-maintenance machinery does not qualify as a problem with the car analogy, because such machinery clearly makes the job of the physician *easier*, not harder, than it would be if that machinery were absent, because the damage which that inbuilt repair machinery repairs need not be repaired by the physician, who can therefore focus on the damage that is not automatically repaired (de Grey, 2003).

Conclusion: what the Tithonus and crème brûlée errors mean for what will work

The bulk of my work focuses not on the misunderstanding of what biogerontology aspires to achieve, but on the nuts and bolts of actually achieving it. My approach to this has long been founded on the logic presented here. The Tithonus error encapsulates the idea that combating aging will be done by developing ever-better geriatrics, capable of keeping people alive in a frail state for longer and longer. I have explained that this approach is futile, and anyway is not what biogerontologists seek to do. The crème brûlée error encapsulates the idea that we can only avoid the twin miseries of premature death and extended frailty by substituting a third misery, the avoidance of many things that make life worth living in the first place, in order to retard the lifelong accumulation of molecular and cellular damage that eventually causes age-related ill health. I have explained that this, too, is inconsistent with known facts. In fact, the best way to maintain a fully active human body in youthful condition for a much longer time than it would naturally survive is a third, in some ways intermediate approach: to let the body lay down molecular and cellular damage at the rate that it naturally lays it down, but periodically to remove or obviate that damage, using comprehensive repair and maintenance technologies, mostly based on stem cells, tissue engineering and gene therapy (de Grey, 2005b; de Grey *et al.*, 2002). Some of those technologies, such as stem cell therapies, are well on the way already; others are probably the best part of a decade away even in mice and a couple more decades in humans, and could be even further away if they encounter yet-unforeseen obstacles. But the approach is foreseeable, and indeed it may well materialise in time for many of those alive at the time of writing. It is devoutly to be hoped that misconceptions and short-sightedness on the part of those in positions of relevant intellectual and political authority, such as those discussed in this chapter, will not continue to slow that process down.

REFERENCES

de Grey, A. D. N. J. (2003). The foreseeability of real anti-aging medicine: Focusing the debate. *Experimental Gerontology*, 38(9) 927–934.

(2004a). Biogerontologists' duty to discuss timescales publicly. *Annals of the New York Academy of Sciences*, 1019, 542–545.

(2004b). Leon Kass: Quite substantially right. *Rejuvenation Research*, 7(2) 89–91.

(2004c). Three self-evident life-extension truths. *Rejuvenation Research*, 7(3) 165–167.

(2004d). Aging, childlessness, or overpopulation: The future's right to choose. *Rejuvenation Research*, 7(4) 237–238.

(2005a). Resistance to debate on how to postpone ageing is delaying progress and costing lives. *EMBO Reports*, 6(S1), S49–S53.

(2005b). A strategy for postponing aging indefinitely. *Studies in Health Technology Informatics*, 118, 209–219.

(2005c). Life extension, human rights, and the rational refinement of repugnance. *Journal of Medical Ethics*, 31(11), 659–663.

(2006a). Compression of morbidity: The hype and the reality, part 1. *Rejuvenation Research*, 9(1), 1–2.

(2006b). Compression of morbidity: The hype and the reality, part 2. *Rejuvenation Research*, 9(2), 167–168.

(2006c). Has Hippocrates had his day? *Rejuvenation Research*, 9(3), 371–373.

(2007a). Life span extension research and public debate: Societal considerations. *Studies in Ethics, Law and Technology*, 1(1), 5.

(2007b). The need to debalkanize gerontology: A case study. *Rejuvenation Research*, 10(4), 431–434.

(2007c). Old people are people too: Why it is our duty to fight aging to the death. *Cato Unbound*, 2007(12): lead essay.

de Grey, A. D. N. J., Ames, B. N., Andersen, J. K., *et al.*,(2002). Time to talk SENS: Critiquing the immutability of human aging. *Annals of the New York Academy of Sciences*, 959, 452–462.

de Grey, A. D. N. J., and Rae, M. J. (2007). *Ending aging: the rejuvenation breakthroughs that could reverse human aging in our lifetime*. New York: St. Martin's Press.

Fries, J. F. (1980). Aging, natural death, and the compression of morbidity. *New England Journal of Medicine*, 303(3) 130–135.

Los Angeles Gerontology Research Group (2006). Living and all-time world longevity record-holders over the age of 110. *Rejuvenation Research*, 9(2), 367–368.

Lynch, T. (1999). Why buy more time? *New York Times*, March 14 (Sec. 4), 15.

Olshansky, S. J., Carnes, B. A., and Butler, R. N. (2001). If humans were built to last. *Scientific American*, 284, 50–55.

Olshansky, S. J., Perry, D., Miller, R. A., and Butler, R. N. (2007). Pursuing the longevity dividend: Scientific goals for an aging world. *Annals of the New York Academy of Sciences*, 1114, 11–13.

Sykes C., and Ogden M. (2006). *Do you want to live forever?* (documentary). Windfall Films, London.

4   You can teach an old dog new tricks: harnessing neuroplasticity after brain injury in older adults

Gitendra Uswatte and Edward Taub

Abstract

Animal and human research has shown that the brain can reorganize and even remodel itself to restore function in response to central nervous system (CNS) injuries, such as stroke, traumatic brain injury, and spinal cord injury. This chapter will discuss the phenomenon of neuroplasticity after damage to the CNS demonstrated in animal and human experiments. Research on Constraint-Induced Movement therapy or CI therapy, which is a behaviorally based approach to physical rehabilitation, will be a major focus. This body of work, among other contributions, overthrew the reigning clinical wisdom that stroke survivors more than 1-year post-event can not benefit from additional physical rehabilitation. It also provided the first evidence that physical rehabilitation can produce large improvements in real-world arm function and change CNS organization and structure. This evidence provides a neurophysiological basis for continued plasticity in behavior among older adults.

Introduction

Clinical wisdom, and even the scientific view, until relatively recently was that older adults who suffered damage to their brain had little hope that this vital organ could repair itself or adapt how it functioned to overcome the injury. The scientific view was based on the long-held tenet that the mature central nervous system (CNS) had little capacity to repair or reorganize itself. Though contrary views were expressed (e.g., Flourens, 1842; Fritsch and Hitzig, 1870; Lashley, 1938; Munk, 1881), the mature CNS was generally believed (Kaas, 1995, p. 735) to exhibit little or no plasticity (e.g., Hubel and Wiesel, 1970; Ruch, 1960, p. 274).

In hindsight, the strength with which this view was held seems odd in the face of the spontaneous recovery of function that not uncommonly takes place after CNS injury. The belief that the adult mammalian nervous system does not have the capacity to reorganize itself functionally after injury began to be convincingly challenged in the 1970s, when animal studies from a number of laboratories showed the contrary (e.g., Kaas, Merzenich, and Killackey, 1983; Merzenich *et al.*, 1984; Wall and Egger, 1971). Studies in humans from the 1990s by Taub, Elbert, Flor, Miltner, and others (reviewed in Taub, Uswatte, and Elbert, 2002) showed not only that brain reorganization occurs after disuse or abolition of a function following nervous system injury but also that brain reorganization can be produced by intense, concentrated use of a function, as Merzenich's laboratory had first demonstrated in New World monkeys (e.g., Jenkins *et al.*, 1990). More recent studies have shown that when the proper conditions are present the brain even has the capacity to repair or structurally remodel itself; that is, that adaptive structural change in brain tissue can take place (e.g., Gauthier *et al.*, 2008).

This chapter will review the revolutionary work that overthrew the traditional model of lack of plasticity in the adult CNS, briefly describe work on spontaneous recovery from neurological injury, and in greater depth discuss research on how the substantial plasticity that now appears to be present in the CNS can be harnessed to help survivors of CNS damage to recover and flourish. Research on Constraint-Induced Movement therapy (Taub *et al.*, 1993), which is a physical rehabilitation method derived from behavioral neuroscience studies of deafferented monkeys (Taub, 1977, 1980), is presented as a model for therapeutically harnessing neuroplasticity to improve motor function degraded by either focal injury to the CNS, as in stroke and traumatic brain injury, or by slow dementing processes. We also touch on approaches for enhancing cognitive function that take advantage of neuroplasticity in older adults who are aging normally.

Overthrowing the view that the adult brain is static

Animal studies

Changes in how particular motor or sensory functions are represented in the CNS, were observed by researchers such as Sherrington and Lashley in the first third of the twentieth century. By repeatedly stimulating the motor cortex with an electrode in a fixed position, Sherrington found that the movement evoked could change from flexion to extension and even occur in parts of the body other than the initial evoked movement (Brown and Sherrington, 1912). In the middle of the twentieth century, Gelhorn and Hyde (1953) discovered that simply repositioning a limb could change which part of the cortex required stimulation to evoke the limb's movement, suggesting that a change in the periphery could also influence the nature of cortical activity.

This dynamic relationship between cortex and periphery was not generally understood as plasticity in the currently accepted sense, nor did the authors discuss it as such. The work of Michael Merzenich, Jan Kaas and others in the 1980s demonstrated with clarity the phenomenon of injury-related brain plasticity, the idea that a physically induced change in afferent input from an extremity affects its representation in the brain. The best-known study in this series involved removing input from a digit in monkeys by amputation instead of cutting the median nerve. Cortical representations for the hand area were identified using microelectrode mapping from two to eight months after surgical amputation of either digit 3 only or both digits 2 and 3. In both types of surgery, the cortical representation field of the intact digits expanded to occupy most of the original cortical territory of the now amputated fingers (Merzenich *et al.*, 1984). This study showed that inputs can cross borders of the representation zones of separate digits to invade nearby cortical representations. The study also suggested to its authors that the extent of reorganization did not extend beyond 2 mm from the original representational boundary of the digit.

Jenkins and co-workers determined that reorganization could happen without injury. If elimination of afferent inputs could produce a change in cortical representation, perhaps a modification of behavior that increased input could result in similar changes, that is, what has come to be known as use-dependent or skill-related reorganization. In their study (Jenkins *et al.*, 1990), microelectrode maps were obtained of the hand representation in cortical area 3b before, immediately after, and three weeks after monkeys underwent behavioral training. Some of the monkeys were conditioned to keep the fingertips of one or more of the longest digits of this hand in contact with a *rotating grooved* disk to receive a reward. (The grooves and rotation of the disk required that the monkeys finely regulate that amount of pressure they applied to the disk with their fingertips to maintain contact with it.) This "behaviorally relevant" stimulation of the fingers produced an expansion of their cortical areas and shifting of some representation borders. The rest of the monkeys were conditioned to keep their fingertips in contact with a *stationary smooth* disk to receive a reward. These animals, whose task did not require as much attention as the task for the first group of monkeys, did not show reorganization of their cortex.

The work of Pons *et al.* (1991) challenged the idea of a 2-mm limit in the amount of reorganization that could occur. Fingers, palm, upper limb, and neck of monkeys were deafferented so that their cortex was deprived of inputs from these areas. Tactile evoked responses recorded from the cortex twelve years after the deafferentation indicated that the area representing the face had invaded the deafferentation zone, that is, the cortical area that had once received input from the deafferented parts of the body. The expansion of the border of the representation zone of the face greatly exceeded 2 mm. It was observed to take place over the entire representation of the arm (10–14 mm), and was designated "massive" cortical reorganization (Pons *et al.*, 1991). This work aroused the interest of investigators because it suggested that plastic brain reorganization could take place over an area large enough to have potential relevance to the rehabilitation of function after brain injury.

Even the tenet that new neurons are not produced in the adult mammalian brain (e.g., Rakic, 1985) has come under challenge, and been overthrown (reviewed in Gould, 2007). In the early 1990s, Gould and co-workers published data that persuasively confirmed earlier work (Altman and Das, 1965), which was largely ignored, that demonstrated the formation of new neurons, that is, neurogenesis, in the adult rat hippocampus (Cameron *et al.*, 1993; Gould *et al.*, 1992). Two other groups of researchers, at close to the same time, showed that neurogenesis takes place in the olfactory bulb in the adult mammalian brain (Corotto, Henegar, and Maruniak, 1994; Lois and Alvarez-Buylla, 1994). Although several reports of neurogenesis in other parts of the adult mammalian brain, including the neocortex, have been published, this phenomenon has still not been demonstrated conclusively (see review by Gould, 2007). As with other forms of plasticity (see above), neurogenesis appears to be experience-dependent: both enriched environments and exercise increase neurogenesis in the hippocampus (reviewed in van Praag, Kempermann, and Gage, 2000).

By the middle of the 1990s, the view that the adult brain had substantial capacity for plasticity gained a strong foothold. CNS reorganization was shown to occur in adult animals following a variety of interventions, including nerve dissection, amputation, and behavioral modification. The concept that the borders between the receptive fields of individual digits were fixed gave way to the idea of borders that were dynamically determined by the amount of sensory input to each receptive field. An upper limit to the expansion of the cortical representation of discrete somatic areas has yet to be identified. The importance of the behavioral relevance of any changes in sensory input for stimulating plastic changes was also established. Furthermore, investigators showed that the production of new neurons, the most radical form of plasticity, takes place even in the adult brain.

Human studies

Modern neuroimaging methods have permitted researchers to test whether the remarkable plastic brain changes observed in animals have parallels in humans. Magnetic source imaging (MSI) studies by Elbert, Flor, Taub, and co-workers have shown that when the amount of sensory input to a particular brain region increases with increased use of a body part, this region expands. Blind individuals who employed three fingers on a hand simultaneously to read Braille showed substantial enlargement of the hand area compared with sighted non-Braille-reading persons (Sterr *et al.*, 1998). Additionally, the medial to lateral order of the representations of the three "reading" fingers on the convexity of the cortex was altered or "smeared" in the three-finger Braille readers. This alteration in topography correlated with impaired ability to detect which finger was being touched. It appears that a "smearing" of cortical representations may be adaptive for Braille readers because it facilitates integrating sensory information from all three reading fingers, which would help in the perception of words. Consistent with the findings from blind readers of Braille, string instrument players also have an increased cortical representation for the left hand, which performs the complex task of fingering the strings, but not the right hand, which has the less dexterity-demanding task of bowing the strings (Elbert *et al.*, 1995).

An increase in cortical representation areas has been observed in the auditory cortex of blind persons, and is thought to be due to increased reliance on audition for information about their environment (Elbert *et al.*, 2002). Blind persons receive the same amount of auditory stimulation as those who are sighted. Therefore, this result suggests again that cortical reorganization is not merely a passive response to increases in sensory stimulation, but rather depends on the behavioral relevance of input into the nervous system and the attention devoted to it. This property would appear to permit the brain to adapt itself to the functional demands placed on an individual.

Recent studies employing structural magnetic resonance imaging (MRI) have shown that brain plasticity in humans not only involves reorganization, that is, one region of the brain representing a function it had not previously, but also the growth of new tissue. Maguire and co-workers showed that London taxi cab drivers, compared with people who do not drive taxis, have differences in the volume of their hippocampus, a structure known to encode spatial information. Furthermore, the amount of time spent driving a taxi was associated with the magnitude of these structural differences (Maguire *et al.*, 2000). Draganski *et al.* (2004) showed that training healthy volunteers to juggle over the course of three months increased the density of cortical tissue in anterior occipital regions involved in visual motor coordination.

In addition to such "input-increase"-driven expansion of cortical representations or increases in gray matter density, "input-decrease" cortical reorganization has been observed subsequent to the abolition of sensation from a body part or its decreased use (Weiss et al., 2004). Elbert et al. (1994) demonstrated that in upper extremity amputees the topographic representation for the face shifted an average of 1.5 cm into the cortical space normally receiving input from the lost hand and fingers. Reorganization of primary somatomotor cortex has also been observed within an hour of abolishing sensation from the radial and medial three-quarters of the hand by pharmacological blockage of the radial and median nerves (Weiss et al., 2004). Amputation has been found to produce a thinning of tissue in the thalamus (Draganski et al., 2006). Casting the ankle joint has been shown to lead to a decrease in its motor representation (Liepert, Tegenthoff, and Malin, 1995). This reduction in cortical area was related to the duration of time spent in the cast and could be reversed by removing the cast and permitting striate muscle contraction.

Ingenious studies in humans have replicated the evidence for neurogenesis in the hippocampus and olfactory bulb in adult rats and even primates (Curtis et al., 2007; Eriksson et al., 1998). Gage and co-workers in a remarkable study showed that neurogenesis takes place in the hippocampus in aged adults (Eriksson et al., 1998). They examined brains post-mortem from cancer patients who had been injected with BrdU, an analog of the DNA nucleoside thymidine, to monitor the proliferation of cells in their tumors; the BrdU tagged new cell production in many tissues including the brain.

These studies established that CNS plasticity is a rapidly occurring, bidirectional process in adult humans. Increases in the area of cortex representing a function, as well as increases in brain tissue density or volume, have been shown to accompany increased use of the function. Shrinking cortical representations and reduced gray matter have been shown to accompany decreased use of a function or sensory input. Plasticity, thus, has emerged as a mechanism by which the brain can respond to changes in functional demands placed on an individual.

Role of brain plasticity in spontaneous recovery after brain injury

Animal models

To now, we have only discussed brain plasticity subsequent to a change in behavior or injury in the periphery. Plastic changes also occur after direct damage to the CNS, and have been studied in animal models of stroke, traumatic brain injury (TBI), and spinal cord injury (SCI) (Brant-Zawadzki *et al.*, 1996). Nudo and colleagues mapped the cortical representation in Brodmann area 4 of distal forelimb movement in New World monkeys after creating focal ischemic infarcts by surgically occluding arteries (Nudo and Milliken, 1996). The lesions generated a deficit in coordinated movements of the digits of the contralateral hand. Five months after the initial damage the representation of the digits in the contralateral cortex decreased in areas adjacent to the lesion, while the representation of the proximal arm and shoulder increased. Studies involving rat models of TBI have found that the hippocampus can actually restore synaptic connections that were lost due to injuries. Scheff *et al.* produced cortical contusion injuries in rats in which there was a 60 percent loss of synapses in the CA1 region of the hippocampus. Sixty days after injury, the total number of synapses approached normal levels and there was an improvement in spatial memory (Scheff *et al.*, 2005). In animal models of SCI, inhibitory GABA signaling is increased as well as the number of astroglial cells around the injury site. Weight bearing or step training returns these levels to near normal (Edgerton *et al.*, 2001; Tillakaratne *et al.*, 2000).

The animal literature on aging and recovery after CNS injury is slim (reviewed in Bogdan Petcu *et al.*, 2008). The available literature, which is dominated by rat models of stroke, suggests that after experimenter-induced stroke, aged animals, compared with young ones, have higher mortality and slower and poorer recovery of function. Worse outcomes in aged animals appear to be mediated by the build-up of more scar tissue around the infarct, a larger inflammatory response, and greater production of neurotoxins relative to young animals. Encouraging evidence for resiliency after CNS injury in aged animals is that processes that promote self-repair in the young brain still persist in the older brain. Popa-Wagner and co-workers report that older rats after stroke show up regulation of molecular markers of CNS structural repair, albeit at a lower level than younger rats (Badan *et al.*, 2004; Popa-Wagner *et al.*, 1999). Furthermore, Darsalia *et al.* (2005) and Popa-Wagner *et al.* (1999) report that stroke stimulates the production of new neurons in the aged brain, although again at a lower level than in the younger brain.

Studies in humans after neurological injury

Brain plasticity after CNS injury in humans has been best studied in stroke survivors (Schaechter, 2004). During the first eight months after the stroke, there appear to be two shifts in cortical activation. The first shift occurs as soon as one week after stroke in which activation from the cortex in the same hemisphere as the lesion decreases and activation from the cortex in the other hemisphere increases. In three to six months, this shift reverses to favor the cortex on the same side as the lesion (Marshall *et al.*, 2000). By the end of this eight-month time frame the activation of the two hemispheres seems to normalize. This normalization is associated with gains in the functional abilities of patients, which suggests that plastic brain changes are occurring during spontaneous recovery that are related to functional motor recovery (Calautti *et al.*, 2001), and could possibly involve a compensatory role of motor pathways other than corticospinal tract that do not cross the midline (Cramer *et al.*, 2001). The findings on aging and recovery after stroke parallel those in the animal literature. Older adults have higher mortality rates and worse functional recovery than younger adults (e.g., Weimar *et al.*, 2002). Studies following traumatic brain injury have produced evidence that although the areas of activation are similar in persons with TBI when compared to controls, the former show more diffuse activation during working memory tasks. Christodoulou *et al.* (2001) suggested that this might indicate a recruitment of additional cerebral areas to help perform tasks that stress working memory.

Harnessing plasticity to restore function after neurological injury in older adults

CI therapy as a model

Few rehabilitation treatments for chronic CNS disease have actually been shown in a controlled manner to benefit real-world behaviors. The approach with the most evidence of efficacy is Constraint-Induced Movement therapy (CI therapy) for rehabilitating use of the more-impaired arm in stroke survivors (Ottawa Panel, Khadilkar, Phillips *et al.*, 2006). The treatment, which is provided over ten or fifteen consecutive weekdays, involves the following: (1) intensive task practice with the more-impaired arm; (2) restraint of the less-impaired arm for 90 percent of waking hours; and (3) a "transfer package" of behavioral techniques to induce and reinforce adherence to the prescription to increase use of the more-impaired arm in the home environment (Taub *et al.*, 1993; Taub *et al.*, 2006). In two separate single-site controlled trials, CI therapy, compared to two types of placebo interventions, produced prolonged improvement in use of the more-impaired arm in daily life in older adults more than one year after stroke (Taub *et al.*, 1993; Taub *et al.*, 2006; see

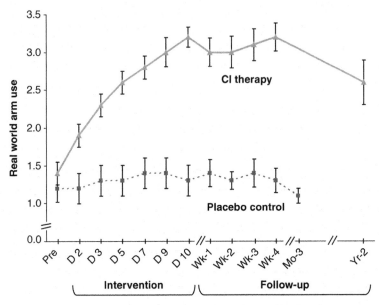

Figure 4.1. Changes in real-world use of the arm on the side of the body more affected by stroke after CI therapy and a placebo control procedure. CI therapy patients showed very large improvements in use of the more-impaired arm in daily life immediately after treatment, while participants in the control procedure showed little change, F (1, 39) = 122, p < 0.0001, d = 1.6. (A d value of 0.8 is considered a large difference between groups in the meta-analysis literature). Two years afterwards, CI therapy patients showed only a 23 percent decrease in arm use. Real-world use of the more-impaired was measured with a structured interview named the Motor Activity Log (Taub *et al.*, 1993; Uswatte *et al.*, 2005); this instrument has been validated against an objective measure of more-impaired arm movement outside the treatment setting (Uswatte *et al.*, 2005a, 2005b, 2006). From "A Placebo Controlled Trial of Constraint-Induced Movement Therapy for Upper Extremity after Stroke" by E. Taub, G. Uswatte, D. K. King, D. M. Morris, J. E. Crago, and A. Chatterjee, 2006, *Stroke*, *37*, 1048.

Figure 4.1). In addition, CI therapy has been shown to be superior to customary care in a large, blinded, randomized, multi-site clinical trial of CI therapy for mild to moderate weakness of the more-impaired arm in individuals from three to nine months after stroke (Wolf *et al.*, 2006). Participants in the CI therapy group (*n* = 106) showed significantly larger gains in real-world use of the more-impaired arm up to one year after treatment than did participants who were permitted access to any care available on a clinical basis ($n = 116$). CI therapy group participants also showed significant improvements in quality of life up to two years after treatment.

Several aspects of the clinical gains following CI therapy deserve attention from students of aging and resiliency. First, the gains in real-world use of the more-impaired arm are very large. For example, effect sizes range from 1.6 to 2 for everyday use of the more-impaired arm produced by CI therapy in the two placebo-controlled studies mentioned above. In the meta-analysis literature, values of 0.8 are considered large for this type of effect size index, that is, d (Cohen, 1983). Some anecdotes from CI therapy patients whose outcomes ranged from average to exceptional help to flesh out what the improvements in more-impaired arm function mean for stroke survivors. A dentist returned to practicing his profession. A pilot returned to flying, and met his true love in between flights. A mother regained sufficient dexterity and confidence in using her more-impaired arm that she started picking up her child again. Second, treatment gains are independent of time since injury. Third, treatment gains are independent of age at time of treatment (Taub, Uswatte, and Pidikiti, 1999; Taub *et al.*, 2006a). Patients in our laboratory who are more than 20 years post-stroke and 80 years old have had gains equal to or better than the average outcome.

CI therapy, as noted, was derived by Taub and co-workers from basic research using a deafferented monkey model (reviewed in Taub, 1977, 1980). When a single forelimb is deafferented in a monkey by surgically severing the sensory nerves that innervate that limb as they enter the spinal cord, the animal does not use the forelimb in the free situation (Knapp, Taub, and Berman, 1963; Mott and Sherrington, 1895). Several converging lines of evidence suggest that nonuse of a single deafferented limb is a learning phenomenon involving a conditioned suppression of movement; the phenomenon is termed "learned nonuse." (For a description of the experimental analysis leading to this conclusion, see Taub, 1977, 1980.) As a background for this explanation, one should note that substantial neurological injury usually leads to a depression in motor and/or perceptual function. Recovery processes then come into operation so that after a period of time movements can once again, at least potentially, be expressed. In monkeys the initial period of depressed function lasts from two to six months following forelimb deafferentation (Taub, 1977; Taub and Berman, 1968). Thus, immediately after operation, the monkeys cannot use a deafferented limb; recovery from the initial depression of function requires considerable time. An animal with one deafferented limb tries to use that extremity in the immediate postoperative situation but it cannot. It gets along quite well in the laboratory environment on three limbs and is therefore positively reinforced for this pattern of behavior, which, as a result, is strengthened. Moreover, continued attempts to use the impaired limb often lead to painful and otherwise aversive consequences, such as incoordination and falling, as well as to loss of food objects, and, in general, failure of any activity attempted with the deafferented limb. These aversive consequences condition the animal to avoid using that limb. (Many learning experiments have demonstrated that punishment results in the suppression of behavior; Azrin and Holz, 1966; Catania, 1998; Estes, 1944.) This response tendency persists, and consequently the monkey does not learn that several months after operation the limb has become potentially useful. In addition, following stroke (Liepert *et al.*, 2000) and presumably after extremity deafferentation, there is a marked contraction in the size of the cortical representation of the affected limb; this phenomenon is probably related to the reports of persons with stroke that movement of that extremity is effortful. These three processes (i.e., punishment of use of the deafferented limb, reinforcement of use of the intact limb only, and plastic brain reorganization; see Figure 4.2) interact to produce a vicious spiral downward that results in a learned nonuse of the affected extremity that is normally permanent (Taub *et al.*, 2002).

Learned nonuse of a deafferented limb can be overcome by intensive training of that extremity, particularly by shaping. (Shaping is an operant conditioning technique that involves progressively raising the bar for reward in small increments and providing frequent positive feedback; Catania, 1998; Skinner, 1968.) Continuous restraint of the intact limb over a period of a week or more is also effective. Both procedures have the effect of changing the contingencies of reinforcement for the use of the affected extremity. For example, when the movements of the intact limb are restricted several months after unilateral deafferentation, the animal either uses the deafferented limb or it cannot with any degree of efficiency feed itself, walk, or carry out a large portion of its normal activities of daily life. This dramatic change in motivation overcomes the learned nonuse of the deafferented limb. If the movement-restriction device is left on for several days or longer, use of the affected limb acquires strength and is then able to compete successfully with the very well-learned habit of learned nonuse of that limb in the free situation. The conditioned response and shaping techniques, just like the restriction of the intact limb, also involve major alterations in the contingencies of reinforcement; the animal must use its compromised limb or forego food or other reinforcers. Increased use of the more-impaired limb after CI therapy in stroke, and presumably also after forced use and shaping in deafferented monkeys, stimulates an expansion in the cortical representation of the

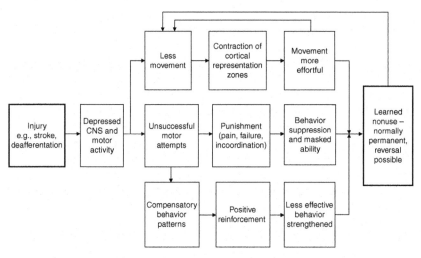

Figure 4.2. Model of the development of learned nonuse. CNS = central nervous system. From "Implications of the Learned Nonuse Formulation for Measuring Rehabilitation Outcomes: Lessons from Constraint-Induced Movement Therapy" by G. Uswatte and E. Taub, 2005, *Rehabilitation Psychology, 50,* 36. Reprinted with permission.

more-impaired limb (Liepert *et al.*, 2000) and other changes in the brain (see next section). One might speculate that such CNS changes support movement that is less effortful and more skillful, in turn encouraging even greater use of the deafferented limb and setting up a "virtuous" cycle.

CNS changes in stroke survivors after CI therapy

As noted, Liepert and co-workers showed a doubling in the cortical region from which electromyography responses of a muscle in the more-impaired hand can be elicited by transcranial magnetic stimulation (TMS) after CI therapy (Liepert *et al.*, 1998, 2000). A review of twenty studies on CI therapy effects on cerebral physiology revealed substantial evidence for brain reorganization based on a wide range of investigational modalities, including TMS, dipole source localization associated with magneto-encephalography (MEG) and electroencephalography (EEG), functional MRI (fMRI), positron emission tomography (PET), and near-infrared spectroscopy (summarized in Mark, Taub, and Morris, 2006). However, findings overall were inconsistent with respect to the location of the changes in regional brain activation. Lack of control over therapy administration, evaluation methods, and participant recruitment are likely to account for these inconsistencies.

Structural MRI is free from some of the methodological challenges faced by fMRI and other functional neurophysiological measures, such as whether the behavior used to elicit brain activation during imaging changes from one testing occasion to another and how to interpret changes in activation. A computational analytic method termed voxel-based morphometry (VBM) was applied to structural MRI scans obtained before and after CI therapy from 16 chronic stroke survivors, and showed widespread increases in gray matter in sensorimotor cortices both contralateral and ipsilateral to the more-impaired arm, as well as in the hippocampi bilaterally (Gauthier *et al.*, 2008). The aforementioned sensorimotor clusters were bilaterally symmetrical and encompassed the hand/arm regions of primary sensory and motor cortices as well as portions of Brodmann's area 6 and the anterior supplementary motor area. Scans from 20 stroke survivors who received a comparison therapy did not show such changes (see Figure 4.3). Moreover, the gray matter changes, across all participants, were correlated with changes in use of the hemiparetic arm in daily life (r's > 0.45, p's < 0.05).

The demonstration of these neuroanatomical changes supports a true remodeling of the brain after CI therapy. Furthermore, the size and location of stroke infarcts prior to treatment did not influence degree of recovery after CI therapy, suggesting that the neuroplastic processes harnessed by CI therapy can to some degree override the severity of the CNS injuries inflicted by stroke (Gauthier *et al.*, 2009; Mark *et al.*, 2008). The specific neuroplastic processes that are responsible for the increases in gray matter have yet to be identified. Three possibilities are as follows: (a) formation of new blood vessels; (b) growth of new connections, for example, axonal sprouting; and (c) growth of new neurons or supporting cells, such as glia (Taub *et al.*, 2002).

Other therapeutic applications of CI therapy approach

A powerful aspect of the learned nonuse formulation is its generality. Learned nonuse was conceptualized as occurring whenever (a) an injury results in an initially reduced ability to use a function so that an animal is punished for attempts to use that function by failure and rewarded for use of other functions and (b) there is slow recovery from the injury so that the animal recovers the physical ability to use that function, but the conditioned suppression of use that developed in the acute phase remains in force. Therefore, even though the type of nervous system injury in the deafferented monkey model was different from that in stroke (i.e.,

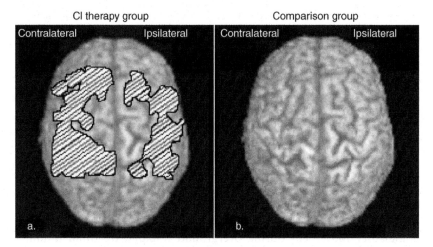

Figure 4.3. Cortical surface-rendered images of gray matter change. Gray matter increases displayed on a standard brain for (a) participants who received CI therapy and (b) those who did not. Surface rendering was performed with a depth of 20 mm. Color bar values indicate t statistics ranging from 2.2 to 6.7. From "Remodeling the Brain: Plastic Structural Brain Changes Produced by Different Motor Therapies after Stroke" by L. V. Gauthier, E. Taub, C. Perkins, M. Ortmann, V. W. Mark, and G. Uswatte, 2008, *Stroke, 39,* 1523.

peripheral vs. central, sensory vs. sensory and motor), it was plausible to hypothesize that the techniques employed to overcome nonuse of deafferented forelimb in monkeys (i.e., restraint of the unimpaired limb and shaping of the impaired limb) would also be effective for rehabilitating hemiparetic arm use in human stroke survivors (Taub, 1980). After stroke, many survivors experience a marked reduction in motor ability of the hemiparetic arm followed by a gradual recovery. Furthermore, a large number of activities can be accomplished using the less-impaired arm alone, and many survivors are encouraged to do so in traditional therapy soon after their stroke.

Other disorders that meet conditions (a) and (b) that have been shown to be amenable to CI therapy include weakness of the more-impaired arm after traumatic brain injury and cerebral palsy, aphasia after stroke, and maladaptive patterns of ambulation after stroke and spinal cord injury (Taub and Uswatte, 2003). The interventions for upper-extremity impairment after traumatic brain injury (Shaw *et al.*, 2005) and cerebral palsy (Taub *et al.*, 2004) are modeled closely on the protocol for upper-extremity hemiparesis after stroke. CI therapy for aphasia "constrains" patients to speak by (a) reinforcing patients for making progressively more articulate responses during a therapeutic language game (i.e., shaping verbal output) that is "played" for 3–4 hours per day for ten consecutive weekdays; (b) withdrawing reinforcement of any nonverbal forms of expression during training; and (c) monitoring and reinforcing speech outside of the training setting (Pulvermüller *et al.*, 2001). Since stroke survivors who recover the capacity to walk at least a short distance must use both of their legs to do so, the primary target of intervention for these individuals is not learned nonuse but "learned misuse," that is, persisting use of maladaptive patterns of ambulation adopted during the acute phase when motor recovery was poor even in later phases of injury after substantial additional motor recovery has taken place (Taub *et al.*, 1999). CI therapy for lower extremity motor impairment constrains patients to ambulate using more adaptive movement patterns by (a) shaping ambulatory movement during overground walking, treadmill training, transfers, and other balance exercises for 6 hours per day for fifteen consecutive weekdays, depending on the severity of the deficit; (b) withdrawing reinforcement of maladaptive patterns of ambulation whenever possible during training; and (c) monitoring and reinforcing the amount and quality of ambulatory activity outside the training setting. Unlike CI therapy for the upper extremity, treatment does not include physically restraining movement of the less-affected lower extremity (Taub *et al.*, 1999). Principles from CI therapy also have been used to derive a treatment for the lack of coordination of the digits in focal hand dystonia associated with maladaptive changes in the cortical representation of those body parts (Candia *et al.*, 2003, 2005; Elbert *et al.*, 1998).

Learned nonuse and frailty in the aged

Two parallels between the development of (a) motor disability and physical inactivity in frail elders and (b) excess motor disability in deafferented monkeys and humans after stroke suggest that learned nonuse might account for a substantial portion of disability in frail individuals. First, the development of frailty is often precipitated by an acute injury or disease from which there is a slow recovery, such as a fractured hip or bout of pneumonia, or an acute episode of a chronic disease, such as a chronic pulmonary disorder. During this period of gradual, spontaneous recovery, individuals are often physically incapable of performing functions that they accomplished successfully prior to injury and that they would be capable of after spontaneous recovery is complete. This situation is very similar to the period of depressed motor function following deafferentation or stroke during which attempts at accomplishing motor activities fail or are extremely effortful, thereby conditioning individuals to avoid these activities and converting a transient decline in physical ability into a permanent reduction in motor activity (see 'CI Therapy as a Model' section, above). Second, an interaction between physiological changes and learned avoidance of movement could produce a vicious spiral down to inactivity. In Rantanen's influential model of frailty (Rantanen et al., 1999), diminished physical activity reduces muscle strength, and in turn diminished muscle strength contributes to motor disability, which in turn reduces physical activity further, and so on. This downward spiral is parallel to that after deafferentation or stroke in which input-decrease cortical reorganization appears to contribute to the learned suppression of motor activity. In addition, it is possible that input-decrease cortical reorganization contributes to the development and maintenance of frailty in the elderly. The reduced amount of ambulation in frail elders might induce contraction of the cortical representation of the lower extremities, which might make ambulation more effortful, which in turn might further reduce the amount of ambulation. If learned nonuse and input-decrease cortical reorganization actually are central factors in the development of frailty, it is possible that CI therapy, which has been shown to be an effective treatment for excess motor disability secondary to other disorders in which these factors operate, would also be an effective treatment for excess motor disability associated with frailty.

Independently of research on learned nonuse, other psychologists have demonstrated that behavioral factors play an important role in the maintenance of frailty. Baltes and co-workers showed in a classic series of studies that dependent behaviors of nursing home residents are regularly reinforced by staff, while independent behaviors are rarely reinforced, with the result that many nursing home residents do not make full use of the physical abilities that they possess (Baltes, Neumann, and Zank, 1994; Baltes et al., 1983). Burgio et al. (1986), using a multiple baseline design and a praise and prompt methodology, demonstrated that verbal reinforcement of ambulation can be used to increase walking distance and independence in elderly nursing home residents. Six out of eight residents showed marked increases in distance walked in the nursing home dining room after they were prompted to walk to the dining table rather than use a wheelchair and were praised for walking. Although the improvement in ambulation did not appear to generalize to other areas of the patients' activity in the nursing home, this study demonstrated an important principle, that is, that even marked physical inactivity can be due to environmental contingencies rather than physical impairment. Their dramatic results replicated and extended previous work on increasing mobility by manipulating environmental contingencies (MacDonald and Butler, 1974; Sachs, 1975; Sperbeck and Whitbourne, 1981).

Harnessing neuroplasticity to help normally aging adults to flourish

Starting in early adulthood, cognitive function declines progressively across multiple domains with age (Salthouse, 2004). Although at one time it was thought this decline was driven by the loss of large numbers of neurons with advancing age, newer research suggests that the structural changes that accompany normal aging are more subtle, involving region-specific changes in dendritic morphology, synapse density, calcium conductance, and gene expression that disrupt the operation of neural networks (reviewed in Burke and Barnes, 2006).

Merzenich and colleagues hypothesize that the steady and progressive declines in both function and neurophysiology with age are not inevitable but rather the fruit of a pernicious type of neuroplasticity (Mahncke *et al.*, 2006). As people age, they commonly develop expertise in a few domains, relying increasingly on this crystallized expertise at the expense of learning new skills. Typically, they also reduce their overall level of engagement in cognitively stimulating activity. This disuse diminishes the neural networks that support learning. At the same time, processing of sensory inputs by the CNS becomes noisy because of degraded inputs from aging sense organs, resulting in slower processing and less effective responding to sensory stimuli. Neuromodulatory systems that support memory, learning, attention, arousal, and reward prediction also degrade with age. In response, people often adopt maladaptive behaviors that amplify these age-related changes. For example, a grandparent who develops trouble hearing their grandchildren over the phone because of the loss of hair cells in the cochlea with age may speak to the children for shorter periods. Thus, these age-related processes interact viciously to generate a powerful downward spiral.

Merzenich and colleagues contend this pernicious cycle can be reversed by intensive training in processing sensory input and paying attention, exercising the brain's reward system, increasing levels of cognitive activity, and learning progressively more challenging cognitive tasks (Mahncke *et al.*, 2006). Although more research is needed to strongly support this claim, a few rigorous studies to date have shown that cognitive training programs consistent with this approach can reverse or slow the rate of cognitive decline for brief (Mahncke *et al.*, 2006; Zelinski *et al.*, 2007) and extended periods (Willis *et al.*, 2006). An alternate approach

to improving cognitive function with strong evidence of efficacy is providing aerobic fitness training (reviewed in Colcombe and Kramer, 2003).
Among the mechanisms thought to be responsible for the positive association between exercise and cognitive function is the salutatory effect of
exercise on neurogenesis in the hippocampus discussed previously (van
Praag *et al.*, 2000).

Discussion

The revolution in the understanding of neuroplasticity in the adult CNS
that has taken place over the last 25 years provides a neurophysiological
basis for resiliency after CNS damage, in older adults even many years
after injury. Equally important, this research provides guidelines for how
clinical researchers and practitioners can therapeutically harness neuroplastic processes to help older adults overcome declines in physical and
cognitive function subsequent to CNS damage. In particular, research
on CI therapy suggests four general principles. They are as follows: (a)
providing extended and concentrated practice in using the function by
scheduling intensive training; (b) increasing use of the impaired function
in the treatment and home setting by providing reinforcement for its use,
forcing its use by preventing the use of compensatory functions, or both;
(c) emphasizing training on tasks rather than small components of the
task such as individual movements; and (d) implementing methods for
transferring gains made in the treatment setting to daily life (Uswatte *et
al.*, 2010).

The last principle, embodied in the "transfer package" component
of CI therapy, is of particular relevance to helping older adults recover
after suffering CNS damage, because retraining is of little worth if the
skills gained do not persist or transfer to everyday living. This package
has seven elements that are commonly employed components of behavioral psychology treatments but are largely foreign to physical rehabilitation: (a) daily structured interview conducted by the therapist with the
patient on how much she has used the impaired function outside of the
treatment setting over the last day; (b) daily diary kept by the patient on
use of the impaired function outside of the treatment setting; (c) problem-
solving conducted by the therapist with the patient about perceived bar-
riers to use of the impaired function; (d) behavioral contract negotiated
by the therapist with the patient and family caregivers specifying when,
where, and how the patient will attempt to use the impaired function
outside of treatment; (e) home practice of individually tailored exercises;
(f) physical restraint of body parts that can be employed to substitute for
the impaired function outside of the treatment setting (for treatment of

motor deficits only); and (g) weekly telephone calls for the first month after treatment during which elements (a) and (c) are repeated (Taub *et al.*, 2006b).

In a 2 × 2 factorial experiment, our laboratory tested the relative contributions of (a) training by shaping and (b) the transfer package to CI therapy outcome in participants with mild to moderate motor impairment of their arm more affected by stroke. While stroke survivors in all groups had similar gains in more-impaired arm motor capacity, those in the two groups that got the transfer package had substantially larger gains in use of their more-impaired arm in daily life than subjects in the two groups that did not. Subjects in the two transfer package groups were also the only ones to show significant increases in gray matter (see above section on 'CNS Changes in Stroke Survivors after CI Therapy').

We speculate that the transfer package is important for producing both CNS changes and gains in everyday arm use because it draws the attention of patients to use of their more-impaired arm, permits therapists to systematically reinforce patients for use of their more-impaired arm outside of the treatment setting, and makes patients accountable for their own improvement. We hypothesize that the transfer package is of general importance for rehabilitation after CNS injury, that is, that transfer package techniques might be combined with other forms of physical rehabilitation than CI therapy to more powerfully harness neuroplastic processes and thereby enhance their real-world effects. The same may be the case for preserving or restoring function in the elderly at risk for frailty. Among questions for future research are testing the relative contributions of the mechanisms listed above and identifying the active ingredients in the now multifaceted transfer package.

Conclusions

Although the capacity for change in patterns of neural activity and brain tissues is less than in young adults, the brains of older adults retain substantial neuroplasticity. Furthermore, this capacity for change in CNS function and structure to adapt to environmental demands can be harnessed therapeutically for enhancing recovery after CNS damage. Thus, advances in neuroscience and their translation into rehabilitation treatments over the last 25 years give the lie to the popular adage "You can't teach an old dog new tricks."

Acknowledgments

Portions of this chapter are adapted from "CNS Plasticity and Rehabilitation" by G. Uswatte *et al.*, 2010. In R. G. Frank, B. Caplan, and M. Rosenthal, *Handbook of Rehabilitation Psychology* (2nd edn), Washington, DC: American Psychological Association. Copyright 2009 by the American Psychological Association. Adapted with permission.

Work on this chapter was supported by National Institutes of Health Grants HD34273 and HD53750, and National Institute of Disability and Rehabilitation Research Grant H133G050222.

REFERENCES

Altman, J., and Das, G. D. (1965). Autoradiographic and histological evidence of postnatal hippocampal neurogenesis in rats. *Journal of Comparative Neurology*, 124, 319–335.

Azrin, N. H., and Holz, W. C. (1966). Punishment. In W. K. Honig (ed.), *Operant behavior: Areas of research and application* (pp. 380–447). New York: Appleton-Century-Crofts.

Badan, I., Dinca, I., Buchhold, B. *et al.* (2004). Accelerated accumulation of N- and C-terminal beta APP fragments and delayed recovery of microtubule-associated protein 1B expression following stroke in aged rats. *European Journal of Neuroscience*, 19, 2270–2280.

Baltes, M. M., Honn, S., Barton, E. M., Orzech, M., and Lago, D. (1983). On the social ecology of dependence and independence in elderly nursing home residents: A replication and extension. *Journal of Gerontology*, 38, 556–564.

Baltes, M. M., Neumann, E., and Zank, S. (1994). Maintenance and rehabilitation of independence in old age: An intervention program for staff. *Psychology and Aging*, 9, 179–188.

Bogdan Petcu, E., Sfredel, V., Platt, D., Herndon, J. G., Kessler, C., and Popa-Wagner, A. (2008). Cellular and molecular events underlying the dysregulated response of the aged brain to stroke: a mini-review. *Gerontology*, 54, 6–17.

Brant-Zawadzki, M., Atkinson, D., Detrick, M., Bradley, W. G., and Scidmore, G. (1996). Fluid-attenuated inversion recovery (FLAIR) for assessment of cerebral infarction. Initial clinical experience in 50 patients. *Stroke*, 27, 1187–1191.

Brown, T., and Sherrington, C. (1912). On the instability of a cortical point. *Proceedings of the Royal Society of London B*, 85, 585–602.

Burgio, L. D., Burgio, K. L., Engel, B. T., and Tice, L. M. (1986). Increasing distance and independence of ambulation in elderly nursing home residents. *Journal of Applied Behavior Analysis*, 19, 357–366.

Burke, S. N., and Barnes, C. A. (2006). Neural plasticity in the ageing brain. *Nature Reviews Neuroscience*, 7, 30–40.

Calautti, C., Leroy, F., Guincestre, J. Y., and Baron, J. C. (2001). Dynamics of motor network overactivation after striatocapsular stroke: A longitudinal PET study using a fixed-performance paradigm. *Stroke*, 32(11), 2534–2542.

Cameron, H. A., Woolley, C. S., McEwen, B. S., and Gould, E. (1993). Differentiation of newly born neurons and glia in the dentate gyrus of the adult rat. *Neuroscience*, 56, 337–344.

Candia, V., Rosset-Llobet, J., Elbert, T., and Pascual-Leone, A. (2005). Changing the brain through therapy for musicians' hand dystonia. *Annals of the New York Academy of Sciences*, 1060, 335–342.

Candia, V., Wienbruch C., Elbert, T. *et al.* (2003). Effective behavioral treatment of focal hand dystonia in musicians alters somatosensory cortical organization. *Proceedings of the National Academy of Sciences of the United States*, 100, 7942–7946.

Catania, A. C. (1998). *Learning*, 4th edn. Upper Saddle River, NJ: Prentice Hall.

Christodoulou, C., DeLuca, J., Ricker, J. H. *et al.* (2001). Functional magnetic resonance imaging of working memory impairment after traumatic brain injury. *Journal of Neurology, Neurosurgery and Psychiatry*, 71(2), 161–168.

Cohen, J. (1983). *Statistical power analysis for the behavioral sciences*, 2nd edn. Hillsdale, NJ: Erlbaum.

Colcombe, S., and Kramer, A. F. (2003). Fitness effects on the cognitive function of older adults; A meta-analytic study. *Psychological Science: a journal of the American Psychological Society*, 14, 125–130.

Corotto, F. S., Henegar, J. R., and Maruniak, J. A. (1994). Odor deprivation leads to reduced neurogenesis and reduced neuronal survival in the olfactory bulb of the adult mouse. *Neuroscience*, 61, 739–744.

Cramer, S. C., Nelles, G., Schaechter, J. D., Kaplan, J. D., Finklestein, S. P., and Rosen, B. R. (2001). A functional MRI study of three motor tasks in the evaluation of stroke recovery. *Neurorehabilitation and Neural Repair*, 15(1), 1–8.

Curtis, M. A., Kam, M., Nannmark, U. *et al.* (2007). Human neuroblasts migrate to the olfactory bulb via a lateral ventricular extension. *Science*, 315(5816), 1243–1249.

Darsalia, V., Heldmann, U., Lindvall, O., and Kokaia, Z. (2005). Stroke-induced neurogenesis in the aged rodent brain. *Stroke*, 36, 1790–1795.

Draganski, B., Gaser, C., Busch, V., Schuierer, G., Bogdahn, U., and May, A. (2004). Changes in grey matter induced by training. *Nature*, 427(6972), 311–312.

Draganski, B., Moser, T., Lummel, N. *et al.* (2006). Decrease of thalamic gray matter following limb amputation. *Neuroimage*, 31, 951–957.

Edgerton, V. R., Leon, R. D., Harkema, S. J. *et al.* (2001). Retraining the injured spinal cord. *The Journal of Physiology*, 533, 15–22.

Elbert, T., Candia, V., Altenmuller, E. *et al.* (1998). Alteration of digital representations in somatosensory cortex in focal hand dystonia. *Neuroreport*, 9(16), 3571–3575.

Elbert, T., Flor, H., Birbaumer, N. *et al.* (1994). Extensive reorganization of the somatosensory cortex in adult humans after nervous system injury. *Neuroreport*, 5(18), 2593–2597.

Elbert, T., Pantev, C., Wienbruch, C., Rockstroh, B., and Taub, E. (1995). Increased cortical representation of the fingers of the left hand in string players. *Science*, 270(5234), 305–307.

Elbert, T., Sterr, A., Rockstroh, B., Pantev, C., Muller, M. M., and Taub, E. (2002). Expansion of the tonotopic area in the auditory cortex of the blind. *The Journal of Neuroscience*, 22(22), 9941–9944.

Eriksson, P. S., Perfilieva, E., Bjork-Eriksson, T. *et al.* (1998). Neurogenesis in the adult human hippocampus. *Nature Medicine,* 4, 1313–1317.

Estes, W. K. (1944). An experimental study of punishment. *Psychological Monographs,* 57 (Serial No. 263).

Flourens, P. (1842). *Recherches expérimentales sur les propriétés et les fonctions du système nerveux, dans les animaux vertébrés [Experiments on the properties and functions of the nervous system of vertebrate animals],* 2nd edn. Paris: Bellière.

Fritsch, G., and Hitzig, E. (1870). Über die elektrische Erregbarkeit des Grosshirns [On the electrical excitability of the cerebral cortex]. *Archiv fuer Anatomie und Physiologie,* 37, 300–332.

Gauthier, L. V., Taub, E., Mark, V. W., Perkins, C., and Uswatte, G. (2009). Improvement after Constraint-Induced Movement therapy is independent of infarct location in chronic stroke patients. *Stroke,* 40, 2468–2472.

Gauthier, L. V., Taub, E., Perkins, C., Ortmann, M., Mark, V. W., and Uswatte, G. (2008). Remodeling the brain: Plastic structural brain changes produced by different motor therapies after stroke. *Stroke,* 39, 1520–1525.

Gellhorn, E., and Hyde, J. (1953). Influence of proprioception on map of cortical responses. *Journal of Physiology,* 122, 371–385.

Gould, E. (2007). How widespread is adult neurogenesis in mammals? *Nature Reviews Neuroscience,* 8, 481–488.

Gould, E., Cameron, H. A., Daniels, D. C., Woolley, C. S., and McEwen, B. S. (1992). Adrenal hormones suppress cell division in the adult rat dentate gyrus. *Journal of Neuroscience,* 12, 3642–3650.

Hubel, D. H., and Wiesel, T. N. J. (1970). The period of susceptibility to the physiological effects of unilateral eye closure in kittens. *Journal of Physiology,* 206, 419–436.

Jenkins, W. M., Merzenich, M. M., Ochs, M. T., Allard, T., and Guic-Robles, E. (1990). Functional reorganization of primary somatosensory cortex in adult owl monkeys after behaviorally controlled tactile stimulation. *Journal of Neurophysiology,* 63(1), 82–104.

Kaas, J. H. (1995). Neurobiology. How cortex reorganizes [news; comment]. *Nature,* 375(6534), 735–736.

Kaas, J. H., Merzenich, M. M., and Killackey, H. P. (1983). The reorganization of somatosensory cortex following peripheral nerve damage in adult and developing mammals. *Annual Review of Neuroscience,* 6, 325–356.

Knapp, H. D., Taub, E., and Berman, A. J. (1963). Movements in monkeys with deafferented forelimbs. *Experimental Neurology,* 7, 305–315.

Lashley, K. S. (1938). Factors limiting recovery after central nervous lesions. *Journal of Nervous and Mental Diseases,* 88, 733–755.

Liepert, J., Bauder, H., Wolfgang, H. R., Miltner, W. H., Taub, E., and Weiller, C. (2000). Treatment-induced cortical reorganization after stroke in humans. *Stroke,* 31, 1210–1216.

Liepert, J., Miltner, W. H., Bauder, H. *et al.* (1998). Motor cortex plasticity during Constraint-Induced Movement therapy in stroke patients. *Neuroscience Letters,* 250(1), 5–8.

Liepert, J., Tegenthoff, M., and Malin, J. P. (1995). Changes of cortical motor area size during immobilization. *Electroencephalograhy and Clinical Neurophysiology*, 97(6), 382–386.

Lois, C., and Alvarez-Buylla, A. (1994). Long-distance neuronal migration in the adult mammalian brain. *Science*, 264(5162), 1145–1148.

MacDonald, M. L., and Butler, A. K. (1974). Reversal of helplessness: Producing walking behavior in nursing home wheelchair residents using behavior modification procedures. *Journal of Gerontology*, 29, 97–101.

Maguire, E. A., Gadian, D. G., Johnsrude, I. S. *et al.* (2000). Navigation-related structural change in the hippocampi of taxi drivers. *Proceedings of the National Academy of Sciences USA*, 97, 4398–4403.

Mahncke, H. W., Connor, B. B., Appelman, J. *et al.* (2006). Memory enhancement in healthy older adults using a brain plasticity-based training program: A randomized, controlled study. *Proceedings of the National Academy of Sciences of the United States of America*, 103, 12523–12528.

Mark, V., Taub, E., and Morris, D. M. (2006). Neuroplasticity and Constraint-Induced Movement Therapy. *Europa Medicophysica*, 42(2), 269–284.

Mark, V. W., Taub, E., Perkins, C., Gauthier, L. V., and Uswatte, G. (2008). MRI infarction load and CI therapy outcomes for chronic post-stroke hemiparesis. *Restorative Neurology and Neuroscience*, 26, 13–33.

Marshall, R. S., Perera, G. M., Lazar, R. M., Krakauer, J. W., Constantine, R. C., and DeLaPaz, R. L. (2000). Evolution of cortical activation during recovery from corticospinal tract infarction. *Stroke*, 31(3), 656–661.

Merzenich, M. M., Nelson, R. J., Stryker, M. P., Cynader, M. S., Schoppmann, A., and Zook, J. M. (1984). Somatosensory cortical map changes following digit amputation in adult monkeys. *Journal of Comparative Neurology*, 224(4), 591–605.

Mott, F. W., and Sherrington, C. S. (1895). Experiments upon the influence of sensory nerves upon movement and nutrition of the limbs. *Proceedings of the Royal Society of London*, 57, 481–488.

Munk, H. (1881). *Über die Funktionen der Grosshirnrinde. Gesammelte Mitteilungen aus den Jahren 1877–1880 [On the functions of the cerebral cortex, collected writing from the years 1877–1880].* Berlin: Hirschwald.

Nudo, R. J., and Milliken, G. W. (1996). Reorganization of movement representations in primary motor cortex following focal ischemic infarcts in adult squirrel monkeys. *Journal of Neurophysiology*, 75(5), 2144–2149.

Ottawa Panel, Khadilkar, A., Phillips, K., *et al.* (2006). Ottawa Panel evidence-based clinical practice guidelines for post-stroke rehabilitation. *Topics in Stroke Rehabilitation*, 2006, 1–269.

Pons, T. P., Garraghty, P. E., Ommaya, A. K., Kaas, J. H., Taub, E., and Mishkin, M. (1991). Massive cortical reorganization after sensory deafferentation in adult macaques. *Science*, 252(5014), 1857–1860.

Popa-Wagner, A., Schroder, E., Schmoll, H., Walker, L., and Kessler, C. (1999). Upregulation of MAP1B and MAP2 in the rat brain following middle cerebral artery occlusion: Effect of age. *Journal of Cerebral Blood Flow and Metabolism*, 19, 425–434.

Pulvermüller, F., Neininger, B., Elbert, T. *et al.* (2001). Constraint-induced therapy of chronic aphasia after stroke. *Stroke*, 32(7), 1621–1626.

Rakic, P. (1985). Limits of neurogenesis in primates. *Science*, 227(4690), 1054–1056.

Rantanen, T., Guralnik, J. M., Sakari-Rantala, R. . *et al.* (1999). Disability, physical activity, and muscle strength in older women: The Women's Health and Aging Study. *Archives of Physical Medicine and Rehabilitation*, 80, 130–135.

Ruch, T. C. (1960). The cerebral cortex: its structure and motor functions. In T. C. Ruch and J. F. Fulton (eds.), *Medical Physiology and Biophysics*, 18th edn. (pp. 249–276). Philadelphia, PA: W. B. Saunders.

Sachs, D. (1975). Behavioral techniques in a residential nursing home facility. *Journal of Behavior Therapy and Experimental Psychiatry*, 6, 123–127.

Salthouse, T. A. (2004). What and when of cognitive aging. *Current Directions in Psychological Science*, 13, 140–144.

Schaechter, J. D. (2004). Motor rehabilitation and brain plasticity after hemiparetic stroke. *Progress in Neurobiology*, 73(1), 61–72.

Scheff, S. W., Price, D. A., Hicks, R. R., Baldwin, S. A., Robinson, S., and Brackney, C. (2005). Synaptogenesis in the hippocampal CA1 field following traumatic brain injury. *Journal of Neurotrauma*, 22(7), 719–732.

Shaw, S. E., Morris, D. M., Uswatte, G., McKay, S., Meythaler, J. M., and Taub, E. (2005). Constraint-Induced Movement therapy for recovery of upper-limb function following traumatic brain injury. *Journal of Rehabilitation Research and Development*, 42, 769–778.

Skinner, B. F. (1968). *The technology of teaching.* New York: Appleton-Century-Crofts.

Sperbeck, D. J., and Whitbourne, S. K. (1981). Dependency in the institutional setting: a behavioral training program for geriatric staff. *The Gerontologist*, 21, 268–275.

Sterr, A., Muller, M. M., Elbert, T., Rockstroh, B., Pantev, C., and Taub, E. (1998). Changed perceptions in Braille readers. *Nature*, 391(6663), 134–135.

Taub, E. (1977). Movement in nonhuman primates deprived of somatosensory feedback. *Exercise and Sports Sciences Reviews*, 4, 335–374.

(1980). Somatosensory deafferentation research with monkeys: implications for rehabilitation medicine. In L. P. Ince (ed.), *Behavioral psychology in rehabilitation medicine: clinical applications* (pp. 371–401). New York: Williams & Wilkins.

Taub, E., and Berman, A. J. (1968). Movement and learning in the absence of sensory feedback. In S. J. Freedman (ed.), *The neuropsychology of spatially oriented behavior* (pp. 173–192). Homewood, IL: Dorsey Press.

Taub, E., Miller, N. E., Novack, T. A. *et al.* (1993). Technique to improve chronic motor deficit after stroke. *Archives of Physical Medicine and Rehabilitation*, 74(4), 347–354.

Taub, E., Ramey, S. L., DeLuca, S., and Echols, K. (2004). Efficacy of constraint-induced movement therapy for children with cerebral palsy with asymmetric motor impairment. *Pediatrics*, 113(2), 305–312.

Taub, E., and Uswatte, G. (2003). Constraint-Induced Movement therapy: Bridging from the primate laboratory to the stroke rehabilitation laboratory. *Journal of Rehabilitation Medicine*, Suppl. 41, 34–40.

Taub, E., Uswatte, G., and Elbert, T. (2002). New treatments in neurorehabilitation founded on basic research. *Nature Reviews Neuroscience*, 3(3), 228–236.

Taub, E., Uswatte, G., King, D. K., Morris, D., Crago, J., and Chatterjee, A. (2006a). A placebo controlled trial of Constraint-Induced Movement therapy for upper extremity after stroke. *Stroke*, 37, 1045–1049.

Taub, E., Uswatte, G., Mark, V. W., and Morris, D. M. (2006b). The learned nonuse phenomenon: Implications for rehabilitation. *Europa Medicophysica*, 42, 241–255.

Taub, E., Uswatte, G., and Pidikiti, R. (1999). Constraint-Induced Movement Therapy: a new family of techniques with broad application to physical rehabilitation – a clinical review. *Journal of Rehabilitation Research and Development*, 36, 237–251.

Tillakaratne, N. J. K., Mouria, M., Ziv, N. B., Roy, R. R., Edgerton, V. R., and Tobin, A. (2000). Increased expression of glutamate decarboxylase (GAD(67)) in feline lumbar spinal cord after complete thoracic spinal cord transection. *Journal of Neuroscience Research*, 60, 219–230.

Uswatte, G., Foo, W. L., Olmstead, H., Lopez, K., Holand, A., and Simms, M. L. (2005a). Ambulatory monitoring of arm movement using accelerometry: An objective measure of upper-extremity rehabilitation in persons with chronic stroke. *Archives of Physical Medicine and Rehabilitation*, 86, 1498–1501.

Uswatte, G. and Taub, E. (2005). Implications of the learned nonuse formulation for measuring rehabilitation outcomes: Lessons from Constraint-Induced Movement therapy. *Rehabilitation Psychology*, 50, 34–42.

Uswatte, G., Taub, E., Mark, V. W., Perkins, C., and Gauthier, L. V. (2010). CNS plasticity and rehabilitation. In R. G. Frank, B. Caplan and M. Rosenthal (eds.), *Handbook of rehabilitation psychology* (2nd edn., pp. 391–406). Washington, DC: American Psychological Association.

Uswatte, G., Taub, E., Morris, D., Light, K., and Thompson, P. (2006). The Motor Activity Log-28: A method for assessing daily use of the hemiparetic arm after stroke. *Neurology*, 67, 1189–1194.

Uswatte, G., Taub, E., Morris, D., Vignolo, M., and McCulloch, K. (2005b). Reliability and validity of the upper-extremity Motor Activity Log-14 for measuring real-world arm use. *Stroke*, 36, 2493–2496.

van Praag, H., Kempermann, G., and Gage, F. H. (2000). Neural consequences of environmental enrichment. *Nature Reviews Neuroscience*, 1, 191–198.

Wall, P. D., and Egger, M. D. (1971). Formation of new connections in adult rat brains following partial deafferentation. *Nature*, 232(5312), 542–545.

Weimar, C., Ziegler, A., Konig, I. R., and Diener, H.-C. (2002). Predicting functional outcome and survival after acute ischemic stroke. *Journal of Neurology*, 249, 888–895.

Weiss, T., Miltner, W., Liepert, J., Meissner, W., and Taub, E. (2004). Rapid functional plasticity in the primary somatomotor cortex and perceptual changes after nerve block. *European Journal of Neuroscience*, 20, 3413–3423.

Willis, S. L., Tennstedt, S. L., Marsiske, M. *et al.* (2006). Long-term effects of cognitive training on everyday functional outcomes in older adults. *The Journal of the American Medical Association*, 296, 2805–2814.

Wolf, S. L., Winstein, C., Miller, J. P. *et al.* (2006). Effect of Constraint Induced Movement therapy on upper extremity function among patients 3–9 months following stroke: the EXCITE randomized clinical trial. *The Journal of the American Medical Association*, 296(17), 2095–2104.

Zelinski, E. M., Yaffe, K., Ruff, R. M., Kennison, R. K., and Smith, G. E. (2007, November). The IMPACT study: A randomized controlled trial of a brain plasticity-based training program for age-related cognitive decline. *The Gerontological Society of America Meeting*. San Francisco, CA.

5 Resilience in the face of cognitive aging: experience, adaptation, and compensation

Christopher Hertzog and Daniela S. Jopp

Abstract

We articulate a lifespan developmental perspective on gains and losses in cognitive functioning during adulthood. This perspective argues that older adults function effectively in ways that preserve goal attainment in cognitively demanding situations despite age-related cognitive decline. Moreover, because individuals grow and age in self-selected contexts, they can successfully use expertise and knowledge, practiced routines of behavior, and reliance on sources of support in their environment to maximize their functional capacity. Metacognitive self-regulation and an active lifestyle can be important means for older adults to preserve cognitive capacity and to effectively compensate for declines in cognitive mechanisms as they occur.

Introduction

A chapter on cognitive resilience should probably start with a definition about it. Is it to think as fast as one did in younger years? Does it involve being as bright and sharp as possible, despite advancing age? Is it about recovering from strokes or other age-related insults to the brain? Is it manifested by showing no signs of decline in all or most cognitive abilities? Or is it about maintaining an active mind until old age? Does it concern keeping one's functional autonomy through preserving the ability to manage one's own affairs in everyday life? Proposing such a definition is not a trivial task, and it requires some insight into theoretical background and ongoing discussions. We begin by treating some core theoretical issues before coming back to propose a definition of cognitive resilience, framed within an important theoretical perspective on development and growth from lifespan developmental psychology. This definition will then be followed by a discussion of factors that we believe play a key role in promoting cognitive resilience in old age, including metacognitive self-regulation, beliefs about cognition and aging, lifestyles that foster cognitive enrichment, and optimal styles of resource utilization.

Theoretical background

The research literature on cognition and aging has traditionally empha-sized age-related decline in basic cognitive mechanisms, intelligence, memory, and related constructs (Birren, 1964; Park and Schwarz, 2000; Salthouse, 1991). Although this view has been challenged with respect to (a) its universality regarding both individuals and cognitive variables (Dixon, 2000; Hertzog, 2008), (b) its relevance to cognition as it func-tions in the natural ecology (Hertzog, 2002), and (c) its immutability (Kramer and Willis, 2002), it remains the dominant perspective in the field of cognitive aging.

Without question, the emphasis on cognitive decline with aging reflects a fundamental descriptive truth supported by a wealth of empirical evi-dence. Older individuals manifest a variety of age-related changes in cog-nitive function, such as slowed information-processing speed, reduced working memory capacity, degraded episodic memory performance, and lower-quality reasoning in new and unfamiliar problem domains (Hoyer and Verhaeghen, 2006; Kausler, 1994; Salthouse, 1991; Zacks, Hasher, and Li, 2000). These changes are regarded as pervasive and are seen by many theorists as beginning early in adulthood (e.g., Baltes, Staudinger, and Lindenberger, 1999; Salthouse, 1991). The attribution of such changes to a senescent neural substrate is also consistent with what is known about how primary biological aging can influence central nervous system structure and function (Cabeza, Nyberg, and Park, 2005; Park and Reuter-Lorenz, 2009; Raz, 2000).

The conceptualization of cognitive aging as a manifestation of declin-ing neurological status has major limitations, however. A fundamental problem with a scientific theory of aging and cognition focused exclu-sively on cognitive decline is its inability to explain why adults in mid-dle age and old age function effectively at work (Colonia-Willner, 1998; Kanfer and Ackerman, 2004; Ng and Feldman, 2008), successfully achieve life goals that are cognitively demanding (Freund and Baltes, 2002), and lead happy and well-adjusted lives (Ong et al., 2006). At best, the decline perspective is an incomplete theoretical account of the rich-ness of cognition as it develops in old age (Dixon, 2000). At worst it is a distortion influenced by scientists' societally shared negative stereotypes about aging that reinforce myths of incapacity, senility, and dysfunction.

In principle, an individual differences perspective (e.g., Hertzog, 2008) can bridge some of the apparent gap between the decline perspective and evidence of positive functioning in old age. Given individual differences in rates of cognitive aging, one can regard successful cognitive perform-ance in old age as a kind of survival of the fittest. Some individuals begin adulthood with better cognitive endowment and maintain high levels of cognitive function into very old age. Neuropsychologists capture this idea under the term 'cognitive reserve' (e.g., Stern, 2002) – people with more initial capacity forestall longer any manifestations of dementia or other brain deterioration. The proportion of persons whose cognitive capacity exceeds environmental demand declines with age, but individuals can remain in good standing, so to speak, for some time. Be that as it may, an allowance for individual differences still cannot explain adaptation, resilience, and successful functioning for many older adults that seems to be the norm, not an exception.

A functional lifespan perspective on cognition

How should we think about cognition in adulthood, then? What are the ways in which we can reconcile the effects of biological aging processes, on the one hand, with the positive aspects of cognitive functioning that enable survival, adaptation, psychological well-being, and successful goal pursuit by persons throughout the lifespan?

The lifespan approach adopted by Baltes (1987) and other developmental psychologists (e.g., Dixon and Hertzog, 1988, 1996; Hertzog, 2008; Hess, 2005; Lerner, 1984; Rybash, Hoyer, and Roodin, 1986; Schaie, 2005; Willis, 2001) offers an alternative perspective on cognition in old age that addresses the competence-performance paradox outlined above. It argues that the dominant mechanistic decline perspective on cognitive aging underestimates the resilience of older adults facing cognitive demands and related life challenges for several reasons: (a) a focus on mechanics while ignoring the pragmatics of cognition; (b) the lack of a functional perspective on cognition and its uses in everyday life; (c) an outmoded view of neurobiology and behavior that neglects the principles of plasticity and adaptation; and (d) the critical importance of context and environmental support.

The pragmatics of cognition

Central to the lifespan view is the idea that cognition as it is required in life is a process of adaptation that involves using knowledge, skills, and experience as the basis for recognizing environmental contingencies and achieving goals in familiar contexts. Moreover, individuals exist in stable and predictable environments and by habit and preference encounter and confront familiar problems and cognitive demands (Hertzog, 2008). For these reasons, knowledge and experience are often more important for successful cognition than the raw computing power of the brain.

Lifespan trajectories are more benign for world knowledge or crystallized intelligence, relative to fluid intelligence (e.g., Horn, 1989; Schaie, 2005), and knowledge accumulation continues throughout adulthood (e.g., Beier and Ackerman, 2005). Moreover, experience promotes both declarative knowledge about the world and procedural knowledge (doing, or acting so as to accomplish goals). The latter is rarely encompassed by the construct of crystallized intelligence. Baltes and colleagues (e.g., Baltes *et al.*, 1999) refer to the procedural and declarative aspects of thinking in the world as the *pragmatics* of cognition.

A distinction between pragmatics and mechanics is helpful in accounting for preserved functional competence, in part because of the relative preservation of pragmatics into old age (Ackerman, 2000). However, the distinction is not always clear-cut. Some basic cognitive mechanisms are well preserved, and accessing knowledge at appropriate times requires retrieval mechanisms that decline with aging (see Hertzog, 2008). Because cognition often involves the interplay between knowledge structures and processing systems, longitudinal studies have observed correlated losses in cognitive variables that would typically be seen as disparate from a mechanics/pragmatics distinction. For instance, world knowledge, a marker of crystallized intelligence, declines in old age, and individual differences in rates of its decline correlate highly with declines in working memory and episodic memory (Hertzog *et al.*, 2003; Hultsch *et al.*, 1998). Hence the pragmatics/mechanics distinction, while helpful in thinking about preserved cognitive function in midlife, also cannot be regarded as a sufficient explanation of why older adults typically function effectively in cognitively demanding situations. It must be combined with additional principles.

A functional perspective on cognition

A comprehensive theory of age-related changes in cognition must consider the functional impact of changes for effective function in everyday life (Dixon and Hertzog, 1988; Hertzog, 2002, 2008) – that is, how cognition evolved to meet environmental demands to ensure survival, how it is typically used and manifested in everyday life, and how its use is supported by contextual factors, including the social context in which most human cognition occurs. A functional perspective emphasizes the practical consequences of age-related changes in cognition. For instance, how much slowing in retrieval time can be tolerated without degrading performance in a given situation? What kinds of knowledge access are well preserved for a given individual, and why? Taking such a functional approach, an age-related decrease in perceptual speed may not hinder an individual to perform cognitively challenging daily tasks despite being slower.

Behavioral and neuronal plasticity

Plasticity, or the capability of organisms to change and adapt to shifting environmental contingencies, is another important principle incorporated into a lifespan perspective. Brains and behaviors are not fixed and unchanging, even though – from a psychological perspective – humans are creatures of habit and often show inertial resistance to change (Hertzog, 2008). Instead, individuals have options to improve their function by learning. They can gain new knowledge and skills, choose environments with different challenges and stimulation (Stine-Morrow, 2007), can behave in ways that optimize functioning, and can act to preserve and enhance physiological and psychological status through health- and mind-promoting behaviors (Wilson and Bennett, 2003). Certainly, there are constraints on learning, and the obstacles one encounters may become more formidable in old age, given normative age-related changes in cognitive mechanisms required for learning. Old humans do learn new tricks, they just do so more slowly and with greater invested effort (e.g., Hertzog, Cooper, and Fisk, 1996; Kausler, 1994).

Likewise, evidence is accumulating that there is considerable brain plasticity in adulthood and even old age (e.g., Kempermann, 2008; see Park and Reuter-Lorenz, 2009, for a review). The nervous system responds to use of functionally differentiated areas by increasing neuronal activity, synaptic connections, increasing blood flow, and growing new neurons in areas that support the cognitive function being exercised. More important, this plasticity continues into old age (Greenwood, 2007) and may have important consequences for rethinking the potential for optimizing cognitive function in later life (Hertzog *et al.*, 2009).

Environmental context and social support

A lifespan perspective on cognition emphasizes the importance of understanding cognition in its context. Cognition occurs in self-selected contexts and relies on practical intelligence and social expertise (Cianciolo *et al.*, 2006; Wagner and Sternberg, 1985). Cognition in everyday life is governed by flexible use of heuristics and strategies to achieve goals, in which one learns through experience and mentorship by skilled social partners what works and what does not work for achieving commonly held goals. Pragmatic knowledge is often knowledge about how to behave in social contexts. Development within such contexts typically involves integration of new knowledge and information into existing social knowledge structures.

Adults have a substantial degree of choice and control regarding the features of contexts in which they live, and they both modify and are influenced by those contexts. Major life decisions are rarely undertaken without consulting a spouse, family, friends, advisors, or relevant experts and professionals. Individuals of all ages, including older adults, develop and grow social networks of persons who can support and assist them, especially in times of stress or crisis. If an individual encounters major cognitive loss (e.g., onset of Alzheimer's disease [AD]), they can receive support and assistance from caregivers and informal support networks that mitigate some of the functional consequences of cognitive loss.

The SOC framework and lifespan cognitive development

A lifespan perspective on human development has generated theoretical frameworks that aim at a better understanding of age-related changes by specifying mechanisms underlying successful adaptation to change (Boerner and Jopp, 2007). In particular, Baltes and Baltes' (1990) Selection, Optimization, and Compensation (SOC) framework (see also Baltes, 1997; Riediger, Li, and Lindenberger, 2006) provides a context that can be used to conceptualize cognitive resilience.

Selection refers to a choice of domains, tasks, or goals. Because the world is complex, time is limited, and available resources are constrained, adults necessarily select domains in which they develop and pursue goals, gain experience, and create new knowledge. These domains co-occur with specific social contexts that provide the milieu for goal-directed action. Contexts differ widely in their demands (including cognitive demands), and individuals are also selected by social mechanisms and by personal choices into niches in which they can function effectively. There are two types of selection decisions. Elective selection occurs when individuals choose a specific goal based on his or her preference. Loss-based selection involves choices triggered by anticipated or perceived loss. For instance, deciding to engage no longer in intellectually challenging activities could be the result of avoiding the consequences of cognitive loss for performance.

The second mechanism specified by the SOC theory, optimization, refers to enhancing and refining the means available for goal pursuit. It can include picking the right moment, working on acquiring a skill, or training in order to become better. Optimization with respect to cognition includes exercising a certain capacity such as memory to enhance one's function-ing (e.g., when learning for an exam) or keeping current in one's area of expertise (e.g., when exploring the features of your newest camera).

The third mechanism proposed by the SOC theory is compensa-tion. Compensation comes into play when the means usually applied for achieving a desired goal are no longer available. With respect to cognition, compensation can be required because of the age-related constraints imposed by biological aging, disuse, and accumulating effects of maladaptive habits (e.g., Bäckman and Dixon, 1987). When cognitive functions are compromised, individuals can adjust their strategies for achieving goals, using different approaches to achieve the same ends (Ebner, Freund, and Baltes, 2006). For instance, when it becomes difficult to remember all the items needed at the grocery shop, individuals can either engage in using internal memory strategies (e.g., such as picturing all the items in a certain sequences, or building sentences as keys) or they could use an external aid such as a list of the groceries needed. Both types of alternative action for supporting memory (internal mnemonic strategy or external aids) could help to reach the original goal, namely to buy all groceries, despite a reduction in memory capacity.

Alternatively, individuals can downgrade the importance of the goals that have become difficult or even impossible to attain and, eventually, abandon them. This usually happens in cases of severe loss, representing an instance of loss-based selection.

Although compensation and loss-based selection are the two processes which are most likely to play a role in the context of dealing with age-related changes, older individuals benefit also from the other SOC processes if they are used at the same time. The SOC theory argues that adaptation is best when the processes are applied in a coordinated way. For instance, selecting a goal is necessary, but not sufficient; instead, applying the right means effectively by optimization is required to achieve the goal, as is replacing lost means to excel in the face of obstacles. For instance, just setting the goal of wanting to have a good memory (selection) is not enough to actually have a good memory. Rather, training may be required (optimization) as well as the use of mnemonic strategies if the individual's capacity gets exceeded by the material to be memorized (compensation). Empirically, there is evidence from a study with old and very old individuals, showing that outcomes were best when individuals used loss-based selection in combination with optimization or compensation (Jopp and Smith, 2006). Giving up a goal or changing goal priorities had the best effect on well-being when individuals applied the remaining means effectively or used alternative means at the same time.

Synthesis: a lifespan perspective on cognition

An important feature of a modern lifespan perspective on cognition, then, is that it does not attempt to deny or negate the phenomena of cognitive decline that have captured the dominant mechanistic decline perspective. Instead, these phenomena are viewed as one part of a more complex and diverse set of relevant processes and variables that determine cognitive successes and failures.

One way to understand the synthesis is through arguments about whether individuals can enhance cognitive function in old age. Hertzog *et al.* (2009), in a review of evidence regarding whether cognition can be maintained or enhanced in old age, framed the problem as one of viewing adults as developing within a zone of possible function (see Figure 5.1).

Genetic and environmental factors create a range of possible outcomes for each individual's life-course trajectory of cognitive function in any given domain. Individuals' selection and optimization behaviors shape their movement within the zone. The zone of possibility may become narrower as a function of biological aging, but upward movement in the zone is still possible in old age if one engages in behaviors that optimize functioning. For example, adopting an aerobic exercise program can have salutary effects on brain functioning and cognitive performance, even in late life (Colcombe and Kramer, 2003). Improvement in cognitive function – even in the face of normative decline in cognitive mechanisms – is possible because individuals often function well below their maximum potential, and because they can learn how to behave so as to improve function. Efforts to improve may have less beneficial impact late in life, owing to age-related declines in plasticity, and declines may occur even when one engages in behaviors that optimize function, especially if one is close to the maximum performance that could be achieved. The main point, however, is that improvement and decline are neither mutually exclusive nor polar opposites, but can co-occur.

The perspective as applied to adult cognitive development argues that personal investment in goal-directed behavior shapes the individual's profile of cognitive skills, knowledge, and competencies, setting the stage for further growth and development even as it places constraints on alternative possibilities that have not been pursued. Given the importance of social and practical intelligence, experience, and learned scripts and schemata for successful behavior, and given the opportunities for adjustments and changes in behavior to maximize cognition-demanding function, even in the face of mechanistic decline, older adults perform well in self-selected, familiar environments where their knowledge and experience provides a basis for goal attainment.

Cognitive resilience in adulthood and old age

Based on a lifespan perspective on cognitive aging, resilience in old age can be defined as a process of successfully adapting to new environmental

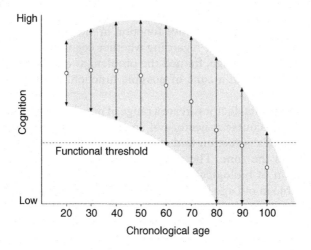

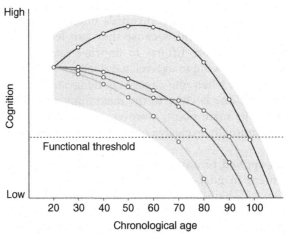

Figure 5.1. Top panel: Depiction of zone of possible cognitive development across the adult lifespan for a given individual. The upper and lower curves indicate optimal and suboptimal boundaries that define the zone of possibility (shaded gray area). Upward and downward movements at a given age are influenced by biological, behavioral, and environmental influences. Bottom panel: Depiction of four possible developmental curves for a single individual, with different trajectories resulting as a function of interactions among behavioral, environmental, and genetic factors that permit vertical movement within the zone at different points in the lifespan. Adapted with permission from Hertzog *et al.* (2009). Copyright: Association for Psychological Science.

demands and to constraints introduced by cognitive changes (Fry, this volume). Adaptation, in this sense, consists of either adjusting one's behaviors to achieve goals or redefining one's goals given that goal attainment has become unlikely or too effortful given the nature of one's current cognitive aptitude (e.g., Brandtstädter, 1999). In this sense resilience seems to be closely related to efforts to cope with adversity and thriving despite of it. In old age, adversity in the cognitive domain is associated with increasing risks of cognitive, motor, and perceptual decline due to normal aging, age-related diseases (such as Parkinson's disease or macular degeneration), and non-normative events, such as exposure to environmental hazards (e.g., Baltes and Willis, 1977). Baltes (1987) noted that increasing age was associated with increasing prevalence of losses in many domains, and gains in fewer domains. Over the course of the lifespan, losses start outnumbering gains, and this imbalance gets especially pronounced in the so-called fourth age (very old age). Whereas individuals in their third age, usually referring to age 65 to 75 or 80 years, are characterized by relatively sound cognitive functioning, good health, and sufficient resources to function effectively, individuals over 80 years old are usually characterized by a higher risk of cognitive impairment, substantial health issues, and reduced overall resources. In centenarians, sensory impairment and chronic diseases are present in almost all individuals (Andersen-Ranberg, Schroll, and Jeune, 2001), and severe cognitive limitations are quite common, as derived from reports indicating that up to 50 percent are affected by dementia of some sort (Kliegel, Moor, and Rott, 2004).

Resilience in later adulthood, then, can be conceptualized as the effective engagement of processes like compensation to offset the functional impact of age-related changes (Greve and Staudinger, 2006). With respect to cognition, resilience may involve compensatory adjustments for mechanistic cognitive decline, such as slowed speed of perceptual processing, or the use of cognition to generate strategies that address physical and perceptual limitations.

Consider the example of an older individual still pursuing a career in academic psychology. Possessing the cognitive aptitude and skills needed for a career in psychology is perhaps necessary, but hardly sufficient, to insure success, either early or late in the adult lifespan. Success in graduate school and as a new assistant professor also depends on developing important procedural skills of critical thinking, scientific writing, and scholarly research. Faculty mentors and colleagues shape the individual's professional behaviors by task, feedback, and example. Successful professionals learn about the implicit rule structures and expectations of the local environment. As they gain declarative knowledge in their chosen specializations, they also gain pragmatic social knowledge about the successful behaviors and practices in the local environment.

These same principles that governed early career success are likely to operate late in a career, including the importance of tacit knowledge and job-specific skills and expertise. In the face of normal age changes in memory and cognition, the older professor can be faced with new challenges that require cognitive resilience. The individual and the context have changed, as have the tasks and challenges at a different career stage (e.g., by becoming a department chair). Later in one's academic career, success in the face of cognitive decline is afforded by a balance between relying on what one already knows and adaptation to a changing environment (e.g., using new educational technology and mastering new research methods), staying current in the field by participating in conferences, reading literature, attending colloquia. Compensation may be needed – for example, relying less on memory for articles just read, relying more on methods of recording notes and ideas. Compensatory strategies may also involve utilizing social support to overcome age-graded limitations, engaging collaborators and colleagues who can help achieve goals that would otherwise require major new learning (e.g., analyzing data with new and mysterious statistical procedures). Moreover, an individual may adjust their career goals, such as emphasizing administration or teaching over research, due to changes in motives or adaptations to age-related changes.

Simonton (1991) pointed out that age and job experience are associated with a reduced probability of major scientific contributions. Although mechanistic cognitive decline is certainly involved (as it is with age of peak performance in competitive sports; Schulz *et al.*, 1994), other variables are at play, such as motivation, capture by an existing perspective, or attention to alternative goals – including personal and family goals outside of the career. Nevertheless, Simonton's research also shows individual differences in ages of peak career contributions and of one's last major contribution. The expertise that comes from years of experience as a professor may lead to productivity and insights that make important contributions to one's field well into old age.

It is to be hoped that there could also be an experience-related increase in personal wisdom about the nature and meaning of professional life in its larger context of individual development, although wisdom is far from an obligatory outcome of growing older (e.g., Baltes and Staudinger, 2000; Labouvie-Vief, 1982; Smith and Baltes, 1990). Perhaps there is at least some hope for developing personal wisdom in psychologists; clinical psychology professionals were found to score higher than non-clinical professionals and gave wiser answers with respect to age-appropriate life problems (Smith, Staudinger, and Baltes, 1994). Compensation, in the sense implied by SOC, involves behaviors that may or may not be successful in achieving target goals. Like the other SOC strategies, compensatory behavior can be adaptive or maladaptive, and whether it is adaptive is an evolving and changing function of the nature of the mechanistic changes and the contextual demands. A compensatory strategy that was effective at one point in time may become less effective as the age-related loss becomes more severe. Compensatory behavior can also have unintended consequences. An older adult driving in the slow lane on the freeway may be attempting to avoid the hazards of having to react to high-speed lane changes of other drivers. Is this effective compensation for slowed information-processing speed and reduced attentional resources (Edwards *et al.*, 2008)? Perhaps, but it could also bring with it an inadvertent increase in the risk of being involved in an accident by being rear-ended by a driver traveling at the speed limit. For this reason, flexible self-regulation, in which individuals monitor effectiveness of goal-directed behavior and adjust the behavior as needed, is important. We consider self-regulation in cognitive contexts in the next section.

Before doing so, we make two additional points concerning cognitive resilience in old age. First, resilience in the face of cognitive changes may be a critical component of what others have defined as "successful aging" (Rowe and Kahn, 1998). Although the classic definition of successful aging involves preserved cognition and reduced risk for cognitive decline, the functional perspective outlined here would modify this criterion. That is, successful aging would be defined as adaptive use of cognition to maintain the probability of goal attainment, along with flexible adjustment of goals when cognitive decline prevents their attainment. The distinction matters, because cognition in context can often be quite good, even when there has been substantial cognitive decline, as measured by cognitive psychologists (Roring and Charness, 2007). Masunaga and Horn (2001) showed that individuals classified as having age-related loss in fluid intelligence still played the challenging game of Go quite effectively, because they used expertise-based working memory and situated reasoning in the game context in ways not predicted by tests of fluid intelligence. Certainly, there is a connection between cognitive loss and adaptive cognition in familiar contexts, but the critical issue is whether an individual can achieve cognitively demanding goals by whatever means. With respect to successful aging, functional effectiveness, not cognition itself, is the key criterion.

A second point is that the concepts of cognitive resilience and successful aging imply individual differences in the degree to which individuals preserve functional effectiveness in old age (Hertzog, 2008). From this perspective, an important consideration is the degree to which persons with different characteristics, including personality and cognitive style, are more or less well suited for effective adaptation to the contingencies encountered during adult development. A key goal of a positive psychology of aging should be to identify those individuals in need of assistance in shaping use of resources and adaptive strategies to maximize effective functioning in old age (Jopp and Smith, 2006).

Metacognitive self-regulation as a means of achieving effective cognitive function

Older adults appear to be highly skilled at revising behavioral repertoires to achieve desired ends. For example, to deal with declining memory, older adults are more likely to report the use of new strategies, including external memory aids such as list and notes and asking others for help to achieve cognitively demanding goals (e.g., de Frias, Dixon, and Bäckman, 2003; Loewen, Shaw, and Craik, 1990).

Use of effective self-regulatory strategies may also explain why older adults are able to maintain cognitive functioning in the natural ecology. One domain in which this phenomenon has been studied extensively concerns prospective memory (remembering to act on an intention at a later point in time, when it is appropriate or desired). Remembering to take one's medications is a prime example; another one is remembering to stop at the store to buy food for dinner on the way home from work. Cognitive psychologists have developed tasks that simulate prospective memory in the laboratory. The typical finding is that older adults do better on prospective memory tests that provide explicit cues for responding (event-based prospective memory) and do worse on prospective memory tests that require responding at specific points in time (time-based prospective memory; see McDaniel, Einstein, and Rendell, 2008). Nevertheless, older adults do better at prospective memory in the natural ecology than they do on laboratory prospective memory tests (Henry *et al.*, 2004). Park *et al.* (1999) showed that older rheumatoid arthritis patients were better at remembering to take their medications than younger and middle-aged patients, in part because they reported less busy life styles and a more routine pattern of daily existence. Routines afford using external aids, for example, by placing medications in locations one is likely to encounter when the medication should be taken (such as putting one's evening medication on the nightstand next to bed). The older adults in Park *et al.*'s study did show typical patterns of lower functioning on tests of reasoning, working memory, and episodic memory. Furthermore, these variables predicted medication adherence. Nevertheless, the older patients were able to overcome their age-related cognitive limitations to exhibit better adherence behavior, probably through a combination of high motivation and strategic self-management.

Self-regulation in cognitive task environments is often conceptualized within a metacognitive framework (Dunlosky and Metcalfe, 2009). Metacognition is a multifaceted construct domain that includes knowledge about how cognition operates, beliefs about oneself and others in terms of cognitive abilities, and monitoring the state of one's own cognitive system. In many respects, metacognitive monitoring appears to be relatively spared by the aging process (e.g., Butterfield, Nelson, and Peck, 1988; Connor, Dunlosky, and Hertzog, 1997; Hertzog et al., 2002). Older adults' accuracy in predicting items they will remember, versus items they will forget, is comparable to younger adults, even though they remember less information. Older adults are also as accurate in discriminating semantic information they know, but cannot recall, from information they have never learned (Bäckman and Karlsson, 1985; Souchay et al., 2007). Spared monitoring is important because it suggests that older adults can effectively use monitoring to help them regulate their learning and their reliance on information (Dunlosky, Kubat-Silman, and Hertzog, 2003; Dunlosky et al., 2007). For example, older adults are as likely as younger adults to choose to restudy items they have not yet learned (Dunlosky and Hertzog, 1997), showing that they can monitor past performance and base item selections on resulting item recollection or familiarity. Recently, Price, Hertzog, and Dunlosky (in press) showed that older adults are similar to younger adults in selecting new foreign language items to study based on their difficulty, choosing the easiest new words they do not yet know. Likewise, older adults are able to learn from experience which of two learning strategies is more effective for them (Dunlosky and Hertzog, 2000; Price, Hertzog, and Dunlosky, 2008). Such findings are encouraging, because they suggest that older adults' metacognition is functioning well enough to assist them in effectively regulating their own learning.

Older adults can also employ effective learning strategies to enhance learning and subsequent retention. Dunlosky and Hertzog (2001) showed that typical age differences in the likelihood of using effective mediators for learning new associations (i.e., unrelated word pairs) can be eliminated simply by informing older adults of their existence, with subsequent benefits for memory performance. Particularly, individuals were informed that they could increase their memory by building so-called mediators such as creating a sentence or a vivid picture that links both words that they should remember. To be sure, older adults do experience impaired memory for associations, and are less likely to remember the mediators they generate to assist with learning (Dunlosky, Hertzog, and Powell-Moman, 2005). Other studies have also demonstrated that older adults' cognitive performance can be improved by training them how to use effective mediators (e.g., Brehmer *et al.*, 2007; Shing *et al.*, 2007). Likewise, structured experience at using recollection to protect against memory errors can dramatically benefit older adults' ability to reduce memory errors (Bissig and Lustig, 2007; Jennings *et al.*, 2005). Dunlosky *et al.* (2003) also showed that training older individuals to use a metacognitive self-testing strategy improved their learning above and beyond what could be achieved by training mnemonic strategies alone. Particularly, individuals tested themselves to determine whether they had learned an item or needed additional study, controlling whether a mnemonic strategy should be repeated or changed in order to do so. Thus, older adults' cognition in laboratory tasks can be enhanced by training them to be strategic, to monitor their successes and failures, and to adapt their approach to optimize learning (Dunlosky *et al.*, 2007).

The use of appropriate strategies as part of a behavioral approach to compensate for cognitive decline can be highly effective, even in persons experiencing pathologies of memory, such as AD. Camp and colleagues have shown that AD patients can be shaped by the use of spaced retrieval to learn new information and develop new routines (e.g., Camp *et al.*, 1996; see Camp, 2006, for a review). Spaced retrieval is a highly effective means of acquiring new information (such as the name of a person one just met). It involves repeated, self-initiated retrieval of the target information (the name) on an expanding schedule (e.g., lags of 1 minute, 4 minutes, 8 minutes, etc.). Even individuals with moderate dementia have been successfully trained with spaced retrieval to use external aids (e.g., caregiver notes left on a refrigerator) to reduce confusion and support activities of daily living.

Furthermore, older adults can overcome the effects of age-related decline in incidental memory (i.e., remembering something without having explicitly encoding it or rehearsing it) by shifting to a deliberate strategy of attending and noticing. For example, an older adult is less likely to forget where their car is parked if they develop the routine strategy of noticing where it is, finding a nearby landmark and encoding its relation to the car, and returning attention to the location of the car before leaving the parking lot (which also includes encoding what the location is likely to look like upon one's return to the parking area). Replacing reliance on incidental remembering with intentionally learning new information using spaced retrieval and meaning-based encoding affords effective use of memory despite the negative influences of aging. An important part of cognitive resilience, then, is the use of self-management and self-regulatory techniques to optimize function. Referring back to Figure 5.1, self-regulatory practices can move one toward the top of the zone of possible performance, leading to stable levels of function despite declining ranges of possibility.

The role of beliefs about cognition and aging

Older adults' beliefs about their cognition can have influences on their cognitive performance and their behavior in everyday life (Hess, 2006). Older adults, like younger adults, believe that cognition, especially memory, declines as people get older (e.g., Ryan and Kwong See, 1993). Lineweaver and Hertzog (1998) investigated these beliefs by asking individuals to complete visual analog scales in a way that established expected developmental curves from the age of 20 to 90 for different kinds of memory for the average adult. Young, middle-aged, and older individuals all expected a substantial decline. Although there were individual differences in the fitted slopes from these functions – indicating individual differences in how steep the decline function is rated over the adult lifespan – few individuals associated age with improvements in memory.

Hertzog and colleagues (2010) further investigated implicit theories about control over memory by conducting a semi-structured interview after individuals completed a memory test. Younger and older adults were asked in what ways they did and did not have control over memory in both the memory test and in life in general. Age differences emerged in the implicit theories about control over memory. Older adults were more likely to state that their lifestyle choices, such as exercising the mind or good nutrition, helped maintain control over memory. They almost universally stated that use of external memory aids created control over memory. They also perceived a loss of control over memory due to factors like poor health, reduced processing speed, and the costs of retrieval blocks (i.e., searching for but failing to access desired memoranda). Younger adults were more likely than older adults to discuss memory control in task contexts involving metacognitive control, such as working with knowledge about how memory works.

The same older adults who stated that lifestyle choices can influence control over memory expected that control over memory will decline with aging. A likely explanation is that older adults have an implicit theory of memory control not unlike the pattern shown in Figure 5.1. They believe that memory and control over memory declines on average, but that people can still influence their level of functioning through the lifestyle choices they make. Lineweaver, Berger, and Hertzog (2009) showed people descriptions of personality traits of target persons that varied in positive or negative age stereotypes. They then asked those individuals to trace expected developmental functions for the target individuals, as in Lineweaver and Hertzog (1998). The expected developmental functions varied as a function of type of trait. All of the functions had negative slopes, but negative trait descriptions increased the expected magnitude of memory decline. These findings are consistent with the argument that implicit theories about memory and aging are differentiated according to personal attributes of individuals.

It is possible that identifying oneself as having or being at risk for age-related decline is a risk factor for poor cognitive performance. Hess and colleagues (e.g., Hess *et al.*, 2003; see Hess, 2006) have shown that age-related stereotype threat may influence older adults' performance on memory tasks. If one has a high achievement motivation regarding memory, then exposure to information about aging's negative effects on memory can impair subsequent memory task performance. Such effects may operate by inducing anxiety about performance, distracting older adults from exerting effective control over memory in the task context. Levy and colleagues (e.g., Levy, 1996) argue that priming negative age stereotypes has detrimental effects on older adults' cognitive perform-ance. Resilience, in this context, may be influenced by whether one fears the effects of aging and is susceptible to being threatened in perform-ance-demanding situations.

Beliefs about one's own memory changes probably derive in part from internalized stereotypes about cognitive decline. For example, McDonald-Miszczak, Hertzog, and Hultsch (1995) studied perceived personal changes in memory function, a variable known to show robust age differences (Hultsch, Hertzog, and Dixon, 1987). Longitudinal data revealed relatively little relation between perceived memory change and actual memory change; instead, perceived change was more closely related to a person's age and their current beliefs about their memory functioning. Although other studies report relations between perceived and actual memory change (e.g., Lane and Zelinski, 2003), the relation-ships are generally small in magnitude and do not support the hypothesis that perceived change is primarily a function of accurate monitoring of one's own memory decline. Furthermore, unpublished work by Hertzog and colleagues suggests that there is a strong relationship between the magnitude of perceived memory change for the average adult in a given age interval and how much change one perceives having occurred in oneself.

Positive beliefs about one's own memory and control over memory may be seen as bucking the tendencies created by negative stereotypes and implicit theories of age-related memory decline. Elliott and Lachman (1989), drawing an analogy to work with children by Dweck and colleagues (e.g., Dweck and Leggett, 1988), argued that older adults who perceive cognition and memory as skills rather than endowed traits are more likely to exert control over memory when it is needed. From our perspective it is unlikely there is a dichotomy of persons who either believe that memory is a skill they can master versus those who see memory as an endowment that must inevitably decline. Hertzog, McGuire, and colleagues (2010) found that most persons make statements consistent with both viewpoints, a finding also more consistent with the idea of zones of possible development outlined in Figure 5.1; namely, people appear to believe that factors such as genetics and neuronal processes play a role in cognition, but that cognitive function also depends on the person's efforts.

Nevertheless, individuals who regard their own memory performance as potentially controllable behave differently in memory task environments. Several studies indicate that persons with a high sense of personal control over memory are more likely to exert control by using effective mnemonic strategies during encoding (e.g., Hertzog, Dunlosky, and Robinson, 2008; Hertzog, McGuire, and Lineweaver, 1998; Lachman and Andreoletti, 2006; Lachman, Andreoletti, and Pearman, 2006).

Self-efficacy is a construct closely related to perceived control (Bandura, 1997). Specifically, memory self-efficacy (Bandura, 1989; Berry, 1999), defined as a belief that one is capable of remembering information when needed, is correlated with but distinct from a sense of perceived control over memory. Several studies suggest that memory self-efficacy is positively correlated with memory performance, arguably because of its relation to goal-setting (West, Thorn, and Bagwell, 2003), persistence on task, and strategy use (Berry, 1999; Hertzog, Dunlosky, and Robinson, 2008).

As noted by Fry (this volume), self-efficacy and control beliefs may be important sources of resilience in old age because they encourage agency and action, as opposed to avoidance and atrophy. An older adult who is anxious about possible memory change (e.g., Davidson, Dixon, and Hultsch, 1991) can be motivated to compensatory action or drawn to avoidance of situations that demand memory. Assuming that persistence and motivation are more important for older adults compared with younger adults who still have sufficient cognitive resources to perform well, beliefs were found to be more important for performance in older adults (Jopp and Lindenberger, 2009; Luszcz and Hinton, 1995; Soederberg Miller and Gagne, 2005). As such, perceived self-efficacy and control may be essential for maintaining an active and engaged lifestyle, especially in the face of impending cognitive decline (Artistico, Cervone, and Pezzuti, 2003; Jopp and Hertzog, 2007).

Cognitive enrichment effects in adulthood

Adults are to a reasonable degree creators of their own development (Stine-Morrow, 2007), consistent with a lifespan perspective on development that argues for behavioral and contextual influences on developmental outcomes (e.g., Lerner, 1984). This includes, for instance, the choice of one's profession and the decision to stay in a certain job. As individuals usually spend a fair amount of their life time in a certain working environment, it is likely to exert an effect on cognition. Positive effects on cognition have been found, for example, with respect to the degree of cognitive complexity, as shown by work from Schooler and colleagues (e.g., Schooler, Mulatu, and Oates, 1999).

Besides choice of professional challenges, there are also other activities that may enhance or help maintain cognitive functioning. Amongst the factors that seem to be influential are – as one would expect – cognitively stimulating activities such as playing bridge or jigsaw puzzles, attending a college course, or studying a foreign language.

Although the evidence in favor of cognitive enrichment effects is mixed (Salthouse, 2006), a number of longitudinal studies have produced evidence that changes in cognition in adulthood and old age are correlated with an intellectually engaged lifestyle (e.g., Hultsch *et al.*, 1999; see Hertzog *et al.*, 2009; Small and McEvoy, 2008). In one study, we also found that the use of modern technology had an additional effect on cognition, over and above the effect of general activity level (Jopp and Hertzog, 2007). As intellectually stimulating activities seem to promote maintenance of cognitive function (e.g., Schooler, Mulatu, and Oates, 1999; Wilson and Bennett, 2003), engaging in such activities appears to be one factor related to cognitive resilience in old adulthood.

Furthermore, cognitive resilience seems also to be related to two factors that come less easily to mind in the context of cognition – namely physical and social activities. As noted earlier, older adults are likely to believe that lifestyle practices influence memory and cognitive function (Hertzog *et al.*, 2010). There is emerging evidence that this is, to at least some degree, correct. Physical exercise interventions, even in old age, have positive effects on physiological functioning and health, including brain morphology (see Hertzog *et al.*, 2009, for a review). Even though the underlying mechanisms are not clear, animal models suggest that the enhanced cognitive function is related to increased capillary density in the brain (e.g., Black *et al.*, 1990), higher dopamine receptor density (e.g., Fordyce and

Farrar, 1991), as well as new cells in hippocampal areas (Kempermann, 2008). To what extent the same mechanisms are at work in humans still needs to be determined. Other mechanisms discussed include enhanced blood flow and maybe enhanced gait and balance activities, reducing the load to the human cognitive system (Lindenberger and Baltes, 1997). The effects of physical activities in humans are quite robust and have been shown in various studies. In an early study, Clarkson-Smith and Hartley (1990) showed that physical exercise, determined by kilocalories per week, actual hours of strenuous exercise as well as hours of prior exercise, predicted reaction time, working memory, and reasoning. Integrating available intervention studies, Colcombe and Kramer (2003) showed in their meta-analysis that aerobic fitness training boosted various cognitive functions including spatial capacity and perceptual speed, with the strongest effect for executive-control processes. There is also evidence that less strenuous physical activities have substantial cognitive benefit, for example with respect to decreasing the risk for AD. In a study conducted by Abbott and colleagues (2004), individuals who walked less than 2 miles per day had an 1.8 times increased risk of developing AD compared with those who walked 2 miles or more. Unfortunately, individuals engage less and less in physical activities when getting older (e.g., DiPietro, 2001; Schroll, 2003), which is likely to have negative effects on not only health, but also cognition, therefore presenting a risk factor for cognitive resilience. Making physical activities more attractive and offering a physically stimulating environment (e.g., installing a walking parcours, as done by the city of Heidelberg; Rott, 2008), may be a way to counteract resistance to exercise in older adults.

The second factor, social activities, has recently received more attention in the context of cognitive aging (e.g., Lövdén, Ghisletta, and Lindenberger, 2005). Engaging in social activities, such as talking to friends, visiting family, and going to dinner with acquaintances, seems to be linked to cognitive functioning. In a recent study, Jopp and Hertzog (2010) found evidence that it is especially private social activities that are linked to cognition. Data from two cross-sectional samples indicated that private social activities had positive correlations with perceptual speed, inductive reasoning, and a composite of fluid intelligence measures. The correlations were higher for the sample of old and very old individuals. By contrast, public social activities such as attending club meetings or organized social events were not linked to cognition in both samples. Thus, direct interaction with personally meaningful social partners may have protective benefits for older adults' cognition, for reasons that are as yet unknown. It could be that social interaction is in and of itself a cognitively challenging task that maintains social skills while enriching cognition and everyday problem-solving.

There is also evidence that social activities are related to a reduced risk of AD. Andel and colleagues (2005) found, based on the Swedish Twin Study, that individuals who had worked in socially complex settings (e.g., with supervising duties) were less likely to develop AD, despite controlling for genetic and family factors, age, gender, and education. Another study found that higher interpersonal demand in main occupation was related to delayed onset of AD (Stern *et al.*, 1995). Fratiglioni and colleagues (2000) further reported that individuals with larger social networks had a lower risk for AD.

As just outlined, older adults' choices regarding lifestyle, nutrition, exercise, social activities, and general engagement with life likely have an impact on maintaining or enhancing cognitive functioning in late life. Adults also have considerable control over the contexts they choose to experience. Cognitive resilience is from this perspective an outcome of positive aging, one that has benefits for maintaining autonomy and effective functioning for longer periods of the life-course. Attitudes, lifestyle practices, and cognition can in that sense work in a fruitful symbiosis. Being active may enhance well-being and energetic arousal, influence a sense that one is in control over one's cognition, and further promote self-regulation that leads to effective cognitive function (Jopp and Hertzog, 2007).

Resource utilization and positive outcomes in old age

Cognitive functioning is not only important for its own sake, as outlined earlier, but is needed with respect to optimal functioning in everyday life. It is essential in dealing with all small and large challenges and required for solving problems of all kinds. This is why measures of intellectual capacity have always been thought of as a substantial prerequisite of adaptation/coping with life (Birren, 1964; Thomae, 1987). Cognition also represents a strong predictor of the survival of old and very old individuals (e.g., Bosworth, Schaie, and Willis, 1999; Small and Bäckman, 1997). Whether this suggests that poor cognition is likely to result in poor adaptation, and eventually, death, is yet debatable. Findings from Anstey and colleagues (2001) instead propose that reduced cognitive status and cognitive loss may mirror biological aging processes.

Besides being a resource in it own right, cognition also enables the use of other resources. For instance, when it comes to mobilize social support, it is not sufficient to have social partners available, they need to be addressed in an appropriate manner so that they are willing to help. Another example is economic resources, which are good to have, but need to be managed and used appropriately in order to facilitate the individual's wishes. Health also is a resource that stands in some connection to cognition and education, as individuals with higher education are showing more health-promoting and less risky behavior.

Social support and social engagement are especially critical for older adults when facing major constraints and loss in multiple domains of functioning (e.g., Boerner and Jopp, 2009). This is also true when individuals suffer from AD, stroke, or other states that place normal cognitive functioning at risk. A potentially important component of effective functioning in the face of cognitive loss is the availability of social support through multiple sources, including family, spouses, and informal and formal service providers. Resilience is more likely in older adults who are able to seek and receive support for critical activities in the face of challenge or loss. A British study found that three-year survival in AD patients was related to provided social support (Orrell, Butler, and Bebbington, 2000). Nevertheless, social support may have its limits. For instance, social support had no influence on depression in AD patients who had been confronted with a critical life event three months prior to assessment (Waite *et al.*, 2004). Effective emotion-regulation and coping is also likely to be influenced by cognitive functioning, as it allows the individual to evaluate the situation with respect to various criteria and to consider different reactions. Underscoring these assumptions, cognition was found to relate to higher use of life-management strategies in older adults (Freund and Baltes, 1999).

Finally, cognition is correlated with another criterion of successful aging, subjective well-being. For example, Isaacowitz and Smith (2003) reported that general intelligence was a unique predictor for old and very old individuals' positive affect. When splitting both age groups, the positive effect for intelligence only remained for the younger group, the young-old individuals. By contrast, general intelligence predicted negative affect in both groups, the young-old and the old-old, but the effect was reversed: higher levels of intelligence were also associated with higher levels of negative affect. Perhaps an unfortunate consequence of a lifetime of high functioning is greater emotional difficulty in adjusting to late-life physical and cognitive challenges. This conjecture is consistent with data from Jopp (2003) demonstrating that old and very old individuals with poor health but high cognitive functioning were the ones least satisfied with their aging.

Concluding comments

A functional lifespan perspective focuses on potentials for improvement and resilience against losses, not just the limits on cognition imposed by aging. This perspective encourages the pursuit of new research questions. More effort is needed on the cognitive processes and mechanisms that contribute to individuals' effective adaptation to age-related losses, including metacognitive self-regulation, strategic behavior, and personal beliefs. Likewise, research should continue to focus on the ways in which intellectual, physical, and social activities can help maintain the brain and functional cognitive competence. Furthermore, research on cognitive resilience can help modify societal assumptions about cognition in old age. Unchallenged negative stereotypes about aging and cognition can be harmful to the individual and unnecessarily hamper our efforts as a society to enhance the productivity and quality of life of older adults.

REFERENCES

Abbott, R. D., White, L. R., Ross, G. W., Masaki, K. H., Curb, J. D., and Petrovitch, H. (2004). Walking and dementia in physically capable elderly. *Journal of the American Medical Association*, 292, 1447–1453.

Ackerman, P. L. (2000). Domain-specific knowledge as the 'dark matter' of adult intelligence: Gf/Gc personality and interest correlates. *Journal of Gerontology: Psychological Sciences*, 55, P69–P84.

Andel, R., Cowe, M., Pedersen, N. L., *et al.* (2005). Complexity of work and risk of Alzheimer's disease: A population-based study of Swedish twins. *Journal of Gerontology: Psychological Science*, 60B, P251–P258.

Andersen-Ranberg, K., Schroll, M., and Jeune, B. (2001). Healthy centenarians do not exist, but autonomous do: A population-based study of morbidity among Danish centenarians. *Journal of the American Geriatrics Society*, 49, 900–908.

Anstey, K. J., Luszcz, M. A., Giles, L. C. and Andrews, G. R. (2001). Demographic, health, cognitive, and sensory variables as predictors of mortality in very old age. *Psychology and Aging*, 16, 3–11.

Artistico, D., Cervone, D., and Pezzuti, L. (2003). Perceived self-efficacy and everyday problem solving among young and older adults. *Psychology and Aging*, 18, 68–79.

Bäckman, L, and Dixon, R. A. (1987). Psychological compensation: A theoretical framework. *Psychological Bulletin*, 112, 259–283.

Bäckman, L., and Karlsson, T. (1985). The relation between level of general knowledge and feeling-of-knowing: An adult age study. *Scandinavian Journal of Psychology*, 26, 249–258.

Baltes, P. B. (1987). Theoretical propositions of life-span developmental psychology: On the dynamics between growth and decline. *Developmental Psychology*, 23, 611–626.

(1997). On the incomplete architecture of human ontogeny: Selection, optimization, and compensation as a foundation for developmental theory. *American Psychologist*, 52, 366–380.

Baltes, P. B., and Baltes, M. M. (eds.) (eds.). (1990). *Successful aging: Perspectives from the behavioral sciences*. Cambridge: Cambridge University Press.

Baltes, P. B., and Staudinger, U. M. (2000). Wisdom: A metaheuristic (pragmatic) to orchestrate mind and virtue toward excellence. *American Psychologist*, 55, 122–136.

Baltes, P. B., Staudinger, U. M., and Lindenberger, U. (1999). Lifespan psychology: Theory and application to intellectual development. *Annual Review of Psychology*, 50, 471–507.

Baltes, P. B., and Willis, S. W. (1977). Toward psychological theories of aging and development. In J. E. Birren and K. W. Schaie (eds.), *Handbook of the psychology of aging* (pp. 128–154). New York: Van Nostrand Reinhold.

Bandura, A. (1989). Regulation of cognitive processes through self-efficacy. *Developmental Psychology*, 25, 729–735.

(1997). *Self efficacy: The exercise of control*. New York: Freeman.

Beier, M., and Ackerman, P. L. (2005). Age, ability, and the role of prior knowledge on the acquisition of new domain knowledge: Promising results in a real-world learning environment. *Psychology and Aging*, 20, 341–355.

Berry, J. M. (1999). Memory self-efficacy in its social cognitive context. In T. M. Hess and F. Blanchard-Fields (eds.), *Social cognition and aging* (pp. 69–96). San Diego, CA: Academic Press.

Birren, J. E. (1964). *The psychology of aging*. Englewood Cliffs, NJ: Prentice Hall.

Bissig, D., and Lustig, C. (2007). Who benefits from memory training? *Psychological Science*, 18, 720–726.

Black, J. E., Isaacs, K. S., Anderson, B. J., Alcantara, A. A., and Greenough, W. T. (1990). Learning causes synaptogenesis, whereas motor activity causes angiogenesis in cerebellar cortex of adult rats. *Proceedings of the National Academy of Sciences, USA*, 87, 5568–5572.

Boerner, K., and Jopp, D. (2007). Improvement/maintenance and reorientation as central features of coping with major life change and loss: Contributions of three life-span theories. *Human Development*, 50, 171–195.

(2009). Resilience in response to loss. In J. W. Reich, A. J. Zautra, and J. S. Hall (Eds), *Handbook of adult resilience* (pp. 126–145). New York: Guilford.

Bosworth, H. B., Schaie, K. W., and Willis, S. L. (1999). Cognitive and sociodemographic risk factors for mortality in the Seattle Longitudinal Study. *The Journals of Gerontology: Psychological Sciences*, 54B, P273–P282.

Brandtstädter, J. (1999). Sources of resilience in the aging self. In F. Blanchard-Fields and T. Hess (eds.), *Social cognition and aging* (pp. 123–141). New York: Academic Press.

Brehmer, Y., Li, S. C., Müller, V., Oertzen, T. V., and Lindenberger, U. (2007). Memory plasticity across the life span: Uncovering children's latent potential. *Developmental Psychology*, 43, 465–478.

Butterfield, E. C., Nelson, T. O., and Peck, V. (1988). Developmental aspects of the feeling-of-knowing. *Developmental Psychology*, 24, 654–663.

Cabeza, R., Nyberg, L., and Park, D. C. (eds.) (2005). *Cognitive neuroscience of aging.* Oxford: Oxford University Press.

Camp, C. J. (2006). Spaced retrieval: A model for dissemination of a cognitive intervention with persons of dementia. In D. K. Attix and K. A. Welsh-Mohmer (eds.), *Geriatric neuropsychology: Assessment and intervention* (pp. 275–292). New York: Guilford.

Camp, C. J., Foss, J. W., O'Hanlon, A. M., and Stevens, A. B. (1996). Memory interventions for persons with dementia. *Applied Cognitive Psychology,* 10, 193–210.

Cianciolo, A. T., Grigorenko, E. L., Jarvin, L, Gil, G., Drebot, M. E., and Sternberg, R. J. (2006). Practical intelligence and tacit knowledge: Advances in the measurement of developing expertise. *Learning and Individual Differences,* 16, 235–253.

Clarkson-Smith, L., and Hartley, A. A. (1990). Structural equation models of relationships between exercise and cognitive abilities. *Psychology and Aging,* 5, 437–446.

Colcombe, S., and Kramer, A. F. (2003). Fitness effects on the cognitive function of older adults: A meta-analytic study. *Psychological Science,* 14, 125–130.

Colonia-Willner, R. (1998). Practical intelligence at work: Relationships between aging and cognitive efficiency among managers in a bank environment. *Psychology and Aging,* 13, 45–57.

Connor, L. T., Dunlosky, J., and Hertzog, C. (1997). Age-related differences in absolute but not relative memory accuracy. *Psychology and Aging,* 12, 50–71.

Davidson, H., Dixon, R. A., and Hultsch, D. F. (1991). Memory anxiety and memory performance in adulthood. *Applied Cognitive Psychology,* 5, 423–433.

de Frias, C. M., Dixon, R. A., and Bäckman, L. (2003). Use of memory compensation strategies is related to psychosocial and health indicators. *The Journals of Gerontology: Psychological Sciences and Social Sciences,* 58B, P12–P22.

DiPietro, L. (2001). Physical activity in aging: Changes in patterns and their relationship to health and function. *The Journals of Gerontology: Biological Sciences and Medical Sciences,* 56A (special issue II), M13–M22.

Dixon, R. A. (2000). Concepts and mechanisms of gains in cognitive aging. In D. C. Park and N. Schwarz (eds.), *Cognitive aging: A primer* (pp. 23–41). Philadelphia, PA: Psychology Press.

Dixon, R. A., and Hertzog, C. (1988). A functional approach to memory and metamemory development in adulthood. In F. Weinert and M. Perlmutter (eds.), *Memory development: Universal changes and individual differences* (pp. 293–330). Hillsdale, NJ: Erlbaum.

  (1996). Theoretical issues in cognitive aging. In F. Blanchard-Fields and T. Hess (eds.), *Perspectives on cognitive change in adult development and aging* (pp. 25–65). New York: McGraw-Hill.

Dunlosky, J., Cavallini, E., Roth, H., McGuire, C. L., Vecchi, T., and Hertzog, C. (2007). Do self-monitoring interventions improve older adults' learning? *The Journals of Gerontology: Psychological Sciences*, 62B (special issue I), 70–76.

Dunlosky, J., and Hertzog, C. (1997). Older and younger adults use a functionally identical algorithm to select items for restudy during multi-trial learning. *Journal of Gerontology: Psychological Sciences*, 52, 178–186.

(2000). Updating knowledge about encoding strategies: A componential analysis of learning about strategy effectiveness from task experience. *Psychology and Aging*, 15, 462–474.

(2001). Measuring strategy production during associative learning: The relative utility of concurrent versus retrospective reports. *Memory and Cognition*, 29, 247–253.

Dunlosky, J., Hertzog, C., and Powell-Moman, A. (2005). The contribution of five mediator-based deficiencies to age-related differences in associative learning. *Developmental Psychology*, 41, 389–400.

Dunlosky, J., Kubat-Silman, A., and Hertzog, C. (2003). Training metacognitive skills improves older adults' associative learning. *Psychology and Aging*, 18, 340–345.

Dunlosky, J., and Metcalfe, J. (2009). *Metacognition*. Thousand Oaks, CA: Sage.

Dweck, C. S., and Leggett, E. L. (1988). A social-cognitive approach to motivation and personality. *Psychological Review*, 95, 256–273.

Ebner, N. C., Freund, A. M., and Baltes, P. B. (2006). Developmental changes in personal goal orientation from young to late adulthood: From striving for gains to maintenance and prevention of losses. *Psychology and Aging*, 21, 664–678.

Edwards, J. D., Ross, L. A., Ackerman, M. L., *et al.* (2008). Longitudinal predictors of driving cessation among older adults from the ACTIVE clinical trial. *The Journals of Gerontology: Psychological Sciences and Social Sciences*, 63B, P6–P12.

Elliott, E. and Lachman, M. E. (1989). Enhancing memory by modifying control beliefs, attributions, and performance goals in the elderly. In P.S. Fry (ed.), *Psychological perspectives of helplessness and control in the elderly* (pp. 339–367). Oxford: North-Holland.

Fordyce, D. E., and Farrar, R. P. (1991). Enhancement of spatial learning in F344 rats by physical activity and related learning-associated alterations in hippocampal and cortical cholinergic functioning. *Behavioral Brain Research*, 46, 123–133.

Fratiglioni, L., Wang, H. X., Ericsson, K., Maytan, M., and Winblad, B. (2000). Influence of social network on occurrence of dementia: A community-based longitudinal study. *Lancet*, 355, 1315–1319.

Freund, A. M., and Baltes, P. B. (1999). Selection, optimization, and compensation as strategies of life management: Corrections to Freund and Baltes (1998). *Psychology and Aging*, 14, 700–702.

(2002). The adaptiveness of selection, optimization, and compensation as strategies of life management: Evidence from a preference study on proverbs. *The Journals of Gerontology: Psychological Sciences*, 57B, P426–P434.

Greenwood, P. M. (2007). Functional plasticity in cognitive aging: Review and hypothesis. *Neuropsychology*, 21, 657–673.

Greve, W., and Staudinger, U. M. (2006). Resilience in later adulthood and old age: Resources and potentials for successful aging. In D. Cicchetti and A. Cohen (eds.), *Developmental psychopathology* (2nd edn., pp. 796–840).

Henry, J. D., MacLeod. M., phillips, L. H., and Crawford, J. R. (2004). Meta-analytic review of prospective memory and aging. *Psychology and Aging*, 19, 27–39.

Hertzog, C. (2002). Metacognition in older adults: Implications for application. In T. J. Perfect and B. L. Schwartz (eds.), *Applied metacognition* (pp. 169–196). New York: Cambridge University Press.

Hertzog, C. (2008). Theoretical approaches to the study of cognitive aging: An individual differences perspective. In S. M. Hofer and D. F. Alwin (eds.), *Handbook of cognitive aging* (pp. 34–49). Thousand Oaks, CA: Sage Publications.

Hertzog, C., Cooper, B. P., and Fisk, A. D. (1996). Aging and individual differences in the development of skilled memory search performance. *Psychology and Aging*, 11, 497–520.

Hertzog, C., Dixon, R. A., Hultsch, D. F., and MacDonald, S. W. S. (2003). Latent change models of adult cognition: Are changes in processing speed and working memory associated with changes in episodic memory? *Psychology and Aging*, 18, 755–769.

Hertzog, C., Dunlosky, J., and Robinson, A. E. (2008). Intellectual abilities and metacognitive beliefs influence spontaneous use of effective encoding strategies. Unpublished manuscript.

Hertzog, C., Kidder, D. P., Powell-Moman, A., and Dunlosky, J. (2002). Aging and monitoring associative learning: Is monitoring accuracy spared or impaired? *Psychology and Aging*, 17, 209–225.

Hertzog, C., Kramer, A. F., Wilson, R. S., and Lindenberger, U. (2009). Enrichment effects on adult cognitive development: Can the functional capacity of older adults be preserved and enhanced? *Psychological Science in the Public Interest* (Supplement to Psychological Science). Washington, DC: Association for Psychological Science.

Hertzog, C., McGuire, C. L., Horhota, M., and Jopp, D. (2010). Age differences in theories about memory control: Does believing in "use it or lose it" have implications for self-rated memory control, strategy use, and free recall performance? *International Journal of Aging and Human Development*, 70, 61–87.

Hertzog, C., McGuire, C. L., and Lineweaver, T. T. (1998). Aging, attributions, perceived control, and strategy use in a free recall task. *Aging, Neuropsychology, and Cognition*, 5, 85–106.

Hess, T. M. (2005). Memory and aging in context. *Psychological Bulletin*, 131, 383–406.

(2006). Attitudes toward aging and their effects on behavior. In J. E. Birren and K. W. Schaie (eds.), *Handbook of the psychology of aging* (6th edn., pp. 379–406). San Diego, CA: Academic Press.

Hess, T. M., Auman, C., Colcombe, S. J., and Rahhal, T. A. (2003). The impact of stereotype threat on age differences in memory performance. *The Journals of Gerontology: Psychological Sciences*, 58B, P3–P11.

Horn, J. L. (1989). Models of intelligence. In R. L. Linn (ed.), *Intelligence: Measurement, theory, and public policy* (pp. 29–73). Urbana, IL: University of Illinois Press.

Hoyer, W. J., and Verhaeghen, P. (2006). Memory aging. In J. E. Birren and K. W. Schaie (eds.), *Handbook of the psychology of aging* (6th edn., pp. 209–232). San Diego, CA: Academic Press.

Hultsch, D. F., Hertzog, C., and Dixon, R. (1987). Age differences in metamemory: Resolving the inconsistencies. *Canadian Journal of Psychology*, 41, 193–208.

Hultsch, D. F., Hertzog, C., Dixon, R. A., and Small, B. J. (1998). *Memory change in the aged*. New York: Cambridge University Press.

Hultsch, D. F., Small, B. J., Hertzog, C., and Dixon, R. A. (1999). Use it or lose it: Engaged lifestyle as a buffer of cognitive decline in aging. *Psychology and Aging*, 14, 245–263.

Isaacowitz, D. M, and Smith, J. (2003). Positive and negative affect in very old age. *The Journals of Gerontology: Psychological Sciences*, 58B, P143–152.

Jennings, J. M., Webster, L. M., Kleykamp, B. A., and Dagenbach, D. (2005). Recollection training and transfer effects in older adults: Successful use of a repetition-lag procedure. *Aging, Neuropsychology and Cognition*, 12, 278–298.

Jopp, D. (2003). Erfolgreiches Altern: Zum funktionalen Zusammenspiel von personalen Ressourcen und adaptiven Strategien des Lebensmanagements [Successful aging: On the functional interplay between personal resources and adaptive life-management strategies]. Doctoral dissertation, Free University of Berlin, Germany.

Jopp, D., and Hertzog, C. (2007). Activities, self-referent memory beliefs, and cognitive performance: Evidence for direct and mediated effects. *Psychology and Aging*, 22, 811–825.

(2010). Assessing adult leisure activities: An extension of a self-report activity questionnaire. *Psychological Assessment*, 22, 108–120

Jopp, D., and Lindenberger, U. (2009). Adults' beliefs about cognition: Age-based increase in the relation to performance. Unpublished manuscript.

Jopp, D., and Smith, J. (2006). Resources and life-management strategies as determinants of successful aging: On the protective effect of selection, optimization, and compensation. *Psychology and Aging*, 21, 253–265.

Kanfer, R., and Ackerman, P. L. (2004). Aging, adult development, and work motivation. *Academy of Management Review*, 29, 440–458.

Kausler, D. H. (1994). *Learning and memory in normal aging*. San Diego, CA: Academic Press.

Kempermann, G. (2008). The neurogenic reserve hypothesis: What is adult hippocampal neurogenesis good for? *Trends in Neuroscience*, 31, 163–169.

Kliegel, M., Moor, C., and Rott, C. (2004). Cognitive status and development in the oldest old: A longitudinal analysis from the Heidelberg Centenarian Study. *Archives of Gerontology and Geriatrics*, 39, 143–156.

Kramer, A. F., and Willis, S. L. (2002). Enhancing the cognitive vitality of older adults. *Current Directions in Psychological Science*, 11, 173–177.

Labouvie-Vief, G. (1982). Dynamic development and mature autonomy: A theoretical prologue. *Human Development*, 25, 161–191.

Lachman, M. E., and Andreoletti, C. (2006). Strategy use mediates the relationship between control beliefs and memory performance for middle-aged and older adults. *The Journals of Gerontology: Psychological Sciences and Social Sciences*, 61B, P88–P94.

Lachman, M. E., Andreoletti, C., and Pearman, A. (2006). Memory control beliefs: How are they related to age, strategy use, and memory improvement? *Social Cognition*, 24, 359–385.

Lane, C. J., and Zelinski, E. M. (2003). Longitudinal hierarchical linear models of the Memory Functioning Questionnaire. *Psychology and Aging*, 18, 38–53.

Lerner, R. M. (1984). *On the nature of human plasticity*. New York: Cambridge University Press.

Levy, B. (1996). Improving memory in old age by implicit self-stereotyping. *Journal of Personality and Social Psychology*, 71, 1092–1107.

Lindenberger, U., and Baltes, P. B. (1997). Intellectual functioning in old and very old age: Cross-sectional results from the Berlin Aging Study. *Psychology and Aging*, 12, 410–432.

Lineweaver, T. T., Berger, A. K., and Hertzog, C. (2009). Expectations about memory change are impacted by aging stereotypes. *Psychology and Aging*, 24, 169–176.

Lineweaver, T. T., and Hertzog, C. (1998). Adults' efficacy and control beliefs regarding memory and aging: Separating general from personal beliefs. *Aging, Neuropsychology, and Cognition*, 5, 264–296.

Loewen, E. R., Shaw, R. J., and Craik, F. I. M. (1990). Age differences in components of metamemory. *Experimental Aging Research*, 16, 43–48.

Lövdén, M., Ghisletta, P., and Lindenberger, U. (2005). Social participation attenuates decline in perceptual speed in old and very old age. *Psychology and Aging*, 20, 423–434.

Luszcz, M., and Hinton, M. (1995). Domain- and task-specific beliefs about memory in adulthood: A microgenetic approach. (Special issue: Cognitive development). *Australian Journal of Psychology*, 47, 54–59.

Masunaga, H., and Horn, J. L. (2001). Expertise and age-related changes in components of intelligence. *Psychology and Aging*, 16, 293–311.

McDaniel, M. A., Einstein, G. O., and Rendell, P. G. (2008). The puzzle of inconsistent age-related declines in prospective memory: A multiprocess explanation. In M. Kliegel, M. A. McDaniel, and G. O. Einstein (eds.), *Prospective memory: Cognitive, neuroscience, developmental, and applied perspectives* (pp. 141–160). Mahwah, NJ: Erlbaum.

McDonald-Miszczak, L., Hertzog, C., and Hultsch, D. F. (1995). Stability and accuracy of metamemory in adulthood and aging. *Psychology and Aging*, 10, 553–564.

Ng, T. W. H., and Feldman, D. C. (2008). The relationship of age to ten dimensions of job performance. *Journal of Applied Psychology*, 93, 392–423.

Ong, A. D., Bergeman, C. S., Bisconti, T. L., and Wallace, K. A. (2006). Psychological resilience, positive emotions, and successful adaptation to stress in later life. *Journal of Personality and Social Psychology*, 91, 730–749.

Orrell, M., Butler, R., and Bebbington, P. (2000). Social factors and the outcome of dementia. *International Journal of Geriatric Psychiatry*, 15, 515–520.

Park, D. C., Hertzog, C., Leventhal, H. *et al.* (1999). Medication adherence in rheumatoid arthritis patients: Older is wiser. *Journal of the American Geriatrics Society*, 47, 172–183.

Park, D. C., and Reuter-Lorenz, P. (2009). The adaptive brain: Aging and neurocognitive scaffolding. *Annual Review of Psychology*, 60, 173–196.

Park, D. C., and Schwarz, N. (eds.) (2000). *Cognitive aging: A primer.* Philadelphia, PA: Psychology Press.

Price, J., Hertzog, C., and Dunlosky, J. (2008). Age-related differences in strategy knowledge updating: Blocked testing produces greater improvements in metacognitive accuracy for younger than older adults. *Aging, Neuropsychology, and Cognition*, 15, 601–626.

(in press). Self-regulated learning in younger and older adults: Does aging affect cognitive control? *Aging, Neuropsychology and Cognition.*

Raz, N. (2000). Aging of the brain and its impact on cognitive performance: Integration of structural and functional findings. In F. I. M. Craik and T. A. Salthouse (eds.), *Handbook of aging and cognition* (2nd edn., pp. 1–90). Mahwah, NJ: Erlbaum.

Riediger, M., Li, S-C., and Lindenberger, U. (2006). Selection, optimization, and compensation as developmental mechanisms of adaptive resource allocation: Review and preview. In J. E. Birren and K. W. Schaie (eds.), *Handbook of the psychology of aging* (6th edn., pp. 289–310). San Diego, CA: Academic Press.

Roring, R. W., and Charness, N. (2007). A multilevel model of expertise in chess across the life span. *Psychology and Aging*, 22, 291–299.

Rott, C. (2008). Selbständigkeit in einer Gesellschaft des langen Lebens – die Rolle von körperlicher Aktivität [Independence in a society of long lives – the role of physical activities]. In F. Mess, D. Dugandzic, and A. Woll (eds.), *Erfolgreiches Altern durch Sport* (pp. 9–33). Konstanz, Germany: UVK Verlagsgesellschaft.

Rowe, J. W., and Kahn, R. L. (1998). *Successful aging.* New York: Pantheon.

Ryan, E. B., and Kwong See, S. T. (1993). Age-based beliefs about memory changes for self and others across adulthood. *The Journals of Gerontology: Psychological Sciences*, 48, P108–P118.

Rybash, J. M., Hoyer, W. J., and Roodin, P. A. (1986). *Adult cognition and aging: Developmental changes in processing, knowing, and thinking.* New York: Pergamon Press.

Salthouse, T. A. (1991). *Theoretical perspectives on cognitive aging.* Hillsdale, NJ: Erlbaum.

Salthouse, T. S. (2006). Mental exercise and mental aging: Evaluating the validity of the "use it or lose it" hypothesis. *Perspectives on Psychological Science*, 1, 68–87.

Schaie, K. W. (2005). *Developmental influences on adult intelligence: The Seattle Longitudinal Study.* New York: Oxford University Press.

Schooler, C., Mulatu, M. S., and Oates, G. (1999). The continuing effects of substantively complex work on the intellectual functioning of older workers. *Psychology and Aging*, 14, 483–506.

Schroll, M. (2003). Physical activity in an aging population. *Scandinavian Journal of Medicine and Science in Sport*, 13, 63–69.

Schulz, R., Musa, D., Staszewski, J., and Siegler, R. S. (1994). The relationship between age and major league baseball performance: Implications for development. *Psychology and Aging*, 9, 274–286.

Shing, Y. L., Werkle-Bergner, M., Li, S.-C, and Lindenberger, U. (2007). Associative and strategic components of memory: A life-span dissociation. *Journal of Experimental Psychology: General*, 137, 495–513.

Simonton, D. K. (1991). Career landmarks in science: Individual differences and interdisciplinary contrasts. *Developmental Psychology*, 27, 119–130.

Small, B. J. and Bäckman, L. (1997). Cognitive correlates of mortality: Evidence from a population-based sample of very old adults. *Psychology and Aging*, 12, 309–313.

Small, B. J., and McEvoy, C. M. (2008). Does participation in cognitive activities buffer age-related cognitive decline? In S. M. Hofer and D. F. Alwin (eds.), *Handbook of cognitive aging* (pp. 575–586). Thousand Oaks, CA: Sage Publications.

Smith, J., and Baltes, P. B. (1990). Wisdom-related knowledge: Age/cohort differences in response to life-planning problems. *Developmental Psychology*, 26, 494–505.

Smith, J., Staudinger, U. M., and Baltes, P. B. (1994). Occupational settings facilitating *wisdom*-related knowledge: The sample case of clinical psychologists. *Journal of Consulting and Clinical Psychology*, 62, 989–999.

Soederberg Miller, L. M., and Gagne, D. D. (2005). Effect of age and control beliefs on resource allocation during reading. *Aging, Neuropsychology, and Cognition*, 12, 129–148.

Souchay, C., Moulin, C. J. A., Clarys, D., Taconnat, L., and Isingrini, M. (2007). Diminished episodic memory awareness in older adults: Evidence from feeling-of-knowing and recollection. *Consciousness and Cognition*, 16, 769–784.

Stern, Y. (2002). What is cognitive reserve? Theory and research application of the reserve concept. *Journal of the International Neuropsychological Society*, 8, 448–460.

Stern, Y., Alexander, G. E., Prohovinik, I. *et al.*, (1995). Relationship between lifetime occupation and parietal flow: Implications for a reserve against Alzheimer's disease pathology. *Neurology*, 45, 55–60.

Stine-Morrow, E. A. L. (2007). The Dumbledore hypothesis of cognitive aging. *Current Directions in Psychological Science*, 16, 295–299.

Thomae, H. (1987). Altersformen – Wege zu ihrer methodischen und begrifflichen Erfassung. In U. Lehr and H. Thomae (eds.), *Formen seelischen Alterns: Ergebnisse der Bonner Gerontologischen Längsschnittstudie (BOLSA)* (pp. 173–195). Stuttgart, Germany: Enke.

Wagner, R. K., and Sternberg, R. J. (1985). Practical intelligence in real-world pursuits: The role of tacit knowledge. *Journal of Personality and Social Psychology*, 49, 436–458.

Waite, A., Bebbington, P., Skelton-Robinson, M., and Orrell, M. (2004). Life events, depression, and social support in dementia. *British Journal of Clinical Psychology*, 43, 313–324.

West, R. L., Thorn, R. M., and Bagwell, D. K. (2003). Memory performance and beliefs as a function of goal setting and aging. *Psychology and Aging*, 18, 111–125.

Willis, S. L. (2001). Methodological issues in behavioral intervention research with the elderly. In J. E. Birren and K. W. Schaie (eds.), *Handbook of the psychology of aging* (5th edn., pp. 78–108). San Diego, CA: Academic Press.

Wilson, R. J., and Bennett, D. A. (2003). Cognitive activity and risk of Alzheimer's disease. *Current Directions in Psychological Science*, 12, 87–91.

Zacks, R., Hasher, L., Li, K. Z. H. (2000). Human memory. In F. I. M. Craik and T. A. Salthouse (eds.), *The handbook of aging and cognition* (2nd edn., pp. 293–357). Mahwah, NJ: Erlbaum.

6 Why do some people thrive while others succumb to disease and stagnation? Personality, social relations, and resilience

Margaret L. Kern and Howard S. Friedman

Abstract

This chapter focuses on the role that personality plays in resilience across the lifespan. The concept of personality captures a combination of genetic, familial, social, and cultural elements, and thus is very useful in understanding differential patterns of development. In particular, this chapter highlights findings from our work with the Terman Life Cycle Study, the longest longitudinal study conducted to date, to demonstrate how core aspects of the individual may impact how he or she travels life's pathways and reacts to life's challenges. Our findings suggest that temperamental predispositions, internal stress, coping responses, social relationships, and health behaviors may all be relevant to whether an individual will thrive and stay healthy in the face of challenge or succumb to illness and disease. By identifying the mechanisms involved, we can better understand risk and intervene more effectively, with the goal of increasing resilience as people age.

It is easy to observe striking individual differences in healthy aging. Consider these two cases drawn from our lifespan studies of longevity. Elmer was constantly on the go – involved in everything and friends with everyone. In the morning he raised funds for a benefit concert to support the children's hospital; in the afternoon he bowled with his buddies; in the evening he cared for his wife and enjoyed the company of his children and grandchildren. Although he had to change jobs at the age of 50, was diagnosed with prostate cancer at the age of 67, had a major heart attack at the age of 80, and lived through a series of personal and financial setbacks, he recovered from each challenge and lived a productive, fulfilling life up until the day of his death at the age of 92. In stark contrast, Ida was a reserved, sedentary woman. She loved to read, but as she aged, she developed diabetes at the age of 75, gradually lost her vision, and subsequently slipped into depression. Dementia then appeared, and she slowly detached from life until her death at the age of 93.

Trajectories across adulthood and later life outcomes can look very different, depending on the individual. For some, there are chronic illnesses, frayed relationships, cognitive impairment, or deterioration toward an early death. Others lead a life of personal fulfillment and many productive years. What distinguishes these different patterns and outcomes? A web of factors leads to health and resilience or disease and stagnation; in most cases, there is no simple cause or cure. Understanding the details of this complexity allows for better-informed theories, empirical studies, and interventions.

In this chapter, we focus on the role that personality plays in resilience across the lifespan. Personality captures a combination of genetic, familial, social, and cultural elements, and thus is very useful in understanding different patterns of development. Individual differences matter for resilience, health, and longevity, but not in a simple manner; we are influenced by our histories, present circumstances, and future expectations. Across the life-course, lives unfold and personalities interact with both random and non-random social contexts.

Healthy aging and resilience: a multidimensional process

Over the last century, along with the general demographic of a graying population, notions of health and aging have changed considerably. In the early 1900s, the average life-expectancy in developed countries was from 35 to 55 years, with acute infectious diseases such as tuberculosis and influenza being the primary causes of death. The life-expectancy at birth is now over 77 years, and the average healthy adult will live well into his or her eighties (Centers for Disease Control and Prevention, 2007; US Department of Health and Human Services, 2000). Changes in living conditions and public health – better nutrition, vaccinations, sanitary and less-crowded living environments – had the primary influence; but new and improved pharmaceuticals and medical care also substantially contributed. However, there is now a much higher prevalence of chronic illnesses, with cardiovascular disease and cancer being the overwhelmingly predominant causes of diseases and death in adulthood. At both the individual and societal level, there is increasing focus not only on length of life, but also on aging in a healthy, connected, and productive manner. This is termed *successful or healthy aging*.

Health can be conceptualized as a state or as a process. The former derives from the traditional biomedical model; the latter extends from the biopsychosocial model (Friedman and Adler, 2007; Ryff and Singer, 1998). In the traditional biomedical perspective, health is defined as a lack of disease, disability, and pathological breakdown. That is, you are healthy until illness strikes, and medicine aims to identify and fix symptoms to re-establish a state of non-illness. From this perspective, aging is a natural, progressive breakdown of physiological systems until death, and successful aging involves accepting and managing this decline (Aguerre and Bouffard, 2003; Anantharaman, 1979; Chapman, 2005; Havighurst, 1961; Siegler, Bosworth, and Elias 2003). The resilient are those who recover – the heart attack victim who survives, the cancer patient who goes into remission. In contrast, the biopsychosocial perspective defines health as a general sense of well-being that evolves over time, and refers not only to physical well-being, but also includes mental, cognitive, social, and functional components (World Health Organization, 1948). Health is more than a singular outcome to achieve; it involves a process of challenge, negotiation, and adaptation that unfolds across the life-course (Aldwin, Spiro, and Park, 2006; Aldwin *et al.*, 2001; Baltes, Lindenberger, and Staudinger, 2006; Baltes, Staudinger, and Lindenberger, 1999; Clipp, Pavalko, and Elder, 1992). The resilient are those who face major challenges across one or more domains and yet find ways to adapt.

From this life-course biopsychosocial perspective, individuals develop specific skills, select situations, build resources across multiple domains of life, and attempt to maneuver challenges that arise. The person must find ways to cope with or adapt to these changes, either through shaping and controlling the surrounding environment, or by adapting and controlling inner thoughts and feelings (Rook, Charles, and Heckhausen, 2007; Schultz and Heckhausen, 1996). Success involves negotiating interdependent challenges across the lifespan. Health continues when balance across multiple life domains is maintained.

Length of life is also important to consider. After death, there is no health. Although such a formulation may seem simplistic at first glance, there are important reasons, both conceptual and analytical, to consider quality-of-life years (Diehr and Patrick, 2003; Kaplan, 1994, 2003). That is, we need to consider both the number of years lived and the health quality of each year. Further, measures of healthy aging are often subjective in nature (e.g., self-rated health, life satisfaction, mental well-being) and share method and definitional variance with psychosocial predictors of interest. Longevity is a valid, distinct, objective outcome that temporally follows other variables.

Resilience can be defined as successful functioning despite serious challenge or chronic stress (Cicchetti and Valentino, 2006; Masten,

2006). It is a dynamic process that unfolds across the life-course and necessarily involves both the individual's trajectory and his or her current psychosocial context. Together, healthy aging and longevity are consequential outcomes that can serve as markers of personal resilience.

Personality: a framework for studying resilience

Who recovers from challenge, remains alive, and ages in a healthy manner? What distinguishes these individuals from other, less resilient individuals? As our models and theories become more complex, nuanced, and representative of actual real-world processes, personality research can capture the biopsychosocial processes that demonstrate both stability and change across time, providing a framework for understanding personal resilience within the individual's social context (Friedman, 2007; MacKinnon and Luecken, 2008; Smith and Spiro, 2002).

Links between the person and health go back thousands of years. The ancient Greeks thought of the body as consisting of four humors, which were extended to personality-type characteristics and health outcomes: phlegmatic (apathetic, associated with rheumatism); choleric (hostile, associated with feverish diseases); melancholic (sad, associated with depression, degenerative diseases, and cancer); and sanguine (ruddy, associated with optimism and health). Hippocrates, Galen, and their followers believed that disease stemmed from an imbalance of these humors. Because the Greeks were such keen observers, it is perhaps not so surprising that modern research efforts have returned to focusing on linking negative traits such as repression, alexithymia, depression, hostility, and negativity with disease outcomes. For example, hostility has been associated with increased risk of heart disease and greater mortality risk (Bunde and Suls, 2006; Caspi, Roberts, and Shiner, 2005; Smith, 2006; Smith et al., 2004). Neuroticism and depression have been associated with poorer health, although there are still unanswered questions concerning the links to objective health outcomes (such as mortality) versus perceived well-being (Charles et al., 2008; Friedman, 2007; Friedman and Booth-Kewley, 1987; Mroczek and Spiro, 2007; Rosmalen et al., 2007; Shipley et al., 2007; Stone and Costa, 1990; Suls and Bunde, 2005).

The dominant model in modern personality research is the Five-Factor Model (or the Big Five). Although the model has limitations, it offers a general framework for structuring studies on personality and health (Carver and Miller, 2006; Caspi et al., 2005; Duberstein et al.,

1999; Smith and Williams, 1992). The main factors are typically labeled agreeableness (cooperative, trusting, kind, generous); conscientiousness (orderly, achievement motivated, responsible, planful); extraversion (sociable, assertive, active); neuroticism (anxious, depressive, experiencing the world as distressful); and openness intellect (imaginative, creative, tolerant, intellectual).

In recent years, attention in personality research has shifted from a sole focus on negative traits to positive, sanguine-type traits, such as optimism, extraversion, and conscientiousness (Friedman, 2007; Goodwin and Friedman, 2006; Smith, 2006). A recent meta-analysis found that higher levels of conscientiousness are consistently linked to lower mortality risk (Kern and Friedman, 2008). In fact, the predictive value of a conscientious, dependable personality on health and longevity appears as strong as or stronger than many risk factors, including socioeconomic status and IQ (Batty *et al.*, 2009; Deary *et al.*, 2008; Ozer and Benet-Martinez, 2006; Roberts *et al.*, 2007). Individual differences clearly matter when considering later life outcomes such as health and resilience.

Linking personality and health

By studying differential relations between aspects of personality, the social context, and multiple components of health across long periods of time, we can better identify potential mechanisms involved. Conceptually, personality and health can be linked through various pathways (e.g., Friedman *et al.*, 1993; Smith, 2006). For example, Figure 6.1 presents several likely links – through the behaviors people engage in, physiological reactions to internal and external challenges, underlying biological factors that impact both health and personality, and social influences and relationships that occur over time.

According to the *behavioral model*, personality influences the behaviors that people engage in, which subsequently impact health and well-being. Key health behaviors include preventive behaviors such as nutrition, physical activity, sleeping well, and receiving immunizations and regular medical check-ups; and risky behaviors, such as drug and alcohol abuse, smoking, and risky sex (Gochman, 1997). It is commonly acknowledged that engaging in health-protective behaviors and avoiding risky behaviors link to better health and lower mortality risk, with the strongest association evident for smoking (US Department of Health and Human Services, 2000). There is also ample evidence linking personality to health behaviors (e.g., Caspi *et al.*, 1997; Markey, Markey, and Tinsley, 2003), with conscientiousness being most consistently related to more health-protective behaviors and fewer risky

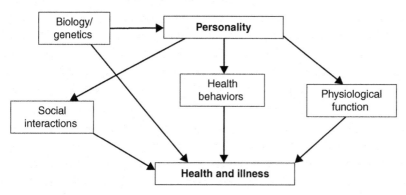

Figure 6.1. Pathways linking personality and health outcomes.
Copyright © Howard S. Friedman.

behaviors (Bogg and Roberts, 2004). Long-term studies have suggested that health behaviors may partially mediate the link between personality and health outcomes, but there remains much unexplained variance, indicating that other pathways are also relevant (Friedman *et al.*, 1995; Hampson *et al.*, 2007).

According to the *internal stress model*, personality influences how people react to stressors encountered in the internal and external environment. People vary tremendously in the amount of objective and subjective stress experienced, perceptions of stressful events, and coping responses; these in turn can affect psychophysiological responses. In particular, high levels of stress can trigger a state in which the heart beats faster, breathing speeds up, cortisol levels increase, inflammation increases, and immune function is depressed – an elaboration of the classic flight-or-fight response first proposed by Walter Cannon in the 1920s (Cannon, 1932; Kemeny, 2007). Although in the short term this reaction may be adaptive, in the long term (i.e., regularly reacting with hostility, anxiety, and depression), such a chronic response pattern becomes detrimental. Over time, negative psycho-emotional reaction patterns disrupt metabolism, immune function, and physiological rhythms, increasing susceptibility to illness, disease, and general breakdown (Kemeny, 2007; McEwen, 2006). Illness in turn further affects psychological functioning, creating a negative cycle toward ill-being.

According to the *genetic* or *temperamental predisposition* model, relations between personality and health or longevity are spurious, stemming from an underlying tendency to be both maladjusted and unhealthy. For example, there is some evidence that serotonin is linked to higher levels of conscientiousness, lower levels of impulsiveness, and genetic variations in systems affecting cortisol responses (Carver and Miller, 2006, Wand *et al.*, 2002). Thus, underlying biological differences may drive personality–health associations. More work with animal and behavioral genetic studies, along with advances in neuroscience, may be informative in high-lighting such nuanced biological processes (Cavigelli, 2005; Friedman, 2008; Mehta and Gosling, 2008; Weiss, Bates, and Luciano, 2008).

Personality also links to health outcomes through *social interactions* – early socialization factors, the situations that people select, relation-ships with others, and the overall social, cultural, and historical context. Socialization begins early in life; temperament and early experiences combine to set positive or negative trajectories, and people are subse-quently pulled toward situations and experiences that maintain those patterns (Caspi and Bem, 1990; Caspi and Roberts, 1999; Caspi *et al.*, 2005; Friedman, 2000; Rutter, Kim-Cohen, and Maughan, 2006; Sroufe, 1997; Sroufe *et al.*, 1999). For example, happy, securely attached infants are more likely to develop better social skills, self-confidence, and cognitive skills than difficult, insecurely attached infants (Fraley, 2002; Ranson and Urichuk, 2008; Schneider, Atkinson, and Tardif, 2001). In turn, interactions between the person and the social context affect per-sonal trajectories toward health or illness. Importantly, although early relationships can set the stage for later outcomes, personality, socio-envi-ronmental factors, and the interaction of the two throughout childhood and beyond can alter trajectories and subsequent outcomes.

Most likely, there is no single pathway involved; rather, multiple bio-psychosocial forces interact to drive the relations we see. This key point is often overlooked by more narrowly focused empirical research.

Insight from the Terman Life Cycle Study

To understand how life processes unfold over time, discover mediating mechanisms, and determine moderators of different relationships, it is essential to use long-term longitudinal studies. Yet to truly understand lifelong biopsychosocial processes, collecting appropriate data would involve a lifelong commitment, extending well beyond the lifetime and resources (both in terms of time and funding) of a single individual. Archival studies offer a way to study processes over time. By creatively using and expanding existing resources, we can address lifespan ques-tions that are impossible in shorter-term studies (Block, 1993; Friedman, 2000).

One such study is the Terman Life Cycle Study. The study was begun in 1922 by Lewis M. Terman, initially as a descriptive study of gifted Californian children (Terman *et al.*, 1925). Between 1922 and 1928, over 1,500 children and adolescents were assessed on a broad array of demographic, familial, psychological, cognitive, health, and social variables. Affectionately known as the "Termites", the participants were followed throughout their lives, completing written assessments every five to ten years, with the last formal assessment in 1999. We have supplemented this information by collecting death certificates and creating new psychosocial measures from the data, presenting a full lifespan picture of most of the participants (see Friedman, 2000 for a more complete description). The Terman study is the longest longitudinal study that has been conducted, and the archived information is an immense resource that offers a unique lifespan portrait of these individuals' lives.

Over the past two decades, our research team has studied the lives of these individuals. Together these studies offer insight into pathways towards resilience or stagnation, as individual lives unfold within the context of broader social contexts. What can we learn from this rather extraordinary sample?

Personality effects on longevity

In the first lifespan study with this sample, Friedman and colleagues (1993) examined the effect of childhood personality on mortality risk. At the initial assessment in 1922, parents and teachers rated the children (average 11 years old) on 25 different personality traits. Using a combination of rational assessment and empirical analyses, six different personality characteristics were identified: sociability, self-esteem/motivation, conscientiousness, cheerfulness, energy/activity, and permanency of moods. We gathered death certificates to ascertain and verify age at death, and the personality traits were used to predict how long people lived. Interestingly enough, children who were rated high on conscientiousness were less likely to die at any given age than those who were rated low on conscientiousness. Thus, personality ratings of conscientiousness were important for a very significant health outcome (longevity) across a seven-decade period.

This intriguing finding has been followed up by other studies, using diverse samples; all have found a certain degree of support for this finding. For example, in a group of chronic renal insufficiency patients, more conscientious individuals lived longer over the course of a two-year period (Christensen *et al.*, 2002). Similar findings were found in a group of elderly clergy members (Wilson *et al.*, 2004) and a group of frail elderly adults (Weiss and Costa, 2005). Even conscientious presidents lived longer (McCann, 2005). Extending from this, we meta-analytically combined the results of 20 studies, and found a significant protective effect of conscientiousness on mortality risk (Kern and Friedman, 2008), similar in magnitude to the effect of IQ, and stronger than the effect of socio-economic status (Roberts *et al.*, 2007).

Taking this a step further, in a lifespan analysis, patterns of personality should be examined. For the Termites, we developed a measure of adult personality, representing four of the Big Five factors (conscientiousness, extraversion, neuroticism, and agreeableness), using the 1940 reports (when the participants were about 30 years old) (Martin and Friedman, 2000). Combining child and adult reports, both childhood and adult conscientiousness independently predicted lower mortality risk (Martin, Friedman, and Schwartz, 2007). That is, individuals who were high on conscientiousness as a child or as an adult were at a lower mortality risk throughout their lives. Further, individuals who were consistently high on conscientiousness were at the lowest mortality risk, individuals who were consistently low on conscientiousness were at the highest mortality risk, and others were in the middle. Personality differences are clearly relevant to later life health and longevity, but the question becomes how personality and health are linked (what are the mechanisms involved) and under what conditions a particular relationship holds (for whom and when).

Early experiences: parental divorce in childhood

Cumulative pathways to older-age health and resilience need to be considered by examining the sequelae of personal inclinations, beginning with early influences that set up trajectories toward or away from health. In several early studies with the Terman participants, we examined the impact of experiencing parental divorce as a child on lifelong health and longevity. Other researchers have linked the experience of parental divorce to poor child, adolescent and adult health and well-being outcomes; we extended this approach across the lifespan. For the Termites, experiencing parental divorce prior to age 21 resulted in an almost four-year decrease in average life-expectancy (Schwartz *et al.*, 1995). The increased mortality risk could not be explained by childhood health status, familial socioeconomic status, or childhood personality traits. Further, losing a parent to death was not associated with such dramatic increases in risk, suggesting that it was something about the conflict of the divorce itself that increased risk for poor outcomes, rather than not having a parent available.

In a follow-up study, we examined potential mediators, including education, health behaviors, social relationships, and psychological well-being (Tucker *et al.*, 1997). The risk of parental divorce could partially be explained by the activities that individuals subsequently engaged in throughout their lives. For example, men who experienced parental divorce were less involved in the community and pursued less education, women were more likely to smoke, and both men and women were more likely to experience conflict and divorce in their own marriages. Supporting developmental theories of the pervasive influence of early experiences, these findings suggest that facing parental divorce as a child may mark the beginning of a trajectory toward ill-being.

Here is where the idea of resilience enters the picture. Although early experiences such as parental divorce increase risk for adverse outcomes, children are not doomed to failure. For the Terman children, many participants who experienced parental divorce did not die prematurely or experience adverse health and well-being consequences. What distinguished these resilient individuals? To examine this matter, we examined pathways leading to health and well-being versus maladjustment and mortality in the face of parental divorce (Martin *et al.*, 2005). Potential predictor variables included positive and negative family attributes, marital stability and satisfaction, life satisfaction and achievement, and risky health behaviors (obesity, smoking, and alcohol abuse). Although parental divorce was related to worse health habits, less marital stability, and adverse health outcomes, this risk was ameliorated among individuals, especially men, who achieved a sense of personal satisfaction by midlife. Figure 6.2 displays this relationship. Despite experiencing early adversity, individuals who managed to get their lives back on track and found a sense of meaning and achievement by midlife tended to avert detrimental outcomes as they aged.

Further, boys from families with more positive family attributes had a slightly higher mortality risk than those with fewer, a finding consistent with the conclusions of other researchers (e.g., Amato, Loomis, and Booth, 1995; Wheaton, 1990) who have found that dismantling a seemingly functional family may be more traumatic than the dissolution of a clearly troubled family. Importantly, although it might be expected that life satisfaction at middle age would be predictive of lower mortality risk for all, we found that it made a difference only for those from divorced homes. That is, it was through challenge that benefit arose; finding meaning in the face of difficult experiences is seemingly relevant for achieving health and well-being in older age.

Social stress: marital history

Modern personality theory suggests that life stresses and events such as marriage and divorce, career outcomes, and health events are not

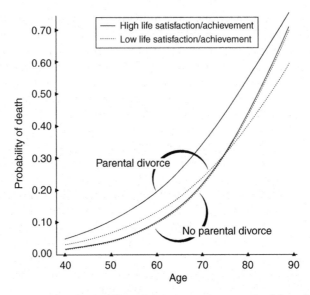

Figure 6.2. Probability of dying at a given age by life satisfaction and parental divorce status. Copyright © Howard S. Friedman.

fully random, but are influenced by personality (Caspi and Roberts, 1999; Caspi *et al.*, 2005). For example, evidence suggests that people self-select into certain marriages that ultimately end in divorce (Johnson *et al.*, 2004; Larson and Holman, 1994). One way that personality and health are linked involves *tropisms* – movements toward or away from suitable environments, situations, and experiences (Friedman, 2000). Early experiences set the individual on a positive or negative trajectory, and then personality-based tropisms pull the individual towards certain environments that subsequently maintain patterned responses and life-styles over time. Such continuity is likely to continue, unless the internal or external milieu changes enough to override habitual patterns (Caspi and Bem, 1990).

Divorce can be one such change in people's lives, with serious dele-terious health effects. It is commonly believed that marriage itself offers important health benefits – there is common advice to "get married to stay healthy." Although married men do tend to live longer, research suggests a more complicated picture. Personality, health behaviors, the social context, the environment, and marriage impact one another over time. For example, using data from the Mills Longitudinal Study of Women, Roberts and Bogg (2004) examined the interrelations of social responsibility (conscientiousness), health behaviors (drug and alcohol use), and socio-environmental factors (marriage and work) over a 30-year period. Individuals who were conscientious developed more stable marriages and used fewer substances, consequently decreasing risk of adverse health outcomes. At the same time, improving health behaviors, entering into a stable marital relationship, and increased work responsibility increased levels of conscientiousness over time. Such findings support a sequential interactional perspective, in which an interplay occurs among personality, behaviors, and situations over time.

Again, the Terman participants offer a fascinating insight into the complexity of these lifespan processes. We examined the association between marital status and mortality risk, focusing on whether links are due to the benefits of being married, the detrimental effects of marital breakup, selection effects (i.e., troubled individuals choosing marriages that are bound for trouble), or some combination (Tucker *et al.*, 1996). Mortality risk was compared across the following four groups: consistently married; inconsistently married (currently married but previously divorced); currently separated or divorced; and never married individuals. In addition, several psychosocial factors were included as follows: childhood personality (conscientiousness, cheerfulness, and permanency of moods); midlife self-reported health; and social ties. As expected, individuals, especially men, who were divorced at midlife were at higher mortality risk as they aged and consistently married individuals were at the lowest risk. Interestingly, for never-married individuals, other social ties ameliorated any increased risk due to staying single; that is, as long as unmarried individuals had other significant social relationships in their lives (such as friends and family members), a lack of a spouse was inconsequential. Importantly, the inconsistent group (individuals who were currently married but had experienced marital dissolution in the past) was at significantly higher mortality risk than the consistently married group (despite their current marriage), suggesting that the earlier conflict may have continued to exert a negative influence. Thus, it is not simply the state of being married that is beneficial.

Moreover, personality played a role. Conscientious individuals were both more likely to be consistently married and to live longer. That is, part of the relation between conscientiousness and longevity was driven by a personality-based tendency toward stable relationships, which in turn related to lower mortality risk. This points to the tropisms of personality; individuals are pulled towards certain relationships that are more or less likely to breed conflict, and subsequently lead towards health or ill-being in older age.

Personality and situation interactions: career success

Work and career can be sources of both stress and social integration. Focusing on the male Terman participants, we examined whether personality characteristics moderate health outcomes. Careers are an integral part of life; during early and mid-adulthood years, more time is spent at work than on any other activity. Aside from the obvious function of providing income, careers relate to social roles, self-concept, ambition, and well-being, and may have long-lasting social and health outcomes. Conscientiousness has been linked to better work performance (Barrick and Mount, 1991; Gelissen and de Graaf, 2006; Ozer and Benet-Martinez, 2006; Roberts *et al.*, 2007; Schmidt and Hunter, 1992), and so we investigated the role of conscientiousness in career and health outcomes.

In 1940, Terman and his colleagues rated male participants on vocational success (Terman, 1942). The 150 most successful and 150 least successful men were identified, based on their occupational prestige, job performance, leadership in the workplace, honors received, and annual income. Terman then compared the two groups on a large range of child and young adult variables. By young adulthood, different pathways were evident. Family background, parental marital stability, personality (including drive to achieve), and marriage separated the successful from the unsuccessful.

Extending these early analyses, we examined the relation between childhood conscientiousness, career success, and mortality risk through 2006 (Kern *et al.*, 2009). Again, the tropisms of personality were apparent – more conscientious children were more likely to have successful careers, which in turn predicted lower mortality risk. However, the two factors independently predicted mortality risk. That is, it is not simply the case that some men are more dependable and in control of their impulses and therefore go on to more successful careers and longer lives. Rather, more complex processes appear to influence mortality risk, likely involving biopsychosocial factors across the lifespan.

The story becomes more interesting when we look at the interaction of personality and success. As shown in Figure 6.3, childhood conscientiousness moderated the effect of career on mortality risk. For successful individuals, conscientiousness made little difference – both career success and conscientiousness related to lower mortality risk. For unsuccessful individuals, however, conscientiousness attenuated the negative effects of low success. Again, these findings point to the need to consider characteristic patterns within the context of life events, and to consider both direct and indirect personality-related pathways underlying resilience.

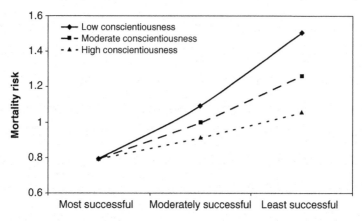

Figure 6.3. Interaction of childhood conscientiousness and adult career success on mortality risk, for men. Copyright © Howard S. Friedman.

Disease-prone versus distress-prone: underlying pathways

There seems little doubt that good mental health is generally associated with good physical health and that neurotic patterns like chronic anxiety and depression are associated with various health problems. Yet the extent to which personal characteristics lead to disease versus simply increasing the report of distress remains unclear.

Two decades ago, Friedman and Booth-Kewley (1987) meta-analytically reviewed the relation between emotional aspects of personality and chronic disease, and suggested a disease-prone personality, in which negative emotions (such as depression, anxiety, and hostility) are generally associated with increased risk of chronic illness. The question remains, however, whether neurotic traits predict actual organic disease, or simply more subjective, distress-prone elements (Stone and Costa, 1990; Watson and Pennebaker, 1989). Increasing evidence suggests that neuroticism indeed predicts increased distress *and* disease, yet pieces of the causal models remain clouded (Charles *et al.*, 2008; DeNeve and Cooper, 1998; Smith and Gallo, 2001; Suls and Bunde, 2005). For example, although personality is generally considered relatively stable, changes in neuroticism may be more important than initial levels in predicting health and well-being outcomes, suggesting the need to consider contextual effects (Mroczek and Spiro; 2007). Similarly, it is unclear whether positive traits predict a lack of disease or simply higher perceptions of health status, especially within the context of lifelong social experiences.

To begin to address these complex conceptual issues, we again turned to the lives of the Termites for insight (Friedman, Kern, and Reynolds, 2010). Using data from the 1986 late-life assessment (when the participants were in their seventies), we empirically developed a multi-component measure of healthy aging that included physical health (absence of serious chronic disease and physical decline), mental well-being (mood, life satisfaction, perceived mental health), social competence (good relations and ties with others), productivity (work, purpose, goals to contribute), and cognitive function (lack of memory and cognitive problems). We also included longevity as an objective and key measure of health. Adult personality (neuroticism, conscientiousness, extraversion, and agreeableness), measured 45 years prior, was used to predict late-life health and longevity.

Importantly, the results suggest that health outcomes differentially related to personality traits measured much earlier in life, and point to some potential underlying pathways linking personality and health. Conscientiousness related to productivity, physical health, and longevity. Combined with the findings from our other studies, this suggests multiple direct and indirect pathways linking conscientiousness to health, likely involving better social relationships, better health habits, and more involvement in life. Extraversion and agreeableness were more relevant to social and subjective outcomes than to physical health or longevity, especially for women. These interpersonal traits have been inconsistently linked to health outcomes and quite possibly work in tangent with other traits and social factors. To the extent that they promote healthy social relationships, good health habits, and interpersonal buffers from stress, they may be helpful, but to the extent that they breed unhealthy habits or dependent relationships, they may be harmful.

Similarly, neuroticism was related more to subjective health outcomes than to longevity. In fact, whereas high levels of neuroticism generally related to poor health outcomes, for the smaller group of men that made it to older age, high neuroticism was protective from mortality risk. Although negative emotionality is often considered detrimental, neuroticism may become beneficial in face of certain life challenges (Taga, Friedman, and Martin, 2009). For example, it may be that distress leads to subsequent beneficial health behaviors, such as better adherence to medical advice and greater avoidance of substances such as alcohol and tobacco when facing the life changes of bereavement. Or, perhaps third variables are relevant; for example, magnified stress and worry experienced by neurotic men when caring for a terminally ill wife may result in a greater degree of emotional relief when the suffering has ended.

Returning to the pathways described earlier in this chapter, it may be that links between conscientiousness, agreeableness, extraversion and later-life health may be more external and socio-behavioral (e.g., staying active, achieving objective success, positive social relationships, and engaging in healthier behaviors), whereas links between neuroticism and later-life health may be more internally based (e.g., negative interpretation of events, increased perceived and actual stress, and negative emotions). Gender also plays a role. Although these data did not allow an explicit tracing of the relevant causal pathways, women were higher on many of the psychosocial dimensions relevant to good health, such as social relationships and health-protective behaviors, whereas pathways were less straightforward for men. Much work remains to be done in this area, but these findings highlight important concepts and pathways that should be pursued in future research.

Conclusion

What does this mean for our understanding of resilience? Resilience is not merely the ability to recover quickly from challenge or misfortune. It involves flexibility and adaptability to stress rather than toughness. Resilience is not a personality trait but rather an emergent attribute – a quality that appears with the appropriate combination of predispositions, behaviors, and socio-environmental circumstances. Further, psychological and physical resilience are not necessarily separate entities, but are often two sides of the same coin. Employing more multifaceted, nuanced, and representative models of real-world processes, we can better understand how individual differences unfold across the lifespan to influence resilience. Core aspects of an individual's personality may affect how he or she travels life's pathways, which in turn impacts later life outcomes, including health and longevity.

What are the practical implications of our findings? Too many interventions are targeted at a single health-relevant behavior or at a single age group. Our studies of personality and health across the lifespan have shown that early experiences carry over and affect later-life challenges and behaviors, and thus important life events should not be ignored. Further, *patterns* of behaviors and reactions, in tangent with consequential experiences and social relationships, need to be considered.

Our findings suggest that temperamental predispositions, internal stress and coping, social relationships, and health behaviors may all be relevant to whether an individual will thrive in the face of challenge or succumb to depression, illness, and disease. In examining why family stability, marital stability, and career success are related to health and longevity, it would be a mistake to design an intervention to promote *states* (e.g., "get married") without considering the effects of the intervention on the various complex long-term patterns that people bring to the intervention. Similarly, because personality is so relevant to the effects of life challenge, interventions should take into account the likely multiple effects on a particular individual. For an individual facing career or social setbacks, his or her personality matters a great deal in understanding and affecting later health outcomes.

By identifying lifespan relationships and the underlying mechanisms involved, we can better identify individuals at risk for negative outcomes, determine critical periods of influence, quantify accumulating risk, and intervene more effectively, with the goal of increasing resilience as people age. Although much work remains to be done in this area, differential associations among personality traits, socio-behavioral activities, and health and longevity outcomes across the decades are clearly important, and will be informative to our overall understanding of personality, health, and resilience.

Acknowledgments

This research was supported by NIA grant AG027001 (C. A. Reynolds, PI).

REFERENCES

Aguerre, C., and Bouffard, L. (2003). Le vieillissement réussi: Théories, recherches et applications cliniques [Successful aging: Theory, research, and clinical applications]. *Revue Québécoise de Psychologie*, 24, 107–129.

Aldwin, C. M., Spiro, A., III, Levenson, M. R., and Cupertino, A. P. (2001). Longitudinal findings from the normative aging study: III. Personality, individual health trajectories, and mortality. *Psychology and Aging*, 16, 450–465.

Aldwin, C. M., Spiro, A., and Park, C. L. (2006). Health, behavior, and optimal aging: A life span developmental perspective. In J. E. Birren, and K. W. Schaire (eds.), *Handbook of the psychology of aging* (6th edn., pp. 85–104). Amsterdam, Netherlands: Elsevier.

Amato, P. R., Loomis, L. S., and Booth, A. (1995). Parental divorce, marital conflict, and offspring well-being during early adulthood. *Social Forces*, 73, 895–915.

Anatharaman, R. N. (1979). Activity vs. disengagement for successful ageing in old age. *Journal of Psychological Researches*, 23, 110–112.

Baltes, P. B., Lindenberger, U., and Staudinger, U. M. (2006). Life span theory in developmental psychology. In R. M. Lerner and W. Damon (eds.), *Handbook of child psychology*, vol. I: *Theoretical models of human development* (6th edn., pp. 569–664). Hoboken, NJ: Wiley.

Baltes, P. B., Staudinger, U. M., and Lindenberger, U. (1999). Lifespan psychology: Theory and application to intellectual functioning. *Annual Review of Psychology*, 50, 471–507.

Barrick, M. R., and Mount, M. K. (1991). The Big Five personality dimensions and job performance: A meta analysis. *Personality Psychology*, 44, 1–26.

Batty, G. D., Wennerstad, K. M., Smith, G. D., *et al.* (2009). IQ in early adulthood and mortality by middle age: Cohort study of 1 million Swedish men. *Epidemiology*, 20, 100–109.

Block, J. (1993). Studying personality the long way. In D. C. Funder, R. D. Parke, C. Tomlinson-Keasey, and K. Widaman (eds.), *Studying lives through time: Personality and development* (pp. 9–41). Washington, DC: American Psychological Association.

Bogg, T., and Roberts, B. W. (2004). Conscientiousness and health-related behaviors: A meta-analysis of the leading behavioral contributors to mortality. *Psychological Bulletin*, 130, 887–919.

Bunde, J., and Suls, J. (2006). A quantitative analysis of the relationship between the Cook-Cedley Hostility Scale and traditional coronary artery disease risk factors. *Health Psychology*, 25, 493–500.

Cannon, W. B. (1932). *Wisdom of the body*. New York: W. W. Norton.

Carver, C. S., and Miller, C. J. (2006). Relations of serotonin function to personality: Current views and a key methodological issue. *Psychiatry Research*, 144, 1–15.

Caspi, A., and Bem, D. J. (1990). Personality continuity and change across the life course. In L. Pervin (ed.), *Handbook of personality: Theory and research* (pp. 549–575). New York: Guilford.

Caspi, A., and Roberts, B. W. (1999). Personality continuity and change across the life course. In L. A. Pervin and O. P. John (eds.), *Handbook of personality: Theory and research* (2nd edn, pp. 300–326). New York: Guilford Press.

Caspi, A., Begg, D., Dickson, N., *et al.* (1997). Personality differences predict health-risk behaviors in young adulthood: Evidence from a longitudinal study. *Journal of Personality and Social Psychology*, 73, 1052–1063.

Caspi, A., Roberts, B. W., and Shiner, R. (2005). Personality development. *Annual Review of Psychology*, 56, 453–484.

Cavigelli, S. A. (2005). Animal personality and health. *Behaviour*, 142, 1223–1244.

Centers for Disease Control and Prevention. (2007). Improving the health of older Americans: A CDC priority. *Chronic Disease Notes and Reports*, 18, 1–7.

Chapman, S. A. (2005). Theorizing about aging well: Constructing a narrative. *Canadian Journal on Aging*, 24, 9–18.

Charles, S. T., Gatz, M., Kato, K., and Pedersen, N. L. (2008). Physical health twenty-five years later: The predictive ability of neuroticism. *Health Psychology*, 27, 369–378.

Christensen, A. J., Ehlers, S. L., Wiebe, J. S., *et al.* (2002). Patient personality and mortality: A 4-year prospective examination of chronic renal insufficiency. *Health Psychology*, 21, 315–320.

Cicchetti, D., and Valentino, K. (2006). An ecological transactional perspective on child maltreatment: Failure of the average expectable environment and its influence upon child development. In D. Cicchetti and D. J. Cohen (eds.), *Developmental psychopathology*, vol. III; *Risk, disorder, and adaptation* (2 nd edn., pp. 129–201). New York: Wiley.

Clipp, E. C., Pavalko, E. K., and Elder, H. H. Jr. (1992). Trajectories of health: In concept and empirical pattern. *Behavior, Health, and Aging*, 2, 159–179.

Deary, I., Batty, G. D., Pattie, A. and Gale, C. R. (2008). More intelligent, more dependable children live longer: A 55-year longitudinal study of a representative sample of the Scottish nation. *Psychological Science*, 19, 874–880.

DeNeve, K. M., and Cooper, H. (1998). The happy personality: A meta-analysis of 137 personality traits and subjective well-being. *Psychological Bulletin*, 124, 197–229.

Diehr, P., and Patrick, D. L. (2003). Trajectories of health for older adults: Accounting fully for death. *Annals of Internal Medicine*, 5, 416–421.

Duberstein, P. R., Seidlitz, L., Lyness, J. M., and Conwell, Y. (1999). Dimensional measures and the five-factor model: Clinical implications and research directions. In E. Rosowsky, R. C. Abrams and R. A. Zweig (eds.), *Personality disorders in older adults: Emerging issues in diagnosis and treatment* (pp. 95–117). Mahwah, NJ: Erlbaum.

Fraley, R. C. (2002). Attachment stability from infancy to adulthood: Meta-analysis and dynamic modeling of developmental mechanisms. *Personality and Social Psychology Review*, 6, 123–151.

Friedman, H. S. (2000). Long-term relations of personality, health: Dynamisms, mechanisms, and tropisms. *Journal of Personality*, 68, 1089–1107.

(2007). Personality, disease, and self-healing. In H. S. Friedman and R. C. Silver (eds.), *Foundations of health psychology* (pp. 172–199). New York: Oxford University Press.

(2008). The multiple linkages of personality and disease. *Brain, Behavior, and Immunity*, 22, 668–675.

Friedman, H. S., and Adler, N. E. (2007). The history and background of health psychology. In H. S. Friedman and R. C. Silver (eds.), *Foundations of health psychology* (pp. 3–18). New York: Oxford University Press.

Friedman, H. S., and Booth-Kewley, S. (1987). The "disease-prone personality": A meta-analytic view of the construct. *American Psychologist*, 42, 539–555.

Friedman, H. S., Kern, M. L., and Reynolds, C. A. (2010). Personality and health, subjective well-being, and longevity as adults age. *Journal of Personality*, 78, 179–216.

Friedman, H. S., Tucker, J. S., Schwartz, J. E., *et al.* (1995). Childhood conscientiousness and longevity: Health behaviors and cause of death. *Journal of Personality and Social Psychology*, 68, 696–703.

Friedman, H. S., Tucker, J. S., Tomlinson-Keasey, C., Schwartz, J. E., Wingard, D. L., and Criqui, M. H. (1993). Does childhood personality predict longevity? *Journal of Personality and Social Psychology*, 65, 176–185.

Gelissen, J., and de Graaf, P. M. (2006). Personality, social background, and occupational career success. *Social Science Research*, 35, 702–726.

Gochman, D. S. (1997). Health behavior research: Definitions and diversity. In D. S. Gochman (ed.), *Handbook of healthy behavior research*, vol. I: *Personal and social determinants* (pp. 3–20). New York: Plenum Press.

Goodwin, R. G., and Friedman, H. S. (2006). Health status and the Five Factor personality traits in a nationally representative sample. *Journal of Health Psychology*, 11, 643–654.

Hampson, S. E., Goldberg, L. R., Vogt, T. M., and Dubanoski, J. P. (2007). Mechanisms by which childhood personality traits influence adult health status: Educational attainment and healthy behaviors. *Health Psychology*, 26, 121–125.

Havighurst, R. J. (1961). Successful aging. *The Gerontologist*, 1: 8–13.

Johnson, W., McGue, M., Krueger, R. J., and Bouchard, T. J., Jr. (2004). Marriage and personality: A genetic analysis. *Journal of Personality and Social Psychology*, 86, 285–294.

Kaplan, R. M. (1994). The Ziggy theorem: Toward an outcomes-focused health psychology. *Health Psychology*, 13, 451–460.

(2003). The significance of quality of life in health care. *Quality of Life Research*, 12, 3–16.

Kemeny, M. E. (2007). Psychoneuroimmunology. In H. S. Friedman and R. C. Silver (eds.), *Foundations of health psychology* (pp. 92–116). New York: Oxford University Press.

Kern, M. L., and Friedman, H. S. (2008). Do conscientious individuals live longer? A quantitative review. *Health Psychology*, 27, 505–512.

Kern, M. L., Friedman, H. S., Martin, L. R., Reynolds, C. A., and Luong, G. (2009). Conscientiousness, career success, and longevity: A lifespan analysis. *Annals of Behavioral Medicine*, 37, 154–163.

Larson, J. H., and Holman, T. B. (1994). Premarital predictors of marital quality and stability. *Family Relations: Interdisciplinary Journal of Applied Family Studies*, 43, 228–237.

MacKinnon, D. P., and Luecken, L. J. (2008). How and for whom? Mediation and moderation in health psychology. *Health Psychology*, 27, S99–S100.

Markey, C. N., Markey, P. M., and Tinsley, B. J. (2003). Personality, puberty, and preadolescent girls' risky behaviors: Examining the predictive value of the Five-Factor Model of personality. *Journal of Research in Personality*, 37, 405–419.

Martin, L. R., and Friedman, H. S. (2000). Comparing personality scales across time: An illustrative study of validity and consistency in life-span archival data. *Journal of Personality*, 68, 85–110.

Martin, L. R., Friedman, H. S., Clark, K. M., and Tucker, J. S. (2005). Longevity following the experience of parental divorce. *Social Science and Medicine*, 61, 2177–2189.

Martin, L.R., Friedman, H.S., and Schwartz, J. E. (2007). Personality and mortality risk across the lifespan: The importance of conscientiousness as a biopsychosocial attribute. *Health Psychology*, 26, 428–436.

Masten, A. S. (2006). Developmental psychopathology: Pathways to the future. *International Journal of Behavioral Development*, 31, 38–45.

McCann, S. J. H. (2005). Longevity, big five personality factors, and health behaviors: Presidents from Washington to Nixon. *The Journal of Psychology*, 139, 273–286.

McEwen, B. S. (2006). Protective and damaging effects of stress mediators: Central role of the brain. *Dialogues in Clinical Neuroscience*, 8, 283–293.

Mehta, P. H., and Gosling, S. D. (2008). Bridging human and animal research: A comparative approach to studies of personality and health. *Brain, Behavior, and Immunity*, 22, 651–661.

Mroczek, D. K., and Spiro, A. III. (2007). Personality change influences mortality in older men. *Psychological Science*, 18, 371–376.

Ozer, D. J., and Benet-Martinez, V. (2006). Personality and the prediction of consequential outcomes. *Annual Review of Psychology*, 57, 401–421.

Ranson, K. E., and Urichuk, L. J. (2008). The effect of parent-child attachment relationships on child biopsychosocial outcomes: A review. *Early Child Development and Care*, 178, 129–152.

Roberts, B. W., and Bogg, T. (2004). A longitudinal study of the relationships between conscientiousness and the social environmental factors and substance use behaviors that influence health. *Journal of Personality*, 72, 325–353.

Roberts, B. W., Kuncel, N. R., Shiner, R., Caspi, A., and Goldberg, L. R. (2007). The power of personality: The comparative validity of personality traits, socioeconomic status, and cognitive ability for predicting important life outcomes. *Perspectives on Psychological Science*, 2, 313–345.

Rook, K. S., Charles, S. T., and Heckhausen, J. (2007). Aging and health. In H. S. Friedman and R. C. Silver (eds.), *Foundations of health psychology* (pp. 234–262). New York: Oxford University Press.

Rosmalen, J. G. M., Neeleman, J., Gans, R. O. B., and de Jonge, P. (2007). The association between neuroticism and self-reported common somatic symptoms in a population cohort. *Journal of Psychosomatic Research*, 62, 305–311.

Rutter, M., Kim-Cohen, J., and Maughan, B. (2006). Continuities and discontinuities in psychopathology from childhood to adult life. *Journal of Child Psychology and Psychiatry*, 47, 276–295.

Ryff, C. D., and Singer, B. (1998). The contours of positive human health. *Psychological Inquiry*, 9, 1–28.

Schmidt, F. L., and Hunter, J. E. (1992). Development of a causal model of processes determining job performance. *Current Directions in Psychological Science*, 1, 89–92.

Schneider, B. H., Atkinson, L., and Tardif, C. (2001). Child-parent attachment and children's peer relations: A quantitative review. *Developmental Psychology*, 37, 86–100.

Schultz, R., and Heckhausen, J. (1996). A life span model of successful aging. *American Psychologist*, 51, 702–714.

Schwartz, J. E., Friedman, H. S., Tucker, J. S., Tomlinson-Keasey, C., Wingard, D. L., and Criqui, M. H. (1995). Sociodemographic and psychosocial factors in childhood as predictors of adult mortality. *American Journal of Public Health*, 85, 1237–1245.

Shipley, B. A., Weiss, A., Der, G., Taylor, M. D., and Deary, I. J. (2007). Neuroticism, extraversion, and mortality in the UK health and lifestyle survey: A 21-year prospective cohort study. *Psychosomatic Medicine*, 69, 923–931.

Siegler, I. C., Bosworth, H. B., and Elias, M. F. (2003). Adult development and aging. In A. M. Nezu, C. M. Nezu, and P. A. Geller (eds.), *Handbook of psychology: Health psychology*, vol. IX (pp. 487–510). Hoboken, NJ: John Wiley and Sons.

Smith, T. W. (2006). Personality as risk and resilience in physical health. *Current Directions in Psychological Science*, 15, 227–231.

Smith, T. W., and Gallo, L. C. (2001). Personality traits as risk factors for physical illness. In A. Baum, T. Revenson, and J. Singer (eds.), *Handbook of health psychology* (pp. 139–172). Hillsdale, NJ: Erlbaum.

Smith, T. W., Glazer, K., Ruiz, J. M., and Gallo, L. C. (2004). Hostility, anger, aggressiveness, and coronary heart disease: An interpersonal perspective on personality, emotion, and health. *Journal of Personality. Special Issue: Emotions, Personality, and Health*, 72, 1217–1270.

Smith, T. W., and Spiro, A. (2002). Personality, health, and aging: Prolegomenon for the next generation. *Journal of Research in Personality*, 36, 363–394.

Smith, T. W., and Williams, P. G. (1992). Personality and health: Advantages and limitations of the five-factor model. *Journal of Personality*, 60, 395–423.

Sroufe, L. A. (1997). Psychopathology as an outcome of development. *Development and Psychopathology*, 9, 251–268.

Sroufe, L. A., Carlson, E. A., Levy, A. K., and Egeland, B. (1999). Implications of attachment theory for developmental psychopathology. *Development and Psychopathology*, 11, 1–13.

Stone, S. V., and Costa P.T., Jr. (1990). Disease-prone personality or distress-prone personality? The role of neuroticism in coronary heart disease. In H. S. Friedman (ed.), *Personality and disease* (pp. 178–200). New York: Wiley.

Suls, J., and Bunde, J. (2005). Anger, anxiety, and depression as risk factors for cardiovascular disease: The problems and implications of overlapping affective dimensions. *Psychological Bulletin*, 131, 260–300.

Taga, K. A., Friedman, H. S., and Martin, L. R. (2009). Early personality traits as predictors of mortality risk following conjugal bereavement. *Journal of Personality*, 77, 669–690.

Terman, L. M. (1942). The vocational successes of intellectually gifted individuals. *Occupations*, 20, 493–498.

Terman, L. M., Baldwin, B. T., DeVoss, J. C. et al. (1925). *Genetic studies of genius*, vol. I: *Mental and physical traits of a thousand gifted children*. Stanford, CA: Stanford University Press.

Tucker, J. S., Friedman, H. S., Schwartz, J. E., et al. (1997). Parental divorce: Effects on individual behavior and longevity. *Journal of Personality and Social Psychology*, 73, 381–391.

Tucker, J. S., Friedman, H. S., Wingard, D. L., and Schwartz, J. E. (1996). Marital history at mid-life as a predictor of longevity: Alternative explanations to the protective effect of marriage. *Health Psychology*, 15, 94–101.

US Department of Health and Human Services . (November, 2000). *Healthy people 2010: Understanding and improving health* (2nd edn.). Washington, DC: US Government Printing Office.

Wand, G. S., McCaul, M., Yang, X., *et al.* (2002). The mu-opinid receptor gene polymorphism (A118G) alters HPA axis activation induced by opioid receptor blockade. *Neuropsychopharmacology*, 26, 106–114.

Watson, D., and Pennebaker, J. W. (1989). Health complaints, stress, and distress: Exploring the central role of negative affectivity. *Psychological Review*, 96, 234–254.

Weiss, A., and Costa, P. T. (2005). Domain and facet personality predictors of all-cause mortality among Medicare patients aged 65 to 100. *Psychosomatic Medicine*, 67, 724–733.

Weiss, A., Bates, T. C., and Luciano, M. (2008). Happiness is a personal(ity) thing: The genetics of personality and well-being in a representative sample. *Psychological Science*, 19, 205–210.

Wheaton, B. (1990). Life transitions, role histories, and mental health. *American Sociological Review*, 55, 209–223.

Wilson, R. S., Mendes de Leon, C. F., Bienias, J. L., Evans, D. A., and Bennett, D. A. (2004). Personality and mortality in old age. *The Journals of Gerontology: Series B: Psychological Sciences and Social Sciences*, 59B, P110–P116.

World Health Organization (1948). Preamble to the constitution of the World Health Organization as adopted by the International Health Conference. *Official Records of the World Health Organization*, 2, 100.

7 Psychosocial resources as predictors of resilience and healthy longevity of older widows

Prem S. Fry and Dominique L. Debats

Abstract

Many factors affect the observed increase of mortality following loss of a spouse. In the research reported in this chapter, we focus on the influence of recently recognized psychosocial resource factors in enhancing the resilience and healthy longevity of older widows. We conducted a 6.5-year longitudinal study of the mortality risk of 385 older widows, who were assessed at baseline on measures of perceived psychosocial resources, health-related self-reports, and psychological traits of challenge and control. A Cox regression analysis of predictor variables was used to examine the mortality risk related to the baseline measures of psychosocial resources and psychological trait measures. Those widows who survived longer were mainly those with higher scores on spiritual resources, and on resources of family stability, social engagement, and commitment to life tasks. In contrast, high scores on control and challenge traits had an unexpected negative effect on longevity. Our findings confirm that psychosocial resource factors have a significant effect on resilience and longevity.

Introduction

A broad range of factors can influence the mortality of women who have become widows. In the research reported in this chapter, we examine the extent to which key psychosocial resources influence the resilience and healthy longevity of older widows.

Widowhood is a common occurrence in the lives of midlife and older women. Almost one half of women over the age of 65 years are widowed (Fields and Casper, 2001). The gerontological literature (e.g., Bowling, 1994; Jacobs and Ostfeld, 1977; Stroebe and Stroebe, 1987; Susser, 1981) has documented the increased vulnerability to death of the recently widowed. Some longitudinal studies have examined mortality risks of pre-widowhood status compared with widowed status (e.g., Johnson *et al.*, 2000) and have compared mortality risks of widowed versus non-widowed older adults (e.g., Mendes de Leon, Kasl, and Jacobs,

185

1994). While an increase in mortality following widowhood seems fairly well established (Kaprio, Koskenvuo, and Rita, 1987; Martikainen and Valkonen, 1996a, 1996b; Mendes de Leon *et al.*, 1994), most studies of the causes have focused on socio-demographic factors of age, race, income, and education, and to a more limited extent on health resources or health limitations and impairments of widowed persons (see Stimpson *et al.*, 2007).

Cross-sectional (e.g., Fry, 2001a, 2001b) and longitudinal studies (e.g., Johnson *et al.*, 2000; Mendes de Leon, Kasl, and Jacobs, 1993; Stimpson *et al.*, 2007), have focused mainly on self-rated health and the effects of widowhood on health outcomes for widows (e.g., Fry, 2001a, 2001b; Wilcox *et al.* 2003). These studies have identified a number of mechanisms (e.g., disability, anxiety, depression, grief) to explain how widowhood might lead to impairments in physical and mental health and health behaviors (Bowling, 1994; Harlow, Goldberg, and Comstock, 1991; Kraaij, Arensman, and Spinhoven, 2002; Manzoli *et al.*, 2007; Umberson, 1992). These impairments are to be expected, given that a woman's loss of her spouse in late life is a stressful experience, and is accompanied by serious debilitating effects on resilience, mental health, and longevity (cf. Campbell and Silverman, 1999; Gallagher-Thompson *et al.*, 1993; Utz *et al.*, 2002). These impairments may be assumed to increase mortality risks (Saz and Dewey, 2001).

Psychologists (e.g., Baltes, 1997; Bandura, 1997; Hobfoll, 1989) have long argued, on both theoretical and empirical grounds, that the contribution of psychosocial resources to understanding resilience and healthy longevity in the face of loss and challenge needs further study. Psychological research has increasingly turned to an examination of the impact of people's psychosocial resources on their stress resistance, well-being, resilience, and longevity (Cowen, 1991; Cozzarelli, 1993; Diener, E., Diener, M., and Diener, C., 1995). More recently, the link between people's psychosocial resources and their resiliency (Seligman and Csikszentmihalyi, 2000) is being pursued in studies involving older persons in general, and older persons who have experienced unique loss, disability, and adversity. However, few longitudinal studies have focused on identifying key psychosocial resource factors that affect widows' resilience following spousal loss, and that are linked with increased or reduced risk of mortality.

In determining what psychosocial resources and personal attributes may be the strongest predictors of longevity and survival, providing protection against mortality, much can be learned from the existing cross-sectional studies of psychosocial factors that predict overall psychological well–being, or shape the resilience of widows and increase longevity (e.g., Fry, 2000, 2001a, 2001b; Ong, Bergeman, and Bisconti, 2004). Previous research has identified a number of psychosocial resources that serve as protective resources and promote health and well-being; for example, familial/community support resources which refer to affectional ties between individuals and their family members and friends, and social engagement ties. These resources protect against stress and promote resilience (see Bergeman and Wallace, 1999; Hintikka *et al.*, 2001). Factors that influence mortality in the general population of community-based older adults include beliefs and perceptions of self-efficacy, self-control, and self-esteem (e.g., Anstey, Luszcz, and Andrews, 2002; Fry and Debats, 2006, 2009; Korten *et al.*, 1999) and five-factor personality traits (e.g., Fry and Debats, 2009; Martin, Friedman, and Schwartz, 2007; McCrae and Costa, 1993; Wilson *et al.*, 2004).

Elsewhere in the literature, spirituality resources have been identified as a protective resource, especially in the case of women, where spirituality and religious beliefs compensate for lack of close relationships following trauma and loss (Granqvist and Hagekull, 2000; Kirkpatrick, 1997). Thus, in community-based non-clinical samples of older adults, it is a plausible hypothesis that their lifespan may be lengthened if they have at their disposal a number of personal and psychosocial resources, including, for example, spirituality, family stability, and social engagement resources.

The present study on the importance of psychosocial resources in contributing to resilience extends the work of Cowen (1991), Cozzarelli (1993), and Diener, E., Diener, M., and Diener, C. (1995) on the impact of people's psychosocial resources on their stress resistance, well-being, resilience, and longevity, and of Seligman and Csikszentmihalyi (2000), who studied both older persons in general, and older persons who had experienced unique loss, disability, and adversity. In the present work we study the implication of these resources in the functioning of elderly widows. We seek to identify key psychosocial resource factors that are assumed to be related to stress, coping and adaptation of older widows, in the hope that the development of these resource factors may possibly contribute to the resilience and well-being of widowed women in advanced old age, and extend their healthy longevity.

The results are expected to have broad implications not only for psychology of aging as a field, but also for the potential contribution of the gerontological research literature to providing insights into what psychosocial resources and interventions may contribute to resilience and healthy longevity of older adults.

Conceptual/theoretical framework of the research

The underlying assumption of our research is derived from a "diathesis-stress to resilience" model proposed with particular reference to old age (see Gatz, 1998; Hobfoll, 1989; Hobfoll and Wells, 1998). According to this model, there is a salient association between access to key psychosocial resources, and stress and health outcomes (Hobfoll, 2002). Our study is conceptualized within a similar theoretical framework arguing for the prevalence of plasticity, resilience, and malleability in old age, and the relationship of key psychosocial resources to resilience, health, and longevity (see discussion by Aspinwall and Staudinger, 2003; Brandtstädter, Rothermund, and Schmitz, 1997). Our work is framed within a paradigm that puts emphasis on how access to key psychosocial resources protects individuals in the face of stress, and at the same time facilitates the development of personal resilience in the face of adversity and threatened losses (Cozzarelli, 1993; Rini *et al.*, 1999). Stress research has focused on the buffering effects of psychosocial resource factors, and a number of developmental scientists (cf. Bergeman and Wallace, 1999; Hobfoll, 1989; Hobfoll and Leiberman, 1987; Hobfoll, Shoham, and Ritter, 1991; Holahan and Moos, 1991; Holahan *et al.*, 1999; Martin, 2002) theorize that persons who have at their disposal robust psychosocial resource reservoirs can endure high levels of stress and sustain resilience in the face of risks to physical and mental health, even in late life. Because individuals derive resilience from a variety of internal and external sources, having a greater awareness of psychosocial resources at their disposal may contribute significantly to individuals' motivation to strive for longevity so as to accomplish more personal goals and commitments (Lawton *et al.* 1999). Thus the relationship between individuals' assessment of their psychosocial resources and mortality may be reciprocal. More concretely, individuals may strive to live longer and more healthy lives as a function of their self-appraisals that they have a variety of psychosocial resources and control resources at their disposal in circumstances of stress and adversity (see Fry, 2001a, 2001b; Fry and Debats, 2002). Furthermore, individuals having a clear sense of personal commitments for the future may strive to live longer in order to accomplish more life goals (see Fry, 2000).

Thus it is argued that those with a larger number of psychosocial resource networks are more protected and guarded against stressful conditions and hence are less negatively affected by loss and challenging encounters, including death encounters and risks to mortality. For example, Cohen and Wills (1985), Kiecolt-Glaser *et al.* (1996), and Yang and Glaser (2000), to mention a few researchers, have argued that individuals' perceptions of their internal and external resources and domains of strengths may influence their immune functions such that individuals are less likely to succumb to infections and stress-induced immunomodulation problems (Ryff and Singer, 1998).

Most of the previous research on widows' mortality has lacked baseline data, obtained shortly after spousal loss, concerning the women's psychosocial resources, which leaves open the possibility that the higher risk of widows' mortality is due, in part, to a relatively rapid loss of psychosocial resources following spousal loss. Thus our major purpose for the study was to examine longitudinally the extent to which key psychosocial resources, including spirituality resources and other resources representing family stability, economic stability, and social engagement assessed at baseline, are enabling with respect to long-term health and longevity. Because such resources are seen as the essential elements of people's stress resistance armamentarium, perceived lack or loss of resources may threaten well-being (Hobfoll, 2002). This association may be especially observable, relevant and significant in the life functioning of older widows. Thus, consistent with previous theorizing, we hypothesized that widows possessing a larger number of psychosocial resources at the time of baseline will have a lower risk of death compared with widows possessing limited psychosocial resources. The extent to which older widows possess resources and draw strength from them may be an important area of inquiry into the determinants of longevity and mortality. The question is of increasing interest to health professionals for both practical and conceptual reasons.

Description of participants

Participants represented a wide range of ages (65 to 80+ years). Educational attainment ranged from 9 years of school to 16 years, with 74 percent reporting an educational attainment of 10 to 14 years. Annual income levels ranged from below $25,000 to above $65,000, with 28 percent reporting an annual income above $65,000. The majority of participants, 85 percent, were retired. Ethnic diversity was limited: 95 percent of participants were Caucasian.

Methods

Sampling frame for the study and recruitment of participants: the target population

The research received "Ethics Approval" from the funding agency and the first author's university. We purposively recruited the sample for the study from the registry listings of six municipal branch offices of Community Services and Community Associations and "Seniors Serving Seniors" boards in southern Alberta (Canada). Participants were recruited by means of fliers that advertised a call for participants from among recently bereaved older adults. These fliers were sent out to 25 regional community associations that organized initial support for seniors in various urban, semi-rural, and rural communities in southern Alberta. The fliers urged the participation of women who had experienced spousal loss in the previous 12 months. Community-residing widows were recruited by word of mouth. The help of pastoral and chaplains' staff was also solicited to encourage the participation of recently bereaved widows.

The purpose of the study was explained as an attempt to understand present and future concerns of older women following spousal loss. Interested women were encouraged to phone one of the assigned research assistants for detailed information. Eligibility criteria included spousal loss within the previous 12 months. For ethical considerations, it was decided not to include persons whose loss had occurred more recently than the previous six months (see discussion by Parkes, 1995). Other eligibility criteria explained to potential participants included being (a) 65 years or older; (b) able to understand, speak and write English; (c) without a diagnosis of cognitive dysfunction in the registered medical files; (d) available for baseline assessments; (e) able to specify by name, address, and phone number one or more family members or permanent care-givers willing to serve as an informant to the research team; and (f) willing to sign a consent form. Participants and informants were given a one-time cash award of 15 dollars for their cooperation.

Procedures

The initial interview with the participants and their family members took approximately one and a half hours. The majority of participants were interviewed in their homes in order to obtain baseline information about health status in relation to chronic conditions presented, and also to obtain participants' formal consent to participate, and permission from their family member or primary care-giver to be contacted periodically. Typically, two family members for each participant contracted to be the informants. We provided informants with postage prepaid envelopes to contact us at regular intervals concerning the participant's health, and in the event of the participant's death, to provide the exact date of death. It should be noted that ascertainment of death was done solely on the basis of report of the informants. Family members preferred that we used this follow-up and contact procedure because it was more personal and private.

Time-line for the study

The study comprised ten waves of data collection. Baseline measures were obtained between October and December of 1998, followed by nine subsequent waves of contact with each participant and/or an approved informant to obtain "summary progress report" data on participants. Contacts with informants were made at approximately 8-month intervals (240 days apart) till early August, 2005. The vital status of each decedent was subsequently also double-checked by the research team with provincial death records. The vital status of 385 respondents could be traced till early August of 2005. For all analyses, participants were classed as living (survivors) or deceased (decedents) in the first week of August, 2005. Thus assessment of mortality and survival was completed at 6.5 years, approximately 2,400 days post-baseline.

Assessment of psychosocial resources and traits of psychological resilience

Participants agreed to complete paper–and–pencil tests at their own pace, at home or in their place of study, and 10 percent sought the help of research assistants to record their responses.

At baseline, participants completed the following measures:

(a) Index of Spirituality; (b) Family Stability measure; (c) Perceived Social Engagement measure; (d) Economic Stability measure; (e) Psychological Resilience measure; and (f) Optimism Trait measure. (Description of each measure and details of psychometric properties of each measure are shown in the Appendix section at the end of the chapter.)

Assessment of health variables and satisfaction with social support

At baseline, participants completed the following measures:

(a) Survey of Number of Visits to Health Providers; (b) IADL Index of Disability; and (c) Measure of Satisfaction with Family and Social Support. (Description of each measure and details of psychometric properties of each measure are shown in the Appendix section at the end of the chapter.)

Data analysis procedures

We assessed the internal consistency of each psychosocial resource factor score and resilience trait score with Cronbach's coefficient alpha, and the association of the scales with each other and with other covariates by means of Pearson correlation coefficients.

For all analyses, differences between survivors and decedents on the date of final censoring were assessed with t-tests and chi-square tests of association. We conducted all analyses by using the Statistical Package for Social Sciences (SPSS) (Version 10) software.

Cox proportional hazard models (Cox, 1972) were fitted to estimate the importance of each predictor of mortality. The regression coefficients were estimated by comparing the risk factors of survivors and deceased individuals. The initial risk ratios (IRR) were calculated by exponentiating the beta weight for the predictor (Kelsey *et al.*, 1996). The Cox regression model assumes that the death rate of the population depends on a continuous time variable. For example, an IRR of 1.10, where the initial incident is defined as death, as in the case of the present study, suggests a 10 percent increase in the death rate with each unit increase in the raw test score compared with the reference category, adjusting for the effects of all other variables in the equation. Interpretation of IRR values as indicative of increased or decreased risk is dependent on the direction in which the predictor variables are scored (Cox, 1972). In the present study the interval between the Wave 1 assessment and date of death was calculated in terms of total number of days. The predictors included psychosocial resource factors (4), individual resilience trait variables and total score (4), and optimism trait (1).

All Cox regression hazard ratios of IRR presented in the present analyses were first adjusted for age. In a subsequent analysis, we controlled for the following health-related covariates: (a) number of medical visits at baseline; (b) global index score for disability at baseline; and (c) global satisfaction with family support score at baseline (see Fry and Debats, 2006, 2009; Korten *et al.*, 1999; Wolinsky and Johnson, 1992, for significance of studying these health variables).

Results

Key differences between survivors and non-survivors (decedents)

Baseline data were originally obtained for 400 widows. However, the data for 15 widows who reported a change in marital status in the course of the study period were removed from the data analyses, reducing the study sample to 385 widows. These 385 participants were followed starting in December of 1998 when baseline assessments were complete. As of August 2005, after approximately 6.5 years of observation, 175 (45.55 percent) deaths had occurred.

Table 7.1. *Baseline characteristics of participants who survived (survivors) or died (decedents)*

Characteristics	Survivors ($N = 210$) = 54.5%	Decedents ($N = 175$) = 45.5%	p Value
Age: (years)	74.2 (5.5)	77.8 (6.1)	> 0.05
Education (years)	14.5 (3.3)	15.9 (3.3)	> 0.05
IADL (12 items)	4.0 (1.0)	5.0 (2.0)	> 0.05
Number of Medical Visits in preceding year at baseline	4.0 (2.0)	5.0 (2.5)	> 0.05
High Satisfaction with Social Support (%)	68	48	< 0.001*
High Physical Fitness Score (%)	32	22	> 0.05*
Spirituality-Religiosity Resource Index Score	82.0 (6.5)	59.5 (4.5)	< 0.001
Family Stability Resource Score	23.1 (3.1)	18.5 (4.0)	< 0.001
Social Engagement Resource Score	56.4 (4.4)	42.5 (4.8)	< 0.001
Economic Stability Resource	27.5 (3.5)	19.5 (3.0)	< 0.001
Optimism Trait	33.5 (3.5)	27.5 (4.5)	< 0.001
Psychological Resilience Resource Total Score	73.5 (4.5)	79.5 (4.0)	< 0.05
Resilience Subscale: *Commitment*	31.5 (4.0)	23.5 (4.5)	< 0.001
Resilience Subscale: *Control*	19.5 (5.0)	32.5 (4.5)	< 0.001
Resilience Subscale: *Challenge*	20.5 (4.0)	31.5 (3.5)	< 0.001

Note: All data are presented as mean ratings and (standard deviations) unless otherwise indicated. p values are based on t-tests; * denotes variables where p values are based on χ^2 tests of association.

Table 7.1 provides crude data at baseline on the two subgroups of decedents and survivors. Those who died during the study period were older and had significantly higher levels of Control and Challenge compared with the survivors. However, they also had significantly lower levels of resources, including resources of Spirituality, Family Stability, Social Engagement, Economic Stability, Commitment to Life Tasks, and Optimism.

At the time of baseline assessment, the respondents in the two subgroups were quite different with respect to physical fitness scores, but did not differ much in the number of visits to health professionals or disability (IADL) scores.

An examination of the correlations of baseline indicators of psychosocial resource factors with one another and with psychological resilience factors, demographic variables, and health-related variables showed that these measures were all related to each other, with correlations ranging from 0.29 to 0.69. The three dimensions of the Psychological Resilience scale measure (Commitment to Life Tasks, Control and Challenge) were related to each other and also to Spirituality, Family Stability, and Social Engagement measures, with correlations ranging from 0.21 to 0.31. Control and Challenge subscale measures of the Psychological Resilience scale, on the other hand, were negatively related to Spirituality, Family Stability, and Social Engagement measures, and to Optimism. Overall, the psychosocial resource factors (Spirituality, Family Stability, Social Engagement, and Economic Stability) were not significantly correlated with age, education, and other diverse health-related variables (i.e., physical fitness, IADL, visits to health professionals, and social support satisfaction).

Psychometric information on four sets of psychosocial resource factors, three dimensions of psychological resilience, and optimism

Table 7.2 (Part A) provides psychometric information on various measures of psychosocial resources and resilience subscales. Internal consistencies of the various scales and subscales, as reported in Table 7.2, are consistent with and converge appropriately with the internal consistencies reported by the authors of the scales and subscales, for the three subscales of Psychological Resilience (Bartone *et al.*, 1989) and for the Spirituality Index (Howden, 1992), Social Engagement (Morgan, Dallosso, and Ebrahim, 1985), Family Stability (Fry and Debats, 2006), Economic Stability (Fry, 2000, 2001a, 2001b), and Optimism (Scheier and Carver, 1985, 1992). Each measure had an approximately symmetric distribution. Skewness and kurtosis coefficients ranged from 0.51 to 0.29 and from 0.52 to 0.34, respectively.

Psychosocial resource factors and mortality

Our initial objective was to examine the relative risk of death associated with psychosocial resource factors (Spirituality, Family Stability, Social Engagement, and Economic Stability) and with Psychological Resilience factors (Control, Challenge, and Commitment to Life Tasks). All variables under study were treated as continuous variables, using Cox proportional hazards models analyses adjusted for age (Cox, 1972). In these analyses (see Table 7.2, Part B), high scores on Control and Challenge were positively related to risk of death. Conversely, high scores on Spirituality, Family Stability, Social Engagement, Optimism and Commitment were inversely related to risk of death. There was no

Table 7.2. *A: Psychometric information on psychosocial resource factors and psychological resilience trait measures* (N = 385).
B: Relative risk of death associated with psychosocial resource factors and psychological resilience trait measures (N = 385).

				B: Relative risk of death associated with psychosocial resource factors and psychological resilience trait measures, derived from Cox separate proportional hazards models adjusted for age	
A: Psychometric information on psychosocial resource factors and psychological resilience trait measures					
Trait	Mean	(*SD*)	*α*	Relative risk	95% Confidence intervals
Spirituality-Religiosity Resource Index Score	74.8	(5.1)	0.81	0.865	0.819, 0.911
Family Stability Resource Score	24.7	(3.5)	0.73	0.842	0.817, 0.867
Social Engagement Resource Score	51.5	(4.0)	0.79	0.799	0.706, 0.892
Economic Stability Resource	23.1	(4.2)	0.74	1.005	0.969, 1.041
Optimism	26.5	(3.3)	0.76	0.955	0.916, 0.994
Psychological Resilience Resource Total Score	85.5	(5.2)	0.76	0.990	0.868, 1.112
Resilience Subscale: *Commitment*	34.7	(5.1)	0.74	0.832	0.817, 0.847
Resilience Subscale: *Control*	31.2	(4.0)	0.80	1.049	0.940, 1.158
Resilience Subscale: *Challenge*	29.5	(3.8)	0.79	1.047	0.939, 1.155

Note: Alpha denotes the coefficient alpha, a measure of internal consistency

significant effect on mortality noted for Economic Stability and the total Psychological Resilience measure.

A subsequent detailed analysis of how deaths across low, average, and high standard scores of all measures were distributed suggested a possible violation of the Cox proportional hazards assumption. In cases of Cox regressions there are often circumstances, such as perhaps in the present study, where a categorical variable procedure such as trichotomization may then be more appropriate for an otherwise continuous variable procedure (see Fry and Debats, 2009; Kalbfleisch and Prentice, 1980; Wasserman and Kutner, 1989; Weiss and Costa, 2005). Although

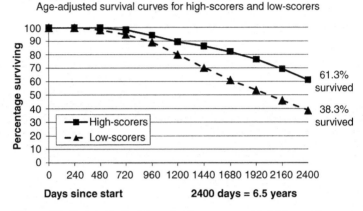

Figure 7.1. Survival of widows in the groups with high and low scores for *Spirituality* over approximately 6.5 years. 61.3 percent of high-scorers survived, 38.8 percent of low-scorers survived. $(1 - 0.613)/(1 - 0.388) = 0.633$. Widows in the high-scorer group had 27 percent less risk of dying within the 6.5 years than widows in the low-scorer group.

trichotomization may reduce statistical power, it has the possible advantage that trichotomized domain scores will be more readily interpreted (Weiss and Costa, 2005). Following Weiss and Costa (2005), we computed tertiles from all standard scores on each of the predictor variables. In the present case, scores that fell in the upper tertile (i.e., 67th to 100th percentile) were seen to be at a level distinctly above the level of usual functioning, and scores that fell in the lower tertile (i.e., 0 to 33rd percentile) were seen to be at a level below the level of usual functioning.

Additionally, an age-adjusted survival curve was plotted showing the relationship of the predictor variables with survival rates over a 6.5 period, for high-scorers (at 67th percentile and above) and low-scorers (at 33rd percentile and below) for each predictor variable. Figures 7.1 to 7.4 (showing age-adjusted survival curves for the predictor variables of Spirituality, Family Stability, Social Engagement, and Commitment to Life Tasks, respectively) suggested that high-scorers compared with low-scorers are at significantly *reduced* risk for mortality. Conversely, the age-adjusted survival curves for Control and Challenge (Figures 7.5 and 7.6, respectively) suggested that high-scorers, compared with low-scorers on these predictor variables, are at significantly *increased* risk for mortality. Percentages of those who survived and the ratio of fractions who died are noted under each figure.

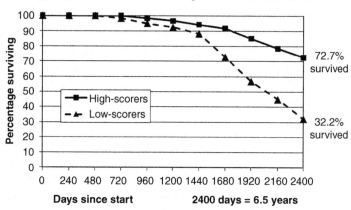

Figure 7.2. Survival of widows in the groups with high and low scores for *family stability*, over approximately 6.5 years. 72.7 percent of high-scorers survived, 32.2 percent of low-scorers survived. $(1 - 0.727)/(1 - 0.322) = 0.402$. Widows in the high-scorer group had 60 percent less risk of dying within the 6.5 years than widows in the low-scorer group.

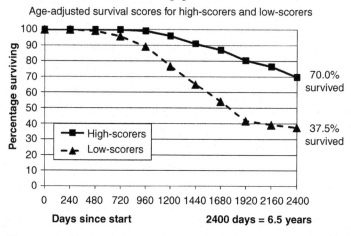

Figure 7.3. Survival of widows in the groups with high and low scores for *social engagement*, over approximately 6.5 years. 69.9 percent of high-scorers survived, 37.5 percent of low-scorers survived. $(1 - 0.699)/(1 - 0.375) = 0.481$. Widows in the high-scorer group had 52 percent less risk of dying within the 6.5 years than widows in the low-scorer group.

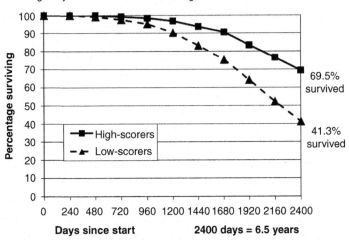

Figure 7.4. Survival of widows in the groups with high and low scores for *commitment to life tasks*, over approximately 6.5 years. 69.5 percent of high-scorers survived, 41.3 percent of low-scorers survived. (1 – 0.695)/(1 – 0. 413) = 0.519. Widows in the high-scorer group had 48 percent less risk of dying within the 6.5 years than widows in the low-scorer group.

Overall, our results as seen in Tables 7.1 and 7.2 suggest a varying magnitude of the predictive ability of various psychosocial resource factors and psychological resilience factors in relation to risk of mortality. The findings from Figures 7.1 to 7.6 further confirm the predictive ability of the resource factors of Spirituality, Family Stability, Social Engagement, and the psychological resilience traits of Commitment to Life Tasks, Control, and Challenge in relation to *increased* or *reduced* risk of mortality as indicated also in Table 7.2 (Part B).

Controlling for health-related variables

In a separate set of regression analyses we explored the influence of three health-related covariates. These analyses were intended mainly to see whether differences in the relationship between the psychosocial resources and resilience traits, and the risks for mortality as predictors of mortality, would hold up after controlling for three health-related covariates assessed at baseline: (a) number of visits in the previous year to medical practitioners and health providers; (b) total index score for the measure of disability

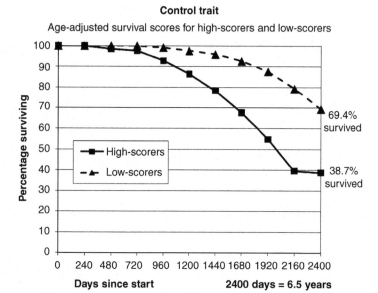

Figure 7.5. Survival of widows in the groups with high and low scores for *control trait*, over approximately 6.5 years. 38.7 percent of high-scorers survived, 69.4 percent of low-scorers survived. (1 – 0.694)/ (1 – 0. 387) = 0.500. Widows in the *low-scorer group* had 50 percent less risk of dying within the 6.5 years than widows in the *high-scorer group*.

in daily life activities; and (c) total score for self-rated satisfaction with social support. Initially, these health-related covariates were controlled for one at a time, using a Cox regression continuous variable analysis procedure. However the results of the Cox regression analyses were ambiguous and largely un-interpretable. These variables were subsequently entered in the multiple regression analyses adjusting for the covariates (Table 7.3).

As seen in Table 7.3, the negative beta values for Spirituality, Family Stability, Social Engagement, and Commitment, and the significant F values observed in the multiple regression analysis, are consistent with the direction of reduced risk ratios shown in the RR and 95 percent CI model. Similarly, after adjusting for the covariates, the positive beta values and the significant F values for control and challenge in the multiple regression analyses are consistent with the direction of increased risk ratios for these variables in the RR and 95 percent CI model. Thus overall, the relationship between psychosocial resources variables and psychological resilience traits and risk for mortality held up after adjusting for the health-related covariates. In other words, the association we

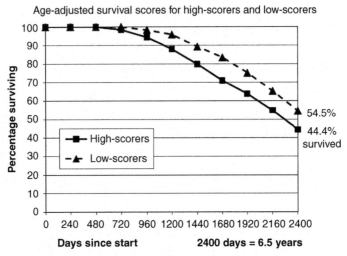

Figure 7.6. Survival of widows in the groups with high and low scores for *challenge trait*, over approximately 6.5 years. 44.4 percent of high-scorers survived, 54.5 percent of low-scorers survived. (1 – 0.545)/ (1 – 0.444) = 0.817. Widows in the *low-scorer group* had 18 percent less risk of dying within the 6.5 years than widows in the *high-scorer group*.

saw in the earlier continuous variable Cox regression analyses (Table 7.2, Part B) between psychosocial resources, psychological resilience traits and risks for mortality remained unchanged after adjusting for the health-related covariates. Economic stability, optimism, and the total of the psychological resilience traits were only weakly associated with the risk ratios even after adjusting for the three health-related covariates. In further analyses we found no statistically significant interaction effects among the socio-demographic variables and health variables relating to the prediction of mortality.

Discussion

Psychosocial resources as predictors of resilience and mortality

A series of age-adjusted Cox regression analyses of psychosocial resource factors and psychological resilience domain traits showed that risk of death during the 6.5-year duration of the study was significantly reduced in those individuals with high scores in the spirituality resource compared with those with low scores in this resource (i.e., 27 percent lower) (see Figure 7.1). This

Table 7.3. *Relative risk of death associated with psychosocial resource factors and resilience traits after adjusting for three covariates entered in the multiple regression analysis*

Trait	β	F	Multiple R	R2	Risk ratio model RR	95% CI
Covariates						
Combined	0.49	6.08**	0.80	0.64	0.872	0.809, 0.935
Spirituality Res.	−0.39	5.79**				
Family Stability Res.	−0.29	5.49**	0.76	0.58	0.849	0.810, 0.888
Social Engagement Res.	−0.27	4.89**	0.75	0.56	0.842	0.816, 0.868
Economic Stability Res.	0.13	< 1.00	0.33	0.11	1.004	0.990, 1.018
Optimism Trait	−0.17	< 1.00	0.34	0.12	0.996	0.921, 1.071
Resilience (Total Score)	−0.19	< 1.00	0.36	0.13	0.970	0.911, 1.029
Commitment: Resilience	−0.26	4.29**	0.69	0.48	0.799	0.705, 0.893
Control: Resilience	0.27	4.68**	0.44	0.19	1.048	1.024, 1.072
Challenge: Resilience	0.29	5.06**	0.69	0.48	1.052	1.026, 1.078
Total				0.72		

*$p < 0.05$; **$p < 0.001$; degrees of freedom for $F = 12, 372$; covariates include: Participants' (a) number of medical visits at baseline; (b) global index score for disability at baseline; and (c) global satisfaction with family support score at baseline. *Note:* covariates were entered simultaneously. RR = relative risk ratio and CI = confidence intervals were determined after means were adjusted for covariates.

finding supports earlier theorizing advocating that aspects of spirituality be built into treatment modalities for bereaved adults (Cole and Pargament, 1999; Fry, 2000), with the objective of enhancing human well-being and resilience. These findings support findings from earlier cross-sectional studies of widows (e.g., Fry, 2001a, 2001b), suggesting that possession of spiritual resources contributed significantly to widows' psychological well-being. Similarly, risk of death was lower in those individuals with high scores in the Family Stability resource (i.e., 60 percent lower) (see Figure 7.2) and Social Engagement resource (i.e., 52 percent lower) (see Figure 7.3), compared in each case with their counterparts having low scores in these psychosocial resource domains. Overall, these results are consistent with our hypothesis that individuals having more psychosocial resources at their disposal are more protected from external stress-inducing forces, and therefore are at a lower risk of mortality. These findings provide more solid evidence in support of the resource-based notion of well-being and resilience versus deterioration proposed by several previous researchers and theorists (e.g., Berkman and Syme, 1979; Caplan, 1974; Thoits, 1994), who have argued that the possession of key psychosocial resources is more keenly instrumental in enhancing resilience than any other mechanisms (Baltes, 1996; Bandura, 1997; Hobfoll, 1989). Our findings provide further support for the theorized and hypothesized link between people's resources and their resiliency in withstanding adversity and loss (Seligman and Csikszentmihalyi, 2000). In short, our findings confirmed that psychosocial resources of Spirituality, Family Stability, and Social Engagement (which we hypothesized to be robust health-related resources) are indeed "enabling" and "protective" in their effects on older widows' longevity. These findings fit well with earlier cross-sectional studies of widowed women (see Fry, 2001a, 2001b) that linked psychosocial resources of spirituality, social embeddedness and long-term goals with the well-being of older widows. It is noteworthy that these associations endure well into the late life of widowed women, regardless of the presence of chronic health conditions.

Psychological resilience traits of Commitment to Life Tasks, Control, and Challenge as predictors of mortality

Concerning the relationship between psychological resilience traits and mortality, we had expected a positive relationship between these traits and a reduced risk of mortality. Consistent, in part, with our hypothesis, the present findings show that widows who scored high in the psychological resilience trait of Commitment to Life Tasks, compared with low-scorers, were at a considerably reduced risk of death (i.e., 48 percent lower) (see Figure 7.4). However, contrary to our hypothesis, our findings showed that widows scoring high on the "Control" and "Challenge" traits of the psychological resilience measure were at increased risk for mortality. Risk of death among individuals who, at the time of baseline assessments, were high-scorers on control was nearly double the risk of their counterparts who were low-scorers on control (see Figure 7.5). When high-scorers on the "Challenge" trait were compared with low-scorers on this trait, the findings show that risk of death was 22 percent greater for the high-scorers than for the low-scorers (see Figure 7.6). This finding is in stern contradiction to the earlier evidence found for Challenge and Control being related to better psychological well-being, better ability to mobilize resources, better ability to withstand midlevel stress effectively, and better physical health (Kobasa, 1979; Kobasa and Puccetti, 1983). Our finding of high Challenge and high Control linked with the outcome of increased risk of mortality defies a simple explanation. However, other earlier research (e.g., Brandtstädter and Renner, 1990; Janoff-Bulman, 1992; Janoff-Bulman and Brickman, 1982) has included aspects of control and challenge that may be particularly relevant to psychological changes in late-life functioning, and which may explain the negative impact of high generalized challenge and control on the lives of older widows. Researchers (e.g., Heckhausen and Schulz, 1995; Janoff-Bulman and Brickman, 1982) who have examined both ends of the continuum of control and challenge have argued that in circumstances in which high levels of control and environmental challenge and mastery are not possible or feasible, as in later life and after loss of a spouse, an individual's inability to relinquish control easily or to take on additional challenges easily may lead to despondency and to a sense of failure, thereby adding to the risk of mortality. Janoff-Bulman and Brickman (1982) suggested that the tendency to take control or the need to control can backfire in circumstances of stress where control is not possible, and can become stress-inducing factors in later-life functioning, to the detriment of older widows' retaining and protecting other resources. We speculate that there may be a threshold for some traits of psychological resilience (e.g., control and challenge) beyond which these traits cease to be an advantage in late life functioning, and instead could increase widows' mortality. Overall, the present findings regarding the effects of control and challenge on risks for mortality suggest that individuals' thresholds for these traits need to be considered in order to determine the nature of the impact the traits may have on resilience and well-being in the context of late life.

Contrary to our hypothesis that economic stability would reduce mortality risk, our findings show that economic stability was very weakly correlated with risk for mortality. However, our finding that economic stability is not strongly related to reduction in risk of mortality gives support to earlier theorizing that income resources are least influential in subjective well-being in later life (see Diener *et al.*, 1999, for a review). We speculate that in order to sustain and protect other key psychosocial resources at their disposal, widows' concerns about income and financial resources may become less influential and important to their well-being and healthy longevity.

Implications

The positive association of psychosocial resources (such as spiritual growth, family stability, social engagement, and commitment to life tasks) with increased longevity may represent important resource domains that contribute significantly to widows' resilience and healthy longevity, assisting them perhaps in meeting the additional challenges that follow spousal loss. Although the body of work on the association of psychosocial resources and mortality, particularly in later adulthood, is still very small, the results of the present study, derived from a limited sample of older widows, have uncovered some robust findings that may provide the basis for designing intervention programs aimed at further preserving and developing older widows' domains of psychosocial resources directly following spousal loss. Taken together, these findings suggest that many of the assumptions that have guided interventions with older widows may need to be re-evaluated. Intervention programs for older widows, in addition to teaching them to cope with the grief of spousal loss, should concentrate equally on the importance of teaching older widows to mobilize and strengthen their psychosocial resources as a means to preserving resilience and longevity. In future research concerning predictors of mortality in later adulthood, psychosocial resource factors should be viewed as health-related dimensions vitally linked with resilience and longevity.

Acknowledgments

Waves 1–5 of this research were supported, in part, by a Population Aging Research Grant (P. S. Fry, File No. 492–87-0006) awarded to the first author from the Social Sciences and Humanities Research Council of Canada (SSHRC) while she was on Faculty at the University of Calgary, Calgary, Alberta. Completion of the study was facilitated, in part, by a Standard Senior Scholars Research Grant award to the first author from the Social Sciences and Humanities Research Council of Canada (P. S. Fry, File No. 410–2004-0152). We greatly appreciate the assistance of Dr. Mark Kolodziej in data tabulation, data analysis, and interpretation.

Appendix: assessment measures

Participants agreed to complete paper-and-pencil tests at their own pace, at home, or in their place of study, and 10 percent sought the help of research assistants to record their responses.

At baseline participants completed:

(1) *Index of Spirituality.* Spirituality was assessed with Howden's (1992) *Spirituality Assessment Scale* (SAS), which is a 28-item Likert-type scale covering four significant domains, including Purpose for Life, Inner Resources, Inner-Connectedness, and Transcendence. The scale is concerned with assessing related constructs of personal

contemplation, private prayer, and connectedness with self and a power higher than oneself. Howden reported inter-item consistency to be 0.92 for the total SAS. Significant reliability coefficients for the scale were reported also by Brennan (1999), who used the scale with older adults. Higher scores reflected higher religious and spiritual involvement, higher degree of peace with self, and easier access to spiritual growth resources. Alpha coefficients ranging from 0.71 to 0.84 were found for the various composite indices of spirituality for the widows. In the current sample, reliabilities for the four domain subscales ranged from 0.69 to 0.81, and inter-item consistency of this measure was 0.81 for the total SAS.

(2) *Perceived Social Engagement* was assessed by means of the original version of *The Brief Assessment of Social Engagement (BASE) scale*. The BASE is a 20-item scale with a previously reported overall reliability alpha of 0.70 (Morgan, Dallosso, and Ebrahim, 1985). All items were measured on a 5-point Likert type scale from "always true" (5) to "never true" (1). Scores were summed to give a total score. Scores on this measure can range between 20 and 100, with higher scores representing higher appraisals of social engagements. In the present study, the alpha coefficient was 0.79, which compares favorably to the alpha reported by the authors of the scale.

(3) *Family Stability* was assessed in terms of seven questions, with each item rated on a 5-point rating scale: regularity of contact with family members; perceptions of authenticity and sincerity of family members' concern/interest; pleasantness of interactions with family members; reliance on family members to provide social support in time of difficulty; degree of emotional closeness ranging from *very close* (5) to *not at all* (1); degree of tenderness shown in terms of gestures of fondness such as hugging and kissing them or being hugged or kissed by them; and degree of mutual confiding about personal or family matters. A total score of family stability was derived from the responses to these seven questions. Alpha coefficient was 0.73 for the present study.

(4) *Economic Stability* was assessed in terms of five questions, with each item rated on a 5-point rating scale: total income coded as per OARS (Older Adults Resources and Services) methodology into five brackets (Very high ... Very low) with a score of 5 for the highest bracket; other specimen questions included "To what extent is your present monthly income from various sources adequate for comfortable living?" (5 = very adequate ... 1 = very inadequate); "How frequently do you feel it is necessary to curtail or cut down your expenses?" (Rarely = 5 ... Frequently = 1); and "To what extent do

you feel sure that you can live financially independent of outside help?" (Very sure = 5 ... very unsure = 1). Alpha coefficient was 0.74.

(5) *Psychological Resilience* was assessed with a modified version of the *Dispositional Resilience Scale* (DRS) (Bartone *et al.*, 1989). The DRS was developed as a measure of personal hardiness and is based on the premise that those who typify personal resilience identify with (a) a sense of control over life's vicissitudes; (b) a sense that stressors represent challenges rather than threats; and (c) a sense of commitment to living and to life's tasks. The DRS is composed of 45 items, with 15 items each assessing three aspects of psychological resilience: *Commitment to living* (e.g., "Most days life is interesting and exciting for me"), *Control* (e.g., "Planning ahead can help me avoid most future problems"), and *Challenge* (e.g., "Changes in routine are interesting to me"). A 4-point Likert scale, ranging from 0 (*not at all true*) to 3 (*completely true*), was used for obtaining a total DR Index score for which scores can range from 0 to 135. Separate scores were derived for each of the three components of Commitment, Control, and Challenge. Reliability data indicated alphas of 0.72, 0.75, 0.79, and 0.77 for the Commitment, Control, and Challenge subscales and for the overall psychological resilience measure, respectively.

(6) *Optimism* was measured by means of Scheier and Carver's (1985) Life Orientation Test (LOT), which measures Dispositional Optimism. This is a 12-item measure rated on a 5-point rating scale ranging from strongly agree (4) to strongly disagree (0). Typical items include "In uncertain times, I usually expect the best"; "I am a believer in the idea that every cloud has a silver lining"; and "I can rarely count on good things happening to me." (reverse-coded). Scheier and Carver (1992) present extensive reliability and validity data of their optimism measure in various clinical and non-clinical samples, and demonstrate the links between optimism and physical and emotional health and well-being (Scheier and Carver, 1985, 1992). Alpha coefficient for the dispositional optimism scale was 0.71, and in the present study the alpha for the widows' sample was 0.76.

Assessment of health variables and satisfaction with social support at baseline

Becoming a widow has been associated with an increase in psychological distress (Avis *et al.*, 1991), higher rates of health-care use (Avis *et al.*,

1991), and higher need for social support (Wolinsky and Johnson, 1992). Thus we felt the need to examine further fluctuations in risk of mortality after controlling for health-related covariates, which were assessed as follows:

(1) *Survey of number of visits to health providers.* As a part of a separate survey, respondents listed the number of visits that they had paid in the previous year to health providers, including visits to family physicians, community health clinics, and emergency health units, including hospital visits.

(2) *IADL index of disability.* We based this index on the self-reported ability for 12 daily living activities included in the IADL. Respondents were asked to indicate whether they had experienced limitations in 12 areas of functioning with responses coded (1) for *yes* and (0) for *no:* for example, able to use a telephone; boarding a bus without assistance; lifting or carrying groceries; personal grooming and personal hygiene care; doing light housework; taking medications; walking one block. All the items were summed to form one index of IADL, with scores ranging from 0 to 12.

(3) *Measure of satisfaction with family and social support* was assessed along a 5-point Likert-type scale ranging from "very satisfied" to "very dissatisfied."

It should be noted that all measures administered to the participants were formatted in terms of language and structure appropriate for adults having a ninth-grade education. All paper-and-pencil tests and self-report measures used in the study were previously piloted on a volunteer group of 20 men and women aged from 60 to 80. Subsequent modifications were made in the instructions and illustrations given for responding to the five-point ratings of test items. This procedure was undertaken to ensure that even those participants who were elderly and had relatively limited education could validly complete the measures.

REFERENCES

Anstey, K. J., Luszcz M. A., and Andrews G. (2002). Psychosocial factors, gender and late-life mortality. *Ageing International*, 27, 71–87.

Aspinwall, L. G., and Staudinger, U. M. (eds.) (2003). *A psychology of strengths: Fundamental questions and future directions for a positive psychology.* Washington, DC: American Psychological Association.

Avis, N. E., Brambilla, D. J., Vass, K., and McKinlay, J. B. (1991). The effect of widowhood on health: A prospective analysis from the Massachusetts Women's Health Study. *Social Science and Medicine*, 33, 1063–1070.

Baltes, M. M. (1996). *The many faces of dependency in old age.* New York: Cambridge University Press.

Baltes, P. B. (1997). On the incomplete architecture of human ontogeny: Selection, optimization, and compensation as foundation of developmental theory. *American Psychologist,* 52, 366–380.

Bandura, A. (1997). *Self efficacy: The exercise of control.* New York: Freeman.

Bartone, P. T., Ursano, R. J., Wright, K. M., and Ingraham, L. H. (1989). The impact of a military air disaster on the health of assistance workers. *Journal of Nervous and Mental Disease,* 177, 317–328.

Bergeman, C. S., and Wallace, K. A. (1999). Resilience in later life. In T. L. Whitman, T. V. Merluzzi, and R. D. White (eds.), *Life-span perspectives on health and illness* (pp. 207–225). Mahwah, NJ: Erlbaum.

Berkman, L. F., and Syme, S. L. (1979). Social networks, host resistance, and mortality: A nine year follow-up of Alameda County residents. *American Journal of Epidemiology,* 109, 186–204.

Bowling, A. (1994). Mortality after bereavement: an analysis of mortality rates and associations with mortality 13 years after bereavement. *International Journal of Geriatric Psychiatry,* 9, 445–459.

Brandtstädter, J., and Renner, G. (1990). Tenacious goal pursuit and flexible goal adjustment: Explication and age-related analysis of assimilative and accommodative strategies of coping. *Psychology and Aging,* 5, 58–67.

Brandstädter, J., Rothermund, K., and Schmitz, U. (1997). Psychosocial resources in later life. *European Review of Applied Psychology,* 47(2), 107–144.

Brennan, M. (1999). Predictors of religiousness and spirituality in middle-aged and older adults. Paper presented at the 52nd Annual Scientific Meeting of the Gerontological Society of America, San Francisco, CA.

Campbell S., and Silverman P. R. (1999). *Widowers: When men are left alone* Amityville, NY: Baywood.

Caplan, G. (1974). *Support systems and community mental health.* New York: Behavioral Publications: Carver.

Cohen, S., and Wills, T. A. (1985). Stress, social support, and the buffering hypothesis. *Psychological Bulletin,* 98, 310–357.

Cole, B., and Pargament, K. I. (1999). Spiritual surrender: A paradoxical path to control. In W. R. Miller (ed.), *Integrating spirituality into treatment* (pp. 179–198). Washington, DC: American Psychological Association.

Cowen, E. L. (1991). In pursuit of wellness. *American Psychologist,* 46, 404–408.

Cox, D. R. (1972). Regression models and life tables (with discussion). *Journal of the Royal Statistical Society,* 34B, 187–220.

Cozzarelli, C. (1993). Personality and self-efficacy as predictors of coping with abortion. *Journal of Personality and Social Psychology,* 65, 124–126.

Diener, E., Diener, M., and Diener, C. (1995). Factors predicting the subjective well-being of nations. *Journal of Personality and Social Psychology,* 69, 851–864.

Diener, E., Suh, E. M., Lucas, R. E., and Smith, H. L. (1999). Subjective well-being: Three decades of progress. *Psychological Bulletin,* 125, 276–302.

Fields, J., and Casper, L. M. (2001). *America's families and living arrangements: March 2000* (Current Population Reports, P20–537). Washington, DC: US Census Bureau.

Fry, P. S. (2000). Religious involvement, spirituality, and personal meaning for life: existential predictors of psychological wellbeing in community-residing and institutional care elders. *Aging and Mental Health*, 4(4), 375–387.

(2001a).The unique contribution of key existential factors to the prediction of psychological well-being of older adults following spousal loss. *The Gerontologist*, 41(1), 69–81.

(2001b). Predictors of health-related quality of life perspectives, self-esteem, and life satisfactions of older adults following spousal loss: An 18-month follow-up study of widows and widowers. *The Gerontologist*, 41(6), 787–798.

Fry, P. S., and Debats, D. L. (2002). Self-efficacy beliefs as predictors of loneliness and psychological distress in late life. *International Journal of Aging and Human Development*, 55, 233–269.

(2006). Sources of life-strengths as predictors of late-life mortality and survivorship. *International Journal of Aging and Human Development*, 62, 303–334.

(2009). Perfectionism and the five-factor traits as predictors of mortality in older adults. *Journal of Health Psychology*, 14(4), 507–518.

Gallagher-Thompson, D., Futterman, A., Farberow, N., Thompson, L.W., and Peterson, J. (1993) The impact of spousal bereavement in older widows and widowers. In W. Stroebe, M. Stroebe, and R. Hansson (eds.), *Handbook of bereavement: Theory, research, and intervention* (pp. 227–239). New York: Cambridge University Press.

Gatz, M. (1998). Toward a developmentally informed theory of mental disorder in older adults. In J. Lomranz (ed.), *Handbook of aging and mental health: An integrative approach* (pp. 101–120). New York: Plenum Press.

Granqvist, P., and Hagekull, B. (2000). Religiosity, adult attachment, and why "singles" are more religious. *International Journal for the Psychology of Religion*, 10, 111–123.

Harlow, S. D., Goldberg, E. L., and Comstock, G. W. (1991). A longitudinal study of the prevalence of depressive symptomatology in elderly widowed and married women. *Archives of General Psychiatry*, 48, 1065–1068.

Heckhausen, H., and Schulz, R. (1995). A lifespan theory of control. *Psychological Review*, 102, 284–304.

Hintikka, J., Koskela, T., Kontula, O., Koskela, K., and Vinamaki, H. (2001). Men, women and friends – are there differences in relation to mental wellbeing? *Quality of Life Research*, 9, 841–845.

Hobfoll, S. E. (1989). Conservation of resources: A new attempt at conceptualizing stress. *American Psychologist*, 44, 513–524.

(2002). Social and psychological resources and adaptation. *Review of General Psychology*, 6, 307–324.

Hobfoll, S. E., and Leiberman, J. (1987). Personality and social resources in immediate and continued stress-resistance among women. *Journal of Personality and Social Psychology*, 52, 18–26.

Hobfoll, S. E., Shoham, S. B., and Ritter, C. (1991). Women's satisfaction with social support and their receipt of aid. *Journal of Personality and Social Psychology*, 61, 332–341.

Hobfoll, S. E., and Wells, J. D. (1998). Conservation of resources, stress, and aging: Why do some slide and some spring? In J. Lomranz (ed.), *Handbook of aging and mental health: An integrative approach* (pp. 121–134). New York: Plenum Press

Holahan, C. J., and Moos, R. H. (1991). Life stressors, personal and social resources and depression: A four-year structural model. *Journal of Abnormal Psychology*, 100, 31–38.

Holahan, C. J., Moos, R. H., Holahan, C. K., and Cronkite, R. C. (1999). Resource loss, resource gain, and depressive symptoms: A 10-year model. *Journal of Personality and Social Psychology*, 77, 620–629.

Howden, J. (1992). *Spirituality Assessment Scale (SES)*. Corsicana, TX: Navarro College.

Jacobs, S., and Ostfeld, A. (1977) An epidemiological review of the mortality of bereavement. *Psychosomatic Medicine*, 39, 344–357.

Janoff-Bulman, R. (1992). *Shattered assumptions: Towards a new psychology of trauma*. New York: Free Press.

Janoff-Bulman, R., and Brickman, P. (1982). Expectations and what people learn from failure. In N. T. Feathers (ed.), *Expectations and actions: Expectancy-value models in psychology* (pp. 207–237). Hillsdale, NJ: Erlbaum.

Johnson, N. J., Backlund, E., Sorlie, P. D., and Loveless, C. A. (2000). Marital status and mortality: The national longitudinal mortality study. *Annals of Epidemiology*, 10, 224–238.

Kalbfleisch, J. D., and Prentice, R. L. (1980). *Statistical analysis of failure time data* (pp. 87–89). New York: Wiley.

Kaprio, J., Koskenvuo, M., and Rita, H. (1987) Mortality after bereavement: A prospective study of 95,647 widowed persons. *American Journal of Public Health*, 7, 283–287.

Kelsey, J. L., Whittemore, A. S., Evans, A. S., and Thompson, W. D. (1996). *Methods in observational epidemiology*. New York: Oxford University Press.

Kiecolt-Glaser, J. K., Glaser, R., Gavenstein, S. and Marlarkey W. B. (1996). Ways in which stress alters the immune response to influenza virus vaccine in older adults. *National Academy of Sciences, USA*, 93, 1043–3047.

Kirkpatrick, L. A. (1997). A longitudinal study of changes in religious beliefs and behavior as a function of individual differences in adult attachment style. *Journal of Scientific Study of Religion*, 36, 207–217.

Kobasa, S. C. (1979). Stressful life events, personality and health: An inquiry into hardiness. *Journal of Personality and Social Psychology*, 37, 1–11.

Kobasa, S. C., and Puccetti, M. C. (1983). Personality and social resources in stress resistance. *Journal of Personality and Social Psychology*, 45, 839–850.

Korten, A. E., Jorm, A. F., Jiao, Z. *et al.* (1999). Health, cognitive and psycho-social factors as predictors of mortality in an elderly community sample. *Journal of Epidemiology and Community Health*, 53, 83–88.

Kraaij, V., Arensman, E., and Spinhoven, P. (2002). Negative life events and depression in elderly persons: A meta-analysis. *The Journals of Gerontology: Medical Sciences*, 57A, M87–M94.

Lawton, M. P., Moss, M., Hoffman, C., Grant, R., Ten Have, T. and Kleban, M. H. (1999). Health, valuation of life, and the wish to live. *The Gerontologist*, 39, 406–416.

Manzoli, L., Villari, P., Pirone, G. M., and Boccia, A. (2007). Marital status and mortality in the elderly: A systematic review and meta-analysis. *Social Science and Medicine*, 64, 77–94.

Martikainen, P., and Valkonen, T. (1996a). Mortality after the death of a spouse: rates and causes of death in a large Finnish cohort. *American Journal of Public Health*, 86, 1087–1093.

(1996b). Mortality after death of a spouse in relation to duration of bereavement in Finland. *Journal of Epidemiology and Community Health*, 50, 264–268.

Martin, L. R., Friedman, H. S., and Schwartz, J. E. (2007). Personality and mortality risk across the life span: The importance of conscientiousness as a biopsychosocial attribute. *Health Psychology*, 26, 428–436.

Martin, P. (2002). Individual and social resources predicting well-being and functioning in later years: Conceptual models, research, and practice. *Ageing International*, 27, 3–29.

McCrae, R. R., and Costa, P. T., Jr. (1993). Psychological resilience among widowed men and women: A 10-year follow-up of a national sample. In M. S. Stroebe, W. Stroebe, and R. O. Hansson (eds.) *Handbook of bereavement: Theory, research, and intervention* (pp. 196–207). New York: Cambridge University Press.

Mendes de Leon, C. F., Kasl, S. V., and Jacobs, S. (1993) Widowhood and mortality risk in a community sample of the elderly: A prospective study. *Journal of Clinical Epidemiology*, 46, 519–527.

Mendes de Leon, C. F., Kasl, S. V., and Jacobs, S. (1994). A prospective study of widowhood and changes in symptoms of depression in a community sample of the elderly. *Psychological Medicine*, 24, 613–624.

Morgan, K., Dallosso, H. M., and Ebrahim, S. B. J. (1985). A brief self-report scale for assessing personal engagement in the elderly: Reliability and validity. In A. Butler (ed.), *Ageing: Recent advances and creative responses* (pp. 298–304). Beckenham,UK: Routledge.

Ong, A. D., Bergeman, C. S., and Bisconti, T. L. (2004). The role of daily positive affect during conjugal bereavement. *The Journals of Gerontology: Psychological Sciences*, 59, 168–176.

Parkes, C. M. (1995). Guidelines for conducting ethical bereavement research. *Death Studies*, 19, 171–181.

Rini, C. K., Dunkel-Schetter, C., Wadhwa, P. D., and Sandman, C. A. (1999). Psychological adaptation and birth outcomes: The role of personal resources, stress, and sociocultural context in pregnancy. *Health Psychology*, 18, 333–345.

Ryff, C. D., and Singer, B. (1998). The role of purpose in life and positive human health. In P. T. P. Wong and P. S. Fry (eds.), *The human quest for meaning: A handbook of psychological research and clinical applications* (pp. 213–235). Mahwah, NJ: Erlbaum.

Saz, P., and Dewey, M. E. (2001). Depression, depressive symptoms and mortality in persons aged 65 and over living in the community: A systematic review of the literature. *International Journal of Geriatric Psychiatry*, 16, 622–630.

Scheier, M. F., and Carver, C. S. (1985). Optimism, coping, and health: Assessment and implications of generalized outcome expectancies. *Health Psychology*, 4, 219–247

(1992). Effects of optimism on psychological and physical well-being: Theoretical overview and empirical update. *Cognitive Therapy and Research*, 16, 210–228.

Seligman, M. E. P., and Csikszentmihalyi, M. (2000). Positive psychology: An introduction. *American Psychologist*, 55, 5–14.

Stimpson, J. P., Kuo, Y.-F., Ray, L. A., Raji, M. A., and Peck, M. K. (2007) Risk of mortality related to widowhood in older Mexican Americans. *Annals of Epidemiology*, 17, 313–319.

Stroebe, W., and Stroebe, M. W. (1987). *Bereavement and health: The psychological and physical consequences of partner loss*. New York: Cambridge University Press.

Susser, M. (1981) Widowhood: a situational life stress or stressful life event? *American Journal of Public Health*, 71(8), 793–795.

Thoits, P. (1994). Stressors and problem-solving: The individual as psychological activist. *Journal of Health and Social Behavior*, 35, 143–160.

Umberson, D. (1992). Gender, marital status and the social control of health behavior. *Social Science and Medicine*, 34, 907–917.

Utz, R. L., Carr, D., Nesse, R., and Wortman, C. B. (2002). The effect of widowhood on older adults' social participation: An evaluation of activity, disengagement, and continuity theories. *The Gerontologist*, 42, 522–533.

Wasserman, N. J., and Kutner, M. H. (1989). *Applied linear regression models* (pp. 377–8). Homewood, IL: Irwin.

Weiss, A., and Costa, P. T. (2005). Domain and facet personality predictors of all-cause mortality among Medicare patients aged 65 to 100. *Psychosomatic Medicine*, 67, 724–733.

Wilcox, S., Evenson, K. R., Aragaki, A., Wassertheil-Smoller, S., Mouton, C. P., and Loevinger, B. L. (2003). The effects of widowhood on physical and mental health, health behaviors, and health outcomes: The Women's Health Initiative. *Health Psychology*, 22, 513–523.

Wilson, R. S., Mendes de Leon, C. F., Bienias, J. L., Evans, D. A., and Bennett D. A. (2004). Personality and mortality in old age. *The Journals of Gerontology: Psychological Sciences*, 59B, 110–116.

Wolinsky, F. D., and Johnson, R. J. (1992). Widowhood, health status, and the use of health services by older adults: A cross-sectional and prospective approach. *The Journals of Gerontology: Medical Sciences*, 47, S8–S16.

Yang, E., and. Glaser, R. (2000). Stress induced immunomodulation: Impact on immune defenses against infectious disease. *Biomedicine and Pharmacotherapy*, 54, 245–250.

8   Resilience and longevity: expert survivorship of centenarians

Peter Martin, Maurice MacDonald, Jennifer Margrett, and Leonard W. Poon

Abstract

Centenarians are survivors, and many among them exemplify sustained competence into very old age. This paper highlights three important resilience domains among centenarians: personal resilience (e.g., personality), cognitive resilience (e.g., intellectual functioning), and social and economic resilience (e.g., social support and economic resources). These psychosocial resources of resilience are linked to overall functioning and survivorship among centenarians. Our findings suggest that a "robust" personality, cognitive reserves, and social and economic resources are salient resilience factors necessary for survival and optimal functioning and well-being. To illustrate, personality traits (e.g., competence) and perceived economic status served as mediators between negative life stress and negative affect. With regard to cognition, some centenarians function very well despite low education or poor physical functioning. Finally, perceived economic status mediates the relation between physical functioning and negative affect. Taken together, we conclude that psychosocial resources and resilience are important components of quality of life in late life.

Introduction

Resilience is a descriptor placed on individuals or groups of individuals who survived in the face of adversities. Resilience has been used to describe survivors of the September 11, 2001 attack at the New York World Trade Center as well as the 2005 Katrina hurricane survivors in New Orleans. Masten (2001) defined resilience as "a class of phenomena characterized as good outcome in spite of serious threats to adaptation or development" (p. 227). The construct of resilience must involve the inclusion of risks or threats toward development such as compelling socioeconomic circumstances, trauma, life events, health, and other adverse conditions which happened in serial, parallel, or concurrent fashion over time. Therefore, to be resilient implies that it is necessary to survive or to meet the condition of a satisfactory or "good" outcome in dealing with the risks and threats. In a review of resilience research Masten (2001) noted a surprising conclusion, which is the ordinariness of the phenomenon. Resilience is a common occurrence within the context of human development. That is, most people encounter adversities over time, and yet many people tend to adapt adequately or successfully in their development.

In this chapter, we outline and discuss a model of successful adaptation in the study of centenarians (Poon *et al.*, 1992a, 2007). Centenarians have met the two major requirements of being resilient. The first requirement concerns the presence of risks or threats. These individuals have accumulated a century of life events, including surviving the deaths of family members and birth cohorts, economic depression, world wars, and health morbidity and co-morbidity. The second concerns successful adaptation in that centenarians have adapted and survived in spite of the cumulative negative as well as positive events. In this respect, longevity, resilience, and successful adaptation are intimately related, and it is likely that they share many of the common mechanisms and characteristics. Long-lived individuals experience risks and adversities over time and the presence of adversity and successful adaptation are the two necessary ingredients present in resilience. Hence, in discussing resilience among centenarians, it is essential to include concepts of longevity and successful adaptation in the face of cumulative risks and threats.

From this perspective, it can be said that centenarians' resilience may be one of the factors in doubling their lifespan. By definition, an American centenarian born in 1900 lived to 2000 and beyond, while their birth cohort survived to an average of 46.3 years for men and 48.3 for women (National Center for Health Statistics, 2007). Not many people are fortunate to achieve centenarian status; however, the proportion of centenarians is increasing at a dramatic rate among industrialized countries around the world. According to the US Census Bureau, there were 37,306 centenarians in 1990, 50,454 in 2000 (Hetzel and Smith, 2001), and it is projected that the number could increase to 324,000 in 2030, 447,000 in 2040, and 834,000 in 2050 (Krach and Velkoff, 1999). It is noted that the accuracy of the American census of centenarians is controversial as it is based on self-reports which are not validated. The number of centenarians in most industrialized countries is about 1 in 10,000, and the trend is toward 1 in 5,000 (Poon and Perls, 2007b).

The pertinent question for this chapter is what individual characteristics potentially contribute to resilience among centenarians. We do not know whether long-lived individuals inherently exhibit the resilience characteristics, acquire these characteristics along the way and hence become long lived, or how resilient people become long-lived individuals. Further, we do not know what heritable and environmental influences combine to inculcate resilience among the oldest-old. While longevity researchers around the world are seeking answers to contributors to longevity, which may have close and important correlates to resilience, there is general consensus on the following conclusions relating to longevity. One, there are large individual differences among centenarians (Gondo and Poon, 2007; Hagberg *et al.*, 2001; Martin, 2007; Poon and Perls, 2007a) along the dimensions of physical, mental, cognitive, and functional health as well as variations in family longevity, support systems, coping, personality, and lifestyles. These findings lead to the second consensus that there are multiple factors that contribute to longevity, and there is no one "secret" to longevity (for reviews see Poon and Perls, 2007b). Similarly, many factors are postulated to contribute to resilience with as many controversies and criticisms as the extant longevity research (Luthar, Cicchetti and Becker, 2000; Masten 1999, 2001; Masten and Coatsworth, 1998). Finally, women, compared with men, are the champion survivors in all the adult age ranges (Poon and Perls, 2007a). Eighty-five percent of centenarians are women, and the ten oldest persons in the world are women. Are long-lived women more resilient as well? We do not know. We do know that some factors contribute to female longevity superiority, while others do not. Further research in both longevity and resilience among the oldest-old is needed.

In this chapter, we begin by introducing a model of adaptation employed by the Georgia Centenarian Study (Poon *et al.*, 1992a). Within this model, we discuss resilience associated with three types of psychosocial contributors that could act as risks or threats toward successful adaptation on the one hand and positive or protective mediators on the other hand. These are personality/coping styles, cognition, and social and economic resources.

Theoretical and conceptual background

The outcome of successful adaptation is one contributor to resilience (Masten, 2001). Figure 8.1 outlines a conceptual model of Phase 1 (1988–1992) of the Georgia Centenarian Study (Poon *et al.*, 1992a), ,which examined successful adaptation of cognitively-intact and community-dwelling centenarians, octogenarians, and sexagenarians. The predictors in this model measure the direct and indirect impact of family longevity, environmental support, individual characteristics, coping abilities and styles, and nutrition on physical health, mental health, and life satisfaction.

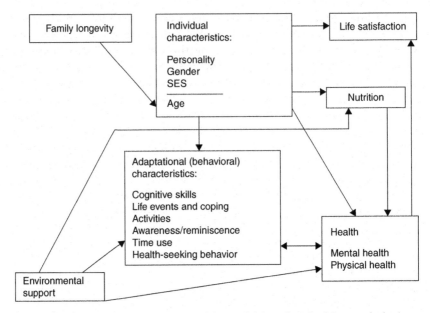

Figure 8.1. Georgia adaptation model (reprinted with permission).

Taken together, this model meets all the expectations of a study of resilience (Masten, 2001) in which the impacts of risks and adversities are examined against "good" outcomes or successful adaptation. Phase 2 (1992–1998) of the study examined longitudinal changes of the model components. The basic question of Phase 2 was whether centenarians could exceed all expectations of survival and continue to extend their individual lifespan. For these unusual centenarians, we were wondering whether there were any resilience factors contributing to continued survival. Phase 3 (2001–2009) is a population-based study examining both biomedical (genetics, neuropathology, blood chemistry, nutrition, health) and psychosocial (neuropsychology, adaptation, resources) contributors to longevity (Poon *et al.*, 2007). Our current study also addresses resilience, as we are comparing those centenarians who adapt well with those who may not adapt well in very late life.

This chapter is designed to focus on three aspects of the Georgia Centenarian Study that could potentially contribute to our understanding of resilience among the oldest-old: personality and coping styles (i.e., individual and adaptational characteristics), cognition (i.e., behavioral skills and functional status), and economic and supportive resources (i.e., environmental support). As noted by Masten (2001), resilience occurs in the context of ordinary everyday lives and, among adversities, good outcomes may occur. In the study of lives and patterns of centenarians, paradoxes present themselves as a matter of course. For example, centenarians may have poor resources in that their income and assets are frequently below the poverty level. Centenarians may also lack in family and support systems as they frequently outlive their families, and yet they may have good everyday problem abilities and coping skills that help them survive with good mental health and excellent perceived quality of life. On the other hand, some centenarians may have a sufficient support system to be cared for in a private nursing home or at home; however, they may have severe dementia that compromises their quality of life at the end stage. Owing to the prevalence of dementia in late life, our study attempts to triangulate self- and proxy reports, actual performances, as well as an interviewer's assessment to ascertain different points of view of the same situation. From this perspective, we have expected complex interactions in both direct and indirect assessment in the study of adaptation among the oldest-old. Our study represents an attempt to take a first few steps to better understand longevity and successful aging in the midst of challenges among the oldest-old.

Personality and coping resilience

The first resilience domain we discuss is concerned with personality and coping behaviors. It is easily noticeable that many centenarians experience a number of limitations. Notwithstanding those limitations, many centenarians continue to astonish family members, nursing staff, and community service providers. What makes centenarians so fascinating? We have noted that, among other things, centenarians have a robust or resilient personality (Martin, 2007). In addition, centenarians have found effective ways to cope with their own limitations (Martin et al., 2008). Personality and coping are considered personal or individual resources that help to adapt during times of change.

Consistent with the definition of resilience provided by Masten (2001), suggesting that resilience refers to beneficial outcomes even if individuals experience threats to their adaptation, personality traits and coping behaviors are resources available during challenging times. For example, centenarians as survivors have lost many family members and friends, yet their unique personality may help them overcome these loss events. Likewise, centenarians may employ unique coping behaviors that help them to adjust to age-associated changes. Resilience is therefore dependent on personal resources available in times of crises.

If these personal resources are characteristic of centenarians, then they should show up in the overall personality profile of centenarians.

In previous publications, we have pointed to a number of important traits and states that are consistently noticeable in the profile or config-uration of centenarians. In Phase 1 of the Georgia Centenarian Study, we reported that centenarians had higher scores in dominance, sus-piciousness, and shrewdness, whereas they were lower in imagination and tension when compared with two younger groups (Martin, 2002). Our longitudinal Phase 2 data showed that when retesting centenar-ians after approximately 20 months, centenarians had decreased scores in sensitivity, but demonstrated higher scores in "openness to change" (Martin, Long, and Poon, 2002). We argued that a relaxed but up-front personality describes the "robust personality" among these highly selected centenarians and that this distinct personality pattern was not only an indication of survivorship but also an important resource helping centenarians to adapt well in later life (Martin, 2002, 2007). In Phase 3 of the Georgia Centenarian Study, we have used the Big 5 framework and reported that centenarians overall had low levels of neuroticism, but relatively high levels of extraversion, competence (a facet of conscientiousness), and trust (a facet of agreeableness; Martin *et al.*, 2006).

Caspi (1998) suggested three personality patterns can be directly related to the Big 5: the "well adapted" or resilient personality (i.e., per-sons who score moderately high on extraversion, openness, conscientious-ness, and agreeableness but low on neuroticism); the "overcontrolled" personality (i.e., persons particularly low on extraversion and emotional stability); and the "undercontrolled" personality (i.e., persons who score high on extraversion, but low on agreeableness, and conscientiousness). Based on this definition of a resilient personality, our results confirmed a tendency toward this special combination of traits among centenarians (i.e., low levels of neuroticism, high conscientiousness, and moderately high extraversion; Martin *et al.*, 2006).

Other centenarian studies have reported similar results. For example, centenarians in a Swedish centenarian study were described as depend-able, reliable, mature, and conscientious (Samuelsson *et al.*, 1997). Furthermore, centenarians on average were responsible, easygoing, cap-able, relaxed, efficient, and not prone to anxiety. A Japanese centenarian study indicated that centenarians scored higher in openness when com-pared with younger controls (Masui *et al.*, 2006). In addition, relatively high scores for conscientiousness and extraversion were found among female centenarians when compared with elderly individuals aged from 60 to 84 years. These studies suggest a common pattern of resilience: low scores in neuroticism and relatively high scores in conscientiousness and extraversion.

Table 8.1. *Cross-tabulation of stressful life events and mental health outcome*

		Negative affect	
		Low	High
Negative life events	Low	43 (A)	23 (B)
		33.9%	18.1%
	High	25 (C)	36 (D)
		19.7%	28.3%

Note: A median split was used to distinguish low and high negative life events and negative affect.

Resilience may also directly relate to effective coping. Centenarians are faced with many adverse changes, and how they deal with these late-in-life changes may be informative as to their ability to survive under unusual circumstances. In our previous research we noted two different aspects of coping: first, whereas centenarians are less likely to use behavioral coping styles (e.g., "made a plan of action"), continued high levels of cognitive coping (e.g., "went over the situation in my mind") are noticeable in these expert survivors (Martin *et al.*, 1992, 2008). Second, when individual coping items were evaluated, we noticed that centenarians were more likely to accept adverse situations, use religious coping, and to take one day at a time. Furthermore, centenarians were less likely to worry about stressful situations (Martin *et al.*, 2001). Taken together, the coping literature on centenarians suggests resilient behaviors rooted primarily in cognitive coping, acceptance, and religious coping.

In the next section, we will provide illustrative examples of how centenarians might use their individual resilience characteristics (i.e., personality and coping behaviors) in challenging situations. We will relate these characteristics to mental health and, with reference to Masten (2001), we will first take a person-focused and then a variable-focused approach to resilience among centenarians.

Illustrative examples: life events, personality, and mental health

Person-focused approaches to resilience, as outlined by Masten (2001), "attempt to capture the configural patterns of adaptation that naturally occur" (p. 232). A simple example would include a cross-tabulation of risk variables and outcomes. Table 8.1 summarizes an illustrative example with our centenarian data. In this example, cumulative or lifetime negative events were conceptualized as a risk factor and the outcome is mental health (i.e., degree of negative affect).

We used a life event checklist and summarized all events that reportedly occurred at any time of the centenarians' lives and that were rated as negative experiences. The negative affect subscale of Bradburn's Affect Balance Scale (Bradburn, 1969) was used as a mental health measure. We would expect that centenarians who reported many negative events throughout their lives would show higher levels of negative affect.

Group A includes centenarians who do not report many negative life events and who show low levels of negative affect. Perhaps these could be termed our "fortunate" centenarians, and it includes the highest percentage of centenarians. Group B includes centenarians who did not experience many negative events but who show high levels of negative affect. These centenarians may show mental health problems for perhaps different reasons not captured in our life events list. It is the smallest group of centenarians and we may label them the "dissatisfied" group. Group C contains centenarians who have experienced many negative events but do not show high levels of negative affect. These are our "resilient" centenarians, and about 20 percent of our centenarians fall in this category. Finally, Group D contains centenarians who have experienced many negative life events and show relatively high levels of negative affect. This is the second largest group, and we label them as our "vulnerable" group of centenarians.

The cross-tabulation alone does not show us whether one group of centenarians is more likely to emerge than others. We therefore computed configural frequency analyses to test for types and antitypes in this cross-classification (von Eye, 1990). This procedure allows us to conduct a probability test for each cell to evaluate whether a configuration of rows and columns in a cross-tabulation occurs more (or less) than expected by chance. Configurations that occurred more often than expected by chance are considered "types," while configurations that occurred less often than expected by chance are "antitypes."

The results suggest that Group A membership (i.e., "fortunate") occurred more often than would be expected by chance ($p = 0.02$), whereas group B membership (i.e., "dissatisfied") occurred less often than would be expected by chance ($p = 0.04$). There was a statistical trend suggesting that the resilient group C (i.e., "resilient") occurred less often than would be expected by chance ($p = 0.09$).

Taken together, our person-centered data illustrate that resilient centenarians exist, but the group of resilient centenarians was not the most frequent group. The strongest group contained individuals who had not

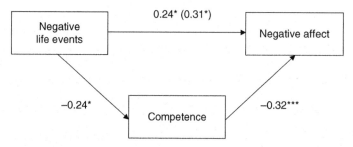

Figure 8.2. Mediation model of negative life events, competence, and negative affect.

experienced many negative life events and reported very low negative affect scores, perhaps pointing to a pattern of advantaged survivorship. Few negative events and high levels of mental health might have moved these centenarians into an elite group of survivors to begin with.

In addition to taking a person-focused approach, Masten (2001) noted that variable-focused approaches "use multivariate statistics to test for linkages among measures of the degree of risk or adversity, outcome, and potential qualities of the individual or environment that may function to compensate for or protect the individual from the negative consequences of risk of adversity" (p. 229). In the following illustrative example we again chose cumulative negative life events as the risk or adversity measure, personality (specifically competence, a facet of conscientiousness in the Big 5 framework) as the personal asset, and negative affect as a potentially negative consequence of adversity. As outlined by Masten (2001), we tested independent, mediating, and moderating effects. When testing the independent effect of negative life events and competence on negative affect, both competence ($\beta = -0.32, p < 0.01$) and negative life events ($\beta = 0.31, p < 0.05$) predicted negative affect. The model suggests that competent centenarians are less likely to show high levels of negative affect. Those centenarians, however, who have experienced many negative events throughout their lives are more likely to show poorer mental health.

An alternative model would place competence as a mediator between cumulative life events and negative affect. The illustrative results are shown in Figure 8.2. The model suggests that competence is a mediator between cumulative negative life events and negative affect. Those centenarians who had experienced many negative events throughout their lives were less likely to be competent, and lower levels of competence were associated with higher levels of negative affect. According to Baron and Kenny (1986), a mediator reduces or eliminates the effect of a risk factor on negative outcomes. In this example, the personality trait competence reduced the effect of negative life events on mental health problems (i.e., the path is reduced from 0.31 to 0.24), suggesting partial mediation.

The final model tested was a model of statistical moderation. The effect of competence as a moderator is established through the interaction term of negative life events and competence. The interaction term was not significant and, more importantly, the interaction entered as a separate regression block did not explain significantly more variance in the dependent variable, $F\Delta(1,99) = 0.73$, $p > 0.05$. Competence, therefore, did not serve as a moderator in the stress–outcome relationship.

This example illustrates the importance of personality as a resilience factor when very old people reflect on their long lives. A long life replete with negative events could be disconcerting, but individual resources may change the overall nature of this relationship. Even though negative events erode the feelings of competence, competence – as a mediator – reduces the effect of stress on negative outcomes. Of course, we only provided illustrative examples; other personality traits (e.g., neuroticism or extraversion) or coping variables (e.g., cognitive or behavioral coping) may also function as salient mediators in the stress – outcome relationship. In the next section, we will discuss our approach to cognitive resilience.

Cognitive resilience

Given the multifaceted nature of "cognition" and the synergistic relation between cognition and functioning throughout the lifespan, the conceptualization of cognitive resilience is complex and its meaning can vary across age. Several issues arise when considering cognitive resilience in late life, including the following: (a) distinguishing the type of cognition assessed such as domain-specific abilities (e.g., memory, reasoning) or mental status (e.g., impaired, at-risk, or intact) and whether assessments are performance-based or subjective reports; (b) identifying criteria to distinguish a minimum level of acceptable performance or, as Masten (2001) notes, specifying what constitutes a "good" outcome; and (c) understanding the interconnectedness of cognition with other systems and functional outcomes (e.g., sensory functioning). Depending on perspective, cognitive abilities and status could be characterized as assets/risks or outcomes in their own right. As an outcome, cognitive resilience might describe individuals who are able to maintain adequate levels of cognitive functioning throughout very late life despite adversity and cumulative risk. For various individuals, an optimal cognitive outcome may include enhancement or maintenance of cognitive abilities, avoidance of impairment, or achievement of minimal, legal cognitive competence. As a predictor, late-life cognitive resilience may typify individuals who maintain adequate everyday functioning despite initially low, currently declining, or impaired cognitive functioning. This section describes the cognitive abilities of oldest-old adults, followed by a review of findings on the impact of cognition on longevity, and finally by borrowing from the resilience literature we postulate how variations in cognition, including dementia, could contribute to successful adaptation of the oldest-old.

Cognition in later life

As previously mentioned, the conceptualization and assessment of cognition vary. For one, prior research has differentiated two broad classes of cognitive abilities comprised of several individual intellectual skills, and this distinction appears to remain important through very late life. Crystallized abilities, or those skills which rely on accumulated knowledge and experience, are generally maintained well into the seventies; however, fluid abilities which are considered more biologically driven peak in the early twenties and exhibit a gradual decline throughout adulthood (Schaie, 2005). Across studies, centenarians demonstrated a greater range of performance on measures of crystallized abilities; however, centenarians' performance on fluid measures tended to be more similar, suggesting a possible floor effect in respect to these more age-sensitive abilities (Hagberg et al., 2001).

In contrast to the first approach, which focuses on more narrowly defined individual cognitive skills, assessments of problem-solving ability tend to be more contextual and incorporate actual real-life stimuli (e.g., prescription labels). "Everyday" problem-solving ability is considered to be a higher-order cognitive skill which depends upon the constituent intellectual abilities (e.g., Marsiske and Willis, 1995). In contrast to marked age-related differences observed in individual intellectual abilities, everyday problem-solving assessments may better capture the skills needed in late life. For instance, Poon and colleagues note the robust ability of oldest-old and centenarian participants to generate solutions to everyday problems (Poon et al., 1992a, 1992b). The ability to navigate everyday challenges is particularly important as we consider successful adaptation and resilience in very late life. The resilience of such abilities may be masked by reliance on domain-specific assessments.

A third approach to understanding cognitive aging stems from a more clinical and neuropsychological perspective aimed at understanding the mechanisms underlying non-normative cognitive changes such as the occurrence of dementia. From this perspective, global indicators of cognitive functioning and neuropsychological measures are typically employed to distinguish individuals with dementia from those without cognitive impairment. Dementia prevalence rates vary with age, and the Alzheimer's Association (2007) estimates that one in eight persons in the USA over the age of 65 has dementia or Alzheimer's disease; this rate dramatically increases among adults aged 85 and older to one in two persons. However, despite an increased risk associated with greater age, not all centenarians have dementia. This raises doubts regarding the "eventuality" of dementia and establishes the need to identify factors related to cognitive resilience, including "functional and cognitive reserves" (e.g., Perls, 2004).

The impact of cognition and dementia on survivorship

The literature has shown with high consistency that cognition and survivorship are positively related; however, there remain many unanswered questions (see Gondo and Poon, 2007, for a review). The foremost question is which types of cognition are particularly important to survival? Second, if cognition is positively related to survival, then there exists a paradox that a good portion of centenarians are cognitively impaired; how can this paradox be resolved? A number of centenarian studies have shown that higher levels of cognitive and functional performances among centenarians predict survival (Gondo and Poon, 2007). The French Centenarian Study (Robine, Romieu, and Allard, 2003) found that mental status was predictive of eight-year survival in addition to health status, activities of daily living (ADL), and independent activities of daily living (IADL). The Tokyo Centenarian Study (Shimizu *et al.*, 2001) found that the Clinical Dementia Scale (CDR) was predictive of survival; however, this effect disappeared after controlling for physical conditions. Another finding from the Tokyo Study (Gondo *et al.*, 2006) was that the total functional scores of physical and cognitive functions predicted one-year survival above and beyond the predictive power of cognitive function alone. Finally, the Georgia Centenarian Study (Poon *et al.*, 2000) showed that cognition was one of four predictors of the number of days of survival after 100 years; the other predictors were being female, father's age of death, and nutrition sufficiency.

If higher levels of cognition are predictive of survival, then how would one reconcile the prevalence of dementia among centenarians? This is indeed a paradox. The prevalence of dementia varies from about 42 to 80 percent from different studies around the world (Gondo and Poon, 2007), with a mean around 50 percent. Given that the average length of life after contracting dementia is about eight years, it is reasonable to postulate that dementia among centenarians is most likely to be late onset. If this postulation is correct, then it could be further hypothesized that distal experiences and cognitive abilities prior to the onset of dementia may be important factors in the determinants of survival, and not just current-state cognition alone. Among models of resilience, Masten (2001) postulated that both the positive influence of "assets" and the negative influence of risks-adversities could work independently or jointly to impact outcome behavior or through moderator variables which in turn impact the outcome behavior. From this perspective, cognition could be an asset that is protective, dementia could be the risk-adversity, and both could impact longevity or resilience through a variety of mechanisms.

Variable and person-focused approaches to cognitive resilience

As noted by Masten (2001), it may be helpful to consider variable (i.e., individual and contextual factors) and person-related (i.e., profiles over time) predictors related to cognitive resilience. Both approaches are applicable to the study of cognitive resilience in later life, as cognitive aging is a dynamic process and one likely to occur with concomitant changes in both the individual and their environment. Examples of individual and contextual variables which affect cognitive development and adaptation in later life are early education, birth cohort, ethnicity, gender, and socioeconomic environment. More dynamic person-related variables include influences such as genetics (e.g., presence of APOE $\epsilon4$ allele), health and physical status, mental health, emotional regulation, as well as developmental changes to the cognitive (e.g., dedifferentiation of abilities and terminal change and drop in ability level prior to death; de Frias et al., 2007; Siegler and Bosworth, 2002) and other systems (e.g., sensory functioning; Li and Lindenberger, 2002).

Illustrative examples: cognitive resilience as an outcome and a predictor

Similar to the cross-tabular approach taken with personality, we examined cognitive resilience as an outcome as well as a predictor. Table 8.2 depicts an indicator of cognitive resilience (i.e., global cognitive or mental status, as assessed by the Mini-Mental Status Examination; Folstein, Folstein, and McHugh, 1975) and educational attainment, an important precursor to late-life mental status.

Table 8.2. *Cross-tabulation of educational attainment and cognitive status outcome*

		Education	
		Less than high school	High School Diploma
Cognitive status	Low	59 (A)	19 (B)
		40.1%	12.9%
	High	38 (C)	31 (D)
		25.9%	21.1%

Note: Cognitive status was dichotomized: $0 = MMSE < 17$; $1 = MMSE \geq 17$.

Similar to the findings for personality, individuals falling into each category can be categorized in terms of risk and resilience. As shown in Group A, lack of early education was a risk for some centenarians; individuals without a high school diploma or its equivalent were more likely to demonstrate a low Mini-Mental Status Examination (MMSE) score. However, a substantial number of individuals could be described as cognitively "resilient" (i.e., Group C). These centenarians maintained a high level of cognitive functioning in later life despite a relatively low level of educational attainment. Consistent with expectations, individuals in Group D could be described as "fortunate" because they possessed high educational attainment and maintained higher cognitive status. Although the smallest group, some centenarians (Group B) attained a high school diploma yet did not maintain high cognitive functioning in late life. The configural frequency analyses suggested that this configuration occurred less often than would be expected by chance ($p < 0.001$). In contrast, Group A occurred more often than would be expected by chance, resulting in a significant "type" for centenarians ($p < 0.001$).

Next, we examined cognition as a conceptual prerequisite of more complex functioning. Table 8.3 depicts the cross-tabular relation between MMSE score and centenarians' ability to perform activities of daily living (i.e., ADL) as assessed by the Direct Assessment of Functional Status (DAFS; Loewenstein *et al.*, 1989). The DAFS assesses objective ability to perform tasks in critical life domains such as communication, finances, personal care, and shopping. As evident in the table, cognitive status and functional ability were highly related. As shown in Group D, many centenarians in the sample could be described as "fortunate" because they exhibited high levels of both cognitive and functional performance. The second most frequent group was Group A, in which individuals can be described as "vulnerable," given the correspondence between lower

Table 8.3 *Cross-tabulation of cognitive status and activities of daily living outcome*

| | | Activity of daily living performance | |
		Low	High
Cognitive status	Low	76 (A)	13 (B)
		39.0%	6.7%
	High	20 (C)	86 (D)
		10.3%	44.1%

Note: Cognitive status was dichotomized: $0 = \text{MMSE} < 17$; $1 = \text{MMSE} \geq 17$; A median split was used to distinguish relatively low and high ADL functioning within the sample.

cognitive status and lower ADL functioning. It is interesting to note that, as illustrated by Group B, very few individuals (6.7 percent) could be described as functionally "resilient" despite low cognitive status. Finally, individuals in Group C demonstrated high cognitive functioning yet have low ADL performance, thus suggesting other influential factors such as poor physical health. Based on configural frequency analyses, Groups A and D are "types," meaning they occur more often than would be expected by chance (both $p < 0.001$). Groups B and C, on the other hand, are "antitypes," meaning that they occur less often than expected by chance (again, both $p < 0.001$).

Social and economic resilience

The third resilience domain relevant to long-lived survivors concerns their social and economic resources. Centenarians have lived well beyond the years for which their social and economic resources were expected to last. Their ADL impairment may inhibit conversations and participation in social activities or restrict their mobility for obtaining support services. Centenarians may also be concerned about their dependency, along with the adequacy of their own resources to meet future consumption and health needs. However, friends, family, and government services do respond to those unique circumstances to support them, and some centenarians may have managed to maintain sufficient wealth to confront increased need. Hence Masten's (2001) conceptualization of resilience in the face of extreme disadvantage seems quite apt for investigating the extent to which social and personal economic resources contribute to centenarian well-being. For that purpose, we will again focus on mental health as measured by negative affect, and thus define social and economic resilience for centenarians as having sufficient socioeconomic resources to restrict negative affect below what would be expected because of deficits in functional health alone, or because of their negative life experiences.

The question of interest is how extremely old individuals are able to maintain a mental outlook that is as positive as among younger-old adults despite their relative deprivation on almost all other accounts. Based on a meta-analysis of 286 empirical studies of influences on subjective well-being in later life, Pinquart and Sörenson (2000) found no age-associated decline and they concluded that social networks were one of the most important positive influences. In the most comprehensive analysis available for the Berlin Aging Study, Smith and colleagues (1999) found that, except for subjective health, satisfaction with social activities had the strongest effects on overall well-being. Additionally, their path analysis revealed that satisfaction with finances was very important and that age was positively related to financial satisfaction, which suggests that reduced financial obligations or consumption needs may change the context of mental health assessment in very old age.

Results from the first two phases of the Georgia Centenarian Study are a prominent feature of the international literature concerning the influences of social support and centenarians' economic resources on mental health (MacDonald, 2007). For example, we reported that Georgia centenarians' annual incomes and poverty status were disadvantaged compared with Georgia sexagenarians and octogenarians and that centenarians were more likely to get help in the form of in-kind assistance (meals, food, and Medicaid) or income assistance (Goetting *et al.*, 1996). Still, centenarians were not significantly different from sexagenarians and octogenarians on most aspects in a self-assessment of economic resource adequacy (e.g., "enough for emergencies," or "to buy extras"). However, about one in five centenarians reported that their resources were insufficient (i.e., they did not have enough for their needs in the future, to meet emergencies, and that they needed financial assistance).

With respect to social resources, we noted that centenarians had fewer potential visitors, were much less likely to talk on the phone daily, and were more likely to list offspring as caregivers than were sexagenarians and octogenarians (Martin *et al.*, 1996). Using the Georgia Study interviewer's rating of the quality of social interactions, we also found that the measure of social resources was negatively affected by adverse cumulative life events, but that there were direct and positive effects of social resources on activities of daily living, and the interviewer's rating of the centenarians' mental health (Martin, 2002). Furthermore, adverse life events were negatively related to centenarians' economic resources, and those adverse events had a negative influence on mental health (Martin, 2002). The current Phase 3 study is based on a population-based sample including residents of nursing homes and skilled nursing facilities, whereas the earlier phases of the Georgia study were restricted to community-dwelling centenarians. Presumably those centenarians requiring constant nursing care are the most disadvantaged, so new evidence of resilience due to social and economic variables in this sample would strongly confirm what those previous findings suggest.

Measures of social and economic resources

We focused on the percentage distributions of three measures for social and economic resources of centenarians, all of which are obtained from centenarians' responses to the Duke Older Adults Resources and Services (OARS) questions (Fillenbaum, 1988). For social resources there are two measures, which are the social interactions scale and the number of types of care services the centenarians received. The social interactions scale is the sum of responses about how many people they knew well enough to visit them in their own or another person's home, how many times they had talked with someone on the telephone in the past week, and how many times in the past week they had spent time with someone who did not live with them. To gauge the level of instrumental social support that centenarians receive, the number of care services counts how many of five types of caregiving they received, which could include personal care, nursing, supervision, household chores, and meal preparation help. The OARS perceived economic status scale is from self-report items that assess the centenarians' perceptions about their economic resources (e.g., with respect to whether financial resources were sufficient to meet emergencies, and how well the amount of money they had took care of their needs). A large majority (81.1 percent) scored six or more for social interactions (nine-point scale maximum) and 79.2 percent received two or more of the five types of care services. Furthermore, over three-quarters scored seven or eight on perceived economic status.

Illustrative examples: life events, social and economic resources, and mental health

Cross-tabulations with social interactions and perceived economic status were obtained (Tables 8.4 and 8.5) to provide a person-focused assessment of the extent to which those resources are associated with ADL functioning from the OARS (Fillenbaum, 1988). For social interactions,

Table 8.4. *Cross-tabulation of social interactions and activities of daily living outcome*

		Social interactions	
		Low	High
Activities of daily living	Low	36 (A)	23 (B)
		28.3 %	18.1%
	High	25 (C)	43 (D)
		19.7%	33.9%

Note: A mean split was used to distinguish low and high ADL functioning and social interactions.

Table 8.5. *Cross-tabulation of perceived economic status and activities of daily living outcome*

		Perceived economic status	
		Low	High
Activities of daily living	Low	15 (A)	32 (B)
		14.0%	29.9%
	High	9 (C)	51 (D)
		8.4%	47.7 %

Note: A mean split was used to distinguish low and high ADL functioning and perceived economic status.

a large percentage of centenarian outcomes were as expected (i.e., Groups A and D: lower ADL functioning was associated with less social interaction and higher ADL functioning was associated with greater social interaction). Twenty percent of individuals (i.e., Group C) could be classified as "resilient"; these centenarians maintained superior ADL functioning despite lower social interaction. For Group B, greater social interaction and presumed support did not translate into superior ADL functioning, and that group included about 18 percent of individuals.

In terms of perceived economic status, the majority of centenarians reported greater economic sufficiency as well as higher ADL functioning (i.e., Group D). Interestingly, for a substantial proportion of individuals (i.e., Group B), higher perceived economic status was actually related to worse ADL functioning. Thus, greater resources did not appear to serve as a buffer against lower functional ability for these individuals. A small proportion of centenarians (i.e., Group C) could be described as "resilient," that is despite lower perceived economic status these individuals maintained superior ADL functioning. The final group (i.e., Group A) represented 14 percent of the cases in which individuals were lower on both perceived economic resources and ADL ability. Configural frequency analysis tests confirmed that Group D was a more frequent type for both sources of support: greater social interaction and higher perceived economic status were positively related to ADL functioning.

However, neither the social interactions scale nor the perceived economic status scale provides an unambiguous standard for assessing what levels of those resources are sufficient to create resilience despite limitations due to functional health impairment or the impact of distal negative events. Hence additional variable-focused analyses were conducted to test whether those measures of socioeconomic resources mediate or moderate the influence of ADL impairment on negative affect. Similar analyses assessed whether the resource measures influenced the relationship of distal negative events on centenarians' negative affect. In that manner, the centenarians' negative affect scores provide a standard to compare the influences of the two types of limitations with those for social and economic resources.

As would be expected from the person-focused cross-tabulation discussed earlier, there was a significant negative relationship ($\beta = -0.19$, $p < 0.05$) between ADL impairment and social interactions. When social interactions was included in the model to predict negative affect, the effect of ADL impairment ($\beta = -0.08$) was not significant. However in that same model, there was a statistical trend for a negative influence of social interactions ($\beta = -0.16$, $p < 0.10$). Hence, there is some potential for concluding that support from the centenarians' social network mediates the negative influence of ADL impairment on their mental health.

The model for considering how perceived economic status may support mental health despite ADL impairment provided strong support for economic resilience of that type. In this case, there was a strong negative effect of ADL impairment on perceived economic status (Figure 8.3). When perceived economic status and ADL were both used as predictors of negative affect, the effect of ADL was not significant but perceived economic status had a significant negative effect. These results demonstrate the importance for centenarians of maintaining a resilient attitude that their economic resources are still sufficient to meet their needs despite the economic stress that is created by their functional impairments.

As an extension, we computed additional models to learn whether and how centenarians' social and economic resources may moderate the effect of stress from distal negative life events on their affect. That effort

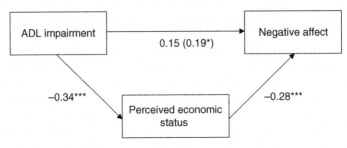

Figure 8.3. Mediation model of perceived economic status, ADL impairment, and negative affect.

yielded little support for the hypothesis that perceived economic status or social interaction moderates the direct effect of negative events on affect. However the use of an interaction term involving negative life events and perceived economic status provided evidence that centenarians' current economic resources do moderate the distal influence of negative events. Centenarians with low economic status were predicted to have a higher mean value for negative affect than those with high economic status, regardless of the number of negative life events. Furthermore, centenarians' negative affect was expected to increase to some extent due to negative events. By contrast, for centenarians with high perceived economic status, more negative events were associated with better affect. Evidently, centenarians with sufficient economic resources are able to resolve or pay for the consequences of negative life events such as health setbacks and thus maintain better mental health.

To summarize briefly, we found that perceived economic status mediates the negative influence of decreased functional ability on mental health. Additionally, the influence of negative life events as a stressor that may increase negative affect was moderated by perceived economic status, so that those who were economically better off managed to maintain positive mental health. Although the results of tests for mediation by social interactions were not as clear cut, the findings also suggested some protective influence for mental health. In our earlier work we reported that centenarians' adverse life events were negatively related to both the quality of their social interactions and perceived economic status, and that both types of resources still contributed to their mental health (Martin, 2002). The present study yields the additional result that economic resources moderate the influence of negative life events on mental well-being. Furthermore, the negative influence of functional health impairment appeared to be entirely mediated by economic resource adequacy. This result may be an important clue for resolving the puzzle about how oldest-old individuals construct positive well-being despite severe health restrictions. Pinquart and Sörenson (2000) have suggested that the oldest people maintain their well-being through "downward age comparisons" and thus feel fortunate simply because they have survived. The findings reported here suggest that maintaining centenarians' economic resources may be sufficiently protective for social and economic resilience that enhances mental health. Further research to examine how social support may enhance resources for meeting centenarians' needs may be in order, particularly with respect to caregiving services and medical assistance.

Conclusion

We noted in the introduction that longevity and successful adaptation are intimately tied to resilience, and these concepts share many of the common mechanisms. Among these mechanisms are the accumulation of risks and threats throughout one's lifetime and successful adaptation in dealing with these risks to achieve exceptional longevity. We also noted that researchers generally agree that there is not one secret to longevity, and it has been shown that different individuals employ diverse paths to achieve longevity. We believe this conclusion also applies when addressing individual differences in resilience among the oldest-old.

We introduced three types of psychosocial domains that could be major contributors to resilience among the oldest-old. First, we have identified specific personality types that are more prevalent among centenarians compared with octogenarians and sexagenarians and that centenarians tended to employ these characteristics to cope in challenging situations. As this point of our research, we postulated these "robust" personality types could be important facilitators toward successful adaptation and resilience. It is not known whether the absence of these characteristics would inhibit adaptation, or that these individuals would use other compensatory behaviors for their adaptation.

Second, cognition was found to positively relate to longevity (Gondo and Poon, 2007). It is clear that maintenance of cognitive abilities is an important facilitator to resilience associated with problem solving in the face of everyday challenges. In contrast, dementia hinders resilience. In the absence of pathology (e.g., dementia of the Alzheimer's type), there are known normative changes in aging that are shown to be facilitative (e.g., crystallized intelligence or dictionary-type knowledge) and significantly lower in old age (e.g., fluid intelligence or learning of new materials). At this point of research, we do not have answers to the important question of which types of cognitive skills are particularly important to survival and resilience.

Finally, data from the Georgia Centenarian Study show that maintenance of social and economic resources facilitates independence and secures care services which are intricately related to resilience. It is quite clear that personality and coping style, cognition, and social and economic resources played important protective roles in ameliorating risks and threats accumulated over the lifetime of the oldest-old. It is most likely that these contributors play direct, indirect, and interactive roles which could vary in different times in one's lifetime. However in times of diminished capacities, these contributors to resilience may be most important at the end stage of life.

The three forms of resilience discussed in this chapter also have practical implications for all aging individuals. Because advancing to very old age does not come without challenges, it would be valuable for all adults to "prepare" for hardships in late life. A rich repertoire of resources and reserves can be helpful when challenges ensue. Older adults who maintain a robust personality and who have optimized cognitive resilience through life-long practice should be better prepared to master expected and unexpected challenges. Furthermore, it is important to maintain a strong social network or replace lost members so that support is available in times of adversity. Finally, solid economic resources can help take care of expenses that often accompany crises. These three resource areas are not obtained instantly during emergencies. Instead, building resources and reserves is a lifespan task for aging individuals, and building resources should be encouraged by educators, family members, and public policy leaders.

It is without question that personal, cognitive, and socioeconomic resilience make up a complex system of lifespan reserves. These levels of complexity remind us of a hypothetical question posed in lectures on centenarians by one of the authors (Poon). He often posed this scenario to his audience. A genie will grant one wish to prolong your longevity. One could pick only one of the following: wealth, health, or good cognitive functioning. Which one would you pick? The answer[1] can be found below.

---

[1] Health, wealth, or cognitive functioning – choose one. In surveying graduate students at the University of Georgia, 18 percent picked health, 5 percent chose wealth, and 77 percent chose good cognition. In surveying older adults in the Learning in Retirement group at the University, 5 percent chose health, 10 percent chose wealth, and 85 percent chose good cognition.

Acknowledgments

The Georgia Centenarian Study (Leonard W. Poon, PI) is funded by 1P01-AG17553 from the National Institute on Aging, a collaboration among The University of Georgia, Tulane University, Boston University, University of Kentucky, Emory University, Duke University, Wayne State University, Iowa State University, and University of Michigan. Authors acknowledge the valuable recruitment and data acquisition effort from M. Burgess, K. Grier, E. Jackson, E. McCarthy, K. Shaw, L. Strong, and S. Reynolds, data acquisition team manager; S. Anderson, E. Cassidy, M. Janke, and J. Savla, data management; M. Poon for project fiscal management.

REFERENCES

Alzheimer's Association. (2007). Alzheimer's Disease facts and figures. Chicago, IL. Retrieved April 20, 2007, from http://www.alz.org/national/documents/report_alzfactsfigures2008.pdf

Baron, R. M., and Kenny, D. A. (1986). The moderator-mediator variable distinction in social psychological research: Conceptual, strategic, and statistical considerations. *Journal of Personality and Social Psychology*, 51, 1173–1182.

Bradburn, N. M. (1969). *The structure of psychological well-being*. Chicago, IL: Aldine.

Caspi, A. (1998). Personality development across the life course. In W. Damon and N. Eisenberg (eds.), *Handbook of child development*, vol.III: *Social, emotional, and personality psychology* (5th edn., pp. 311–388). New York: Wiley.

de Frias, C. M., Lövdén, M., Lindenberger, U., and Nilsson, L. G. (2007). Revisiting the dedifferentiation hypothesis with longitudinal multi-cohort data. *Intelligence*, 35, 381–392.

Fillenbaum, G. G. (1988). *Multidimensional functional assessment of older adults: The Duke Older Americans Resources and Services Procedures.* Hillsdale, NJ: Erlbaum.

Folstein, M. F., Folstein, S. E., and McHugh, P. R. (1975). Mini-mental state: A practical method for grading the cognitive state of patients for the clinician. *Journal of Psychiatric Research*, 12, 189–198.

Goetting, M., Martin P., Poon L. W., and Johnson, M. (1996). The economic well-being of community-dwelling centenarians. *Journal of Aging Studies*, 10, 43–55.

Gondo, Y., Hirose, N., Arai, Y., *et al.* (2006). Functional status of centenarians in Tokyo, Japan: Developing better phenotypes of exceptional longevity. *Journal of Gerontology*, 61, 305–310.

Gondo, Y., and Poon, L.W. (2007). Cognitive function of centenarians and its influence on longevity. *Annual Review of Gerontology and Geriatrics*, 27, 129–150.

Hagberg, B., Alfredson, B. B., Poon, L. W., and Homma, A. (2001). Cognitive functioning in centenarians: A coordinated analysis of results from three countries. *Journal of Gerontology: Psychological Sciences,* 56B(3), P141–P151.

Hetzel, L., and Smith, A. (2001). *The 65 years and over population: 2000.* Washington, DC: US Census Bureau.

Krach, C. A., and Velkoff, V. A. (1999). *Centenarians in the United States.* Washington, DC: US Bureau of the Census, Current Population Reports, Series P23–199RV. US Government Printing Office.

Li, K. Z. H., and Lindenberger, U. (2002). Connections among sensory, sensorimotor, and cognitive aging: Review of data and theories. *Neuroscience and Biobehavioral Reviews,* 26(7), 777–783.

Loewenstein, D. A., Amigo, E., Duara, R. *et al.* (1989). A new scale for the assessment of functional status in Alzheimer's disease and related disorders. *Journal of Gerontology,* 44, 114–121.

Luthar, S. S., Cicchetti, D., and Becker, B. (2000). The construct of resilience: A critical evaluation and guidelines for future work. *Child Development,* 71, 543–562.

MacDonald, M. (2007). Social support for centenarians' health, psychological well-being and longevity. In L. W. Poon and T. T. Perls (eds.) *Annual review of gerontology and geriatrics,* vol. XXVII: *Biopsychosocial approaches to longevity* (pp. 107–127). New York: Springer.

Marsiske, M., and Willis, S. L. (1995). Dimensionality of everyday problem solving in older adults. *Psychology and Aging,* 10, 269–283.

Martin P. (2002). Individual and social resources predicting well-being and functioning in later years: Conceptual models, research, and practice. *Ageing International,* 27, 3–29.

(2007). Personality and coping among centenarians. In L. W. Poon and T. T. Perls (eds.), *Annual review of gerontology and geriatrics,* vol. XXVII: *Biopsychosocial approaches to longevity* (pp. 89–106). New York: Springer.

Martin, P., da Rosa, G., Siegler, I. *et al.* (2006). Personality and longevity: Findings from the Georgia Centenarian Study. *Age,* 28, 343–352.

Martin, P., Kliegel, M., Rott, C. Poon, L. W., and Johnson, M. A. (2008). Age differences and changes of coping behavior in three age groups: Findings from the Georgia Centenarian Study. *International Journal of Aging and Human Development,* 66, 97–114.

Martin, P., Long, M. V., and Poon L. W. (2002). Age changes and differences in personality traits and states of the old and very old. *The Journals of Gerontology: Psychological Sciences,* 57B, 144–152.

Martin, P., Poon, L. W., Clayton, G. M., Lee, H. S., Fulks, J. S., and Johnson, M. A. (1992). Personality, life events, and coping in the oldest-old. *International Journal of Aging and Human Development,* 34, 19–30.

Martin, P., Poon, L., Kim, E., and Johnson, M. A. (1996). Social and psychological resources in the oldest old. *Experimental Aging Research,* 22, 121–139.

Martin, P., Rott, C., Poon, L. W., Courtenay, B., and Lehr, U. (2001). A molecular view of coping behavior in older adults. *Journal of Aging and Health*, 13, 72–91.

Masten, A. S. (1999). Resilience comes of age: Reflections on the past and outlook for the next generation of research. In M. D. Glantz, J. Johnson, and L. Huffman (eds.), *Resilience and development: Positive life adaptations* (pp. 282–296). New York: Plenum.

(2001). Ordinary magic: Resilience processes in development. *American Psychologist*, 56, 227–238.

Masten, A. S., and Coatsworth, J. D. (1998). The development of competence in favorable and unfavorable environments: Lessons from successful children. *American Psychologist*, 53, 205–220.

Masui, Y., Gondo, Y., Inagaki, H., and Hirose, N. (2006). Do personality characteristics predict longevity? Findings from the Tokyo Centenarian Study. *Age*, 28, 353–361.

National Center for Health Statistics. (2007). *Health, United States, 2007 with chartbook on trend in the health of Americans*. Hyattsville, MD: US Department of Health and Human Services.

Perls, T. (2004). Dementia-free centenarians. *Experimental Gerontology*, 39, 1587–1593.

Pinquart, M., and Sörenson, S. (2000). Influences of socioeconomic status, social network, and competence on subjective well-being in later life: A meta-analysis. *Psychology and Aging*, 15, 187–207.

Poon, L. W., and Perls, T. T. (2007a). The trials and tribulations of studying the oldest old. *Annual Review of Gerontology and Geriatrics*, 27, 1–10.

Poon, L. W., and Perls, T. (eds.) (2007b). *Annual review of gerontology and geriatrics: Biopsychosocial approaches to longevity*. New York: Springer.

Poon, L. W., Clayton, G. M., Martin, P., et al. (1992a). The Georgia Centenarian Study. *International Journal of Aging and Human Development*, 34, 1–17.

Poon, L. W., Jazwinski, S. M., Green, R. C., et al. (2007). Methodological considerations in studying centenarians: Lessons learned from the Georgia Centenarian Studies. *Annual Review of Gerontology and Geriatrics*, 27, 231–264.

Poon, L. W., Johnson, M. A., Davey, A., Dawson, D. V., Siegler, I. C., and Martin, P. (2000). Psycho-social predictors of survival among centenarians. In P. Martin, Ch. Rott, B. Hagberg, and K. Morgan (eds.), *Centenarians: Autonomy versus dependence in the oldest old* (pp. 77–89). New York: Springer.

Poon, L. W., Messner, S., Martin, P., and Noble, C. A. (1992b). The influences of cognitive resources on adaptation and old age. *International Journal of Aging and Human Development*, 34(1), 381–390.

Robine, J. M., Romieu, I., and Allard, M. (2003). French centenarians and their functional health status. *Le Presse Medicale*, 32, 360–364.

Samuelsson S. M., Alfredson B. B., Hagberg B., et al. (1997). The Swedish Centenarian Study: A multidisciplinary study of five consecutive cohorts at the age of 100. *International Journal of Aging and Human Development*, 45, 223–253.

Schaie, K. W. (2005). *Developmental influences on adult intelligence: The Seattle Longitudinal Study.* Oxford University Press.

Shimizu, K., Hirose, N., Arai, Y., Gondo, Y., and Wakida, Y. (2001). Determinants of further survival in centenarians. *Geriatrics and Gerontology International,* 1, 14–17.

Siegler, I. C., and Bosworth, H. B. (2002). Terminal change in cognitive function: an updated review of longitudinal studies. *Experimental Aging Research,* 28, 299–315.

Smith, J., Fleeson, W., Geiselmann, B., Settersten Jr., R., and Kunzmann, U. (1999). Sources of well-being in very old age. In P. B. Baltes and K. U. Mayer (eds.), *The Berlin Aging Study: Aging from 70 to 100* (pp. 450–471). New York: Cambridge University Press.

von Eye, A. (1990). *Introduction to configural frequency analysis: The search for types and antitypes in cross-classification.* New York: Cambridge University Press.

9 The socioemotional basis of resilience in later life

Anthony D. Ong and C. S. Bergeman

Abstract

Resilience has numerous meanings in prior research, but generally refers to a pattern of functioning indicative of *positive adaptation* in the context of significant *risk* or adversity. Underlying this broad definition are two specific conditions: (a) exposure to significant risks; and (b) evidence of positive adaptation despite serious threats to development. In this chapter, we examine the relevance of positive emotions and social connection as basic building blocks of resilience in later life. We put forth a dynamic conception of resilience to illuminate, theoretically and empirically, how some individuals are able to maintain, recover, or improve their health and well-being in the face of life challenges. We then summarize select parts of ongoing studies to illustrate how our formulation of resilience guides our program of empirical research on positive emotions. We conclude with a brief consideration of future research directions to advance understanding of later life resilience.

The socioemotional basis of resilience in later life

The gross national product does not allow for the health of our children, the quality of their education, or the joy of their play. It does not include the beauty of our poetry or the strength of our marriages; the intelligence of our public debate or the integrity of our public officials. It measures neither our wit nor our courage; neither our wisdom nor our learning; neither our compassion nor our devotion to our country; it measures everything, in short, except that which makes life worthwhile. (Kennedy, 1968)

What do we know about human well-being? The answer is surprisingly little, compared with what is known about human illness, dysfunction, and disorder. With little exception, there remain few countervailing studies of the positive side of human functioning (see Keyes, Shmotkin, and Ryff, 2002; Ryff and Keyes, 1995), particularly in later adulthood where assessments of psychopathology have been the norm. But the keys to the kingdom are changing hands. An emerging literature is documenting the extraordinary capacity of some individuals to thrive in the face of life's challenges and setbacks. This chapter is about those very individuals.

Historically, resilience research has been largely the purview of developmental researchers dealing with early childhood and adolescence. This research primarily focused on at-risk children who were exposed to significant and severe life adversities (e.g., extreme poverty, parental mental illness, community violence). The study of resilience in adulthood and later life, by comparison, remains largely understudied. In this chapter, we describe select parts of ongoing studies to illustrate how previous conceptualizations of resilience have guided our program of empirical research with older adults. Although this research involves multiple methods of data collection (i.e., longitudinal, diary, life history interviews), we highlight findings derived from the daily diary process component of our work. We examine the importance of positive emotions and social connectedness for the stresses of everyday life, even the stresses of interpersonal loss. We summarize findings from this research to illustrate the ways in which daily process approaches can be used to examine key issues about resilience as it unfolds, both within individuals and across everyday life circumstances. Finally, drawing on these findings, as well as relevant work by others, we discuss priority recommendations for future research.

An intra-individual approach to studying resilience

A primary goal of our research has been to investigate the daily context in which resilience arises in response to challenge. Here we have adopted a daily process approach (i.e., diary methods) to examine how the nature of stressors, the social context, and the affective experiences of those involved can affect the process of resilience in adulthood. This approach involves intensive, day-to-day monitoring of study variables, allowing us to view change in fluctuating processes, such as stress and mood, closer to their real-time moments of change. In addition to providing a framework in which to study inherently intra-individual (within-person) questions (Bolger, Davis, and Rafaeli, 2003), diary methods confer specific methodological advantages for the study of resilience. As has been suggested (e.g., Almeida, 2005), perhaps the primary advantage of this methodology is its ability to reveal dynamic processes (e.g., stress duration and recovery) that are of particular interest to resilience researchers. In addition, diary methods allow individuals to report their behavior and experiences over the range of potentially stressful circumstances encountered in everyday life, thereby facilitating ecologically valid research (Reis and Gable, 2000). Finally, diary designs have the potential for greater internal validity, because the shorter lag between experience and reporting minimizes memory distortions (Stone, Shiffman, and DeVries, 1999).

In our research we have embarked on the study of resilience in everyday life by utilizing statistical methodologies that are responsive to complex, dynamic changes over time. A major strength of the analytic approaches we utilize is the ability to model processes that may be simultaneously occurring within individuals and across contexts. The emphasis on multiple pathways and multiple levels of analysis is prominent in recent reviews of both child and adulthood resilience (Cicchetti and Dawson, 2002; Luthar and Brown, 2007; Masten, 2007). The contemporary statistical approaches that we adopt (e.g., multilevel modeling, dynamic systems analysis) have enabled us to address a variety of questions, including some that are difficult, if not impossible, to address with traditional cross-sectional methods. In particular, processes that involve patterns of change (e.g., cycles or rhythms), rate of change (e.g., duration or recovery), speed of change (e.g., nonlinear processes), and covariation in change (e.g., co-occurrence, lagged associations) are all ideally suited for study using multilevel modeling (MLM) and dynamic systems analysis.

Positive emotions in the context of stress

More than two decades ago, Lazarus, Kanner, and Folkman (1980) suggested that under intensely stressful conditions, positive emotions may provide an important psychological time-out, sustain continued coping efforts, and restore vital resources that had been depleted by stress. Until recently, there has been little empirical support for these ideas. Foundational evidence for the adaptive function of positive emotions is beginning to accrue, however. Multiple studies have now shown that positive emotions have a wide range of effects on individuals (for reviews, see Ashby, Isen, and Turken, 1999; Lyubomirsky, King, and Diener, 2005; Pressman and Cohen, 2005).

Both theoretical and empirical work indicate that positive emotions promote flexibility in thinking and problem solving (Fredrickson and Branigan, 2005; Isen, Daubman, and Nowicki, 1987), counteract the physiological effects of negative emotions (Fredrickson and Levenson, 1998; Fredrickson et al., 2000), facilitate adaptive coping (Folkman and Moskowitz, 2000, 2004), build enduring social resources (Fredrickson and Branigan, 2001; Keltner and Bonanno, 1997), and spark upward spirals of enhanced well-being (Fredrickson, 2000; Fredrickson and Joiner, 2002). Notably, positive emotions can co-occur with negative emotions with relatively high frequency, even in the midst of personally significant stress (Moskowitz *et al.*, 1996). For instance, in a study of AIDS-related caregiving and bereavement, Folkman (1997) reported that with the exception of the period immediately before and after their partner's death, the positive emotion scores of men whose partners had died of AIDS did not reliably differ from their negative emotion scores, and at three months post-loss had returned to pre-bereavement levels. Similarly, Keltner and Bonanno (1997) observed that Duchenne laughter and smiling were exhibited at least once by a majority of conjugally bereaved participants as they discussed their interpersonal loss.

A major objective of our research with older adults has focused on the role of positive emotions as one important mechanism underlying resilient adaptation. Our efforts to date have largely explored the degree to which positive emotions may serve as a bulwark against the normal disruptions and setbacks of day-to-day life, as well as the pangs of conjugal bereavement. When we look at the problem in a multivariate way, we do not find a single, simple answer to the question of how positive emotions influence health. Instead, the most accurate assessment is to say that it is an intra-individual process that proceeds along at least three intersecting pathways.

Positive emotions strengthen stress resistance

Converging empirical work on positive emotions in our lab (e.g., Ong, Bergeman, and Bisconti, 2004) and by others (e.g., Zautra *et al.*, 2001) raises the possibility that positive emotions are important facilitators of stress resistance, counteracting the short-term arousal generated by stress. One way by which positive emotions may play a pivotal role in stress adaptation has been proposed by Zautra and colleagues (2001) in their dynamic model of affect (DMA). In contrast to other models of stress and coping, which view emotional adaptation entirely in terms of regulating psychological distress, the DMA takes into account both negative and positive emotions in the stress process. The model predicts that under ordinary circumstances, positive and negative emotions are relatively independent, whereas during stressful encounters an inverse correlation between positive and negative emotions increases sharply (for a review, see Reich, Zautra, and Davis, 2003). One implication of the DMA is that positive emotions are more likely to diminish negative emotions on days of elevated stress. The model also predicts that a relative deficit in positive emotional experience should leave individuals more vulnerable to the effects of stress.

Supportive evidence for the DMA comes from research demonstrating that during stressful periods, emotions are experienced along a single continuum in adults coping with everyday hassles, as well as major life

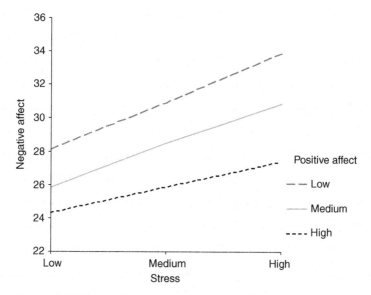

Figure 9.1. The relationship between daily stress and negative affect as a function of positive affect.

events. Figure 9.1 illustrates the results of a daily diary study of stress and emotion with older adults (Ong and Bergeman, 2004). The figure shows how elevations in positive emotion during times of heightened stress are particularly important in the regulation of daily stress, a finding that is in line with predictions from the DMA (Davis, Zautra, and Smith, 2004; Zautra et al., 2001). Although these findings help to establish the adaptational significance of positive emotions, a number of methodological features limit their generality. Foremost, the findings were limited to relatively minor stressors, and as such, examining the generality of these findings to major life events would also be necessary. In a subsequent study (Ong et al., 2004), we sought to examine how profiles of daily emotional responses to stress intersect with the significant adaptive pressures associated with conjugal loss. Figure 9.2 illustrates how positive emotions can interact with stress to interrupt its influence on negative emotions. These findings provide additional empirical footing for the DMA.

Positive emotion facilitates stress recovery

In addition to offsetting the immediate adverse consequences of stress, positive emotions may also play an important role in recovery processes. Fredrickson's (1998, 2001) broaden-and-build model of positive

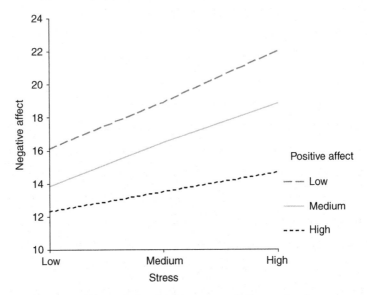

Figure 9.2. The relationship between daily conjugal stress and negative affect as a function of positive affect.

emotions suggests that positive emotions are important facilitators of adaptive recovery, quieting or *undoing* the autonomic arousal generated by negative emotions. In several laboratory studies in which positive and negative emotions were experimentally induced, Fredrickson and colleagues (Fredrickson and Levenson, 1998; Fredrickson *et al.*, 2000) found that positive emotions were linked to faster cardiovascular recovery from negative emotional arousal. More recent investigations confirm the importance of positive emotions in fostering *recovery* from stressful life events (Fredrickson *et al.*, 2003; Tugade and Fredrickson, 2004; see also Zautra, Johnson, and Davis, 2005).

Data from a daily diary study of recently bereaved widows (Ong *et al.*, 2006) afforded us the opportunity to test the prediction that part of the impact that stress may have on negative emotional recovery may be due to decreases in positive emotion brought about by stress. In contrast, the presence of positive emotion, according to the broaden-and-build theory, should function to speed recovery from stress (Fredrickson *et al.*, 2003; Tugade and Fredrickson, 2004). Our analyses of daily relationships revealed that when positive emotion was included in the analysis of emotional recovery, the association between stress and next day's negative emotion was reduced to nonsignificance (0.08), whereas it was significant in an analysis without positive emotion (0.31), suggesting that positive emotion mediates the relationship between stress and next-day negative emotion. To the extent that such results can be used as a basis for making inferences about directionality of effects, it would appear that changes in emotional recovery from stress are due to changes in positive emotion.

Taken together, the above findings add to and strengthen the generality of extant empirical work on positive emotion. In particular, the results extend previous research through empirical attention to the real-life challenges and stresses of later life. A primary finding emerging from our research is that a significant proportion of older adults manage to experience positive emotion, even in the midst of overwhelming loss. Despite variation in the types of stressors experienced, however, the results across multiple studies are remarkably consistent: positive emotions have demonstrably beneficial effects when present during times of stress.

Positive emotion broadens attention and thinking
Scientific evidence for the proposition that positive emotion broadens peoples' modes of attention and thinking comes from two decades of pioneering experiments conducted by Cornell psychologist Alice Isen (see Isen, 2000). Isen and her colleagues were the first to document that people experiencing positive affect show patterns of thought that are notably flexible, integrative, and efficient. Fredrickson's (1998, 2001) broaden-and-build theory of positive emotions suggests that positive emotions function to broaden the scope of attention and, over time, build lasting personal resources.

One central tenet of the broaden-and-build theory of positive emotions is the *broadening* hypothesis. This hypothesis posits that positive emotions function, in part, to broaden the scope of momentary visual attention and facilitate more holistic processing of information (Fredrickson and Branigan, 2001, 2005). Additional empirical support for the broadening hypothesis comes from recent investigations that suggest that positive emotions may enhance the ability to see the "big picture" by reducing and, in some cases, even eliminating the own-race bias in face recognition (Johnson and Fredrickson, 2005). Drawing on the broaden-and-build theory, Johnson and Fredrickson (2005) suggest that positive emotions may reduce the own-race bias by (a) facilitating more holistic processing of facial information (Fredrickson and Branigan, 2005) and (b) promoting more inclusive social categorization (Isen, Niedenthal, and Cantor, 1992), thereby decreasing the salience of racial categories.

Importantly, the cognitive broadening that accompanies positive emotional states is believed to bolster the ways individuals cope resourcefully with adversity (Fredrickson *et al.*, 2003). Supportive evidence that high levels of positive affect characterize those who are resilient in the face of major life stressors comes from a study of ethnic minority youth. Ong and Edwards (2008) examined the possibility that positive affect would have incremental effects, above and beyond related personality characteristics (i.e., optimism) in promoting adjustment to perceived racism. Their analyses revealed that the broadened mindsets sparked by positive affect function, in part, to moderate chronic perceptions of racism. That these relationships held even after controlling for variables thought to influence these processes (i.e., frequency of daily race-related stress, ethnic/racial status, optimism) is noteworthy. The results, thus, provide additional empirical support for the broaden-and-build model of positive emotions (Fredrickson, 2001) by providing an important conceptual link to previous laboratory studies with young, predominantly European-American, adults. Specifically, this work provides a model of how positive affect serves to moderate the emotional consequences of perceived racism in a sample of racial and ethnic minority young adults.

Finally, several studies indicate that coping styles marked by situational meaning (Park and Folkman, 1997) and perspective-taking (Fredrickson and Joiner, 2002) may facilitate adjustment to acute and persistent stress. Findings from our ongoing investigations with older adults suggest that changing the appraised personal significance of stressful conditions may be one mechanism by which to cultivate positive emotions in the midst of stress (Ong, Bergeman, and Boker, 2009). Taken as a whole, these findings provide the basis for underscoring the importance of *building* positive emotional experiences into the ecology of older adults' everyday lives.

Positive emotion fuels psychological resilience

What psychological traits are implicated in the generation and maintenance of positive emotions in the face of stress? One stable personality trait that has emerged as an important psychological asset is "ego resiliency," defined as the capacity to overcome, steer through, and bounce back from adversity (Block and Kremen, 1996). In longitudinal studies of personality, "ego-resilient" children were described as confident, perceptive, insightful, and able to have warm and open relations with others (Block, 1971). "Ego-brittle" children, by contrast, exhibited behavioral problems, depressive symptoms, and higher levels of drug use in adolescence (Block, Block, and Keyes, 1988).

Recent research from our lab and others suggests that positive emotions are a crucial component of trait resilience in adults as well (Ong *et al.*, 2006; Tugade and Fredrickson, 2004). Rather than being a simple by-product of resilience, however, the experience of positive emotion is thought to have adaptive benefits in the coping process (Folkman and Moskowitz, 2004). Empirical support for this prediction comes from our research with older adults demonstrating that resilient individuals tend to draw on positive-emotion-eliciting coping strategies, such as humor and infusing ordinary events with positive meaning (Ong and Bergeman, 2004; Ong *et al.*, 2004; Ong *et al.*, 2006) to regulate negative emotional experiences. Taken as a whole, our research indicates that traits (e.g., psychological resilience) with functional properties associated with positive emotion may serve to facilitate successful adaptation to stress by affording greater access to positive emotional resources (Ong *et al.*, 2006; Tugade, Fredrickson, and Barrett, 2004), which, in turn, may help to provide a momentary respite from ongoing stressful experiences (Folkman and Moskowitz, 2000; see also Zautra *et al.*, 2005).

Protective social relationships

Studies of resilient children and adults have repeatedly underscored the significance of quality social relationships (Masten and Obradovic, 2006; Ryff and Singer, 2000). In her synthesis of resilience research across five decades, Luthar concluded that "Resilience rests, fundamentally, on relationships" (Luthar, 2006, p. 780). Reviewing the adult literature, Ryff and Singer added, "Advancing the science of positive human health requires linking critical goods in life, such as quality social relationships, to biology" (Ryff and Singer, 2000, p. 37). The question of how *social connectedness*, defined as having quality social ties to others (Ryff and Singer, 2001), is linked to biological and emotional resilience is of particular importance for older adults given the stability and centrality of interpersonal relationships in late life (Carstensen, 1992; Lang and Carstensen, 1994).

Social connectedness and biological resilience

Our first evidence that having quality social ties contributes to resilience in the face of life challenges came from a daily process study of older adults, who participated in a 60-day diary assessment of emotions and cardiovascular functioning (Ong and Allaire, 2005). Our major hypothesis was that compared with those low in social connectedness, socially connected individuals would show diminished cardiovascular reactivity and more rapid recovery following negative emotional arousal. We found strong support for this hypothesis. Figure 9.3 illustrates that the individual slopes relating negative affect to systolic blood pressure (SBP) were predictable from individual differences in

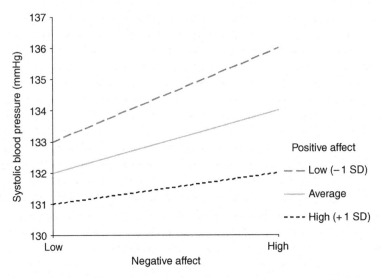

Figure 9.3. The relationship between daily negative affect and systolic pressure as a function of social connectedness.

social connectedness. Specifically, socially connected individuals displayed less systolic blood pressure reactivity on days characterized by high negative emotional arousal. Importantly, these relations were not limited to concurrent effects, but extended to influence each other as much as two days later. In particular, individuals who reported lower levels of social connectedness were more likely to have difficulty modulating the intensity of negative emotion once it had been triggered. Conversely, those high in social connectedness showed greater ability to inhibit the detrimental impact of negative emotion on subsequent cardiovascular responses. These findings remained significant when controlling for other methodological factors known to predict cardiovascular changes (e.g., time of day, trait affect, age, gender, marital status).

In support of the undoing hypothesis (Fredrickson and Levenson, 1998; Fredrickson et al., 2000), we also found that positive emotion served to dampen the cardiovascular impact of daily negative emotions. For individuals high in social connectedness (1 SD above the mean in social connectedness), there was a significant reduction in the magnitude of the negative affect–SBP association on days in which greater positive affect was also present. These results provided additional empirical footing for the broaden-and-build model of positive emotions (Fredrickson, 1998, 2001; Fredrickson et al., 2003) by identifying an individual difference

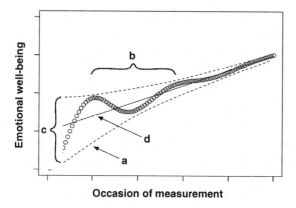

Figure 9.4. A damped linear oscillator model with parameters (a) damping, (b) 1/frequency (days/cycle, which is sometimes called the period of the cycle or the wavelength), (c) amplitude, and (d) trend.

variable (i.e., social connectedness) thought to influence the underlying undoing benefits occasioned by positive emotions.

Social support and adjustment to widowhood

A central focus of our research on bereavement has been to explore the social underpinnings of resilience to loss in later adulthood. Here we have used dynamic systems analysis as an investigative tool to study the adjustment patterns of widows following conjugal loss. In our early work (Bisconti, Bergeman, and Boker, 2004), we examined the intra-individual variability in emotional well-being following partner loss using a *damped linear oscillator model* (see Figure 9.4). The equation for a damped linear oscillator can be expressed as a linear regression formula in which the acceleration, or second derivative, is the outcome variable (i.e., the change in the slope in emotional well-being), and the displacement from equilibrium (i.e., the value of emotional well-being relative to the point around which it is oscillating) and velocity (i.e., change in emotional well-being) are the predictor variables (Boker, 2001; Boker and Bisconti, 2006).

Figure 9.4 illustrates the prototypic patterns of change implied by the damped linear oscillator model. The displacement from equilibrium is represented by the distance from the trend line at each occasion of measurement and the velocity is the first derivative, or slope, of the trajectory at each occasion. Note that the slope of the trajectory changes from one occasion to the next. The acceleration is the second derivative, or curvature, of the trajectory (i.e., the change in the slope) at each occasion. As depicted in Figure 9.4, these four parameters – (a) damping, (b) frequency, (c) amplitude, and (d) trend – constitute a dynamical system in which the relationships between parameters define a central tendency of a family of trajectories.

The results of our research on bereavement processes indicated that the trajectory of emotion regulation following conjugal loss resembled a damped linear oscillator. In particular, the frequency parameter indicated that the mean frequency of the oscillations that characterized the emotional well-being of widows was relatively slow, with a single cycle lasting on average approximately 47 days. In addition, the damping parameter was also significant and negative, suggesting that oscillations in well-being following the death of a spouse evidenced significant reduction across a 98-day period. This research provided us with initial empirical "guideposts" for understanding the process by which widows typically adjust to conjugal loss (Bisconti and Bergeman, 2007; Bisconti *et al.*, 2004).

In a subsequent study (Bisconti, Bergeman, and Boker, 2006), we examined how social support predicted individual differences in adjustment trajectories. Of particular interest to us were the structural components of support from family and friends (i.e., quantity and frequency of support), perceived control over supportive relationships (psychosocial resources), and emotional- and instrumental-support seeking behaviors (coping responses). Because emotional well-being and the regulation of emotional states are intimately tied to social interactions (Carstensen, 1992), we hypothesized that the structural and functional aspects of social support would represent two important pathways by which emotion regulation is established and maintained throughout the grieving process. Our results partially supported this prediction. Overall, 47 percent of the variance was explained by our social support constructs as predictors in the model. In comparison with structural support (i.e., quantity and frequency of support from both family and friends), our findings suggested that the functional components of support figured more prominently in predicting adjustment to loss. Specifically, we found that engagement in emotional support-seeking behaviors was related to a quicker return to equilibrium and a more positive trend in overall adjustment. In contrast, instrumental support seeking significantly predicted a slower damping rate and weaker overall adjustment. When viewed together, our results suggest that differential utilization of support seeking for emotional versus instrumental needs early in the bereavement process may help to distinguish different pathways of later functioning.

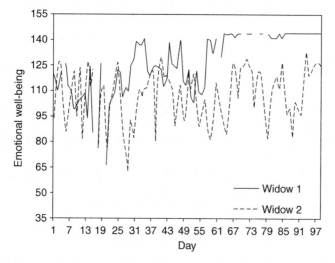

Figure 9.5. Emotional well-being of two widows, in which a higher score indicates better well-being. Widow 1 scored high on emotional support seeking and low on instrumental support seeking; Widow 2 scored low on emotional support seeking and high on instrumental support seeking.

Our findings also joined with past research (e.g., Bonanno *et al.*, 2005) by identifying groups of widows who follow different outcome trajectories over time. As an illustration, Figure 9.5 represents the trajectories of two women from our widowhood study that correspond to the prototypical *resilience* and *chronic* distress outcome trajectories identified by Bonanno (2004). Importantly, our research uncovered important factors that might explain divergent reactions in the early months following the loss of a spouse. Widow 1 primarily utilized emotional support seeking and had a trajectory similar to the prototypical resilience trajectory, characterized by an initial brief influx of lability in emotional responses, followed by a high level of positive and stable emotional well-being. Conversely, Widow 2 relied on instrumental support seeking and had a trajectory similar to the prototypical chronic distress trajectory, characterized both by low levels of well-being and high levels of emotional oscillation across the duration of the study.

Summary and conclusion

We began this chapter by underscoring how little we know about the nature of human resilience and well-being. In his book *Outliers* (2008, pp. 19–20), writer Malcolm Gladwell sums up the idea with the observation:

Biologists often talk about the "ecology" of an organism: the tallest oak in the forest is the tallest not just because it grew from the hardiest acorn; it is the tallest also because no other tree blocked its sunlight, the soil around it was deep and rich, no rabbit chewed though its bark as a sapling, and no lumberjack cut it down before it matured. We all know that successful people come from hardy trees. But do we know enough about the sunlight that warmed them, the soil in which they put down the roots, and the rabbits and lumberjacks they were lucky enough to avoid?

In this chapter, we have described a program of research, the results of which evoke the metaphor that resilience is not about trees. It's about forests. This research has yielded important clues about the nature of daily resilience as it unfolds in real life. We have argued that resilient adaptation to daily stress is likely to be multi-determined by various protective pathways. At the affective level, our research suggests that positive emotions may have adaptive benefits when present during times of stress. Overall, our findings dovetail with past research (e.g., Fredrickson and Levenson, 1998; Lazarus *et al.*, 1980; Zautra *et al.*, 2005) in demonstrating that positive emotions may function in the service of well-being not only by interrupting the ongoing experience of daily stress, but also by averting delays in adaptation to subsequent stressors. Additionally, our findings link up with prior research (e.g., Fredrickson *et al.*, 2003; Tugade and Fredrickson, 2004) in demonstrating positive emotions' enduring connection to personality. Our data suggest that individual differences in psychological resilience may constitute an important route to understanding differential resistance to and recovery from daily stress in later adulthood. In particular, trait resilience may contribute to positive adaptation by helping older adults sustain access to daily positive emotions, which, in turn, may lead to adaptive recovery from stress. Finally, our research suggests that resilient qualities do not emerge without the scaffolding of quality social supports (e.g., Rutter, 2002; Ryff and Singer, 2000).

We have outlined a program of research that integrates affective, psychological, and social processes to illuminate the unique challenges and opportunities associated with investigations of resilience in later life. The consequences of these processes increase the need to translate our understanding of basic research into effective interventions that target not just older adults themselves, but also their families and surrounding communities. Among leading candidates for further attention are the role of family supports (e.g., nurturing intergeneration ties), community resources (e.g., quality neighborhoods), and the natural environment (e.g., access to nature). We underscore, however, that it is critical that future studies examine the extent to which these factors are salient in the specific risk condition examined (Luthar, Cicchetti, and Becker, 2000). Similarly, our research program has focused on minor daily problems as sources of stress. Other researchers have studied major life events (Pillow, Zautra, and Sandler, 1996) and chronic difficulties (Eckenrode, 1984). Currently, little is known about the circumstances of life – the combined impact of major, chronic, and daily stressors – that so dangerously ignite the brain's vulnerabilities. Another related question is whether positive events buffer the effects of stress and the extent to which high-resilient individuals actively recruit and cultivate positive experiences to cope with stress. Finally, our analyses of daily stress and emotion relied heavily on self-reports from respondents. Future investigations should take a multi-method approach to stress assessment by including not only self-reports from respondents, but also physiological outcomes, biochemical assessments, and behavioral measures of stress. Detailed analyses of these and other variables will surely deepen our understanding of the resilience process.

Acknowledgment

Preparation of this paper was supported in part by grants from the National Institute on Aging (1 R01 AG023571-A1–01; 1 R01 AG02357-A1–01).

REFERENCES

Almeida, D. M. (2005). Resilience and vulnerability to daily stressors assessed via diary methods. *Current Directions in Psychological Science*, 14, 64–68.

Ashby, F., Isen, A. M, and Turken, A. U. (1999). A neuropsychological theory of positive affect and its influence on cognition. *Psychological Review*, 106, 529–550.

Bisconti, T. L., and Bergeman, C. S. (2007). Understanding the adjustment to widowhood: using dynamical systems to assess and predict trajectories of well-being. In M. H. M. van Dulmen and A. D. Ong (eds.), *Oxford handbook of methods in positive psychology* (pp. 395–408). New York: Oxford University Press.

Bisconti, T. L., Bergeman, C. S., and Boker, S. M. (2004). Emotional well-being in recently bereaved widows: A dynamical systems approach. *The Journals of Gerontology: Psychological Sciences and Social Sciences*, 59B, P158–P167.

  (2006). Social support as a predictor of variability: An examination of the adjustment trajectories of recent widows. *Psychology and Aging*, 21, 590–599.

Block, J. (1971). *Lives through time.* Berkeley, CA: Bancroft Books.

Block, J., Block, J. H., and Keyes, S. (1988). Longitudinally foretelling drug usage in adolescence: Early childhood personality and environmental precursors. *Child Development,* 59, 336–355.

Block, J., and Kremen, A. M. (1996). IQ and ego-resiliency: Conceptual and empirical connections and separateness. *Journal of Personality and Social Psychology,* 70, 349–361.

Boker, S. M. (2001). Differential models and differential structural equation modeling of intraindividual variability. In L. M. Collins and A. G. Sayer (eds.), *New methods for the analysis of change* (pp. 5–27). Washington, DC: American Psychological Association.

Boker, S. M., and Bisconti, T. L. (2006). Dynamical systems modeling in aging research. In C. S. Bergeman and S. M. Boker (eds.), *Methodological issues in aging research* (pp. 185–229). Mahwah, NJ: Erlbaum.

Bolger, N., Davis, A., and Rafaeli, E. (2003). Diary methods: Capturing life as it is lived. *Annual Review of Psychology,* 54, 579–616.

Bonanno, G. A. (2004). Loss, trauma, and human resilience: Have we underestimated the human capacity to thrive after extremely aversive events? *American Psychologist,* 59, 20–28.

Bonanno, G. A., Moskowitz, J. T., Papa, A., and Folkman, S. (2005). Resilience to loss in bereaved spouses, Bereaved parents, and bereaved gay men. *Journal of Personality and Social Psychology,* 88, 827–843.

Carstensen, L. L. (1992). Social and emotional patterns in adulthood: Support for socioemotional selectivity theory. *Psychology and Aging,* 7, 331–338.

Cicchetti, D., and Dawson, G. (2002). Editorial: Multiple levels of analysis. *Development and Psychopathology,* 14, 417–420.

Davis, M. C., Zautra, A. J., and Smith, B. W. (2004). Chronic pain, stress, and the dynamics of affective differentiation. *Journal of Personality,* 72, 1133–1159.

Eckenrode, J. (1984). Impact of chronic and acute stressors on daily reports of mood. *Journal of Personality and Social Psychology,* 46, 907–918.

Folkman, S. (1997). Positive psychological states and coping with severe stress. *Social Science and Medicine,* 45, 1207–1221.

Folkman, S., and Moskowitz, J. T. (2000). Positive affect and the other side of coping. *American Psychologist,* 55, 647–654.

(2004). Coping: Pitfalls and promise. *Annual Review of Psychology,* 55, 745–774.

Fredrickson, B. L. (1998). What good are positive emotions? *Review of General Psychology,* 2, 300–319.

(2000). Cultivating positive emotions to optimize health and well-being. *Prevention and Treatment,* 3, 1–25.

(2001). The role of positive emotions in positive psychology: The broaden-and-build theory of positive emotions. *American Psychologist,* 56, 218–226.

Fredrickson, B. L., and Branigan, C. (2001). Positive emotions. In G. A. Bonanno and T. J. Mayne (eds.), *Emotions: Current issues and future directions.* (pp. 123–151). New York: Guilford Press.

(2005). Positive emotions broaden the scope of attention and thought-action repertoires. *Cognition and Emotion*, 19, 313–332.

Fredrickson, B. L., and Joiner, T. (2002). Positive emotions trigger upward spirals toward emotional well-being. *Psychological Science*, 13, 172–175.

Fredrickson, B. L., and Levenson, R. W. (1998). Positive emotions speed recovery from the cardiovascular sequelae of negative emotions. *Cognition and Emotion*, 12, 191–220.

Fredrickson, B. L., Mancuso, R. A., Branigan, C., and Tugade, M. M. (2000). The undoing effect of positive emotions. *Motivation and Emotion*, 24, 237–258.

Fredrickson, B. L., Tugade, M. M., Waugh, C. E., and Larkin, G. R. (2003). What good are positive emotions in crisis? A prospective study of resilience and emotions following the terrorist attacks on the United States on September 11th, 2001. *Journal of Personality and Social Psychology*, 84, 365–376.

Gladwell, M. (2008). *Outliers*. New York: Little Brown.

Isen, A. M. (2000). Some perspectives on positive affect and self-regulation. *Psychological Inquiry*, 11, 184–187.

Isen, A. M., Daubman, K. A., and Nowicki, G. P. (1987). Positive affect facilitates creative problem solving. *Journal of Personality and Social Psychology*, 52, 1122–1131.

Isen, A. M., Niedenthal, P. M., and Cantor, N. (1992). An influence of positive affect on social categorization. *Motivation and Emotion*, 16, 65–78.

Johnson, K. J., and Fredrickson, B. L. (2005). We all look the same to me: Positive emotions eliminate the own-race bias in face recognition. *Psychological Science*, 16, 875–881.

Keltner, D., and Bonanno, G. A. (1997). A study of laughter and dissociation: Distinct correlates of laughter and smiling during bereavement. *Journal of Personality and Social Psychology*, 73, 687–702.

Keyes, C. L., Shmotkin, D., and Ryff, C. D. (2002). Optimizing well-being: The empirical encounter of two traditions. *Journal of Personality and Social Psychology*, 82, 1007–1022.

Lang, F. R., and Carstensen, L. L. (1994). Close emotional relationships in late life: Further support for proactive aging in the social domain. *Psychology and Aging*, 9, 315–324.

Lazarus, R. S., Kanner, A. D., and Folkman, S. (1980). Emotions: A cognitive-phenomenological analysis. In R. Plutchik and H. Kellerman (eds.), *Theories of emotion* (pp. 189–217). New York: Academic Press.

Luthar, S. S. (2006). Resilience in development: A synthesis of research across five decades. In D. J. Cohen and D. Cicchetti (eds.), *Developmental psychopathology: Risk, disorder, and adaptation* (pp. 739–795). Hoboken, NJ: Wiley.

Luthar, S. S., and Brown, P. J. (2007). Maximizing resilience through diverse levels of inquiry: Prevailing paradigms, possibilities, and priorities for the future. *Development and Psychopathology*, 19, 931–955.

Luthar, S. S., Cicchetti, D., and Becker, B. (2000). The construct of resilience: A critical evaluation and guidelines for future work. *Child Development*, 71, 543–562.

Lyubomirsky, S., King, L., and Diener, E. (2005). The benefits of frequent positive affect: Does happiness lead to success? *Psychological Bulletin*, 131, 803–855.

Masten, A. S. (2007). Resilience in developing systems: Progress and promise as the fourth wave rises. *Development and Psychopathology*, 19, 921–930.

Masten, A. S., and Obradovic, J. (2006). Competence and resilience in development. *Annals of the New York Academy of Sciences*, 1094, 13–27.

Moskowitz, J. T., Folkman, S., Collette, L., and Vittinghoff, E. (1996). Coping and mood during AIDS-related caregiving and bereavement. *Annals of Behavioral Medicine*, 18, 49–57.

Ong, A. D., and Allaire, J. (2005). Cardiovascular intraindividual variability in later life: The influence of social connectedness and positive emotions. *Psychology and Aging*, 20, 476–485.

Ong, A. D., and Bergeman, C. S. (2004). The complexity of emotions in later life. *The Journals of Gerontology: Psychological Sciences and Social Sciences*, 59B, P117–P122.

Ong, A. D., Bergeman, C. S., and Bisconti, T. L. (2004). The role of daily positive emotions during conjugal bereavement. *The Journals of Gerontology: Psychological Sciences and Social Sciences*, 59B, P168–P176.

Ong, A. D., Bergeman, C. S., Bisconti, T. L., and Wallace, K. (2006). Psychological resilience, positive emotions, and successful adaptation to stress in later life. *Journal of Personality and Social Psychology*, 91, 730–749.

Ong, A. D., Bergeman, C. S., and Boker, S. M. (2009). Resilience comes of age: Defining features in later adulthood. *Journal of Personality*, 77, 1777–1804.

Ong, A. D., and Edwards, L. M. (2008). Positive affect and adjustment to perceived racism. *The Journal of Social and Clinical Psychology*, 27, 105–126.

Park, C. L., and Folkman, S. (1997). Meaning in the context of stress and coping. *Review of General Psychology*, 1, 115–144.

Pillow, D. R., Zautra, A. J., and Sandler, I. (1996). Major life events and minor stressors: Identifying mediational links in the stress process. *Journal of Personality and Social Psychology*, 70, 381–394.

Pressman, S. D., and Cohen, S. (2005). Does positive affect influence health? *Psychological Bulletin*, 131, 925–971.

Reich, J. W., Zautra, A. J., and Davis, M. C. (2003). Dimensions of affect relationships: Models and their integrative implications. *Review of General Psychology*, 7, 66–83.

Reis, H. T., and Gable, S. L. (2000). Event-sampling and other methods for studying everyday experience. In C. M. Judd and H. T. Reis (eds.), *Handbook of research methods in social and personality psychology* (pp. 190–222). New York: Cambridge University Press.

Rutter, M. (2002). Family influences on behavior and development: Challenges for the future. In W. S. Grolnick and J. P. McHale (eds.), *Retrospect and prospect in the psychological study of families.* (pp. 321–351). Mahwah, NJ: Erlbaum.

Ryff, C. D., and Keyes, C. L. M. (1995). The structure of psychological well-being revisited. *Journal of Personality and Social Psychology*, 69, 719–727.

Ryff, C. D., and Singer, B. (2000). Interpersonal flourishing: A positive health agenda for the new millennium. *Personality and Social Psychology Review*, 4, 30–44.

Ryff, C. D., and Singer, B. H. (eds.). (2001). *Emotion, social relationships, and health*. London: Oxford University Press.

Stone, A. A., Shiffman, S. S., and DeVries, M. W. (1999). Ecological momentary assessment. In E. Diener and D. Kahneman (eds.), *Well being: The foundations of hedonic psychology* (pp. 26–39). New York: Russell Sage Foundation.

Tugade, M. M., and Fredrickson, B. L. (2004). Resilient individuals use positive emotions to bounce back from negative emotional experiences. *Journal of Personality and Social Psychology*, 86, 320–333.

Tugade, M. M., Fredrickson, B. L., and Barrett, L. F. (2004). Psychological resilience and positive emotional granularity: Examining the benefits of positive emotions on coping and health. *Journal of Personality*, 72, 1161–1190.

Zautra, A. J., Johnson, L. M., and Davis, M. C. (2005). Positive affect as a source of resilience for women in chronic pain. *Journal of Consulting and Clinical Psychology*, 73, 212–220.

Zautra, A. J., Smith, B., Affleck, G., and Tennen, H. (2001). Examinations of chronic pain and affect relationships: Applications of a dynamic model of affect. *Journal of Consulting and Clinical Psychology*, 69, 786–795.

10 Emotional resilience and beyond: a synthesis of findings from lifespan psychology and psychopathology

Eva-Marie Kessler and Ursula M. Staudinger

Abstract

The aim of the chapter is to attempt a synthesis of age-comparative research on emotional resilience. To do so, we integrate extant studies on age-related differences in indicators of normal and successful aging and indicators of psychopathology (emotional well-being/depressive disorders). Our review of empirical findings underscores the enormous emotional reserve capacity of aging individuals proposed by previous research. For example, in contrast to old-age stereotypes, negative affect as well as major depression do not occur more often in old age compared with younger ages; in young old age, negative emotional states even seem to be less frequent. However, positive states decrease in very old age. This is indicated by increasing levels of subsyndromal forms of depression based on anhedonia, but also by decreasing levels of positive, high-arousal affect and social vitality. We also demonstrate that the positive age trends in emotional resilience are to be seen in combination with a flattening of measures of emotional maturity during adulthood and old age.

Introduction

Over the last 20 years, an increasingly large number of studies has provided evidence on age differences and changes in emotional functioning across adulthood and old age, including lifespan psychology (e.g., Carstensen *et al.*, 2000; Charles, Reynolds, and Gatz, 2001; Kessler and Staudinger, 2009), personality psychology (e.g., Donnellan and Lucas, 2008; McCrae *et al.*, 1999) as well as clinical psychology and epidemiology (e.g., Blazer *et al.*, 1991; Wernicke *et al.*, 2000). The growing body of evidence from these different research disciplines has brought us closer to an answer to one of the most challenging questions in aging research: how well are we able, as we age, to maintain or regain relatively high levels of mental health and emotional well-being in the face of multiple losses? We would like to propose that this question may be investigated under the heading of "*emotional resilience.*" On the most general level, resilience is achieved if sufficient internal and external resources are available to deal with increasing constraints in and decreasing opportunities for replenishment of societal and material as well as biological resources. Emotional resilience must be distinguished from physical and cognitive resilience.

In this chapter, we investigate how emotional resilience changes across adulthood and old age by integrating extant research on age trajectories in two categories of indicators which have rarely been discussed conjointly: that is, indicators of normal and successful aging as well as indicators of psychopathology. In terms of normal and successful aging, we will summarize the empirical literature on age trajectories of *emotional well-being*, as indexed by the experience of positive and negative affect. We will also refer to indirect indicators of emotional well-being as covered by specific dimensions of the Big Five (neuroticism and extraversion) (Costa and McCrae, 1984) and of "Psychological Well-being" (environmental mastery, self-acceptance) (Ryff, 1989). In sum, this facet of emotional resilience refers to how good an individual feels about the self in a world of others (Bauer and McAdams, 2004).

When it comes to indicators of psychopathology, we consider age trajectories in the presence (versus absence) of specific forms of psychopathology, namely *depressive disorders*. Even though depressive disorders encompass a relatively complex and variegated system of manifestations involving biomedical and cognitive aspects, their specific feature is the breakdown of the affect-regulatory system (Staudinger, Marsiske, and Baltes, 1995). Therefore, prevalence rates of depressive disorders at different ages represent age differences in the (in)ability to regulate basic affect and emotional states. In fact, until very recently, emotional resilience has mostly been assessed in the context of psychopathology rather than in the context of normal or successful aging. Our synthesis of clinical and non-clinical research on emotional resilience should contribute to a better understanding of the heterogeneity of emotional resilience in the aging process and the factors that cause developmental pathways to diverge toward adaptive or maladaptive emotional outcomes (see also Greve and Staudinger, 2005; Staudinger *et al.*, 1995).

Beyond the issue of emotional resilience, there has been another question that has inspired lifespan psychologists to investigate emotional functioning across the lifespan. Namely, does increasing chronological age contribute to increasing *emotional maturity*? In the literature, unfortunately, emotional resilience and emotional maturity are often treated as if they were dealing with the same phenomenon (but see also Staudinger and Kessler, 2009; Staudinger and Kunzmann, 2005). However, they tap into very different criteria of what constitutes "good" emotional functioning throughout the adult lifespan[1] (Labouvie-Vief, 2003). Emotional maturity is expressed in emotional differentiation and the complexity of emotion regulation (Heckman, Coats and Blanchard-Fields, 2008; Labouvie-Vief and Medler, 2002). Various constructs have been introduced in order to investigate age differences and changes revolving around emotional maturity, including affect complexity, self-concept maturity, personal wisdom as well as (the absence of) "defense mechanisms" in the sense of suppression and denial (Staudinger and Kessler, 2009). Overall, we regard emotional complexity as part and parcel of the more global construct of "personality growth." The two types of emotional functioning (emotional resilience, emotional maturity) with the respective indicators are listed in Table 10.1.

In subjective theories of development, aging is commonly associated with depression, dissatisfaction and increasing levels of negative feelings and neuroticism (Heckhausen, Dixon, and Baltes, 1989; Nelson, 2002). At the same time, it is part of lay wisdom that if there is anything positive about aging it is that, as we grow older, we gain in life experience and that we are better able to integrate emotion and cognition. In this chapter, we will challenge lay theories of development by proposing that we seem to normatively experience fewer negative emotional states with age, while emotional maturity seems to stay stable or to decline.

The purpose of the following three sections is to summarize previous research on how the two types of emotional resilience (Section 1: emotional well-being; Section 2: prevalence/absence of depressive disorders) as well as emotional maturity (Section 3) develop across adulthood and old age. In addition to descriptive findings, each section aims to elucidate how age-related increases in emotional resilience and emotional maturity may be achieved. In the fourth section, we will summarize and integrate our review and discuss avenues for future research.

Emotional resilience and aging: age differences and changes in emotional well-being

In the non-clinical literature on emotional developmental across the adult lifespan, positive and negative affect are traditionally used as the central

---

[1] In contrast to this distinction, the concept of resilience as defined in humanistic psychology also includes phenomena subsumed under "personality growth." Accordingly, resilience refers to an individual's capacity to thrive and fulfill potential despite or perhaps *even because* of such stressors (Ryff *et al.*, 1998). Accordingly, strains and stressors are conceptualized as learning and development opportunities.

Table 10.1. *Overview of facets of emotional functioning and measurement indicators*

Indicators of "good" emotional functioning	Subdimensions	Measurement indicators
Emotional resilience	Emotional well-being	Positive affect/negative affect
		Emotional stability/ extraversion/environmental mastery/self-acceptance
	(Absence of) depressive disorders	Major depression
		Subsyndromal forms of depression (dysthymia, minor depression, depressive symptoms)
Emotional maturity		Affect complexity
		Low level of defense mechanisms
		Self-concept maturity: high complexity, medium integration in content and valence, self-transcendent values, moderate self-esteem
		Personal wisdom: high ratings on all five criteria
		Personal growth/purpose in life

indicators of emotional resilience. Positive and negative affect have been shown to represent two distinct dimensions rather than the poles of a one-dimensional construct (Watson and Tellegen, 1985). Overall, the effects of aging on these two dimensions are small to moderate in size when compared with age effects, for instance, in cognitive functioning (Kessler and Staudinger, 2009). With a few exceptions, the large majority of extant studies found that – compared with older age groups – young adults score highest in overall *negative affect* (Barrick, Hutchinson, and Deckers, 1989; Carstensen *et al.*, 2000; Diener and Suh, 1998) as well as in negative states of both high arousal (e.g., anger, fear) and low arousal (e.g., sadness) (Gross *et al.*, 1997; Lawton, Kleban, and Dean, 1993; Stoner and Spencer, 1986). In line with these cross-sectional findings, longitudinal studies demonstrated a decrease in negative affect from young to middle-aged adults and stability into old and very old age (Charles *et al.*, 2001; Herbrich, 2006; Kunzmann, Little, and Smith, 2000).

In contrast, the picture that has emerged from previous studies on age differences and changes in positive affect is still rather mixed. Some cross-sectional studies have found no significant differences in *positive affect* between younger and older adults (Barrick *et al.*, 1989; Carstensen *et al.*, 2000; Malatesta and Kalnok, 1984). One cross-sectional study found a slight and non-linear increase with age, but only among women (Mroczek and Kolarz, 1998). However, in one large cross-sectional and three longitudinal studies, there was stability from young adulthood to middle age, but in very old age, decreases in positive affect were found (Charles *et al.*, 2001; Diener and Suh, 1998; Ferring and Filipp, 1997; Herbrich, 2006). Most of these studies, however, have used measures that distinguish only between the positive and negative valence and neglect the arousal dimension of affect (Kessler and Staudinger, 2009). Usually high-arousal states of positive affect are overrepresented in such scales (Carroll *et al.*, 1999).

In this vein, some research has suggested that such inconsistencies in the literature on positive affect can be explained by differential age patterns for low-arousal forms versus high-arousal states of positive affect. In two studies, there were stronger negative age effects for high-arousal states of positive affect (excitement, interest) compared with low-arousal positive affect (Carstensen *et al.*, 2000; Diener and Suh, 1998). In a recent age-comparative study, we directly tested this assumption by applying a newly developed questionnaire that systematically represents the valence as well as the arousal dimension of affect (Kessler and Staudinger, 2009). In the investigated sample of 277 participants, older participants showed a higher level of positive, low-arousal affect (e.g., serene). Furthermore, older participants did not significantly differ from the two younger age groups in positive, high-arousal affect (e.g., excited). However, this study did not include participants older than 80 years, so the findings are restricted to "young-old age" and cannot be generalized into oldest age group.

Besides positive and negative affect, trait-like personality characteristics, namely neuroticism and extraversion, have also been used as indicators of emotional well-being across the adult lifespan. *Neuroticism* (versus emotional stability) shows strong links with negative affect and has often been viewed as the dispositional underpinning of negative affect (Costa and McCrae, 1980; Diener and Fujita, 1995; Watson and Clark, 1984). Furthermore, *extraversion* shows strong links with positive affect and has been discussed as reflecting positive affect on the level of personality characteristics. It seems that extraversion is associated with subjective well-being by engendering conditions and behaviors that facilitate or maintain subjective well-being (Costa and McCrae, 1980). It has been argued that extraversion is a fairly complex characteristic that is composed of two subdimensions, that is, social assurance (e.g., dominance, independence) and social vitality (e.g., sociability, social presence)

(Helson and Kwan, 2000). Social dominance reflects self-confidence and low levels of energy, whereas social vitality is related to gregariousness and high levels of energy. Therefore, we would like to argue that social vitality corresponds closely to the high-arousal and social assurance in the low-arousal category of positive affect.

Taking into account cross-sectional and longitudinal evidence, neuroticism has been found to decrease across adulthood (Mroczek and Spiro, 2003; Roberts, Walton, and Viechtbauer, 2006) and may show a small, albeit significant, increase again in late life (Small *et al.*, 2003; Steunenberg *et al.*, 2005). In an interesting cross-sectional study comparing samples between the ages of 14 and 83 from Korea, Portugal, Italy, Germany, Czech Republic, and Turkey, McCrae and others (McCrae *et al.*, 2000) found a highly similar pattern of mean-level age differences in neuroticism across these different nations. However, in a recent study using a sample of people aged from 16 to 85 years, neuroticism was slightly negatively correlated with age in Great Britain, but positively in Germany (Donnellan and Lucas, 2008). Whereas research has found that extraversion decreases with age (McCrae *et al.*, 1999), recent research found evidence for differential development in social assurance and social vitality. Specifically, social assurance seems to increase with age, whereas social vitality showed age-related decreases (Helson and Kwan, 2000; Roberts *et al.*, 2006).

Another theoretical framework that informs us about emotional well-being across adulthood is the conception of "psychological well-being" as defined by Carol Ryff (Ryff, 1989, 1995). She developed a measure of psychological well-being based on extant theoretical models of personality development. This measure encompasses six dimensions, two of which can be regarded as indicators of emotional well-being, that is, environmental mastery and self-acceptance: *Environmental mastery* refers to choosing or creating environments matching one's self. *Self-acceptance* is defined as holding positive attitudes toward oneself. In factor analyses, the dimensions, environmental mastery, and self-acceptance load on the same factor conjointly with indicators of adjustment such as life satisfaction and positive/negative affect (Compton, 2001; Keyes, Shmotkin, and Ryff, 2002; Mickler and Staudinger, 2008). Replicating the trends of prior findings, in a large representative sample ($N = 1108$) environmental mastery and self-acceptance show positive age differences (Ryff and Keyes, 1995).

Emotional well-being and aging: psychological dynamics

The fact that older adults seem to be able to maintain their emotional well-being in the face of adversity that often comes with higher ages, has also been labeled as "the well-being paradox of old age" (Baltes and Baltes, 1990; Kunzmann, Little, and Smith, 2000; Staudinger, 2000). Initial attempts have been undertaken to understand the underlying mechanisms (Brandtstädter and Greve, 1994; Staudinger and Fleeson, 1996). On the level of self-regulatory mechanisms, it has been suggested that people become increasingly better at adjusting to losses and negative events with age – for example, by disengaging from blocked goals, re-scaling personal expectations to the given, or letting go of self-images that do not fit the actual self anymore (Rothermund and Brandtstädter, 2003; Wrosch *et al.*, 2003)

There is reason to assume also that certain affect-regulatory processes contribute to the maintenance of emotional well-being in old age. One line of research has argued that older individuals might be better able to proactively cope with emotion-laden situations (Gross, 1998; Gross *et al.*, 1997; Magai, 2001), owing to an increase in the richness and effectiveness of available emotion schemata. Other authors have argued that affect regulation may improve as people age due to learning and practice (Lawton, 1996). In other words, through years of practice we learn to regulate our affective responses and thus in old age we report to be better able to deal with and to control emotions than younger people. Indeed, there is first empirical evidence that older people have advantages in affect-regulatory capacities. First, older adults report higher levels of success in managing positive and negative emotional states, including controlling external signs of emotions and maintaining a neutral state (Labouvie-Vief, DeVoe, and Bulka, 1989; Lawton *et al.*, 1992). Supporting the self-report data, in one recent experimental study, inhibiting emotions resulted in dampened emotional reactions in older, but not in young and middle-aged, adults (Magai *et al.*, 2006). Second, older adults have been shown to display a greater flexibility in adjusting their strategies of emotion-regulation (e.g., passive strategies such as suppression, denial versus active strategies such as directly confronting emotions, seeking out emotional support) to the contextual features of a situation (Blanchard-Fields, 2007).

Despite this growing empirical research on age differences in emotion regulation, to the best of our knowledge, the explanatory power of emotion regulation concerning the observed age-related differences in affective experiences has not yet *directly* been tested. We have shown in a recent study that age-related advantages in the regulation of affect seem to be a central component of emotional resilience in old age (Kessler and Staudinger, 2009). Specifically, older participants' higher efficiency in increasing positive affect in difficult situations and reducing negative affect after negative events and failures emerged as central processes by which older people seem to maintain or regain high levels of emotional well-being. That is, the efficiency of affect regulation in the face of difficulties and/or threatening situations emerged as a central mediator in the age–affect relationship.

Yet, it is still unclear how the improvement in emotion regulation comes about. Socioemotional selectivity theory (SST) argues that high levels of emotional well-being in old age are not primarily a result of better regulatory capacity due to learning and practice, but a result of perceived time left in life (Carstensen, Fung, and Charles, 2003; Mather and Carstensen, 2005). As people move through adulthood, due to the social-cognitive construal of time, they shift their motivational orientation away from information search towards emotion regulation. Accordingly, as people age, they gear their lives, especially their social lives, toward maximizing positive and minimizing negative affect. In contrast, young people see the future as being largely open. Therefore, they are more focused on the acquisition of new knowledge. In support of this assumption, studies on attention and memory for positive/negative stimuli have found three major pieces of evidence: first, during *initial attention*, older adults seem to avoid negative information (Mather and Carstensen, 2003), unless this information is threatening or extremely aversive (Mather and Knight, 2006). Second, older adults *remember* a lower proportion of negative stimuli than younger adults do (Charles, Mather, and Carstensen, 2003). Third, there is a positivity effect in older adults' *autobiographical memories* (Kennedy, Mather, and Carstensen, 2004; Sneed and Whitbourne, 2003). This so-called "positivity bias" in attention and memory was consequently cited as the regulatory mechanisms underlying emotional adjustment. Surprisingly, in our own study reported above (Kessler and Staudinger, 2009) future time perspective did not contribute to an explanation of the age–affect relationship, as suggested by SST (Kessler and Staudinger, 2009). This finding suggests that future studies should more directly test future time perspective as a mechanism underlying age differences and changes in emotional well-being.

The protective power of emotion-regulatory resources needs to be seen in concert with the detrimental effects of increasing losses in physical functioning and limitations on emotional resilience (see also Staudinger *et al.*, 1999). For example, in the Berlin Aging Study, the more people were confronted with functional health limitations, the more likely they were to report low positive affect and to show decline in positive affect over the following years (Kunzmann *et al.*, 2000). However, it has been shown that physical limitations demonstrate neither cross-sectional nor longitudinal relationships with negative affect. A similar pattern also emerged in another longitudinal study. In a sample of 2117 participants aged from 55 to 85 years, older adults' physical health status did not predict changes in trajectories of neuroticism over a six-year period

(Steunenberg *et al.*, 2005). Differential associations with positive and negative affect are also found for other objective indicators of functioning. In the Berlin Aging Study, levels of social involvement and test intelligence were cross-sectionally and longitudinally associated with positive affect, but not with negative affect (Kunzmann, 2008).

Summary

In sum, we suggest that the developmental pattern discussed above is indicative of stability or even an increase in emotional well-being across adulthood. This is reflected in the mean-level decrease in negative affect combined with a decrease in neuroticism, and an increase or at least stability in extraversion (social dominance), environmental mastery, and self-acceptance. Recent results have suggested that age-related advantages in the regulation of affect seem to be one central component of emotional resilience in old age.

However, it also seems that, in very old age, one facet of emotional well-being, that is positive emotions (particularly of high arousal), does not increase but even decreases. Research has suggested that this negative age trend may be due to the detrimental effects of increasing losses in physical functioning and other objective limitations which cannot anymore be completely compensated. The finding that physical losses affect positive, but not negative affect, might speak for the high emotion-regulatory capacity to protect the system or recover from being overwhelmed by negative emotions.

Emotional resilience and aging: age differences and changes in depressive disorders in old age

Whereas research on emotional well-being directs our attention towards the upper limits of emotional resilience in late life, the majority of research on emotional resilience in late life has focused on how aging leads to emotional disorders and dysfunction. Indeed, a large percentage of the investigations of emotional functioning in old age have been conducted in the context of psychopathology. Building on this literature, we want to explore the prevalence of affective states related to depression in old age.

When investigating age differences and changes in depressive symptoms, major depression as well as the various forms of subsyndromal depression must be considered (Geiselmann and Bauer, 2000). Across research designs and classification criteria, there is consensus that the prevalence of *major depressive disorder* in the community is not higher in older adults than in other age groups (Blazer, 2003). While some studies have found a fairly constant prevalence of depressive episodes across the adult lifespan (Blazer *et al.*, 1991; Lindesay, Briggs, and Murphy, 1989), even into extreme old age (Heeren *et al.*, 1992), several epidemiological studies even found a cross-sectional decrease with age (Henderson, Jorm, and Mackkinnon, 1993; Robins and Regier, 1991). According to current epidemiological data, from 1 percent to 5 percent of the general population of older people in the USA and Europe have been diagnosed with a major depression (Alexopoulos, 2005; Helmchen, Baltes, and Geiselmann, 1999). Twice as many women as men are affected, that is, the gender difference observed in younger age groups is also carried through into old age. Research has suggested that these estimates cannot be accounted for by selective mortality of people with anxiety or depression (Simon and Van Korff, 1992).[2] Given the cross-sectional character of most of this research, we still do not know exactly to what degree these results are driven by cohort membership and lifetime occurrence of depression (Lewinsohn *et al.*, 1993). To determine whether there is a "true" aging phenomenon, cohort sequential designs are needed (Baltes, Reese, and Nesselroade, 1988). Note, however, that cross-sectional stability of rates of major depression has been replicated in different nations at different historical points in time.

In contrast to the low rates in major depression, there seems to be higher prevalence of *subsyndromal forms of depression* in older adults (Gatz, Kasl-Godley, and Karel, 1996). Minor depression and dysthymic disorder are typical forms of depressive disorders, which require therapeutic intervention according to clinical judgment, but do not fulfil the criteria for major depression. Minor depression refers to a depression in which at least two symptoms of a major depression are present for two weeks. Dysthymic disorder is a chronic, milder mood disturbance where a person reports a low mood almost daily over a span of at least two years. Referring to more recent studies of DSM-IV classification criteria, the prevalence of minor depression ranges from 4 percent to 13 percent in old age, whereas about 2 percent of older individuals suffer from dysthymic disorder (Helmchen *et al.*, 1999; Nordhus, 2008). The increase in subsyndromal forms of depression is most evident in syndrome rating scales and self-rating scales

---

[2] Past literature has emphasized certain aspects of depressive disorder that are thought to be typical of old age, including a preponderance of somatic complaints, hypochondrias, and greater agitation compared wih young adults. However, more recent studies did not find differences in the clinical features of major depression between older and younger adults, at least if there are no co-morbid conditions. Nevertheless, a common difficulty arises from associated physical ill health that may accentuate certain aspects of the clinical picture or that may rather mask the diagnosis. Furthermore, subtle organic cerebral change may predispose to late-onset depression in a significant minority of cases (for a detailed discussion, see Baldwin and O'Brien, 2002).

in particular (Ernst and Angst, 1995). Interestingly, research has suggested that the positive age trends are based on loss of interest, poor ability to concentrate and anhedonia rather than in negative affective states (i.e., tearfulness, a wish to die, negative emotions) (Prince, Beekman, and Deeg 1999). This is in line with a population-based, longitudinal study of people aged 80 that demonstrated that lack of well-being, as opposed to an increase in negative affect, was the biggest contributor to the overall changes of the depression score (Haynie *et al.*, 2001). Note that these findings are completely in line with the age-comparative results concerning affective well-being reported above.

Two aspects warrant mentioning. First, the prevalence of both major depression and less severe forms of depressive symptomatology is higher in medical and institutional settings than for older people living in the community. Unfortunately, the large majority of studies was conducted using community-based samples (Ernst and Angst, 1995). This may to a certain degree bias, but by no means fully explain, the low prevalence estimates of major depression in old age (Snowdon, 1990). Second, much epidemiological research comprises only a very small proportion of the very old, and extrapolation to this fastest growing sector of the aging population may be inaccurate. Therefore, it is still unclear whether the prevalence of depressive symptoms increases in very old age, that is, whether the "young olds" differ from the "old olds." Indeed, while some studies found a small increase in depression into very old age (Helmchen *et al.*, 1999), others found no clear age trends or even further decrease (Lindesay *et al.*, 1989).

Depression and aging: psychological dynamics

Aging research on depression has almost exclusively been concerned with identifying risk factors of depression in old age rather than with psychological resources and mechanisms that protect aging individuals from depression. Among the stressors associated with depression in old age, physical limitations have been discussed as a particularly strong predictor of depressive symptoms in old age (Blazer, 2003). A longitudinal study has shown that intervening levels of pain and, to a lesser extent, daily discrimination (i.e., the experience of a stigma associated with being impaired), seem to be among the mechanisms by which physical limitations are translated into increased mental health risk (Gayman, Turner, and Cui, 2008). Furthermore, research has shown that it is an accumulation of daily hassles and life events rather than a single event that acts as risk factor/antecedent of depression (Kraaij, Arensman, and Spinhoven, 2002). Unfortunately, the field of clinical psychology and epidemiology has not contributed much to our understanding of why rates of major depression do *not* increase with age despite increasing numbers of losses and limitations.

Summary

It is commonly assumed that the accumulation of losses with age is an obvious cause of depression in old age. The lack of an increase in major depression in old age as described in the empirical literature contradicts this common-sense view and highlights the relative reserve capacity of the affect-regulatory system in old age. Furthermore, the increase in depressive symptomatology most probably reflects increases in anhedonia and functional limitations rather than breakdowns in the ability to deal with negative states. Extant research has not investigated the specific regulatory mechanisms that contribute to the relatively low level of depression in old age.

Emotional maturity and aging

In the two prior sections, we elucidated age differences and changes in emotional resilience and its limits, that is, the question of how emotional well-being in old age is regained or maintained in the face of adversity. Beyond emotional resilience, lifespan psychologists have also pursued the question of age-related changes in emotional growth. On the most general level, there is consensus among growth theorists that emotionally mature individuals are able to process new information or new events in an open-minded and non-repressive fashion. More specifically, the defining characteristic of emotional maturity is the ability to integrate multiple emotional perspectives to form flexible and differentiated representations of oneself, others, and situations (Allport, 1937/1961; Heckman Coats and Blanchard-Fields, 2008; Labouvie-Vief, 2003; Labouvie-Vief and Medler, 2002; Loevinger, 1976). Consequently, a high degree of affective differentiation and the co-existence of positive and negative emotions (at one point in time) are at the gist of emotional maturity (Labouvie-Vief, 2003; Staudinger and Kessler, 2009; Staudinger, Mickler, and Dörner, 2005). From a regulatory perspective, this ability requires the flexible interplay between automatic emotional processes and executive processes over time. Some researchers assume that emotional maturity enables the individual to differentiate self-chosen emotional standards from societal standards (Labouvie-Vief and Medler, 2002). Compared with the growing body of aging literature on depressive disorders and emotional well-being, findings on age differences and changes in emotional maturity are rare. And virtually no study targets "old old" people. Moreover, there is a profound lack in longitudinal, let alone cohort-sequential analyses. In the following, we will summarize extant research that has provided at least some evidence on age differences in emotional maturity.

Emotional maturity, like personality maturity in general, has often been investigated by referring to individuals' self-conceptions (Campbell, Assanand, and Di Paula, 2003). Labouvie-Vief's research on emotional maturity is most prominent in this literature. Her concept of emotional maturity builds on the conceptual complexity, openness, and multivalence of adults' self-representations (Labouvie-Vief and Medler, 2002). In her studies, people ranging from preadolescents up to 80 years are given five minutes to write a brief paragraph about him- or herself. Judges then rate the protocols on a five-point scale according to the degree to which the answers are complex and multivalent (rather than uniformly positive or negative). On average, middle-aged adults scored the highest, while complexity scores were lowest in the preadolescent and older adult age groups. Furthermore, older adults' narratives on average were characterized by a low degree of blending of emotions and high levels of repression (Labouvie-Vief et al., 1995). A similar pattern emerged when patterns of *coping and defense mechanisms* were used as indicators of affective complexity (Labouvie-Vief and Medler, 2002). In a sample of people aged from 15 to 86 years, older participants engaged less strongly in strategies related to the exploration and amplification of affect (e.g., tolerance of ambiguity, intellectuality). Rather, the older participants more strongly engaged in suppression, denial, and concentration.

Affective complexity has also been used in the sense of the covariation of self-reported positive and negative emotions within short periods of time. A high intraindividual correlation between positive and negative affect is interpreted as a high degree of "poignancy" (Carstensen et al., 2000). This definition and operationalization does not exclude the possibility that older adults, for instance, use positive emotions more often than younger adults to "undo" negative emotions. Neither is it possible to investigate exactly which kind of emotions co-occur when using this operationalization. Further, one would need to find a way to differentiate the dialectical character of emotional experience from insecurity in assigning emotional states. Thus, this definition would need to be refined in order to reflect the notion of emotional maturity proposed here.

Emotional maturity is not only reflected in the level of affective experience, but also in other indicators of the self. Thus, it is informative when interested in the age trends of emotional maturity to check for age-related differences and changes in indicators of personality maturity. Two such indicators are considered below: self-concept maturity and personal wisdom (for a more detailed overview of this research, see Staudinger, Kessler, and Dörner, 2006; Staudinger, Mickler, and Dörner, 2005). Stability or even negative age trends in emotional maturity are reflected in recently developed measures of personality maturity such as a measure of *self-concept maturity* (Dörner and Staudinger, 2010). This measure consists of a profile of five self-concept indicators. These indicators are: complexity of self-concept content (the number of perspectives an individual adopts with regard to himself or herself, as indicated by the number of non-redundant self-aspects or content categories of the self-definition) (Linville, 1987); self-concept integration (the similarity of self-aspects, as indicated by the correlation of trait ratings across different domains of the self-concept) (Donahue *et al.*, 1993); balance of self-related affect; self-esteem; and value orientation. Each of the five indicators has to show a specific value, and all five have to be considered jointly in order to assess personality maturity: high complexity, medium integration, a balanced experience of positive as well as negative self-related emotions, self-transcending values and a medium level of self-esteem were defined to index personality maturity. As expected, self-concept maturity did not show age differences (Dörner and Staudinger, 2009).

Moreover, no evidence for positive age trends in emotional maturity was found when a measure of *personal wisdom* was used to assess emotional maturity. Mickler and Staudinger (2008) showed that in contrast to younger people (20–40 years), older people (60–80 years) were less likely to reflect on and have insight into the possible causes of their feelings and behaviors (interrelating the self), were less likely to evaluate themselves as well as others from a distanced view (self-relativism) and had fewer strategies available in order to manage the uncertainty of life through openness to experience and the development of flexible solutions (tolerance of ambiguity). Overall, personal wisdom as one indicator of personality maturity has shown stability or even slight decline with age and thus supports the assumption that emotional maturity does not come automatically with age. Interestingly, the rather "objective" indicators of affective complexity, personal wisdom, and self-concept maturity as reported above show the same age pattern as self-perceptions of personality maturity. Self-perceptions of personality maturity are, for example, indicated by Ryff's dimensions of personal growth (continuing to develop one's potential, to grow and expand as a person) and purpose in life (beliefs that give one the feeling there is purpose in and meaning to life). Replicating the trends of prior findings, in a large representative sample ($N = 1108$) purpose in life and personal growth showed negative age differences (with scores of the oldest respondents significantly lower than those of the two younger age groups) (Ryff and Keyes, 1995).

Emotional maturity and aging: psychological dynamics

In the current literature, three alternative lines of interpretation have been proposed for an explanation of the decreasing level of emotional maturity in old age. First, a decline in the cognitive mechanics might contribute to this finding. Accordingly, the negative age differences found for the three meta-criteria of personal wisdom disappeared when fluid intelligence (as well as openness to experience) was controlled (Mickler and Staudinger, 2008). This finding is in line with theoretical and empirical research showing that decreasing levels of cognitive resources put constraints on cognitive-affective complexity (Labouvie-Vief and Medler, 2002).

Second, changes in the motivational system may contribute to decreasing levels of emotional maturity. We have recently argued that the developmental task of integrity, that is, coming to terms with oneself and finding acceptance, may refrain older people from pursuing a realistic perception of oneself and one's own life (Mickler and Staudinger, 2008; Staudinger and Kessler, 2009). In line with this assumption, two studies found that older people try to maintain a consistent and positive autobiography and self-concept and protect it against changes (Kennedy *et al.*, 2004; Sneed and Whitbourne, 2003). Referring back to the findings of socioemotional selectivity theory, one may also argue that the so-called "positivity bias" in old age counteracts the realization of emotional maturity in old age. Indeed, the ability to attend to negative information can be regarded as a central precondition in order to achieve emotional maturity.

A third interpretation relies on the acquisition of knowledge and skills across the lifespan. Specifically, the body of knowledge that an individual has gained across the lifespan serves as a filtering system for incoming information. In early adulthood, the *acquisition of schemata* is necessary in order to acquire new information; however, in later adulthood, the then available schemata may increasingly counteract the acquisition of new information. Specifically, older people may be less able to integrate new and inconsistent information in their schema-based memory representation, thereby reducing the complexity of incoming information (Hess, 1999; Hess, Osowski, and Leclerc, 2005).

Summary

Empirical evidence on age differences and changes in emotional maturity is scare. The few empirical studies on the topic have suggested that the maturity with which we deal with emotional information even decreases in old age. The mechanisms underlying this negative age trend still need further exploration. In addition to changes in fluid and knowledge-based cognition, increases in the tendency to protect the aging self against negative states at the end of life may have a detrimental effect on the development of emotional maturity.

Discussion

In this chapter, we discussed three indicators of "good" emotional functioning which have rarely been examined conjointly, namely emotional well-being, (the absence of) depressive disorders, and emotional maturity. To do so, we reviewed central findings from lifespan developmental psychology, personality psychology, and clinical epidemiology. Drawing on these diverse lines of research is necessary in order to advance our insight into the complex pattern of developmental trajectories in emotional functioning across the adult lifespan. Despite a steadily growing number of studies, emotional aging has to now been less well understood as compared with aging processes in the realm of cognition and personality. Research on age trajectories in emotional maturity is particularly scarce. Furthermore, there is only fragmentary knowledge about emotional functioning in very old age. Despite recent attempts to include nonagenarians and centenarians, very old age is still heavily understudied. Due to strong normative limitations in *sensory*, perceptual, *motor*, and *cognitive* functioning, standard measures of emotional functioning are often difficult to administer to members of that age group. For example, the validity of self-report questionnaires of emotional well-being is clearly threatened if the person is cognitively impaired. Therefore, extant studies on emotional well-being have systematically excluded people suffering from dementia. Unfortunately, we are still far away from a solution to the problem of how emotional resilience and maturity can be assessed in the "fourth age."

Our integrative overview of empirical results from both clinical and nonclinical research tentatively validates the enormous emotional resilience of aging individuals proposed by extant lifespan developmental and psychopathological literature. This is indicated by normative stability or even decreases in the incidence and prevalence of major depressive disorders as well as an increase in emotional stability, extraversion (social dominance), environmental mastery, and self-acceptance, at least until very old age is reached. Overall, this developmental pattern points to a strong capacity to protect the self from getting overwhelmed by the increasing numbers of losses and limitations. In line with these assumptions, we have shown that older people are better able to regulate affect in the face of difficulties and after negative events and failures.

We have shown that general statements about resilience in old age need one qualification, rendering the stability-despite-loss paradox less paradoxical than has often been suggested in the literature. There are limits to resilience that become increasingly visible with old age (cf. Staudinger *et al.*, 1999). Specifically, both clinical epidemiology/psychology as well as lifespan developmental research have demonstrated that positive states may decrease in very old age. This is indicated not only by increasing levels of subsyndromal forms of depression based on anhedonia, but also by decreasing levels of positive affect and social vitality. There is preliminary evidence that this trend may not affect positive affect in general, but rather specific positive states related to high arousal such as excitement and interest. Physical limitations, particularly functional losses, seem to contribute to the decreasing capacity to experience such positive emotions. Kunzmann (2008) recently proposed that age-related declines in objective competencies in general (in contrast to self-evaluations) may explain age-related decreases in positive affect. We would like to propose that the age-related differences in positive affect may also be a product of selecting social environments or being directed in environments such that high arousal states of positive affect are avoided. No study has yet systematically investigated this assumption.

Contrary to the relative age-related stability of emotional resilience, there is a flattening of the emotional-maturity trajectory during adulthood and old age. This is indicated by decreasing levels of affective complexity and by more general impairments in the domain of personality maturity, as indicated by losses in self-concept maturity and personal wisdom. We are only at the very beginning of understanding the dynamics underlying this developmental trajectory.

We would like to argue that a *functionalist perspective* on emotional development and aging may provide an enriching interpretational framework of our synthesis of empirical findings (Consedine and Magai, 2006; Fredrickson, 2003). Specifically, at each phase of the adult lifespan, people are confronted with different developmental tasks which differ in the degree to which they draw on the different modes of emotional functioning (Kessler and Staudinger, 2009). The absence of depressive disorders is a basic human resource and the central prerequisite to satisfy basic human needs such as sleep, nutrition, and communication as well as to function effectively within a society at the most basic level (Jahoda, 1958). Moreover, positive emotional states and emotional well-being ensure the promotion, restoration, and maintenance of social, cognitive, and physical resources at each phase of the lifespan (e.g., Fredrickson, 2003; Fredrickson and Branigan, 2005; Isen, 2003). Emotional maturity reaches beyond mastering given challenges. The gist of emotional maturity is self-transcendence and the emancipation in thinking and feeling (Chandler and Holliday, 1990; Helson and Wink, 1987).

Emotion-regulation in old age calls for the preservation of resources, self-protection, and the avoidance of exhausting physical and mental resources, as it may occur in complex and threatening states and situations (cf. Labouvie-Vief, 2003; Staudinger *et al.*, 1995). In contrast, the developmental task of young adulthood is to explore environments and to acquire more knowledge about ourselves and the world (Izard, 1977; Staudinger *et al.*, 1995). As a consequence of their distinct contributions to adaptation, negative emotional states may normatively tend to decrease, as people age – at least until very old age, when the limits of emotional resilience are reached. In contrast, emotional maturity and positive (high-arousal) affect may be most pronounced in the first half of adulthood and may show normative stability or even decline thereafter.

Our aim was to provide a tentative synthesis of research on emotional resilience and emotional maturity, as based on clinical and non-clinical research. There is still a long way to go before we can claim to understand emotion functioning in old age. An integrative theory of emotional development is need that captures normal, successful as well as pathological aging. Future research should concentrate, for instance, on discerning the specific psychological and biological mechanisms that underlie the age-related changes in emotion regulation. Longitudinal studies are needed to better understand the dynamics between the two trajectories of emotional resilience and emotional growth. Finally, it would seem worthwhile to do more intervention work in the area of emotional maturity.

REFERENCES

Alexopoulos, G. S. (2005). Depression in the elderly. *The Lancet*, 365, 1961–1970.
Allport, G. W. (1961). *Pattern and growth in personality*. New York: Holt, Rinehart & Winston.
Baldwin, R. C. and O'Brien, J. (2002). Vascular basis of late-onset depressive disorder. *British Journal of Psychiatry*, 180, 157–160.
Baltes, P. B., and Baltes, M. M. (1990). Psychological perspectives on successful aging: The model of selective optimization with compensation. In P. B. Baltes and M. M. Baltes (eds.), *Successful aging: Perspectives from the behavioral sciences* (pp. 1–34). Cambridge: Cambridge University Press.
Baltes, P. B., Lindenberger, U., and Staudinger, U. M. (2006). Lifespan theory in developmental psychology. In R. M. Lerner (ed.), *Handbook of child psychology*, vol. I, 6th edn. (pp. 569–664). Hoboken, NJ: Wiley.
Baltes, P. B., Reese, H. W., and Nesselroade, J. R. (1988). *Life-span developmental psychology: An introduction to research methods*. Hillsdale, NJ: Erlbaum.
Barrick, A. L., Hutchinson, R. L., and Deckers, L. H. (1989). Age effects on positive and negative emotions. *Journal of Social Behavior and Personality*, 4, 421–429.

Bauer, J. J., and McAdams, D. P. (2004). Growth goals, maturity, and well-being. *Developmental Psychology*, 40, 14–127.

Blanchard-Fields, F. (2007). Everyday problem solving and emotion: An adult developmental perspective. *Current Directions in Psychological Science*, 16(1), 26–31.

Blazer, D. (2003). Depression in late life: Review and commentary. *The Journals of Gerontology: Medical Sciences*, 58(3), 249–265.

Blazer, D., Burchett, B., Service, C., and George, L. K. (1991). The association of age and depression among the elderly: An epidemiologic exploration. *The Journals of Gerontology: Medical Sciences*, 46(6), 210–215.

Brandtstädter, J., and Greve, W. (1994). The aging self: Stabilizing and protective processes. *Developmental Review*, 14, 52–80.

Campbell, J. D., Assanand, S., and Di Paula, A. (2003). The structure of the self-concept and its relation to psychological adjustment. *Journal of Personality*, 71, 115–140.

Carroll, J. M., Yik, M. S., Russell, J. A., and Barrett, L. F. (1999). On the psychometric principles of affect. *Review of General Psychology*, 3(1), 14–22.

Carstensen, L. L., Fung, H. H., and Charles, S. T. (2003). Socioemotional selectivity theory and the regulation of emotion in the second half of life. *Motivation and Emotion*, 27(2), 103–123.

Carstensen, L. L., Pasupathi, M., Mayr, U., and Nesselroade, J. R. (2000). Emotional experience in everyday life across the adult life span. *Journal of Personality and Social Psychology*, 79(4), 644–655.

Chandler, M. J., and Holliday, S. (1990). Wisdom in a postapocalyptic age. In R. J. Sternberg (ed.), *Wisdom: Its nature, origins, and development* (pp. 121–141). New York: Cambridge University Press.

Charles, S. T., Mather, M., and Carstensen, L. L. (2003). Aging and emotional memory: The forgettable nature of negative images for older adults. *Journal of Experimental Psychology: General*, 132(2), 310–324.

Charles, S. T., Reynolds, C. A., and Gatz, M. (2001). Age-related differences and change in positive and negative affect over 23 years. *Journal of Personality and Social Psychology*, 80, 136–151.

Compton, W. C. (2001). Toward a tripartite factor structure of mental health: Subjective well-being, personal growth, and religiousity. *Journal of Psychology: Interdisciplinary and Applied*, 135(5), 486–500.

Consedine, N. S., and Magai, C. (2006). Emotion development in adulthood: A developmental functionalist review and critique. In C. Hoare (ed.), *The Oxford handbook of adult development and learning* (pp. 209–244). New York: Oxford University Press.

Costa, P. T., and McCrae, R. R. (1980). Influence of extraversion and neuroticism on subjective well-being: Happy and unhappy people. *Journal of Personality and Social Psychology*, 38, 668–678.

(1984). Personality as a lifelong determinant of well-being. In C. Z. Malatesta and C. E. Izard (eds.), *Emotion in adult development* (pp. 141–157). Beverly Hills, CA: Sage Publications.

Diener, E., and Fujita, F. (1995). Resources, personal strivings, and subjective well-being: A nomothetic and idiographic approach. *Journal of Personality and Social Psychology*, 68(5), 926–935.

Diener, E., and Suh, E. M. (1998). Subjective well-being and age: An international analysis. In K. W. Schaie and M. P. Lawton (eds.), *Annual Review of Gerontology and Geriatrics*, vol. VIII (pp. 304–324). New York: Springer.

Donahue, E. M., Robins, R. W., Roberts, B. W., and John, O. P. (1993). The divided self: Concurrent and longitudinal effects of psychological adjustment and social roles on self-concept differentiation. *Journal of Personality and Social Psychology*, 64, 834–846.

Donnellan, M. B., and Lucas, R. E. (2008). Age differences in the big five across the life span: Evidence from two national samples. Age differences in the big five across the life span: Evidence from two national samples. *Psychology and Aging*, 23(3), 558–566.

Dörner, J., and Staudinger, U. M. (2010). *A self-concept measure of personality maturity*. Jacobs University Bremen, Germany.

Ernst, C., and Angst, J. (1995). Depression in old age. Is there a real decrease in prevalence? A review. *European Archives of Psychiatry and Clinical Neuroscience*, 245, 272–287.

Ferring, D., and Filipp, S.-H. (1997). Subjektives Wohlbefinden im Alter: Struktur- und Stabilitatsanalysen. [Subjective well-being in old age: Analyses of stability and structure.]. *Psychologische Beitraege*, 39(3), 236–258.

Fredrickson, B. L. (2003). The value of positive emotions. *American Scientist*, 91, 330–335.

Fredrickson, B. L., and Branigan, C. (2005). Positive emotions broaden the scope of attention and thought-action repertoires. *Cognition and Emotion*, 19(3), 313–332.

Gatz, M., Kasl-Godley, J. E., and Karel, M. J. (1996). Aging and mental disorders. In J. E. Birren and K. W. Schaie (eds.), *Handbook of the psychology of aging* (pp. 365–382). San Diego, CA: Academic Press.

Gayman, M. D., Turner, R. J., and Cui, M. (2008). Physical limitations and depressive symptoms: exploring the nature of the association. *The Journals of Gerontology: Series B: Psychological Sciences and Social Sciences*, 63, 219–228.

Geiselmann, B., and Bauer, M. (2000). Subthreshold depression in the elderly: Qualitative or quantitative distinction? *Comprehensive Psychiatry*, 41, 32–38.

Greve, W., and Staudinger, U. M. (2005). Resilience in later adulthood and old age: Resources and potentials for successful aging. In D. Cicchetti and A. Cohen (eds.), *Developmental psychopathology*, 2nd edn. (pp. 796–840). New York: Wiley.

Gross, J. J. (1998). Antecedent- and response-focused emotion regulation: Divergent consequences for experience, expression, and physiology. *Journal of Personality and Social Psychology*, 74(1), 224–237.

Gross, J. J., Carstensen, L. L., Pasupathi, M., Tsai, J., Skorpen, C. G., and Hsu, A. Y. (1997). Emotion and aging: Experience, expression, and control. *Psychology and Aging*, 12(4), 590–599.

Haynie, D. A., Berg, S., Johansson, B., Gatz, M., and Zarit, S. H. (2001). Symptoms of depression in the oldest old: A longitudinal study. *The*

Journals of Gerontology: Series B: Psychological Sciences and Social Sciences, 56B, 111–118.

Heckhausen, J., Dixon, R. A., and Baltes, P. B. (1989). Gains and losses in development throughout adulthood as perceived by different adult age groups. *Developmental Psychology,* 25(1), 109–121.

Heckman Coats, A., and Blanchard-Fields, F. (2008). Emotion regulation in interpersonal problems: The role of cognitive-emotional complexity, emotion regulation goals, and expressivity. *Psychology and Aging,* 23(1), 39–51.

Heeren, T. H., Van Hemert, A. M., Lagaay, A. M., and Rooymans, G. M. (1992). The general population prevalence of non-organic psychiatric disorders in subjects aged 85 years and over. *Psychological Medicine,* 22, 733–738.

Helmchen, H., Baltes, M. M., Geiselmann, B. *et al.* (1999). Psychiatric illness in old age. In P. B. Baltes and K. U. Mayer (eds.), *The Berlin Aging Study: Aging from 70 to 100* (pp. 167–196). Cambridge: Cambridge University Press.

Helson, R., and Kwan, V. S. Y. (2000). Personality development in adulthood: The broad picture and processes in one longitudinal sample. In S. Hampson (ed.), *Advances in personality psychology,* vol. I (pp. 77–106). London: Routledge.

Helson, R., and Wink, P. (1987). Two conceptions of maturity examined in the findings of a longitudinal study. *Journal of Personality and Social Psychology,* 53(3), 531–541.

Henderson, A. S., Jorm, A. F., and Mackkinnon, A. (1993). The prevalence of depressive disorders and the distribution of depression in late life. *Psychological Medicine,* 23, 719–792.

Herbrich, I. (2006). Developmental patterns of positive and negative affect in old and very old age: Longitudinal findings from the Berlin Aging Study. Unpublished Diploma Thesis. Dresden University, Dresden.

Hess, T. M. (1999). Cognitive and knowledge-based influences on social representations. In T. M. Hess and F. Blanchard-Fields (eds.), *Social cognition and aging* (pp. 237–263). San Diego, CA: Academic Press.

Hess, T. M., Osowski, N. L., and Leclerc, C. M. (2005). Age and experience influences on the complexity of social inferences. *Psychology and Aging,* 20, 447–459.

Isen, A. M. (2003). Positive affect as a source of human strength. In L. G. Aspinwall and U. M. Staudinger (eds.), *A psychology of human strengths: Fundamental questions and future directions for a positive psychology* (pp. 179–195). Washington, DC: American Psychologist Association.

Izard, C. E. (1977). *Human emotions.* New York: Plenum Press.

Jahoda, M. (1958). *Current concepts of positive mental health.* New York: Basic Books.

Kennedy, Q., Mather, M., and Carstensen, L. L. (2004). The role of motivation in the age-related positivity effect in autobiographical memory. *Psychological Science,* 15(3), 208–214.

Kessler, E.-M., and Staudinger, U. M. (2009). Affective experience in adulthood and old age: The role of affective arousal and perceived regulation. *Psychology and Aging*, 24(2), 349–362.

Keyes, C. L. M., Shmotkin, D., and Ryff, C. D. (2002). Optimizing well-being: The empirical encounter of two traditions. *Journal of Personality and Social Psychology*, 82(6), 1007–1022.

Kraaij, V., Arensman, E., and Spinhoven, P. (2002). Negative life events and depression in elderly persons: A meta-analysis. *The Journals of Gerontology: Series B: Psychological Sciences and Social Sciences*, 57B(1), 87–94.

Kunzmann, U. (2008). Differential age trajectories of positive and negative affect: Further evidence from the Berlin Aging Study. *The Journals of Gerontology: Psychological Sciences*, 63B, P261–270.

Kunzmann, U., Little, T. D., and Smith, J. (2000). Is age-related stability of subjective well-being a paradox? Cross-sectional and longitudinal evidence from the Berlin Aging Study. *Psychology and Aging*, 15(3), 511–526.

Labouvie-Vief, G. (2003). Dynamic integration: Affect, cognition, and the self in adulthood. *Current Directions in Psychological Science*, 12(6), 201–206.

Labouvie-Vief, G., Chiodo, L. M., Goguen, L. A., Diehl, M., and Orwoll, L. (1995). Representations of self across the life span. *Psychology and Aging*, 10(3), 404–415.

Labouvie-Vief, G., DeVoe, M., and Bulka, D. (1989). Speaking about feelings: Conceptions of emotion across the life span. *Psychology and Aging*, 4, 425–437.

Labouvie-Vief, G., and Medler, M. (2002). Affect optimization and affect complexity: Modes and styles of regulation in adulthood. *Psychology and Aging*, 17(4), 571–587.

Lawton, M. P. (1996). Quality of life and affect in later life. In C. Magai and S. H. McFadden (eds.), *Handbook of emotion, adult development and aging* (pp. 327–348). San Diego, CA: Academic Press.

Lawton, M. P., Kleban, M. H., and Dean, J. (1993). Affect and age: Cross-sectional comparisons of structure and prevalence. *Psychology and Aging*, 8(2), 165–175.

Lawton, M. P., Kleban, M. H., Rajagopal, D., and Dean, J. (1992). Dimensions of affective experience in three age groups. *Psychology and Aging*, 7(2), 171–184.

Lewinsohn, P. M., Rohde, P., Seeley, J. R., and Fischer, S. A. (1993). Age-cohort changes in the lifetime occurrence of depression and other mental disorders. *Journal of Abnormal Psychology*, 102, 110–120.

Lindesay, J., Briggs, K., and Murphy, E. (1989). The Guy's Age Concern survey: prevalence rates of cognitive impairment, depression and anxiety in an urban elderly community. *British Journal of Psychiatry*, 155, 317–329.

Linville, P. W. (1987). Self-complexity as a cognitive buffer against stress-related depression and illness. *Journal of Personality and Social Psychology*, 52, 663–676.

Loevinger, J. (1976). *Ego development: Conception and theory*. San Francisco, CA: Jossey Bass.

Magai, C. (2001). Emotions over the life span. In J. E. Birren and K. W. Schaie (eds.), *Handbook of the psychology of aging* (pp. 399–426). San Diego, CA: Academic Press.

Magai, C., Consedine, N. S., Krivoshekova, Y. S., Kudadjie-Gyamfi, E., and McPherson, R. (2006). Emotion experience and expression across the adult life span: Insights from a multimodal assessment study. *Psychology and Aging*, 21(2), 303–317.

Malatesta, C. Z., and Kalnok, M. (1984). Emotional experience in younger and older adults. *Journal of Gerontology*, 39, 301–308.

Mather, M., and Carstensen, L. L. (2003). Aging and attentional biases for emotional faces. *Psychological Science*, 14(5), 409–415.

(2005). Aging and motivated cognition: The positivity effect in attention and memory. *Trends in Cognitive Sciences*, 9(10), 496–502.

Mather, M., and Knight, M. R. (2006). Angry faces get noticed quickly: Threat detection is not impaired among older adults. *The Journals of Gerontology: Series B: Psychological Sciences and Social Sciences*, 61, 54–57.

McCrae, R. R., Costa, P. T., de Lima, M. P. *et al.* (1999). Age differences in personality across the adult life span: Parallels in five cultures. *Developmental Psychology*, 35(2), 466–477.

McCrae, R. R., Costa, P. T., Ostendorf, F. *et al.* (2000). Nature over nurture: Temperament, personality, and life span development. *Journal of Personality and Social Psychology*, 78(1), 173–186.

Mickler, C., and Staudinger, U. M. (2008). Personal wisdom: Validation and age-related differences in a performance measure. *Psychology and Aging*, 23(4), 778–799.

Mroczek, D. K., and Kolarz, C. M. (1998). The effect of age on positive and negative affect: A developmental perspective on happiness. *Journal of Personality and Social Psychology*, 75(5), 1333–1349.

Mroczek, D. K., and Spiro, A. I. (2003). Modeling intraindividual change in personality traits: Findings from the Normative Aging Study. *The Journals of Gerontology: Series B: Psychological Sciences and Social Sciences*, 58B(3), P153–P165.

Nelson, T. D. (2002). *Ageism: Stereotyping and prejudice against older persons.* Cambridge: MIT Press.

Nordhus, I. H. (2008). Manifestations of depression and anxiety in older adults. In B. Woods and L. Clare (eds.), *Handbook of the clinical psychology of aging.* Chichester, UK: Wiley.

Prince, M., Beekman, A., Deeg, D. *et al.* (1999). Depression symptoms in late life assessed using the EURO-D scale – Effect of age, gender and marital status in 14 European centres. *British Journal of Psychiatry*, 174, 339–345.

Roberts, B. W., Walton, K. E., and Viechtbauer, W. (2006). Patterns of mean-level change in personality traits across the life course: A meta-analysis of longitudinal studies. *Psychological Bulletin*, 132(1), 1–25.

Robins, L. N., and Regier, D. A. (1991). *Psychiatric disorders in America: The Epidemiologic Catchment Area Study.* New York: Free Press.

Rothermund, K., and Brandtstädter, J. (2003). Age stereotypes and self-views in later life: Evaluating rival assumptions. *International Journal of Behavioral Development*, 27(6), 549–554.

Ryff, C. D. (1989). Happiness is everything, or is it? Explorations on the meaning of psychological well-being. *Journal of Personality and Social Psychology*, 57(6), 1069–1081.

(1995). Psychological well-being in adult life. *Current Directions in Psychological Science*, 4(4), 99–104.

Ryff, C. D., and Keyes, C. L. M. (1995). The structure of psychological well-being revisited. *Journal of Personality and Social Psychology*, 69, 719–727.

Ryff, C. D., Singer, B., Love, G. D., and Essex, M. J. (1998). Resilience in adulthood and later life: Defining features and dynamic processes. In J. Lomranz (ed.), *Handbook of aging and mental health: An integrative approach* (pp. 69–96). New York: Plenum Press.

Simon, G., and Van Korff, M. (1992). Reevaluation of secular trends in depression rate. *American Journal of Epidemiology*, 135, 1411–1422.

Small, B. J., Hertzog, C., Hultsch, D. F., and Dixon, R. A. (2003). Stability and change in adult personality over 6 years: Findings from the Victoria Longitudinal Study. *The Journals of Gerontology: Series B: Psychological Sciences and Social Sciences*, 58B(3), P166–P176.

Sneed, J. R., and Whitbourne, S. K. (2003). Identity processing and self-consciousness in middle and later adulthood. *The Journals of Gerontology: Series B: Psychological Sciences and Social Sciences*, 58B(6), P313–P319.

Snowdon, J. (1990). The prevalence of depression in old age. *International Journal of Geriatric Psychiatry*, 5, 141–144.

Staudinger, U. M. (2000). Viele Gründe sprechen dagegen und trotzdem fühlen viele Menschen sich wohl: Das Paradox des subjektiven Wohlbefindens. [Even though many reasons speak against it, many people are happy] *Psychologische Rundschau* [German Journal of Psychology], 51, 185–197.

Staudinger, U. M., and Fleeson, W. (1996). Self and personality in old and very old age: A sample case of resilience? *Development and Psychopathology*, 8, 867–885.

Staudinger, U. M., Freund, A., Linden, M., and Maas, I. (1999). Self, personality, and life regulation: Facets of psychological resilience in old age. In P. B. Baltes and K. U. Mayer (eds.), *The Berlin Aging Study: Aging from 70 to 100* (pp. 302–328). New York: Cambridge University Press.

Staudinger, U. M., and Kessler, E.-M. (2009). Adjustment and personality growth: Two trajectories of positive personality development across adulthood. In M. C. Smith and T. J. Reio (eds.), *The handbook on adult development and learning* (pp. 241–268). Mahwah, NJ: Erlbaum.

Staudinger, U. M., Kessler, E.-M., and Dörner, J. (2006). Wisdom in social context. In K. W. Schaie and L. Carstensen (eds.), *Social structures, aging, and self-regulation in the elderly* (pp. 33–54). New York: Springer.

Staudinger, U. M., and Kunzmann, U. (2005). Positive adult personality development: Adjustment and/or growth? *European Psychologist*, 10(4), 320–329.

Staudinger, U. M., Marsiske, M., and Baltes, P. B. (1995). Resilience and reserve capacity in later adulthood: Potential and limits of development across the life span. In D. Cicchetti and D. J. Cohen (eds.), *Developmental psychopathology*, vol. II: *Risk, disorder, and adaptation* (pp. 801–947). New York: Wiley.

Staudinger, U. M., Mickler, C., and Dörner, J. (2005). Wisdom and personality. In R. Sternberg and J. Jordan (eds.), *A handbook of wisdom: Psychological perspectives* (pp. 191–219). New York: Cambridge University Press.

Steunenberg, B., Twisk, J. W. R., Beekman, A. T. F., Deeg, D. J. H., and Kerkhof, A. J. F. M. (2005). Stability and change of neuroticism in aging. *The Journals of Gerontology: Series B: Psychological Sciences and Social Sciences*, 60(1), 27–33.

Stoner, S. B., and Spencer, W. B. (1986). Age and sex differences on the State-Trait Personality Inventory. *Psychological Reports*, 35, 263–266.

Watson, D., and Clark, L. A. (1984). Negative affectivity: The disposition to experience aversive emotional states. *Psychological Bulletin*, 96(3), 465–490.

Watson, D., and Tellegen, A. (1985). Toward a consensual structure of mood. *Psychological Bulletin*, 98, 219–235.

Wernicke, T. F., Linden, M., Gilberg, R., and Helmchen, H. (2000). Ranges of psychiatric morbidity in the old and the very old: Results from the Berlin Aging Study (BASE). *European Archives of Psychiatry and Clinical Neuroscience*, 250, 111–119.

Wrosch, C., Scheier, M. F., Carver, C. S., and Schulz, R. (2003). The importance of goal disengagement in adaptive self-regulation: When giving up is beneficial. *Self and Identity*, 2, 1–20.

11 Risk, resilience, and life-course fit: older couples' encores following job loss

Phyllis Moen, Stephen Sweet, and Rachelle Hill

Abstract

A long tradition of research shows job loss to be socially toxic to the health and well-being of individuals and families. In today's economy, seniority no longer means job security, as lay-offs of older workers from their career jobs are increasingly common, but often unexpected by those forced out of work. Older dual-earner couples are in double jeopardy of job lay-offs. What contributes to the resilience of women and men in their fifties and sixties confronting the crisis of job loss, as individuals *and* as couples? With years of adulthood before them, what 'encores' do they seek? We build on a combined ecology of the life-course and stress process framework to theorize four strategic adaptations of older working couples confronting displacement from one or both partners' jobs, drawing on qualitative data to illustrate how they promote resilient life-course fit: (a) changing the situation, (b) redefining the situation, (c) altering relationships, and (d) managing rising strains and tensions. We theorize and find three key resources conducive to and reinforced by a resilient encore of fit: *control* or mastery over one's life, *social connections* and support (within the couple but also with others in one's social network), and making a *meaningful contribution* (through paid work, civic engagement, or family work).

Introduction

A number of demographic trends – including delays in the labor force participation of younger workers, the aging of the large baby-boom cohort, changes in retirement and Social Security policies and programs – are encouraging longer labor force participation among older people, as well as new scholarly and policy interest in the growing proportion of older workers. By 2010 the number of workers aged 55+ will be about 26 million, a 46 percent increase since 2000, and by 2025 this number will increase to approximately 33 million. There is also an increase in the number of workers over the age of 65 (Fullerton and Toosi, 2001).

Unfortunately, this changing workforce demography is occurring just when a global economy has rendered the security of seniority obsolete (Sweet and Meiksins, 2008). For 50 years the social contract between employees and employers privileged those with greater tenure and seniority; it was the last hired (young, women, minorities) who were the first to be fired or laid off (Rubin, 1996; Sweet and Meiksins, 2008). Today, employees in their fifties and sixties – regardless of race, ethnicity, education, or gender – cannot count on job security, no matter how hard they have worked or how long they have contributed value. Job loss is increasingly a risk factor for older workers who are vulnerable to either being laid off or else encouraged to take early retirement/buy-out packages as a result of downsizing, restructuring, mergers, bankruptcies, or closings. Once laid off, most older workers find that they cannot land a comparable job, much less a comparable salary. Young and blue-collar workers have always been at risk of job loss, but today they are joined by middle-class older workers who thought they were working under different rules, earning increased security through their advancing tenure with their employers. Most older working couples have little savings or pension prospects, even as their mortgages, children in college, and/ or other costs require two incomes to stay afloat. When the mortgage or credit card debts are based on both spouses' earnings, a job loss for one becomes a crisis for both. And yet, in our study of a middle-class sample of laid-off workers and their husbands and wives (described below), we find considerable resilience among a subset of couples. What conditions and processes promote such resilience in what effectively becomes an encore life following job loss?

Studies of resilience tend to focus on individuals as the unit of analysis, and to deal with all types of crisis events. In their scholarship on resilience in later life stages, Marziali and Donahue (2001) identify its multifaceted nature. Though they only focus on social support and finances, they call for a more inclusive approach to resilience. In this chapter we (a) move the focus from individuals to couples experiencing job loss; (b) investigate experiences as they unfold over time, both before and after job displacement; and (c) apply an ecology of the life-course, stress process theoretical framing to understand resilience as processes of successful adaptation to weather the loss and even achieve better life-course fit under challenging circumstances.

First, we describe the more general theoretical model of risk, resilience, and life-course fit, including four adaptive strategies theorized to enable individuals and couples to move toward encores of personal and relational renewal. We define and illustrate with qualitative data three key sets of resources as older couples navigate their lives under conditions of insecurity, strategically adapting to one or both spouses' job dislocations.

Theoretical and conceptual bases

Our approach is grounded in an ecology of the life course perspective (Moen and Chesley, 2008; Moen and Kelly, 2009; Moen, Elder, and Lüscher, 1995); combined with stress process theory (Pearlin, 1999; Pearlin et al., 1981). We define stress as resulting from a gap between resources and claims, with individuals at risk when their claims, demands, or needs exceed their available resources. Thus stress is the opposite of a sense of life-course fit, the cognitive appraisal that demands and resources are aligned. The etiology of stress, risk factors, and vulnerability differs over the life-course, as claims and resources shift. Older working couples confronting job loss face ongoing financial obligations, age discrimination, and skill mismatches when seeking re-employment or the prospect of unplanned transitions into retirement.

The loss of a job has long been viewed as a trigger of the stress process (Pearlin and Schooler, 1978; Pearlin et al., 1981), a toxic event in the lives of individuals and families. Studies link lay-offs to lower psychological well-being and less positive self-conceptions, as well as more depressive symptoms, anxiety, somatic complaints, and overall feelings of distress (e.g. Keyes, 1998; Kohn and Schooler, 1982; Lazarus and Folkman, 1984; Ross and Mirowsky, 1992; Ryff and Keyes, 1995; Thoits, 1999; Wheaton, 1990).

Our contribution is to build on and extend prior "ageless" approaches to develop an age-related, life-course fit model of resilience (see Figure 11.1). In other words, we theorize that, although the toxicity of job loss and adaptive strategies are similar, what job losers and their spouses define as a sense of fit (resilience) differs by life stage. In particular, we propose that resilient older working couples come to seek (or else find) an encore, a new lifestyle rather than recovery to the pre-loss status quo. We further theorize that successful strategies of adaptation are the result of and further promote three interconnected resources. Specifically, resilience involves building (or rebuilding) a sense of *control*, social *connectedness*, and meaningful engagement or *contribution*. Control, connectedness, and making a contribution, we argue, are especially of key importance in cultivating resilience in later adulthood, given that job displacement at this life stage is likely to initiate or precipitate either an encore job and/or a retirement transition.

Our analysis focuses both on the ecological circumstances in which planning and response occurs, as well as the agentic capacities of

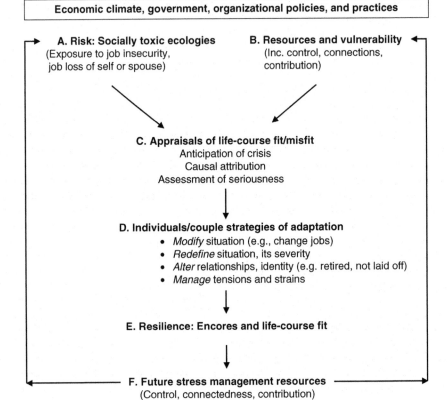

Figure 11.1. Risk, resilience, and life-course fit: a model of toxic ecologies, strategic adaptations, and encores.

individuals to influence their life pathways and their environments. Our model expands upon the thesis of agency advanced by Emirbayer and Mische (1998), who observed that the "projective capacities" of individuals – meaning their capacity to foresee alternatives and to adjust their actions – varies remarkably and is contingent on social positioning. Thus, some individuals, given their social positions, including their prior experiences and pre-existing habits, are better situated than others to sway the direction of their biographies. And, as Figure 11.1 shows, individuals not only have the capacity to adapt, but also to shape the ecologies in which they live. Moreover, the couple relationship takes the form of iterations and feedback loops shaping adaptive strategies; these in turn, give shape to later life encores. We draw on stress process theory and four interrelated life-course concepts – control cycles, life-course fit (or misfit), linked lives, and adaptive strategies – to identify effective strategic responses, that is, the conditions under which older working couples who face job dislocations manage to be resilient, fashioning encore lives that sometimes fit better than their pre-loss lifestyles.

Cycles of control and the toxicity of job loss

The term "toxic" typically refers to harmful things (such as pesticides or waste) in the physical environment. In his study of the social world of children, Jim Garbarino (1995) defines certain *social* environments as toxic, deleterious to children's health and well-being. We build on and expand his approach (see also Moen and Chesley, 2008; Moen and Kelly, 2009) to define chronic job insecurity and layoffs in the face of downsizing, plant closings, restructuring, or mergers as socially toxic for older workers, given the ambiguity around unplanned later life job exits, as well as the age norms, age discrimination, and skill mismatches that make it difficult to find comparable work (see A, Figure 11.1).

Stress at its most basic can be defined as the gap between resources and claims, (such as between A and B on Figure 11.1) leading to life-course mismatch or misfit (C, Figure 11.1; see also Goode, 1960). A tradition of theory and research on family stress (e.g., Hill, 1970), life-course processes (Moen, 1989; Moen and Howery, 1988; Moen and Yu, 1999, 2000), and on stress more generally (e.g., Lazarus and Folkman, 1984) has depicted crises and chronic strains as occurring when there is a gap between resources and demands or claims (or needs), reducing people's sense of control. Elder (1985) defines the shifts in resources and claims over the life-course as *cycles of control*, as individuals move to or from a sense of control (what we term life-course fit or misfit – see also Moen and Chesley, 2008, Moen, Kelly, and Huang, 2008) between what they expect (or perceive is expected of them) and the resources available to meet those expectations. As acute stressors, chronic strains, and resources change across the life-course, so too should individuals' assessments of their own ability to control the circumstances of their lives.

Life-course fit and misfit

The concept of control cycles captures processes of actively strategizing and adapting to seek better "fit" between claims and resources. A sense of mastery or control becomes essential to managing conditions of mismatch or misfit, but paradoxically it is often undermined by the same circumstances (Elder, 1978; Moen, 2003; Moen and Kelly, 2009; Moen and Wethington, 1999).

Research on the deleterious effects of job loss on individuals and families demonstrates that it can have a major impact on finances, health, relationships, and psychological well-being (e.g., Burke and Greenglass, 1999; Dooley, 1994; Hamilton *et al.*, 1990; Iversen and Sabroe, 1988; Jahoda, 1982; Kelvin and Jarrett, 1985; Leana and Feldman, 1992; Perrucci, 1994; Perrucci and Perrucci, 1990; Perrucci, Perrucci, and Targ, 1997; Shamir, 1986a, 1986b; Uchitelle, 2006; Vosler and Page-Adams, 1996; Westman, Etzion, and Danon, 2001). One consequence of job loss is that displaced workers lose their sense of place and purpose, their sense of making a meaningful *contribution*.

Workers in their fifties and sixties have traditionally been the most secure in their jobs, meaning that many come to lay-offs or buy-outs unprepared, as are their husbands and wives. Most expect an eventual role exit (retirement), but 'not yet.' As Powell and DiMaggio (1991, p. 194) point out, existing social arrangements provide a guide to action and produce shared expectations that, in turn, foster psychological security. When such existing arrangements are suddenly upended, older workers and their partners have to come to terms with and create a new vision of reality, and to do so with incomplete blueprints and outdated guideposts (Moen and Roehling, 2005; Rubin, 1996). Complicating their transitions into new jobs, many older workers lack the technological skills to match the needs of rising industries, and often encounter age discrimination as they are commonly perceived as less capable or productive than younger workers (Charness, 2006; Palmore, 2005; Rupp, Vodanovich, and Cred, 2006; Sweet, 2007).

Linked lives

The life-course notion of *linked lives* highlights the ways individuals' responses to exigencies are always embedded in and shaped by the people in their lives. In the wake of a job loss, ties to a spouse can buffer strain, but also constrain options. Employed spouses, for example, can provide income that somewhat ameliorates budgetary shortfalls, as well as provide emotional support (Walsh and Jackson, 1995). At the same time, older working couples confronting job loss on the part of one or both partners must coordinate their responses, engaging in various adaptive strategies as individuals and as couples (Moen and Wethington, 1992). These strategies consist of both taken-for-granted cultural templates as well as *ad hoc* responses to stressful circumstances. Job loss is invariably stressful, but when occurring unexpectedly in later adulthood it can become a focal event, a turning point (Ebaugh, 1988, Wethington, Pixley, and Kavey, 2003) reshaping the arc of the life-course. Riley and

Waring (1976) discuss the potential for *counter point* transitions, changes that a person experiences as a consequence of changes in another person's life. Couples in later adulthood experience just such counter point transitions, when job severance or early retirement of one person affects the life-course of the other. Thus one job displacement produces strains and ambiguity, along with constraints and options, for both members of a couple.

The marital relationship, as well as relations with a network of colleagues and friends, provides a sense of *connectedness*, crucial for an effective response. At the same time, job loss can mean a shrinking social network. As Robert Weiss (1997) points out, the world of work links individuals to a valued collectivity, with events, deadlines, relationships, and schedules providing a structure to life. The loss of such a community can result in a sense of marginality, valuelessness, exile, and anomie.

Adaptive strategies

Adaptive strategies can be individual or couple-level actions. We delineate four types of strategies (see Figure 11.1) that can enhance displaced older couples' sense of control, connectedness, and contribution. One strategy is to *modify* the situation, such as seeking another job. A second strategy is to *redefine* the situation, whether in terms of cognitive assessments of current circumstances or future prospects, or the redefinition of the past, such as redefining the relative salience of, for example, couples' relationships or their career jobs. A third approach is to *alter* relationships or identities, trying on new roles or divisions of labor for example, or else deepening social ties. Fourth is to seek out ways to *manage* tensions and strains, such as exercising more frequently or using alcohol as a reprieve from the pressures of dislocation. Note that not all strategies are equally effective and some strategies (such as alcohol use) may prove to be *maladaptive*. In line with the focus of this volume, we focus on the strategies of adaptation used by couples who proved especially resilient. In the absence of clear norms and institutionalized strategies, older workers facing the uncertain future of job loss adapt in often happenstance ways. There have been few studies of the life-course dynamics and resilience of older workers – much less older couples – confronting what is an increasingly common experience: an unexpected role exit (Ebaugh, 1988) in the guise of lay-offs, early retirement incentives, and/or severance packages. It is important to recognize that individuals and couples construct their own meanings surrounding both job loss and retirement (cf. Wheaton, 1990). Their definitions and assessments, in turn, have repercussions in terms of their strategies of adaptation. Moreover, simply redefining the situation can itself be an adaptive strategy, a way of promoting a greater sense of life-course fit.

Methodology

Study design and sample

To illustrate strategies of adaptation theorized in the life-course fit model depicted in Figure 11.1, we draw on data from a subset of couples from the *Ecology of Careers Panel Study* where one partner was aged 50 or older and one or both partners experienced some type of dislocation. The goal of the larger study was to collect information from a representative sample of middle-class dual-earner couples ($N = 4637$ in 2000, and $N = 3893$ when reinterviewed in 2002) in upstate New York on the challenges and strategies of bridging work and family. The surveys were designed so that both spouses in dual-earner families were interviewed (separately) in order to generate extensive information on each partner's job histories, family histories, educational histories, current family dynamics, current work experiences, and future plans (Moen, 2003; Swisher, Sweet, and Moen, 2004).[1]

These panel data enabled us to identify a sample of couples who experienced job loss in the two years between surveys, as well as couples where at least one partner worked under conditions of chronic low job security. Identifying this sample permitted a subsequent project, the *Couples Managing Change Study*. It involved hour-long telephone interviews with participants answering detailed qualitative questions concerning their preparation for, experiences during, and outcomes of job loss and job insecurity. This study yielded interviews with 260 husband and wife couples conducted in May 2002 (in nearly every case both partners were interviewed separately). We restrict our analysis to couples where at least one spouse is aged 50 or older at the time of the Couples Managing

---

[1] Fully 84 percent of the participants in the baseline survey participated in the second wave of interviews. The high response rate can be attributed to the interest participants expressed in the goals of the study, as well as the compensation they received (from $25 to $35 per participant). To generate the sample, an initial pool of participants was recruited through a random sample in 11 different places of employment (representing a diversity of occupations and economic sectors), and another group of participants was recruited in a random sample from three communities in which the initial pool of participants resided (an average of 26.9 respondents was recruited in each of 57 Census Block Groups in Upstate New York). Although it is not possible to calculate an exact response rate for the organizational sample, it is likely comparable to the 68 percent response rate achieved for the community sample, as specified by one or more members of the household participating.

Table 11.1. *Characteristics of older working couples* experiencing a job loss*

Variable	Mean/Percentage	Standard deviation	Total
N	—	—	72
Women	50.0%	—	36
Men	50.0%	—	36
Marital status			
Married	97.22%	—	70
Living with a partner	2.78%	—	2
Life stage			
No children	9.72%	—	7
Children in the home under the age of 18	33.33%	—	24
Full-time enrolled college student	19.44%	—	14
Empty nester	37.50%	—	27
Number of children	1.944	1.060	72
Age	51.299	4.813	72
Respondent type			
Displaced worker	33.90%	—	41
Spouse of displaced worker	25.60%	—	31
Work status			
Retired, not working	6.94%	—	5
Retired working	2.78%	—	2
Not retired, not working	15.28%	—	11
Working for pay	75.00%	—	54
Work hours	41.818	11.788	55
Household income	$149,652	$212,041	72
Individual income	$88,411	$187,259	72

* With at least one partner over the age of 50.

Change Study and at least one spouse experienced a job loss.[2] Based on the reports of seventy-two participants who met these criteria, this study reports the experiences of four couples in which both partners lost their jobs, nineteen couples in which the husband lost his job, fourteen couples in which the wife lost her job. We include in the analysis information on each partners' prior career experiences and career strategies, data collected in the larger Ecology of Careers Panel Study.

Table 11.1 summarizes the demographic characteristics of this sample. Because the Ecology of Careers Study set out to examine the experiences

[2] The response rate for this study was 95 percent, but owing to interviewer errors five interviews had to be discarded. Interviews were taped and transcribed verbatim, producing over 8000 pages of text that was subsequently coded and analyzed using the text management system 'AskSam.'

of middle-class dual-earner couples, it cannot be generalized to account for the experiences of low-wage workers. Most of the analytic sample consists of empty nesters with adult children who no longer live in the parental home.

Measures and analysis

We define a displaced worker as a worker who lost a job due to an organizational restructuring or downsizing in the two years between survey waves. These workers may or may not be working in new jobs at the time of the (third and fourth) interviews in the Couples Managing Change Study. The spouses of displaced workers are individuals married (or partnered) to a displaced worker. One in three of displaced workers remained out of the labor force by the second survey. Most of their spouses remained employed; only one in ten spouses were out of the labor force by the second survey wave.

To assess resilience in the face of job loss (model 1), we rely on quantitative and qualitative items drawn from the Couples Managing Change Study. We first identify individuals and couples who evidenced resilience on the basis of their response to the following type of interview question: "*In comparison to when you (your spouse) had that previous job, would you say that your physical health is (better, worse, about the same)?*" *(if better or worse)* "*Can you tell me some of the ways your health has changed?*" This same question structure was replicated in respect to "emotional well-being," "relationship with your spouse," "relationships with other people other than your spouse," and "family's financial situation." Those who respond "better" or the "same" are considered to be resilient. Note that we theorize resilience as multifaceted, evident on one or more dimensions, and qualitative data further inform some of the variations evident across resilience domains. As shown in Table 11.2, more than 77 percent of job losers and 73 percent of their spouses responded better or the same on four or more dimensions. Less than 6 percent of the entire sample responded worse. We then performed extensive analysis of the qualitative data on a resilient subgroup who responded better or the same on most dimensions, examining three cognitive and behavioral resources we theorize as key to resilience in the face of job loss: a sense of control or mastery, connectedness with others, and making a contribution or meaningful engagement.

Resilience in practice: the case of older couples

Despite the challenges of job loss, many interviewees report they are "better" or the "same" across the five resilience domains. Table 11.2

Table 11.2. *Resilience measures assessing change among older working couples* experiencing a job loss (N = 72)*

		Displaced worker (%)	–	Spouse of displaced worker (%)	–	Total (%)
Health	Better	39.0		9.7		26.4
	Same	43.9		71.0		55.6
	Worse	17.1		19.4		18.1
	Total	100.0	41	100.0	31	
Emotional	Better	48.8		22.6		37.5
	Same	26.8		58.1		40.3
	Worse	24.4		19.4		22.2
	Total	100.0	41	100.0	31	
Financial	Better	17.1		6.5		12.5
	Same	39.0		41.9		40.3
	Worse	43.9		51.6		47.2
	Total	100.0	41	100.0	31	
Relationship with spouse*	Better	55.0		26.7		42.9
	Same	35.0		60.0		45.7
	Worse	10.0		13.3		11.4
	Total	100.0	40	100.0	30	
Relationship with others	Better	31.7		16.1		25.0
	Same	61.0		80.6		69.4
	Worse	7.3		3.2		5.6
	Total	100.0	41	100.0	31	
Better or same on five measures		37.5		40.0		38.6
Better or same on four measures		40.0		33.3		37.1
Better or same on three measures		10.0		10.0		10.0
Better or same on two measures		7.5		10.0		8.6
Better or same on one measures		2.5		6.7		4.3
Better or same on zero measures		2.5		0.0		1.4
Total		100.0		100.0		100.0

* With at least one partner older than 50. One couple did not indicate how their relationship with their spouse had or had not changed.

describes the proportion of each group responding "better," the "same," or "worse" on these questions. We used these responses to select a resilient group: those responding "better" in some domains, "the same" in others, but who do not generally feel they are "worse" off. We then analyzed the in-depth interviews of a random subsample of resilient couples.

Coding and analysis of themes drawn from the interviews with those demonstrating resilience (as operationally defined by responses above) underscored three resources we theorized as key to resilience: a sense of mastery or *control*, social *connections* with others (including the spouse), and *meaningful contribution* or engagement in some type of paid or unpaid work. These factors interconnect and are interdependent, but we illustrate them separately to emphasize the incidence and importance of each.

A sense of control

We found that redefining the situation and changing relationships (such as the relationship with one's former employer) are key adaptive strategies (see C, Figure 11.1) of dislocated but resilient older workers. To gain or retain a sense of mastery or control, many in this age group chose to redefine their lay-offs from "job loss" to "retirement." Downsizing companies encourage this by offering early retirement or severance packages, so the corporations are able to claim few were actually "laid off," but, instead, either took early retirement or else left "voluntarily."

Consider the case of Joan and Gerald. Joan, a vice-president for a large company, was offered a retirement package two years before her firm completed merging with another company. She ended up defining her exit as retirement, but then took a consulting position back with her same firm following the merger. Joan answered the "same" on four of the five resilience measures, and "better" in terms of her financial situation. When asked if she felt glad about retiring, Joan responded *"Absolutely."* She went on to explain:

We have grandchildren and it gave me a lot more flexibility with my time and, uh, working part time as a consultant I was still able to keep in the business on a much less commitment scale.

Her husband Gerald is 66 but still works full time in his career job as assistant to a high-level administrator at Upstate University. Describing his situation following his wife's lay-off, Gerald responded "same" on all five measures of resilience. Though his wife's transition was not planned, he saw it as welcomed by her, offering her a greater sense of control over her employment and her life. When asked to describe when he first learned his wife's position was being eliminated, Gerald's reaction was positive: "*I was pleased for her that she, could retire and negotiate a retirement.*" Redefining Joan's layoff as a welcome retirement exit increased this couple's sense of control and their appraisals of life-course fit.

Resilient couples confronting job loss display *planful competence* (Clausen, 1968), a degree of control even in this high-risk climate. This is exemplified by Fritz and Pamela. Fritz is a 54-year-old librarian who turned self-employed entrepreneur. He made this career change after being laid off (after 23 years) from a manufacturing company. Though he has not yet found a new job, he has adapted by "changing the situation," specifically, starting his own business. His wife Pamela is working full time at her encore job (following her own lay-off) as a textile artist. Overall, Fritz seems very positive about this job change. He answered "better" on four of the five resilience measures and "worse" about his financial position since the layoff. Still, when asked about his financial situation, he exhibits the sense of control that the couple's planful competence around savings has provided:

We had to cut back some because obviously the money wasn't coming in as much. But we have a significant amount of personal savings, uh that we used for a while to offset the loss of income. And we borrowed some money in the last, oh six months, uh to sort of bridge us until retirement starts. So, in terms of lifestyle changes, uh not significantly, we still planned appropriately.

Preparation and advanced warning seem key to a sense of control. Fritz anticipated that he might well lose his job about six months before he was given official notice; he therefore began taking action early on:

Well you obviously call your contacts, you know look around with what's going on in the community, who's hiring, who wasn't, made a few calls, interviewed with a few people. Thought about what I wanted to do if I started my own business. Things like that.

He also thought of a career change, entering into an entirely different line of work. He describes his thinking:

Well, let's see, maybe going back to school and getting my certificates, and I taught oh 30 years ago and enjoyed it, thought about doing some carpentry, things like that. Getting into some venture capital formation-type projects.

He chose the venture capital route:

I set up a small business on entrepreneurism and capital resources. I have another small business that does information research for start-up companies. Um, a lot of website development for smaller companies.

His explanation underscores his sense of control over the situation, as well as his dual strategies of both changing his situation and redefining it:

If I can't do better than the idiots out there ... [laughter], you know uh ... the entrepreneur type, I've got a small business that essentially links entrepreneurs and capitalists. So making those connections and helping people that are starting out is very satisfying.

We also find that anticipation gives older couples time to adjust, even when both spouses are laid off. Pamela, the 51-year-old self-employed textile artist married to Fritz, lost her job at a manufacturing firm we call Vantech two years before Fritz lost his job with another corporation. Afterwards she too decided to make a career change, pursuing her interest in textile art. She is very positive about the changes that they went through and their ability as a couple to manage problems that arise. She responded 'better' on three of the resilience measures, the 'same' on the health measure and 'worse' regarding their financial situation. Speaking about Fritz's job loss, she says:

Well, I knew that he was going to way ahead of it. It was just a matter of when. How did I first learn? He told me ... I had been anticipating it for so long it was sort of, ah, what do you call that when something is – it was sort of a non-event.

Her initial reaction was one of relief and celebration:

Um, we planned his retirement party. [laugh] I had a retirement party after I got laid off so we planned his retirement party and we had a nice retirement party for him. It's one of the things I learned years ago when I was working for another company where people were getting laid off, they all went out to drink at a bar together – the people who stayed and the people who got laid off – and they just kind of, I don't know, it wasn't a sorrowful moment. They all rather had a joyous time. [laugh] Um, you know, well you just can't get upset about these kinds of things.

Prior to his actual layoff, Fritz and Pamela did some planning:

We probably, you know, spent some time looking at our financial situation to see, you know, what it was going to do to us. How we needed to live. Already having been laid off from my job and having lost my salary for two years, [previously] we'd already gone through one level of adjustment, so, you know, taking the next stage of adjustment, though not always the most exciting thing to happen to, it just becomes easier to do. Man am I a coupon clipper, you know. [laugh]

Pamela reports being very prepared for Fritz's job loss, pointing out the importance of their life stage and life-course fit in promoting their resilience:

I think we are in a better situation than an awful lot of people. It's not – I have one friend who has, you know, four children – the youngest of which is about four years old – and he still has a mortgage. You know, when you're facing a situation where you've got to raise children and send them to college and you've got to pay mortgage and all that kind of stuff, losing your job is a terrifying thing. Um, whereas we were in a better position for that.

Another example of the importance of a sense of control for resilience is 58-year-old Patricia, laid off from New Wave, an information technology company, two and a half years earlier. About three years before losing her job permanently, the firm offered her early retirement benefits if she transitioned to contract work. Then, following the contract work, she was told that she was no longer needed. Her husband Hal is still employed as the VP of Accounting Operations at New Wave. She seems very resilient in her conversation with the interviewer, talking a great deal about her new ability to focus on herself, her relationships, and the control she has over her future employment, as well as the importance of being able to anticipate the layoff. She said she was the "same" on four of the five resilience measures and "better" on the measure gauging her emotional situation. When asked about her initial reaction, she responded by saying that she had had her suspicions, despite only being given two days' notice:

I wasn't surprised at all. Because I had, I'm pretty well tapped, I was tapped in, and I, I knew that these were, that these things were going to happen ... Actually, you know, I – it was more matter-of-fact for me, because I suspected that it would happen, I was prepared for it, and I truly wasn't devastated, because I have a pension, and – I don't know. In a way I felt, I felt some measure of freedom. Because I didn't really like doing what I was doing. And so – and it was really, really good money so I wouldn't have walked away from it, but I, I was kind of happy to be free of it.

Narratives about control permeate the interviews of those reporting resilience. A prime example is Nadia, a 42-year-old registered nurse in an ICU raising a 6-year-old. Though Nadia is young for our sample, her husband Oswald is 51. Both Nadia and Oswald experienced recent job loss. This is a situation – young family at home, two job losses – rife for life-course misfit and considerable stress. His job exit was not anticipated and much more difficult for him (based on his interview) while hers was expected. In fact, she took control of the situation by resigning a week prior to when they would have officially let her go. She found a new job and did not have a lapse between jobs. She sounded very much in control in her discussion of her family, her proactively searching for a job, and her priorities in life. She answered "better'" on three of the five resilience measures and the "same" on measures of her present health and financial situation. Nadia described how she learned that her position was being eliminated and her strategies to maintain a sense of control:

Well, I think it was actually one of those situations where I knew that we pretty much had finished training the agency on computers. And I knew at that point that they were just going to have the new employees that were hired be trained. And that they probably wouldn't need two trainers. So, before I actually lost the job, I went ahead and resigned, and found out a week or two later that they were going to eliminate my position anyway. So, it was kind of a decision that I made beforehand, and part of the reason why I made the decision to resign and do something else was the long hours, and the taking work home and that kind of thing. Because that was really starting to bother me. So I decided to just try working weekends. So I could spend more time with my son and with my family.

Lay-offs among older workers can be challenging – employees in this age group often cannot afford to retire and yet find it difficult to get another job. Still, many demonstrate a sense of resilience, as in the case of Madeline and Morton. Madeline, a 51-year-old who lost her job at a large company found another job three months later while still receiving severance pay from her previous employer. She is not overly positive about her situation but seems confident in their ability to weather the change, describing very few changes following the transition. She answered the "same" to all five resilience measures. When asked how she has changed the management of her career after losing her job, Madeline explains that job loss no longer seems as major as it used to be: *"I wouldn't say less concerned about losing a job, but you know, it's not life threatening thing."*

Her 54-year-old husband Morton was transferred out of his design job from Utilco (a utility firm) during a sale of a portion of the business. He continued to remain with the original company through the transfer, but in a lower office-worker position. He answered "better" to the questions about changes in his emotional and physical health and the "same" to the remaining three resilience measures. Similar to his wife, Morton explains that his career has changed for the better because:

It's given me a chance to be able to sit down and evaluate myself ... Uh, evaluate, just my situation ... And evaluate what I really want to do with my life for the next I'd say, oh, 47 years if I live to be 100.

Connections with others

Research shows that social connectedness or integration is key to well-being (House *et al.*, 1992; Pillemer *et al.*, 2000). One key source of connectedness is the couple's own relationship, which can provide important support for the dislocated worker. One person we interviewed, 58-year-old retiree Patricia, lost her job at New Wave, a telecommunications company. The day she was laid off her husband Hal took her out for dinner. He was very encouraging, Patricia recalls:

You know, we were so prepared for it, that really, um, and you know I think the only other thing I would say about my husband is that he just said, "take some time, figure out what you want to do, and whatever it is, I'll support it." So I guess the support, you know, offering the support, regardless of how I decided to spend my time, is helpful.

Dawn, a 54-year-old school librarian, described offering her husband Jeffrey similar support after he lost his job as an accountant due to downsizing at Upstate University. He was very committed to finding a new position and in fact started a new job only two months after losing his old one. Dawn seems fairly positive about the experience and was not fazed by the challenges that came with the process. She answered the "same" to all five resilience measures. After finding out that he lost his position, she

encouraged him to – not to give up on himself and go out and, you know, seek um, network with other, um, take advantage of career counseling, um, just being actively open to things.

Though positive relationships with a spouse are an important resource to draw upon in order to weather the challenges of job dislocation, acquaintances and co-workers may play an even more important role in helping older laid-off workers find new employment. Recall Oswald, the 51-year-old technical writer who lost his contract job (writing curricula materials) a few years prior to the interview. He was able to find a new job as a technical writer for a software training company only after using many contacts and experiencing what he termed a bout of depression. His wife Nadia remains employed as an ICU nurse. In terms of resilience, losing his job was clearly hard on Oswald; the tensions and strains culminated in a range of depressive symptoms and he talks about his former job very negatively. However, he defines his current situation very positively. He answered "better" on four resilience measures and the "same" on the measure gauging relationships with others besides his wife. Oswald refers to the importance of social connections when asked to explain the resources that he utilized to locate his current position:

Well, I, let's see. I was checking in the, on the internet, on the State Job Line. Um, I was, I did some networking with people that I knew in my professional society for technical writers. And with, uh, my, one of my professors at Upstate University for my writing program. He in fact got me the next job that I had ... He'd gotten me the first job, and then he got me the second job too [chuckles].

And Madeline, the 51-year-old who lost her job at a large company as a training manager, found a job three months later. Though Madeline did not find her position through networking she does mention the importance of supportive friends and co-workers. She explains that:

They were just very supportive and encouraging. Professional-type friends who were more than willing to help with, uh, resumes and networking opportunities, and very supporting in that way.

Connections with others can become important for weathering the challenges around job loss. Rosa is a 40-year-old woman who lost her job as a customer service/distribution manager at Lake University when it eliminated her department. She transitioned into massage therapy and is preparing to start her own practice in her home. Her 56-year-old husband Kane is also self-employed as an industrial design consultant out of their home. Rosa feels very engaged by her new calling and talks a great deal about the excitement and changes it made in her life. It seems possible that there may be some future challenges with Kane but otherwise she is very connected with others. She answered "better" on three and "worse" on the two measures about their financial situation and her relationship with her spouse. Concerning the support received from Rosa's co-workers, she reports some help:

It was more sort of like an emotional support sort of thing … Their encouragement for my choices and I've known these people for years and years.

However, not all relationships are a resource, as Rosa's relationship with her husband Kane demonstrates. After being asked how her relationship with her husband compares to the time prior to the job loss, Rosa explains:

Um, I think it may be a little worse off in some respects only because I – I'm less apt to just go to work and come home and survive. You know, I have – I want more fulfillment from my career, thus I want more fulfillment in my life.

In addition to the emotional and psychological support that relationships provide, many family members also provide economic stability. Couples dealing with job loss are then able to draw upon these resources to maintain a standard of living while searching for a new job or using their time for community service activities. Erwin and Lani lean on one another to adjust to new employment situations. Erwin is 58 years old, formerly employed at Vantech until he was offered an early retirement package. He now spends his time volunteering while his wife Lani is working in the school district as an administrator. Erwin describes some of the ways in which Lani has provided emotional support:

Being supportive and, ah, and striving to be flexible and accommodating with, you know, the conflicts and so forth that come about. Both doing different things, coming home at different times, and that sort of thing. So I guess it's [unintelligible] that support that she provides and also just keeping a good even, you know, climate at home climate. [An] accepting home, peaceful climate at home.

But Lani's support does not stop with emotional and psychological aspects. Erwin explains that Lani's work situation and commitments influence his choices "a lot":

That is, it allows some earnings coming in that takes the heat off of my obligations to continue high income work. A very big influence on the things that I'm able to do ... [Her income] allows me to be able to take on opportunities that are strictly in the volunteer realm.

The support goes both directions, even though it may entail different means from Erwin than it does from Lani. Erwin describes his role in supporting Lani now that he is no longer working for pay. He says that he is

trying to make it so, again, when she comes home and goes, try to, you know, make that, try to be flexible and that, trying to take care of things that frees her up to do, frees her up so her mind is free when she has to do the stressful things that she has to do daily.

Meaningful contribution/engagement

As we have seen in the preceding sections, resilient couples in the face of job loss find alterative ways to continue to contribute, whether through paid jobs, unpaid community work, or family care work. Often they redefine their previous career job as less than ideal, seeing their post-layoff "encores" providing them with better sense of life-course fit. Recall Morton, the 54-year-old man transferred out of his job as a designer from Utilco after the sale of a portion of the business. He was able to remain with his original company by taking a lower-level job as an office manager. Though he continues to work full time, his new job requires fewer hours and he is no longer on call. His wife Madeline also lost her job as a training manager three years later. She received a severance package and found another full-time job in human resources with a trucking company within three months. They have two children, including a 17-year-old still living at home. Morton reports that, in terms of his physical health, the job change has affected him "a lot":

Yeah, I lost weight, I feel a lot better. Uh, I'm less stressed out. I used to have acid reflux. I don't have that anymore. I used to [get] migraine headaches at least every other day, I don't have those anymore. Uh, let's see. I get to walk around a lot, get a great amount of exercise. Get to meet a lot people and talk to them. God, what else could you ask for in life? [chuckles] I'm a lot happier. I get to do things now that I've always wanted to do, never got to do.

It is obvious that for Morton, his sense of meaningful engagement is closely tied with the connections he has in his current job. It is also interconnected with his sense of control and his sense of meaningful contribution in an encore arrangement, not simply returning to business as usual: "*Why would I say I'm happier? Because of the fact that I can just get to live life the way I've wanted always to live it.*"

And 58-year-old Erwin who accepted an early retirement package is now very engaged in an encore of service, helping community organizations while his wife Lani continues to work for pay. When asked to describe his current work he gives a long explanation of the projects he is involved in, all offering a sense of contribution to the greater good:

It's quite broad, it's quite broad. Like town-based type activities, you know, some planning board, master plan committees, bicentennial planning committees, you know, within town type things, [I'm] still a member of the flying club, which I earned a license during the past years. Able to help them and do things, help in some of their programs.

He is finding real rewards in his encore career of service:

Just the, you know, it's just the, it's a time in life when you can give back some, give back more than you've received over the years. [I've] been able to do that more, and so I see this time. It's satisfying being very helpful and seeing things happen that wouldn't happen if we weren't here. And I feel very good about that kind of a thing.

Erwin goes on to explain that though this was an intentional transition, the progression to community leader was gradual, allowing him to shape his experience:

It was evolution of something we've done where we've lived in other communities before, and it's just really, just allowed me more time to do that kind of a thing. Flexibility and the freedom to tackle things that before you really couldn't get into cause you'd sacrifice your work environment, the things that you needed to do to support yourself ... It's been adapted to the community we live in since we moved. So we're doing things that are relative to this community and also more tempered with the age we are. We're no long supporting soccer teams, can't be with Boy Scouts, but we're doing other things that are more fitting to our lifestyle and age at the moment.

More than anything Erwin recognizes this phase in life as a continuation of his previous commitment and productive engagement:

Well it was, couple comments. One, I was very happy before I retired. I was very happy in my work, I was very happy with the company and the folks I worked with.

So you know [unintelligible] a logical flow kind of thing, and when I did retire, the work environment you know prepared me for other things that were to follow, prepared me economically and prepared me educationally, and exposed me to many good people. And some I still contact for help and things like that; we still keep in touch. And the fact that I have the time now to do these things, it's very satisfying. It's very satisfying to put in place things that you know will help people for long after I'm gone. It's very, very satisfying to know these things.

Erwin's wife Lani's own encore is also civic engagement, but in a paid job in school district administration, building upon her past skills, providing better life-course fit, and contributing to her school system:

Because it was a new initiative, um, in the sense that unlike industry, education has never really looked at data to make a difference in what they did about it ... And, that was kind of exciting to me, I don't know if it was my science background, but I thought it was about time that we did this sort of thing ... Um, I liked um, I liked moving out of the school building, which I was in before, a high school building, into a district-wide, you know, the broadening of that into the different levels. And the different curricular areas. So both of those things, um, I think attracted me. It was, it was more pay but I can't, I can't tell you that that was a motivator.

Similar to her husband, Lani was able to shape the future of her new position. This process helped Lani create a position where she is giving back and will be able to continue doing so in the future:

I actually was able to take a new position and kind of mold it and evolve it the way I, and have a lot of influence over how that position was going to look. So I've only been in it for a year, but within that year, um, I've been able to establish some of the processes, and some of the um, projects that will be the hallmark of that job when I leave. So, it's been satisfying in that way. I've, you know, it hasn't been perfect, but ...

Rosa, the 40-year-old in massage therapy encore, is very excited about her new career and the positive impact it is having on her life. Though she says that she liked her previous job "a lot," Rosa describes her old job in retrospect, redefining the situation:

It could – it could – it was a little routine at times. It can be a little routine. And, um, you know, thinking about it now, I just don't like getting up everyday and spending my whole entire day at a job working for somebody else to turn around and come home and live a life, you know, that's my whole revelation the last year. You know, life is more than going to work ... So it became inconvenient to breathing really.

She goes on to explain how the transition and the new position allowed her to re-evaluate and to make choices that reflect her new priorities:

It gave me the opportunity to kind of slow down just a little bit. And to really see what I had around me. And to objectively and selfishly, for myself, look at my future and, um, where I'm at right now as in just kind of live each day as it comes. And make choices for myself instead of working for someone else or doing something for a corporation that. I'm much more kind of selfish in the way of – and, you know, I don't ever want to work for anybody again in that situation. You know, it's just too much.

The opportunity to re-evaluate proved to Rosa that her career did not define her and she would be able to be happy in many other jobs and situations. She explained that she can make her new position into whatever she would like:

I can make it as big or do as little as I want and I have the opportunity to adapt myself and my lifestyle to either working my butt off at my profession or skating it by and I'll still be all right. But I know that I'll be a lot happier than I used to be.

Conclusions

Being laid off in later adulthood is for many an "ambiguous loss" (Boss, 1999). Older workers, presumably the most secure segment of the workforce, often feel blindsided, not knowing what or when it is happening, not feeling any control over their displacement, and not clear as to what are next steps. But an unplanned exit from the career job for workers in their fifties or sixties can also be a positive turning point (Ebaugh, 1988). Strategies of adaptation on the part of displaced workers and their spouses can reduce its ambiguous nature. We theorized, and demonstrated with case examples, three resources that reduce the toxicity of job loss and facilitate successful adaptive strategies that, in turn, promote resilience. Specifically, increasing a sense of *control*, nourishing *social connections,* and continuing to *contribute* in some capacity – all constitute interrelated resources essential for building and sustaining resilience.

It is often said that when one door closes another opens. That seems the case for the displaced but resilient middle-class couples in their fifties and sixties we interviewed. Their stories capture the multiple tactics couples use to successfully manage job displacement, a range of effective strategies – redefining and/or changing the situation, altering their relationships with work and with one another, and seeking ways to reduce tensions and strains. These couples' narratives suggest that effective adaptive strategies for this age group often involve carving out alternative, less stressful 'encores,' not trying to reproduce but, rather, to move beyond the career jobs they have lost. These encores appear to promote a greater life-course fit, enhancing older couples' sense of control, connectedness, and contribution at a pace that seems more doable and less stressful than the jobs they were displaced from.

Leonard Pearlin coined the term "role captivity" to denote being in an unwanted role. The idea of life-course fit or misfit similarly encapsulates cognitive and emotional assessments of captivity or control – as they play out at different ages and life stages. One adaptive strategy for displaced older workers appears to be to redefine the jobs they were displaced from, concluding in retrospect that they had lacked the resources in those jobs to achieve their goals, needs, and demands, much like divorced people tend to redefine the quality of their previous marriages. Another redefinition is to view job loss as an opportunity to fashion an encore, replete with new ways of living. The people we interviewed actively engaged in restructuring their lives following their own or their partners' job displacement. In doing so, many felt the yoke of what may have been unrecognized role captivity in their previous job lift, offering new and better fitting arrangements.

It is important to recognize, however, that these strategies of adaptation represent *constrained* choices. Here we return to our initial observations concerning toxic ecologies. Resilience implies recovery, when an individual or family "bounces back" or, perhaps more relevant for this group, "moves on" from adversity. In the couples we studied, adaptation reflected personal strategies of readjusting lives in the wake of job loss, which in turn shaped their subsequent resources and options. What these displaced workers could *not* do was reshape the socially toxic environments of job insecurity and displacement; instead, they viewed global forces of competition precipitating their own job displacement as simply the way things are. Ultimately the question for policy makers may not be how to promote resilience, but rather, setting standards for acceptable thresholds of toxicity (e.g., rights to advance notification, reasonable work schedules, access to breaks, etc.) and expanding the resources and options available to individuals (e.g., training, unemployment compensation, family leave, etc.) vulnerable to displacement. If the global economy continues to sustain flexibility for *employers* (that is the ability to lay off workers regardless of their contract, tenure, or performance), it may be possible to reduce the toxicity of this condition by instituting supports for flexible careers, replete with retraining, bridge incomes, and alternative retirements (Moen and Sweet, 2004). For older workers, policies and practices that facilitate the creation of second, third, or fourth "encore" careers would greatly facilitate recovery and renewal in the face of an uncertain economy and an uncharted course in the second half of life.

REFERENCES

Boss, P. (1999). *Ambiguous loss*. Cambridge, MA: Harvard University Press.
Burke, R. J. and Greenglass, E. (1999). Work-family conflict, spouse support and nursing staff well-being during organizational restructuring. *Journal of Occupational Health Psychology*, 4, 327–336.

Charness, N. (2006). Work, older workers, and technology. *Generations*, 30, 25–30.

Clausen, J. (ed.). (1968). *Socialization and society*. Boston, MA: Little, Brown. and Co.

Dooley, D. (1994). Depression and unemployment. *American Journal of Community Psychology*, 22, 745–765.

Ebaugh, H. R. F. (1988). *Becoming an ex: The process of role exit*. Chicago, IL: University of Chicago Press.

Elder, G. H., Jr. (ed.). (1985). *Life course dynamics: Trajectories and transitions, 1968–1980*. Ithaca, NY: Cornell University Press.

(1978). Family history and the life course. In T. Hareven (ed.), *Transitions: The family and the life course in historical perspective* (pp. 17–64). New York: Academic Press.

Emirbayer, M., and Mische, A. (1998). What is agency? *American Journal of Sociology*, 103, 692–1023.

Fullerton, H. N., and Toosi, M. (2001). Labor force projections to 2010: Steady growth and changing composition. *Monthly Labor Review*, 124, 21–38.

Garbarino, J. (1995). *Raising children in a socially toxic environment*. San Francisco, CA: Jossey-Bass.

Goode, W. I. (1960). A theory of role strain. *American Sociological Review*, 25, 483–496.

Hamilton, V. L., Broman, C. L., Hoffman, W. S., and Renner, D. S. (1990). Hard times and vulnerable people: Initial effects of plant closing on autoworkers' mental health. *Journal of Health and Social Behavior*, 31(2), 123–140.

Hill, R. (1970). *Family development in three generations*. Cambridge, MA: Schenkman.

House, J. S., Kessler, R. C., Herzog, A. R., Mero, R. P., Kinney, A. M., and Breslow, M. J. (1992). Social stratification, age, and health. In K. W. Schaie, D. Blazer, and J. S. House (eds.), *Aging, health behaviors, and health outcomes* (pp. 1–32). Hillsdale, NJ: Erlbaum.

Iversen, L., and Sabroe, S. (1988). Psychological well-being among unemployed and employed people after a company closedown: A longitudinal study. *The Journal of Social Issues*, 44, 141–152.

Jahoda, M. (1982). *Employment and unemployment: A social psychological analysis*. New York: Cambridge University Press.

Kelvin, P., and Jarrett, J. E. (1985). *Unemployment: Its social psychological effects*. Cambridge, MA: Cambridge University Press.

Keyes, C. L. M. (1998). Social well-being. *Social Psychology Quarterly*, 61, 121–140.

Kohn, M. L., and Schooler, C. (1982). Job conditions and personality: A longitudinal assessment of their reciprocal effects. *American Journal of Sociology*, 87, 1257–1286.

Lazarus, R. S., and Folkman, S. (1984). *Stress, appraisal and coping*. New York: Springer.

Leana, C. R., and Feldman, D. C. (1992). *Coping with loss: How individuals, organizations and communities respond to layoffs*. New York: Lexington Books.

Marziali, E., and Donahue, P. (2001). Resilience indicators of post retirement well-being. Social and economic dimensions of an aging population, Hamilton, Ontario. Unpublished manuscript.

Moen, P. (1989). *Working parents: Transformations in gender roles and public policies in Sweden.* Madison, WI: University of Wisconsin Press.

(2003). *It's about time: Couples and careers.* Ithaca, NY: Cornell University Press.

Moen, P., and Chesley, N. (2008). Toxic job ecologies, time convoys, and work-family conflict: Can families (re)gain control and life-course "fit"? In K. Korabik, D. S. Lero, and D. L. Whitehead (eds.), *Handbook of work-family integration: Research, theory, and best practices* (pp. 95–122). New York: Elsevier.

Moen, P., Elder, G. H. Jr., and Lüscher, K. (1995). *Examining lives in context: Perspectives on the ecology of human development.* Washington, DC: American Psychological Association.

Moen, P., and Howery, C. B. (1988). The significance of time in the study of families under stress. In D. Klein and J. Aldous (eds.), *Social stress and family development* (pp. 131–156). New York: Guilford Press.

Moen, P., and Kelly, E. (2009). Working families under stress: Socially toxic job ecologies and time convoys. In E. J. Hill, and D. R. Crane, (eds.), *Handbook of families and work* (pp. 31–61). Lanham, MD: University Press of America.

Moen, P., Kelly, E. L, and Huang, R. (2008). 'Fit' inside the work-family black box: An ecology of the life course, cycles of control reframing. *Journal of Occupational and Organizational Psychology*, 81, 411–433.

Moen, P., and Roehling, P. (2005). *The career mystique: Cracks in the American dream.* Boulder, CO: Rowman & Littlefield.

Moen, P., and Sweet, S. (2004). From "work-family" to "flexible careers": A life course reframing. *Community, Work and Family*, 7, 209–226.

Moen, P., and Wethington, E. (1992). The concept of family adaptive strategies. *Annual Review of Sociology*, 18, 233–251.

(1999). Midlife development in a life course context. In S. L. Willis, and J. D. Reid (eds.), *Life in the middle* (pp. 3–23). San Diego, CA: Academic Press.

Moen, P., and Yu, Y. (1999). Having it all: Overall work/life success in two-earner families. In T. Parcel, and R. Hodson (eds.), *Work and family: Research in the sociology of work*, vol. VII (pp. 109–139). Greenwich, CT: JAI Press.

(2000). Effective work-life strategies: Working couples, work conditions, gender, and life quality. *Social Problems*, 47, 291–326.

Palmore, E. (2005). Three decades of research on ageism. *Generations*, 29, 87–90.

Pearlin, L. I. (1999). The stress process revisited: Reflections on concepts and their interrelationships. In C. S. Aneshensel and J. Phelan, (eds.), *Handbook on the sociology of mental health* (pp. 395–415). New York: Plenum Press.

Pearlin, L. I., Menaghan, E. G., Lieberman, M. A., and Mullan, J. T. (1981). The stress process. *Journal of Health and Social Behavior*, 22, 337–356.

Pearlin, L. I., and Schooler, C. (1978). The structure of coping. *Journal of Health and Social Behavior,* 19, 2–21.

Perrucci, C. C. (1994). Economic strain, family structure and problems with children among displaced workers. *Journal of Sociology and Social Welfare,* 21, 79–91.

Perrucci, R., and Perrucci, C. C. (1990). Unemployment and mental health: Research and policy implications. *Research in Community and Mental Health,* 6, 237–264.

Perrucci, C. C., Perrucci, R. and Targ, D. B. (1997). Gender differences in the economic, psychological and social effects of plant closings in an expanding economy. *The Social Science Journal,* 34, 217–233.

Pillemer, K. A., Moen, P., Wethington, E., and Glasgow, N. (2000). *Social integration in the second half of life.* Baltimore, MD: Johns Hopkins University Press.

Powell, W. W., and DiMaggio, P. (1991). *The new institutionalism in organizational analysis.* Chicago, IL: University of Chicago Press.

Riley, M. W., and Waring, J. (1976). Age and aging. In R. K. Merton and R. Nisbet, (eds.), *Contemporary social problems* (pp. 355–413). New York: Harcourt Brace Jovanovich.

Ross, C. E., and Mirowsky, J. (1992). Households, employment, and the sense of control. *Social Psychology Quarterly,* 55, 217–235.

Rubin, B. A. (1996). *Shifts in the social contract: Understanding change in American society.* Thousand Oaks, CA: Pine Forge Press.

Rupp, D., Vodanovich, S., and Cred, M. (2006). Age bias in the workplace: The impact of ageism and causal attributions. *Journal of Applied Social Psychology,* 36, 1337–1364.

Ryff, C. D., and Keyes, C. L. M. (1995). The structure of psychological well-being revisited. *Journal of Personality and Social Psychology,* 69, 719–727.

Shamir, B. (1986a). Protestant work ethic, work involvement and the psychological impact of unemployment. *Journal of Occupational Behavior,* 7, 25–38.

(1986b). Self-esteem and the psychological impact of unemployment. *Social Psychology Quarterly,* 49, 61–72.

Sweet, S. (2007). The older worker, job insecurity and the new economy. *Generations,* 31, 45–49.

Sweet, S., and Meiksins, P. (2008). *Changing contours of work: Jobs and opportunities in the new economy.* Thousand Oaks, CA: Pine Forge Press.

Swisher, R., Sweet, S. A., and Moen, P. (2004). The family-friendly community and its life course fit for dual-earner couples. *Journal of Marriage and Family,* 66, 281–292.

Thoits, P. A. (1999). Self, identify, stress, and mental health. In C. S. Aneshensel and J. Phelan, (eds.), *Handbook on the sociology of mental health* (pp. 345–368). New York: Plenum Press.

Uchitelle, L. (2006). *The disposable American: Layoffs and their consequences.* New York: Knopf.

Vosler, N. R., and Page-Adams, D. (1996). Predictors of depression among workers at the time of a plant closing. *Journal of Sociology and Social Welfare,* 23(4), 25–42.

Walsh, S., and Jackson, P. R. (1995). Partner support and gender: Contexts for coping with job loss. *Journal of Occupational and Organizational Psychology*, 68(3), 253–268.

Weiss, R. (1997). Family life cycle, work, and the quality of life: Reflections on the roots of happiness, despair, and indifference in modern society. In B. Gardell and G. Johannson (eds.), *Working life: A social science contribution to work reform* (pp. 235–265). New York: Wiley.

Westman, M., Etzion, D., and Danon, E. (2001). Job insecurity and crossover of burnout in married couples. *Journal of Organizational Behavior*, 22(5), 467–481.

Wethington, E., Pixley, J., and Kavey, A. (2003). Turning points in work careers. In P. Moen (ed.), *It's about time: Couples and careers* (pp. 168–182). Ithaca, NY: Cornell University Press.

Wheaton, B. (1990). Life transitions, role histories, and mental health. *American Sociological Review*, 55, 209–223.

12 Resilience in mobility in the context of chronic disease and aging: cross-sectional and prospective findings from the University of Alabama at Birmingham (UAB) Study of Aging

Patricia Sawyer and Richard M. Allman

Abstract

The purpose of this chapter is to provide a conceptual basis for using life-space to assess mobility resilience and maintenance of social participation among community dwelling older adults. The Life-Space Assessment (LSA) measures mobility and the geographic scope of participation in society over one month. It reflects distance, frequency, and use of equipment or personal help while ambulating through the environment. An LSA score of 60 or higher defines an unrestricted life-space – a level of mobility and participation that operationalizes resilience among older adults. After reporting results of a qualitative study examining attitudes toward life-space mobility, we report cross-sectional and prospective data from an observational cohort study of community-dwelling older adults. Significant associations between life-space mobility with social participation, as well as specific correlates and predictors of life-space mobility resilience, are defined.

The importance of life-space resilience as a reflection of mobility and social participation among community-dwelling older adults

An important aspect of resilience is the ability to maintain function in the context of chronic disease and age-associated physiological changes. Available data suggest that 80 percent of persons over the age of 65 years have at least one chronic condition and 20 percent have four or more such conditions (Chodosh *et al.*, 2005). Age-associated physiological changes have been well documented in all organ systems (Hazzard *et al.*, 2003).

Previous gerontological research has focused on how chronic diseases and age-associated physiological changes are associated with functional declines characterized by the development of difficulty in carrying out

310

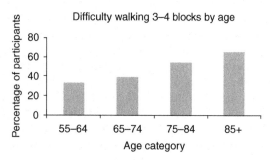

Figure 12.1. Difficulty in walking among community-dwelling older adults.

specific activities or in performing particular tasks (Jette *et al.*, 2002). However, most older adults continue to maintain independent function into late life despite chronic disease, age-related physiological changes, and disability with specific activities. Identification of the factors associated with such functional independence and resilience in late life should guide the development of future interventions designed to optimize the function and quality of life of older adults.

The most commonly reported disability among older adults living in the community is in relation to specific mobility-related activities, such as walking or climbing stairs. For example, the prevalence of difficulty walking from three to four blocks (1/4 mile) increases from 33 percent of persons aged from 55 to 64 years to 65 percent among those aged 85 years and older (Figure 12.1) (Baker and Allman, 2004). However, older adults reporting difficulty with specific mobility-related activities may still continue to move about in society, participating in an array of social activities such as visiting friends or neighbors, attending religious services, participating in clubs or organizations, or traveling with family. Maintenance of this mobility is thus an important component of better quality of life (Metz, 2000; Muldoon *et al.*, 1998). Understanding the factors associated with the maintenance of mobility among community-dwelling older adults should not only provide insights into the underlying mechanisms of resilience in this important functional domain, but also provide clues to factors that permit older adults to maintain active participation in social activities.

Traditional measures of function such as Activities of Daily Living (ADLs – bathing, dressing, transferring, toileting, and eating) and Instrumental Activities of Daily Living (IADLs – light and heavy housework, preparing meals, shopping, and managing money) measure specific abilities of which mobility is an integral component (Kovar and

Lawton, 1994). In contrast, life-space reflects integration and social participation in geographically defined areas, providing a measure of how far, how often, and how independently individuals move in their environments. The assessment thereby provides a measure of mobility across the full continuum of function observed among community-dwelling older adults who may have different and multiple chronic conditions and differing levels of disability. Life-space mobility also reflects participation in society to the degree to which movement within one's environment is required to be involved in social activities. According to the 2005 Institute of Medicine (IOM) Workshop on Disability in America, the maintenance of social participation is perhaps the most important functional outcome for individuals, families, and society and is closely related to quality of life. The IOM report suggested that social participation may be more amendable to interventions than are difficulties with specific activities. As Whiteneck (2006, p. 59) asserted in the IOM report, "although all disabilities cannot be cured, society is in a position, at least theoretically, to return people to active, productive lives that are well integrated into family and community life. Society is better prepared to maximize *participation* [our italics] than to maximize activity." Older adults who maintain life-space may do so without ever experiencing precipitous decline or may have the resources (physical, therapeutic, social, cognitive, and emotional) to recover from conditions and events compromising participation. Therefore, the identification of factors and/or behaviors associated with maintenance or improvement of life-space is particularly salient to developing interventions that are both feasible and meaningful to individuals and society.

Despite the importance of participation as a component of functioning, epidemiological studies commonly focus on disability and decline associated with aging, particularly in the domain of activities of daily living. In contrast, three components of functioning and disability have been identified by the International Classification of Function, Disability, and Health (ICF): (a) body function and structure (the physiological and psychological functions of body systems and the body's anatomical parts); (b) activity (the execution of a task or action by an individual, such as walking); and (c) participation (defined as an individual's involvement in a social situation, such as that represented by movement from one life-space level to another) (Field, Jette, and Martin, 2006).

The growing numbers of older adults will impact society in general, although immediate concerns have been in the area of health care. Between 2000 and 2030, the number of Americans over age 65 will double to 72 million and by 2050 will reach 82 million (Guralnik and Ferrucci, 2003). During this time, projections show a shift in proportion of the age categories such that those over the age of 75 will constitute over half of the adults aged 65 and older in the USA (Hooyman and Kiyak, 2005); much of this change derives from the unprecedented four fold increase in those over the age of 85 (Guralnik and Ferrucci, 2003). In addition to maintenance of mobility, the potential for improvement of mobility and social participation in accordance with individual desires represents a primary component of resilience and should be a priority for older adults and those who care for older adults.

The UAB Study of Aging Life-Space Assessment (LSA) (Baker, Bodner, and Allman, 2003) measures the full continuum of mobility experienced among community-dwelling older adults in both rural and urban settings and also reflects their social participation to the degree that mobility is associated with such social activities (Baker *et al.*, 2003; Parker, Baker, and Allman, 2001).

The purpose of this chapter is to provide a conceptual basis for using life-space to assess mobility resilience and maintenance of social participation among community dwelling older adults. Using cross-sectional data analyses and prospective data from an observational cohort study of community-dwelling older adults, we document the significant associations between life-space mobility with social participation as well as specific correlates and predictors of life-space mobility resilience. These analyses can guide the development of future efforts to develop interventions to optimize the proportion of older adults who achieve life-space mobility resilience and maintain social participation in late life, despite the presence of age-associated physiological changes, chronic diseases, self-reported difficulties with specific activities of daily living, and/or intervening acute events or exacerbations of chronic disease.

Conceptual basis for measuring life-space

The UAB Study of Aging Life-Space Assessment (LSA) measures mobility and participation based on the areas through which a person reports moving during the four weeks preceding the assessment (Baker *et al.*, 2003). Questions establish movement to specific life-space levels ranging from within one's dwelling to beyond one's town. For each life-space level, frequency of movement and use of assistance with mobility (from equipment or persons) are assessed by asking: "During the past four weeks, have you (a) been to other rooms of your home besides the room where you sleep; (b) been to an area outside your home such as your porch, deck or patio, hallway of an apartment building, or garage; (c) been to places in your neighborhood other than your own yard or apartment building; (d) been to places outside your neighborhood, but within your town; and

(e) been to places outside your town?" Persons are asked how many days within a week they attained that level and whether they used help from another person or from assistive devices to move to that level.

Scoring is based on the assumption that persons able to get to a level by themselves are the most independent, that using only equipment represents a mid-level of independence, and requiring the help of another person represents dependence. At the same time, getting out with any type of assistance reflects an important aspect of one's lifestyle. The life-space score is calculated based upon the life-space level, the degree of independence in achieving each level, and the frequency of attaining each level. Values are computed for each life-space level by multiplying the level (1–5), the degree of independence (2 if independent, i.e., no assistance from persons or equipment was reported; 1.5 if equipment was used; or 1 if personal assistance was reported), and the frequency of attainment (1 = less than once a week; 2 = 1–3 times a week; 3 = 4–6 times a week; and 4 = daily). The level-specific values are summed to create a score ranging from 0 to 120, with higher levels representing greater mobility. Although different combinations of responses for the questions about the frequency of movement and the use of equipment or help from another person at different life-space levels can give similar scores on the life-space assessment, higher scores represent greater distance, frequency, or independence of movement (Baker *et al.*, 2003). Figure 12.2 shows the distribution of life-space scores at baseline. Although declines over time are noted, the assessment remains normally distributed in the population.

Although scoring the UAB Life-Space Assessment provides a score ranging from 0 to 120, we have found that a score of 60 and higher (unrestricted life-space) corresponds well with a person's ability to get out of one's neighborhood independently (Allman, Sawyer and Roseman 2006; Peel *et al.*, 2005). Examination of personal feelings about life-space from the qualitative interviews (see below) showed a clear demarcation of persons scoring below and above 60 on the life-space assessment. Cross-sectional associations of ADL and IADL limitation as well as mortality over 4 years differed dramatically for persons scoring below and above 60 (see results).

Examination of scoring possibilities to reach a score of 60 on the life-space assessment further supports this cut-off as a marker of resilient aging. To attain a score of 60, a person must be independent within their home environment and able to go to a porch or hallway outside their dwelling. For example, persons independent at the neighborhood level on a daily basis (perhaps walking a few blocks each day) would need a minimum of 12 additional points accumulated from travel into or out

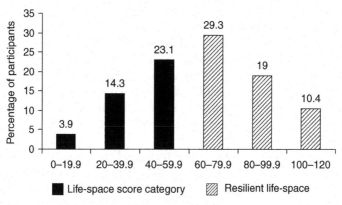

Figure 12.2. Distribution of life-space scores.

of town (perhaps going to town once a week using an assistive device if necessary). A person using an assistive device to get outside of their home (level 2) could attain a score of 60 by a greater frequency of activity at the higher levels. A score of 60 thus represents a level of self-sufficiency and independent mobility, consistent with optimal and adaptive aging.

The UAB Study of Aging utilizes a conceptual model showing the central and important role of life-space in the pathway from disease, geriatric syndromes, and impairments to the development of adverse outcomes in older adults such as ADL disability, nursing home placement, and death. We have conceptualized that diseases, syndromes, and impairments occur in the context of socioeconomic, environmental, neuropsychological, and behavioral factors. While there are bidirectional relationships among these variables, our focus has been to identify the specific predictors of life-space mobility decline that may be potentially modifiable and thus targets for future intervention efforts to enhance mobility and prevent adverse outcomes. Previous analyses have confirmed that specific risk factors in each of these domains predict life-space mobility declines (Allman *et al.*, 2004). We have also found that a large part of life-space is explained by physical ability to carry out specific activities of daily living (ADLs), instrumental activities of daily living (IADLs), and performance on specific mobility-related tasks, that is, walk speed, timed chair stands, and standing balance (Peel *et al.*, 2005). However, these data also confirmed that life-space reflects more than physical capacity. Indeed, as suggested by Stalvey and colleagues (1999), multiple factors other than performance may be included in determining the scope of individual life-space, including environmental characteristics, socioeconomic and emotional resources.

While much of our prior research has been on life-space decline, we have found that life-space trajectories studied at six-month intervals are dynamic at the individual level. Indeed, we have found that 20 percent of persons over the age of 75 had at least one interval with an improvement of 10 or more points in life-space over 4 years of follow-up. These findings are consistent with others who note that a small but significant percentage of persons demonstrate improved function over time (Guralnik and Ferrucci, 2003; Hardy *et al.*, 2005; Wolf, Mendes de Leon, and Glass, 2007).

Research with a focus on factors predicting declines in life-space mobility provides clues for factors that may predispose to maintenance or resilience in life-space mobility. For example, decrements in psychosocial factors have been shown to be associated with declines in mobility (Ayis *et al.*, 2006; Boyd *et al.*, 2005). Social support and social capital have the potential to affect health through both instrumental and emotional mechanisms, by promoting healthy behaviors and discouraging unhealthy ones, by increasing access to health services and amenities, and by enhancing psychosocial well-being through the provision of emotional support in trusting relationships and environments (Locher *et al.*, 2005). Strong and compelling theoretical and empirical evidence links the presence of social networks and the provision of social support with positive health outcomes (House, Landis, and Umberson, 1988; Mendes de Leon *et al.*, 2001; Thoits, 1995). Recently, Giles *et al.* (2004) linked the protective effects of social networks with relatives on the development of mobility disability. A number of social network and social support factors have been found to correlate specifically with both better function and better nutrition in older adults (Stuck *et al.*, 1999; Thoits 1995).

Life-space measures mobility reflecting "participation" in society, rather than simply the ability to carry out a specific mobility-related activity, such as walking or climbing stairs. Persons move from one life-space zone to another for specific purposes. For example, a person may exercise or visit friends within one's neighborhood; go shopping or attend religious meetings within town; or visit family or go on vacation outside of town. Purposeful movement through these life-space zones requires multiple, different mobility-related activities (walking, driving a car, or perhaps using public transportation), and also provides opportunities for many social interactions. We have found that older adults with a score of at least 60, defined as resilient life-space, describe themselves as being moderately or very socially active. In contrast, 77.9 percent of persons with life-space scores of less than 60 describe themselves as being minimally or not socially active. In the UAB Study of Aging, church attendance was the most commonly reported social activity, with 78.6 percent of those with resilient life-space (scores ≥60) reporting attending "church or other religious meetings" at least one time per week, while 48.0 percent of those with life-space scores <60 reported this frequency of attendance. In fact, 17.7 percent of those with scores <60 reported never attending church, while only 4.0 percent of persons with resilient life-space reported never attending church. These data confirm that while life-space not only measures mobility, it also reflects social participation. Clearly, there are close associations between movement in one's environment and participation in social activities such as church attendance.

It can also be expected that cognition will be an important determinant of life-space, although Guralnik and Ferrucci (2003) note the generally ignored role of cognition on functional change and the development of disability in epidemiological studies. Major sociodemographic factors that have been considered in relation to cognitive level include age, education, gender, and race/ethnicity. With regard to cognitive outcomes, the general pattern, paralleling that found earlier in the lifespan, is that there are cognitive advantages for younger (Lindenberger, Mayr, and Kliegl, 1993), more educated (Cagney and Lauderdale, 2002), and non-minority individuals, although this is complicated by the confounds of educational quality and health (Crowe et al., 2008; Dick et al., 2002).

Maintenance of life-space with aging represents resilience in the face of chronic disease as well as the presence of symptoms (such as balance problems, fatigue, pain, shortness of breath, stiffness, and weakness), all of which may increase with age. Symptoms, perhaps an indication of severity of disease, are more likely to be what patients report as limiting their social participation. Likewise, symptoms, not specific diseases, are more often noted as reasons for utilizing health care (Gill et al., 2001). Older adults are at increased risk for acute events that have the potential to compromise life-space, particularly events such as hospitalization and decreased health or mortality of a spouse (Guralnik and Ferrucci, 2003; Williams et al., 2007). Although life-space may precipitously decline in response to such an event, restoration of participation over time is perhaps true resilience.

We first report on results of a pilot qualitative study to develop the UAB Study of Aging Life-Space Assessment instrument and to understand the meaning of life-space in individual lives. Following that discussion, we present analyses of cross-sectional correlates and predictors of life-space resilience in the UAB Study of Aging, a prospective longitudinal study of life-space mobility in community-dwelling older adults.

The meaning of life-space – a qualitative study

To pilot test the UAB Study of Aging Life-Space Assessment and explore the meaning of life-space mobility in persons' lives, a semi-structured interview was developed. Standardized measures as well as open-ended responses to questions about feelings about life-space limitations, possible changes in life-space experienced, and factors attributed to change were included. The study was approved by the Institutional Review Board and informed consents were obtained before interviews were conducted.

Sampling and method

Potential participants were screened by telephone in an attempt to balance the sample by independent life-space level and race. Participants had to be able to answer correctly five of eight cognitive screening items from the Short Portable Mental Status Questionnaire (Erkinjuntti *et al.*, 1987) to be eligible for the interview. Trained interviewers conducted the interviews and were instructed to allow the participant say as much as they wanted before proceeding to the next question, even for closed-ended questions. The study sample ($N = 49$) included 37 community-dwelling adults recruited from participants in other research studies at UAB, older adults recruited from a rural medical practice ($N = 5$), and volunteers from an upscale, urban independent living continuing care community (CCRC) ($N = 7$).

Standardized measures included sociodemographic factors and included race, gender, and marital status. Co-morbidity was measured by a count of self-reported physician diagnoses based on the Charlson co-morbidity index (Charlson *et al.*, 1986). Symptoms potentially limiting mobility (problems with falls, balance or dizziness, fainting, any pain, incontinence, shortness of breath, feeling tired or fatigued, feeling sleepy, stiffness, or weakness in legs) were also assessed. Participants were asked to describe their health as excellent, very good, good, fair, or poor (range 1–5, higher scores represent poorer health). The Geriatric Depression Scale (short-form), a 15-item scale (Sheikh and Yesavage, 1986), was used to measure mental health.

After using the life-space assessment to establish the highest level of life-space a person attained, questions focused on that level (for example, neighborhood) and previous travel that might have occurred beyond that level. Persons were asked whether there had been a change in their mobility, and if so, when and why it occurred. Additional questions probed: "If you could change anything about the way you get around, what would it be?" What differences have changes in the way you get around made in your life?" "Are there any places you would like to get do but can't?"

Interviews were taped and subsequently transcribed. Content analysis (Taylor and Bogdan, 1998) was used to identify themes in the transcribed interviews. Relevant codes were based on the predetermined topics of definitions of life-space terminology, limitations, and change in life-space mobility as well as emergent themes noted during analyses. Three researchers independently read and evaluated each transcript. SPSS (SPSS, 2008) was used for statistical analyses.

The mean age of the 49 persons who participated in qualitative interviews was 79.7 years (SD = 7.5). There were 17 males (35 percent) and 32 females; 8 of the men were married (47 percent) and 6 of the women were married (19 percent). The sample was approximately half African American (24 persons). Thirty-one percent of persons (15) lived in housing specifically for the elderly. Of the five persons living in rural areas, one lived in retirement housing. More than half the sample traveled outside of their neighborhoods (20 without assistance of any type and 8 used assistive equipment). The mean composite life-space score was 48.6 (SD = 27.7) and ranged from 12 to 120. Using a cut-point of 60 to define unrestricted life-space (resilience), 33 percent (16 persons) had maintained resilience in life-space despite 12 of the 16 reporting that they had some decrease in life-space associated with aging. The four who said they had not changed were able to get around independently within their town or get beyond town had a mean composite life-space score of 87.7 (SD = 18.5), ranging from 71 to 110.

Life-space mobility scores were significantly lower for women compared with men (39.5 vs. 64.2; $p = 0.002$) and adults 80 years and older compared with adults 65–79 (40.6 vs. 50.5; $p = 0.043$). There were no differences by race (49.0 for Whites and 47.1 for African Americans), but there were clear differences in life-space mobility by residence, with community-dwelling urban older adults ($N = 30$) having a mean life-space of 57.2 (SD = 29.6); community-dwelling rural adults ($N = 4$) 47.6 (24.5); CCRC residents ($N = 7$) 35.7 (8.6); and other retirement housing ($N = 8$) 24.6 (10.8). Although not significant (two-tailed tests), married participants had a higher life-space than not married (55.3 vs. 45.1; $p = 0.246$) and those living with someone had a higher life-space than those living alone (52.5 vs. 44.7; $p = 0.322$). The number of medical conditions was not correlated with life-space (-0.06; $p = 0.67$); however, the number of symptoms was significantly associated with lower life-space scores ($r = -0.389$; $p = 0.006$).

Emotional aspects of life-space mobility

Initial analyses ranked the participants by life-space score to explore the association of life-space and feelings about mobility. A pattern of emotional expressions linked to life-space scores emerged when the transcribed interviews were ranked by life-space score. There appeared to be a continuum of comments about their situation corresponding to life-space scores, with increasingly less said about mobility limitation as the scores increased. Using the standard cut-off of six or more symptoms on the Geriatric Depression Scale (Sheikh and Yesavage, 1986), seven persons (14 percent) were classified as potentially depressed and their scores reflected restricted life-space (Mean 23.7; SD = 7.7; range 15–38). A majority (62 percent) of persons with life-space scores under 30 reported having poor or fair health. Although there was overlap, general patterns emerged that corresponded to the life-space score categories defined by 0–29 (category 1), 30–59 (category 2), 60–89 (category 3), and 90 and higher (category 4). Table 12.1 describes characteristics of the persons within the life-space category groups. Differing comments about mobility were noted, roughly corresponding to the four quartiles of scores. Further analyses identified profiles associated with each category. These are briefly described below.

Life-space category 1 (0–30): reluctant resignation or "learning to be old but not liking it"

A common theme was an acknowledgment of the aging process and the associated decrease in mobility. This was often accompanied by a statement that the person had accepted the situation and was not "worried" (10 of 16 persons).

"I never realized my age before. I thought as long as I lived that I would go on and things would be normal. I would like to go to church but I know my limitations" (life-space score = 18; 90-year-old white female).

"I'd rather go out and do things, but I can't so I realize that I just go by what I can do and can't do. As far as I can do, I am, but the things I can't do, I don't worry about it (life-space score = 25; 86-year-old white male). An 80-year-old African American woman (life-space score = 12) told us at length that she went when she could: "You know I went when I could, and since I can't go, it don't even worry me at all. 'Cause I did what I could while I could."

A white male (aged 67) told us that "I would like to go and just go, go, go constantly" but acknowledges that this is not possible, saying "I can't do nothing except get up and walk to the table and eat, and walk back here, then I'm give out" (life-space score = 23); and a 71-year-old African American woman (life-space score = 22) expressed regret at her situation saying: "If my legs weren't sore I wouldn't mind getting around more, if I feel good, you know. Sometimes I don't feel good, you know, going nowhere." In summary, 10 persons indicated acceptance of their limited life-space (mean age = 84, SD = 6.0); 4 persons were ambivalent (mean age = 77.5, SD = 10.0) and 3 indicated unhappiness (mean age = 74.3; SD = 8.6).

Life-space category 2 (30–60): fearful coping or "not taking any chances"

Eleven of the 17 persons in this category expressed feelings of vulnerability and the perception that "it could be worse." They were afraid of problems related to their health.

"I'm afraid I'm going to have a heart attack sometimes and then I'm not prepared for it. So now I live in fear whenever I go someplace I might suddenly have a heart attack" (life-space score = 38; 92-year-old white female). An 82-year-old African American female (life-space score = 57) said: "Look like my balance is not as good as it used to be. I'm afraid I might fall." An 81-year-old white female (life-space score = 44) told us: "I enjoy staying at home and I had just rather not take chances that I don't have to … I might fall and break myself up …"

This group expressed gratitude that things were weren't worse. "I just thank God I'm able to get up and get around and help myself. It could be worse; thank God I ain't no worse. I could be in a nursing home or I could be laying in there sick and couldn't move without somebody helping me, you know. It's just a blessing, so I'm satisfied" (life-space score = 52; 68-year-old African American female); and "I just thank God that I can get up and move" (life-space score = 33; 81-year-old African American female).

Life-space category 3 (60–90): adaptive living or "pretty well satisfied"

This group had a much more positive outlook, with 8 of 12 persons making affirmative statements to that effect, even after admitting that they have changed.

"I don't have as much energy as I did years ago … [but] I'm a busy man" (life-space score = 80; 92-year-old white male); and a 90-year-old white female (life-space score = 71) joked about her age and lack of energy but summarized the situation saying: "I can get around, and I can go to bed at night and don't have a pain in the world. So many people my age are just in a wheelchair or walker and I thank the Lord that I'm not." A 70-year-old African American female (life-space score = 76) talked about how she "loves" going to the casinos.

Life-space category 4 (90–120): positive independence or "I can't complain"

Mobility was taken for granted and was not even a topic of conversation in this group. Although two of the four persons in this category reported fair to poor health, their conversations revealed a positive attitude about their lives as well as an awareness of changes associated with aging. Even though she said her health was poor, a 74-year-old white female (life-space score = 100) reported: "There's not nobody better off than me. I do pretty good. I got a husband that's still living, got a pretty good income, got a comfortable home." In response to a question about anything they would like different in their lives, an African American male of 76 years (life-space score = 120), who reported fair health, replied: "I don't want to change anything, but if I could stop my knee from hurting ..."; and a white 75-year-old male (life-space score = 96) commented: "Well, it ain't no use in thinking about getting younger, so I just go ahead and take everyday one day at a time."

These qualitative interviews demonstrated the association of life-space with quality of life. As noted by the persons we interviewed and previous research (Gill *et al.*, 2006; Patla and Shumway-Cook, 1999), independent mobility is an integral component of quality of life. We noted that persons demonstrating life-space resilience lived their lives over a broader geographic environment, providing a greater potential for social interaction. Their communication indicated active participation in society, often in spite of physical limitation.

Maintaining resilience – the UAB Study of Aging

The UAB Study of Aging is a prospective, observational study of a racially balanced sample of 1000 community-dwelling older African Americans and Whites designed to investigate the impact of the aging process on life-space mobility. Participants were a random sample of Medicare beneficiaries aged 65 and older living in five counties of central Alabama, selected from a list of Medicare beneficiaries provided by the Centers of Medicare and Medicaid Services (CMS) and stratified by county, race, and sex. Recruitment was set to achieve a balanced sample in terms of race, gender, and rural/urban residence and has been described in other publications (Allman *et al.*, 2006). The study protocol was approved by the UAB Institutional Review Board.

Methods

After obtaining informed consent, in-home assessments lasting approximately 2 hours were conducted by trained interviewers between November 1999 and February 2001. Factors assessed represented the basic domains hypothesized to affect life-space mobility: socio-demographic and economic factors (race, gender, residence, age, income, education, marital status, and transportation availability); general health (diseases, medications, symptoms, self-rated health status, and unintended weight loss); mental health (depression, cognition, and anxiety); and traditional functional measures including observed physical performance. Telephone follow-up interviews were conducted at 6-month intervals. The following analyses use data over 4 years of follow-up. As an example of an event with consequences for declines in life-space we explored the impact of overnight hospitalizations on the maintenance and/or restoration of life-space. Variables used in the analyses are listed in the appendix to this chapter.

Statistical analyses

After determining cross-sectional (baseline) bivariate associations of factors with life-space scores 60 and higher versus life-space scores lower than 60, hierarchical models using logistic regression were used to evaluate the independence of the associations. The same procedures were used to evaluate baseline factors predictive of life-space 60 or greater at 4 years, controlling for baseline life-space score. In exploratory analyses of persons who scored 60 or greater at the 4-year follow-up, data from the six-month telephone follow-up interviews were used to determine the number of times a person might have scored under 60 through 4 years of follow-up (nine assessment intervals). Persons who were placed in a nursing home or who had died were considered to have declined in life-space. Calculations were repeated excluding deceased.

Results

Figure 12.3 shows the distribution of the sample by life-space score below and above 60 at baseline and 4 years. At baseline, the mean value of life-space was 64.1 (SD 24.9) with a median of 65.0, and thus slightly over half of the sample had scores of 60 and higher (N = 588), even

Participant status by life-space over 4 years

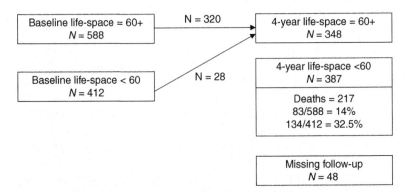

Figure 12.3. The UAB Study of Aging.

though the mean age of the sample was 75 years. Of particular note, the number of co-morbid conditions was 2.0, even among the participants with resilient life-space mobility at baseline (Table 12.1). In fact, 86 percent of the resilient life-space mobility group had at least one Charlson co-morbidity condition at baseline, confirming that life-space mobility permits identification of resilience in older adults despite the presence of chronic disease.

Bivariate associations with life-space are shown in Table 12.1. Except for urban/rural residence, all socioeconomic factors were significantly different for the two groups, as were measures of physical and emotional health, cognition, health behaviors, and other measures of function. Persons with resilient life-space differed in the degree of ADL and IADL difficulty reported (ADL mean 0.41, SD = 0.98 for resilient vs. 2.1; SD = 2.7 for those with life-space <60 and IADL mean 0.85, SD = 1.6 for resilient vs. 3.9, SD = 4.3 for those with life-space <60; $p < 0.001$ for both).

Multivariable analyses found that younger age, white race, male gender, rural residence, higher income, adequate transportation, fewer symptoms of depression, higher leisure time physical activity levels, and better observed physical performance were significant and independent correlates of resilient life-space at baseline (Table 12.2). Rural residence became significant and strongly correlated with resilient life-space mobility after adjusting for other socioeconomic factors and remained significant even after adjusting for measures of health, cognition, emotional status, health behaviors, and physical performance. The odds of having a resilient life-space level for rural participants

Table 12.1. *Odds ratios for resilient life-space at baseline*[a]

Factors	Model 1	Model 2	Model 3	Model 4	Model 5	Model 6
Socioeconomic						
Age (continuous)	0.910***	0.909***	0.920***	0.916***	0.923***	0.936***
African American (vs. Caucasian)	0.595**	0.482***	0.579**	0.512**	0.489***	0.594*
Female gender (vs. male)	0.548**	0.526**	0.467***	0.454***	0.462***	0.465**
Rural (vs. urban)	2.199***	2.705***	2.862***	2.832***	2.908***	3.065***
Education[b]	1.259*	1.270*	1.100*	1.131	1.132	1.192
Income[c]	1.327***	1.258***	1.267***	1.225***	1.232***	1.240***
Married (vs. not married)	1.036	1.161	1.134	1.148	1.059	0.943
Transportation difficulty	0.183***	0.217***	0.230***	0.256***	0.242***	0.261***
Health						
Co-morbidity score[d]		0.802***	0.819***	0.814***	0.849**	0.912
Symptom count[e]		0.821***	0.821***	0.881**	0.898*	0.969
Unintentional weight loss[f]		0.605*	0.663*	0.718	0.764	0.834
Cognitive						
MMSE score			1.094***	1.083**	1.079**	1.048
Emotional						
Geriatric depression score				0.828***	0.837***	0.861**
Anxiety				1.009**	1.012	1.017
Health behaviors						
Irregular meals					1.364	1.301

Table 12.1. (cont.)

Factors	Model 1	Model 2	Model 3	Model 4	Model 5	Model 6
Pack years					1.001	1.001
Alcohol use					1.041	1.017
Leisure-time physical activity					1.519***	1.348***
Physical performance						
Short physical performance battery						1.331***

[a] All models control for baseline life-space.
[b] Education categories: 1 = completed 6th grade or less; 2 = completed 7th through 11th grade; 3 = completed high school or GED; and 4 = any higher education.
[c] Income categories: 0 = less than $5,000; 1 = $5,000–$7,999; 2 = $8,000–$11,999; 3 = $12,000–15,999; 4 = $16,000–$19,999; 5 = $20,000–29,999; 6 = $30,000–$39,000; 7 = $40,000–$49,000; and 8 = greater than $50,000.
[d] Co-morbidity count (range 0–12) sum of items from the Charlson comorbidity index (Charlson et al., 1986) (see Appendix).
[e] Symptom count (range 0–10), simple count of symptoms (see Appendix).
[f] Unintentional weight loss = previous year weight loss of 10 or more pounds without trying* p < 0.05; **p < 0.01; ***p < 0.001.

Table 12.2. *Odds ratios for resilient life-space at 4 years*[a]

Factors	Model 1	Model 2	Model 3	Model 4	Model 5	Model 6
Socioeconomic						
Age (continuous)	0.899***	0.895***	0.905***	0.907***	0.903***	0.909***
African American (vs. Caucasian)	1.380	1.222	1.507	1.470	1.349	1.453
Female gender (vs. male)	1.295	1.181	1.047	.998	.817	0.825
Rural (vs. urban)	0.868	1.019	1.080	1.091	1.077	1.083
Education[b]	1.244*	1.307*	1.120	1.131	1.128	1.153
Income[c]	1.206***	1.170**	1.165**	1.161**	1.134*	1.127*
Married (vs. not married)	0.969	1.083	1.088	1.071	1.043	1.013
Transportation difficulty	0.178***	0.187***	0.195***	0.198***	0.195***	0.198***
Health						
Co-morbidity score[d]		0.731***	0.741***	0.738***	0.744***	0.759***
Symptom count[e]		0.897*	0.890**	0.893*	0.906*	0.933
Unintentional weight loss[f]		0.508*	0.565*	0.577*	0.580	0.613
Cognitive						
MMSE score			1.134***	1.134***	1.126***	1.115**
Emotional						
Geriatric depression Score				0.933	0.940	0.953
Anxiety				0.975	0.978	0.983
Health behaviors						
Irregular meals					0.807	0.799
Pack years					0.993*	0.993*

Table 12.2. (*cont.*)

Factors	Model 1	Model 2	Model 3	Model 4	Model 5	Model 6
Alcohol use					1.009	1.004
Leisure-time physical activity					1.116	1.080
Physical performance						
Short physical performance battery						1.133**

[a] All models control for baseline life-space.
[b] Education categories: 1 = completed 6th grade or less; 2 = completed 7th through 11th grade; 3 = completed high school or GED; and 4 = any higher education.
[c] Income categories: 0 = less than $5,000; 1 = $5,000–$7,999; 2 = $8,000–$11,999; 3 = $12,000–$15,999; 4 = $16,000–$19,999; 5 = $20,000–$29,999; 6 = $30,000–$39,000; 7 = $40,000–$49,000; and 8 = greater than $50,000.
[d] Co-morbidity count (range 0–12) sum of items from the Charlson co-morbidity index (Charlson *et al.*, 1986) (see Appendix).
[e] Symptom count (range 0–10), simple count of symptoms (see Appendix).
[f] Unintentional weight loss = previous year weight loss of 10 or more pounds without trying.
* $p < 0.05$; ** $p < 0.01$; *** $p < 0.001$.

were 3.065 times greater than for urban participants (model 5, Table 12.2). In contrast, educational level and unintentional weight loss were not significantly correlated with resilient life-space after adjusting for baseline depression and anxiety, suggesting that the negative association between weight loss and resilient life-space may be mediated by emotional factors. The associations between general health measures such as the number of co-morbid conditions and symptoms and cognitive status with resilience were no longer significant after adjusting for observed physical performance, suggesting that the impact of chronic disease, symptoms, and cognitive function on life-space are mediated by their impact on physical performance, that is, walking speed, timed chair stands, and standing balance. While these associations may provide clues to potential predictors for life-space resilience, they cannot prove cause and effect due to their cross-sectional nature. For example, life-space mobility scores may be 60 or greater in rural areas, because participants living in these areas had to go farther distances to shop, go to church, or get needed personal services than persons in urban areas rather than rural residence predicting an increase in life-space. Resilient life-space may be a key factor in the ability to continue residence in rural areas. Persons with greater levels of physical performance may have greater life-space mobility simply because they have greater capacity to move about, or maintenance of life-space levels of 60 or greater may help ensure physical performance.

To identify predictors of resilient life-space, we examined the association between baseline characteristics with a life-space mobility score of 60 or greater after 4 years of follow-up. Data for 96.2 percent of the baseline sample of 1000 participants were available at 4 years. Baseline life-space, age, race, gender, urban/rural residence, and transportation difficulty did not differ for participants missing data at 4 years in comparison to those for whom data were available at 4 years of follow-up. Those missing data were had significantly lower education, income, Mini-Mental Status Examination (MMSE) scores, reported more depressive symptoms, and were less likely to be married. Because of their potential impact on life-space, these variables are included in all models.

At 4 years, 348/962 (36.2 percent) of participants had life-space scores 60 and higher (i.e., resilient life-space mobility). Of the 348 with resilient life-space at 4 years, 28 (8.0 percent) had improvement from baseline life-space scores under 60. Thus resilient life-space (score 60 or greater) at 4 years represented maintenance of mobility for 92 percent of the participants. Those with resilient life-space mobility at 4 years had a mean baseline life-space of 81.3, while the mean for those with a life-space score <60 was 54.3 at baseline.

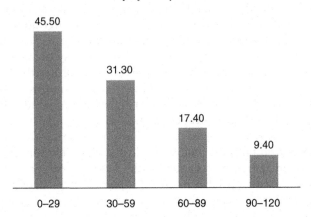

Figure 12.4. Mortality (%) over 4 years.

To obtain a broad sense of outcomes associated with baseline levels of life-space mobility, mortality rates over the 4 years by baseline life-space scores were calculated. Lower life-space scores were associated with significantly higher 4-year mortality. Participants with scores ≥60 had 4-year mortality of 14.7 percent, in contrast to 34.5 percent for those with lower baseline life-space scores (Figure 12.4). Although Figure 12.4 shows unadjusted mortality, a logistic regression model adjusting for age, race, and sex showed statistically significant odds ratios of mortality in a direct association with the four categories of life-space scores. With 90–120 as the referent category, lower life-space was significantly predictive ($p < 0.001$ for all) of increased mortality: scores 60–89 (OR = 2.3), scores 30–59 (OR = 5.1), and scores 0–29 (OR = 10.6).

Of the 348 persons with life-space scores over 60 at 4 years, 45.5 percent ($N = 158$) had no interviews with a life-space under that threshold; 23 percent had one interview under 60; 12 percent had two periods with life-space under 60 and 18 percent had 3 or more periods with life-space under 60. Of the 348 persons with life-space above 60 at 4 years, 28 percent (99 persons) had been hospitalized overnight in contrast to 43 percent of those with life-space below 60 at 4 years. In spite of hospitalizations, 25 percent of persons never reported a life-space under 60 and 21 percent had only one period under 60. Many of the hospitalizations were surgical ($N = 37$), including 19 restorative surgeries reported: 9 knee replacements (7 persons), 7 rotator cuff repairs, and 3 hip replacements. In addition to hospitalizations, we noted that 161/348

(48 percent) reported at least one new co-morbidity and that 112 persons (32 percent) reported at least one fall.

Discussion

Increasingly, the focus of aging research is on the maintenance of all aspects of health, yet there has been much discussion and vacillation about appropriate measurement. As noted by Muldoon *et al.* (1998), it is important to go beyond the immediate effects of disease to examine the impact on persons' daily lives. Traditional measures have focused on function and the ability to perform specific tasks (Peel *et al.*, 2005). Yet, difficulty in these measures may not be apparent until a much later stage in models of disability. In contrast, life-space provides a measure of the full continuum of mobility, allowing differentiation at the upper bounds of "healthy aging."

As indicated in previous research (Kington and Smith, 1997), social factors are strongly associated with health status, particularly deficits in education and income. At the beginning of the UAB Study of Aging, lower education, lower income, and problems with transportation were associated with life-space scores lower than 60. These economic characteristics might also have been reflected in other factors related to socio-economic situations, such as co-morbidity, weight loss, and symptoms. At the same time, life-space of 60 and higher was associated with better mental function (cognition, lack of depression, and anxiety) as well as physical ability and activity.

Logistic regression models indicated independent contributions of socioeconomic factors to life-space, with the exception of marital status. Younger aged, white, educated, higher-income males living in rural environments with no transportation problems were the most likely to have higher life-space at study enrollment. Better health, measured by lower co-morbidity, fewer symptoms, and no unintended weight loss-additionally contributed to higher life-space. Better cognitive functioning and fewer depressive symptoms also had an independent association with higher life-space. Leisure-time physical activity was associated with higher life-space, even when physical ability measured by the Short Physical Performance Battery was included in the model.

The second set of models shows what happened over 4 years of follow-up. These results controlled for baseline life-space, showing factors contributing to maintenance (or decline) over the 4-year period, given that individuals were at different starting life-space levels. After determining baseline life-space, it was observed that life-space maintenance was greater for persons who were younger, with higher education, higher income, and without transportation difficulty, all markers of social advantage. Similar to cross-sectional findings, the absence of health conditions and the maintenance of cognitive ability predicted maintained life-space. However, depression was not associated with the maintenance of life-space, nor was baseline leisure time physical activity. Over 4 years, the impact of smoking history, measured in pack years, was a barrier to the maintenance of life-space. It is important to note the impact of socioeconomic factors over the 4 years of the study, even after controlling for baseline physical performance, for both African Americans and Whites, suggestive that racial disparities are largely a product of earlier life-experience, and older age a residual effect of economics.

Resilience in life-space can be illustrated by the 348 persons with life-space of 60 and higher over 4-year period. Our results suggest that older adults can maintain resilience through stability, that is not having a challenge, and that resilience may come from resources providing the capacity to recover from the vicissitudes of life. These resources might reside within the individual (i.e., reserve capacity) or come from social and economic support available.

Acknowledgments

The project described was supported by award numbers AG15062 and 1P30AG031054 from the National Institute on Aging and a grant from the AARP Andrus Foundation. The content is solely the responsibility of the authors and does not necessarily represent the official views of the National Institute on Aging or the National Institutes of Health.

Presented in part at the Gerontological Society of American annual meeting (Symposium title, "Psychosocial Frontiers of Resilience in Later Life"), November 2008, Baltimore, MD.

Appendix: Measures

Demographic factors

All factors were self reported and included age, race, marital status. Locale was defined as urban or rural based on county population (Alabama Rural Health Association, 1998).

Socioeconomic factors

Educational status

Education was categorized as: 1 = completed 6th grade or less; 2 = completed 7th through 11th grade; 3 = completed high school or GED; and 4 = any higher education.

Income levels

Total combined family income before taxes was reported in the following nine categories: 0 = less than $5000; 1 = $5000–$7999; 2 = $8000–$11,999; 3 = $12,000–$15,999; 4 = $16,000–$19,999; 5 = $20,000–$29,999; 6 = $30,000–$39,000; 7 = $40,000–$49,000; and 8 = greater than $50,000. The following question also was asked about subjects' perceived income: "All things considered, would you say your income is (a) not enough to make ends meet, (b) gives you just enough to get by on, (c) keeps you comfortable, but permits no luxuries, or (d) allows you to do more or less what you want." For persons who did not report income (165 subjects), responses indicating perceived income were used to calculate income categories based on the correspondence of income categories and perceived income among persons with answers to both questions. The coding to impute income levels for perceived income categories was: 1 = $5000–$7999; 2 = $8000–$11,999; 3 = $16,000–$19,999; 4 = $30,000–$39,999.

Availability of transportation

Transportation resources were assessed by asking: "Over the past four weeks, have you had any difficulty getting transportation to where you want to go?", and "Do you limit your activities because you don't have transportation?" Persons responding positively to either question were classified as having transportation difficulty.

General physical health measures

ADL/IADL

Both ADL and IADL were measured by self-report (Kovar and Lawton, 1994). The five ADL items included eating, using the toilet, dressing, transferring, and bathing. The six IADL items included using the telephone, managing money, preparing meals, doing light housework, shopping, and doing heavy housework. For each item, subjects were asked: "Do you have any difficulty performing the task?" If subjects answered "no," a score of zero was assigned. If subjects answered "yes," they were asked to rate the level of difficulty as "some," "a lot" or "unable to do the task." The answer "some" was assigned a score of 1, "a lot" was assigned a score of 2, and "unable to do the task" was assigned a value of 3. Subjects also could answer that they "did not perform the task for other reasons," an answer that was coded as a missing value.

Composite scores for ADL and IADL were calculated using the sum of the items. For ADL, the scores could range from 0 to 15, with a score of 15 indicating that they could not perform any of the tasks. For IADL, the scores could range from 0 to 18, with a score of 18 indicating inability to perform any of the tasks. For ADL and IADL, lower scores indicated less reported difficulty with the functional tasks.

Co-morbidity

Respondents were asked whether a physician had told them they had specific medical conditions, based on items of the Charlson co-morbidity index (Charlson *et al.*, 1986), used to predict mortality. These conditions included congestive heart failure, myocardial infarction, valvular heart disease, peripheral artery disease, hypertension, diabetes, COPD, kidney failure, liver disease, non-skin cancer, neurological disease, and gastrointestinal disease. A condition was validated if the participant reported taking a medication for the disease or condition, if the primary physician returned a questionnaire indicating that the participant had the disease, or if a hospital discharge summary for a hospitalization in the previous 3 years listed the condition. A count of validated conditions was used.

Number of medications

Participants were asked to show the interviewer all prescription medications that they currently used. A count of medications was determined.

Symptoms

Symptoms potentially limiting mobility were assessed by participant self-reports, since these conditions are frequently under-reported to physicians. Symptoms included the following: problems with falls, balance or dizziness, fainting, any pain, incontinence, shortness of breath, feeling tired or fatigued, feeling sleepy, stiffness, or weakness in legs. A simple count of these mobility-related symptoms was created.

Self-rated health

Participants were asked to describe their health as excellent, very good, good, fair, or poor (range 1–5, higher scores represent poorer health).

Weight and weight loss

Participants were measured for height and weight. BMI was calculated from the measured height and weight (kg/m^2) for persons able to stand (91 percent of the sample). For participants unable to stand, height and weight were calculated from knee-height and arm circumference measurements obtained at the in-home interview ($N = 89$). If the knee height was unavailable, self-reported height and weight were used to calculate BMI ($N = 37$). Weight loss was determined by asking: "In the past year, have you lost weight (more than ten pounds)?" If participants answered yes to this question, they were then asked: "Did you try to lose weight?" If the participant had lost more than ten pounds without trying, they were defined as having unintentional weight loss.

Cognitive functioning

Cognition

The Mini-Mental State Examination (MMSE) was used to assess cognitive status (Folstein, Folstein, and McHugh, 1975).

Emotional health

Depression

The Geriatric Depression Scale (short-form), a 15-item scale (Sheikh and Yesavage, 1986), was used.

Anxiety

The anxiety scale of the AIMS2 (Arthritis Impact Measurement Scales) (Meenan *et al.*, 1992) was coded such that lower scores represented higher anxiety. This subscale ranges from 5 to 25.

Health behaviors

The Leisure Time Physical Activity Assessment was used to calculate energy expenditure in kcal/week based on the number of sessions per week, average time per session, and kcal/min for each activity of the assessment. Results were adjusted for subject weight (Martin *et al.*, 2006).

Smoking history was calculated in pack years, determined from the number of cigarettes smoked per day multiplied by number of years smoked and divided by 20 (the number of cigarettes in one pack).

Alcohol use was calculated in terms of the number of drinks per week consumed. A drink was defined as a 12-ounce bottle of beer, a 4-ounce glass of wine, or a 1.5-ounce shot of alcohol.

Dietary insufficiency was determined by response to a question about the number of meals eaten per day. Eating fewer than three meals per day was coded as having irregular meals.

Physical performance

The *Short Physical Performance Battery* (SPPB) of timed tests of standing balance, walking, and the ability to rise from a chair was used during the baseline in-home assessment as described in detail by Guralnik *et al.* (1994). For each assessment of physical performance, scores ranged from 0 to 4, with 4 representing the best performance and 0 indicating inability to complete the task. Composite scores were calculated as the sum of the categorical rankings for each of the tests (standing balance, timed walk, timed chair stands) and ranged from 0 to 12, with higher scores indicating better performance.

Hospitalizations that involved an overnight stay were assessed by participant self-report at baseline and at each 6-month telephone follow-up interview.

REFERENCES

Allman, R. M., Baker, P. S., Maisiak, R. M., Sims, R. V., and Roseman, J. M. (2004). Racial similarities and differences in predictors of mobility change over eighteen months. *Journal of General Internal Medicine*, 19, 1118–1126.

Allman, R. M., Sawyer, P., and Roseman, J. M. (2006). The UAB Study of Aging: background and insights into life-space mobility among older Americans in rural and urban settings. *Aging Health*, 2, 417–429.

Alabama Rural Health Association. (1998). *Health status of rural Alabamians.* Montgomery, AL: Alabama Rural Health Association.

Ayis, S., Gooberman-Hill, R., Bowling, A., and Ebraham, S. (2006). Predicting catastrophic decline in mobility among older people, *Age Ageing*, 35, 382–387.

Baker, P. S., and Allman, R. M. (2004). Charting the course: State of Alabama long-term care needs assessment. Retrieved on December 2008 from http://www.aging.uab.edu/SubChannel/Research/pdf/Charting%20 the%20Course.pdf

Baker, P. S., Bodner, E. V., and Allman, R. M. (2003). Measuring life-space mobility in community-dwelling older adults. *Journal of the American Geriatrics Society,* 51(11), 1610–1614.

Boyd, C. M., Xue, Q.-L., Guralnik, J. M., and Fried, L. P. (2005). Hospitalization and development of dependence in activities of daily living in a cohort of disabled older women: The women's health and aging study I. *The Journals of Gerontology. Series A, Biological Sciences and Medical Sciences,* 60(7), 888–893.

Cagney, K. A., and Lauderdale, D. S. (2002). Education, wealth, and cognitive function in later life. *The Journals of Gerontology. Series B, Psychological Sciences and Social Sciences,* 57,(2), P163–P172.

Charlson, M. E., Sax, F., Mackenzie, C. R., Fields, S. D., Braham, R. L., and Douglas, R. G. (1986). Assessing illness severity: Does clinical judgment work? *Journal of Chronic Disease,* 6, 439–452.

Chodosh, J., Morton, S. C., Mojica, W. *et al.* (2005). Meta-analysis: Chronic disease self-management programs for older adults. *Annals of Internal Medicine,* 143, 427–438.

Crowe, M., Clay, O. J., Sawyer, P., Crowther, M. R., and Allman, R. M. (2008). Education and reading ability in relation to differences in cognitive screening between African American and Caucasian Older Adults. *International Journal of Geriatric Psychiatry,* 23, 222–223.

Dick, M., Teng, E., Kempler, D., David, D., and Taussig, I. (2002). The cross-cultural neuropsychological test battery (CCNB): Effects of age, education, ethnicity, and cognitive status on performance. In F. R. Ferraro (ed.), *Minority and cross-cultural aspects of neuropsychological assessment: Studies on neuropsychology, development, and cognition* (pp. 17–41). Bristol, PA: Swets & Zeltlinger.

Erkinjuntti, T., Sulkava, R., Wikström, J., and Autio, L. (1987). Short portable mental status questionnaire as a screening test for dementia and delirium among the elderly. *Journal of the American Geriatrics Society,* 35, 412–416.

Field, M. J., Jette, A. M., and Martin, L. (2006). *Workshop on disability in America: A new look – summary and background papers.* Washington, DC: The National Academies Press.

Folstein, M. F., Folstein, S. E., and McHugh, P. R. (1975). "Mini-mental state". A practical method for grading the cognitive state of patients for the clinician. *Journal of Psychiatric Research,* 12(3), 189–98.

Giles, L. C., Metcalf, P. A., Glonek, G. F., Luszcz, M. A., and Andrews. G. R. (2004). The effects of social networks on disability in older Australians. *Journal of Aging and Health,* 16, 517–538.

Gill, T. M., Allore, H. B., Hardy, S. E., and Guo, Z. (2006). The dynamic nature of mobility disability in older persons. *Journal of the American Geriatrics Society,* 54, 248–254.

Gill, T. M., Desai, M. M, Gahbauer, E. A., Holford, T. R., and Williams, C. S. (2001). Restricted activity among community-living older persons: Incidence, precipitants, and health care utilization. *Annals of Internal Medicine,* 135, 313–321.

Guralnik, J. M., and Ferrucci, L. (2003). Demography and epidemiology. In W. R. Hazzard, J. P. Blass, J. B. Halter, J. G. Ouslander, and M. E. Tinetti (eds.), *Principles of geriatric medicine and gerontology* (pp. 53–76). New York: McGraw Hill.

Guralnik, J. M., Simonsick, E. M., Ferrucci, L. *et al.* (1994). A short physical performance battery assessing lower extremity function: Association with self-reported disability and prediction of mortality and nursing home admission. *The Journals of Gerontology. Series A, Biological Sciences and Medical Sciences*, 49, M85–M94.

Hardy, S. E., Dubin, J. A., Holford, T. R., and Gill, T. M. (2005). Transitions between states of disability and independence among older persons. *American Journal of Epidemiology*, 161, 575–584.

Hazzard, W. R., Blass, J. P., Halter, J. Ouslander, J., and Tinetti, M. (2003). *Principles of geriatric medicine and gerontology.* New York: McGraw Hill.

Hooyman, N. R., and Kiyak, H. A. (2005). *Social gerontology: A multidisciplinary perspective.* Boston, MA: Pearson Education.

House, J. S., Landis, K. R., and Umberson, D. (1988). Social relationships and health. *Science*, 241, 540–545.

Jette, A. M., Haley, M., Coster, J. *et al.* (2002). Late life function and disability instrument: I. Development and evaluation of the disability component. *The Journals of Gerontology. Series A, Biological Sciences and Medical Sciences*, 57, M209–M216.

Kington, R. S., and Smith, J. P. (1997). Socioeconomic status and racial and ethnic differences in functional status associated with chronic diseases. *American Journal of Public Health*, 87, 805–810.

Kovar M. G. and Lawton, M. P. (1994). Functional disability: Activities and instrumental activities of daily living. *Annual Review of Gerontology and Geriatrics*, 14, 57–75

Lindenberger, U., Mayr, U., and Kliegl, R . (1993). Speed and intelligence in old age. *Psychology and Aging*, 8, 207–220.

Locher, J. L., Ritchie, C. S., Roth, D. L., Baker, P. S., Bodner, E. V., and Allman, R. M. (2005). Social isolation, support, and capital and nutritional risk in an older sample: Ethnic and gender differences. *Social Science and Medicine*, 60, 747–761.

Martin, M. Y., Powell, M. P., Peel, C., Zhu, S., and Allman, R. M. (2006). Leisure-time physical activity and health care utilization in older adults. *Journal of Aging and Physical Activity*, 14, 392–410.

Meenan, R. F., Mason, J. H., Anderson, J. J., Guccione, A. A., and Kazis, L. E. (1992). AIMS2. The content and properties of a revised and expanded arthritis impact measurement scales health status questionnaire. *Arthritis and Rheumatism*, 35, 1–10.

Mendes de Leon, C. F., Gold, D. T., Glass, T. A., Kaplain, L., and George, L. K. (2001). Disability as a function of social networks and support in elderly African Americans and Whites: the Duke EPESE 1986–1992. *The Journals of Gerontology. Series B, Psychological Science and Social Science*, 56, S179–S190.

Metz, D. H. (2000). Mobility of older people and their quality of life. *Transport Policy*, 7, 149–152.

Muldoon, M. F., Barger, S. D., Flory, J. D., and Manuck, S. B. (1998). *British Medical Journal*, 316, 542–545.

Parker, M., Baker, P. S., and Allman, R. M. (2001). A life-space approach to functional assessment of mobility in the elderly. *Journal of Gerontological Social Work*, 35, 35–55.

Patla, A. E., and Shumway-Cook, A. (1999). Dimensions of mobility: Defining the complexity and difficulty associated with community mobility. *Journal of Aging and Physical Activity*, 7–19.

Peel, C., Sawyer-Baker, P., Roth, D. L., Brown, C. J., Bodner, E. V., and Allman, R. M. (2005). Assessing mobility in older adults: The UAB study of aging life-space assessment. *Physical Therapy*, 85, 1008–1019.

Sheikh, J. L., and Yesavage, J. A. (1986). Geriatric depression scales (GDS): Recent evidence and development of a shorter version. *Clinical Gerontologist*, 5, 164–174.

SPSS (2008). *SPSS 16 for windows*. Chicago, IL: SPSS.

Stalvey B.T., Owsley, C., Sloan, M. E., and, Ball, K. (1999). The life space questionnaire: a measure of the extent of mobility of older adults. *Journal of Applied Gerontology*, 18, 460–478.

Stuck, A. E., Walthert, J. M., Nikolaus, T., Bula, C. J., Hohmann, C., and Beck, J. C. (1999). Risk factors for functional status decline in community-living elderly people: A systematic literature review. *Social Science and Medicine*, 48, 445–469.

Taylor, S. J., and Bogdan, R. (1998). *Introduction to qualitative research methods*. Hoboken, NJ: Wiley.

Thoits, P. A. (1995). Stress, coping, and social support processes: Where are we? What next? *Journal of Health and Social Behavior*, Special issue, 53–79.

Whiteneck, G. (2006). Conceptual models of disability: Past, present, and future. In M. J. Field, A. M. Jette and L. Martin (eds.),*Workshop on disability in America: A new look – summary and background papers*. Washington, DC: National Academies Press.

Williams, B. R., Sawyer-Baker, P., Allman, R. M., and Roseman, J. M. (2007). Bereavement among African American and white older adults. *Journal of Aging and Health*, 19, 313–333.

Wolf, D. A., Mendes de Leon, C. F., and Glass, T. A. (2007). Trends in rates of onset of and recovery from disability at older ages: 1982–1994. *The Journals of Gerontology. Series B Psychological Science and Social Science*, 62, S3–S10.

13   Positive aging: resilience and reconstruction

Kenneth J. Gergen and Mary Gergen

Abstract

From a social constructionist perspective, conceptions of aging emerge from participation in relationships. Thus, there is reason to counter the Western stereotype of aging as decline with a more robust and positive vision. In the same way, resilience in everyday life may be achieved by engaging creatively and collaboratively in coordinating the flow of circumstances and interpretations making up daily life. We illustrate the potentials of resilience in terms of collaborative attempts to generate positive reconstructions of what are often defined as debilitating circumstances: reduced income, diminished attractiveness in physical appearance, declining physical and mental abilities, physical handicaps, the "empty nest," the loss of loved ones and approaching death. As we propose, sustaining a resilient orientation requires continuous improvization, as one's life conditions continue to change. By drawing on the resources accumulated over a lifetime, and collaborating with one's contemporaries, culturally defined losses may be reconstructed and a positive confluence re-established.

As we look back at our lives, we both agree that when we were in our twenties and thirties, we had not looked forward to "growing old." We never wanted to be identified as "old folks" and we did not look forward to "retiring." Later we viewed with some distress the emergence of wrinkles and gray hair, and we hoped that every forgotten name was not a sign of dementia. It was not so much the signaling of oncoming death that was important in our age anxiety. Rather, as we have come to see, it is the fact that we would now be burdened with an onerous cluster of self-characterizations: declining, feeble, unproductive, over the hill, finished, powerless, irrelevant, unattractive, and so on. We scarcely feel we are alone in this vision of aging life; indeed, we believe that our anxieties merely reflected our participation in a culture of prejudice-at-large; we were victims of the pervasive American stereotype of aging as the worst period of life one could endure: decline, deficits, disaster, and death. We decided to fight back!

Although we can never scrape away the residues of cultural history, we believe we can generate more promising visions. This is the implication of the social constructionist perspective with which we approach research and practice in the social sciences (K. Gergen, 1994, 2009; K. Gergen and M. Gergen, 2000, 2004). From a constructionist standpoint, descriptions and explanations of the world are not demanded by the nature of the world itself. Rather, it is through the active negotiation and collaboration of people that such understandings are constructed. With regard to the concept of aging, constructionist theses are particularly catalytic. They unsettle the widespread tendency within the social and biological sciences to search for the naturalized life-course, that is, to chart the innate development and decline of human capacities over the lifespan (M. Gergen and K. Gergen, 2005). Rather, from a constructionist perspective, to find someone "old" and biologically or cognitively impaired, constitutes a collaborative accomplishment (Gubrium, Holstein, and Buckholdt, 1994; Hazan, 1994). There is nothing about changes in the human body that requires a concept of aging or of decline. In accord with Michel Foucault (1979), we propose that cultural constraints imposed on older people encourage them to accept themselves as undesirable, and thus delimit their own options for living. As research suggests, when one approaches aging as a burden, the lifespan is substantially shortened (Levy et al., 2002). And it is when we avoid tendencies to naturalize that we begin to appreciate possibilities of a cultural transformation of aging (Gubrium and Holstein, 2003).

From this perspective, the negative definition of aging is neither objective nor immutable. Even the bulk of scientific findings that portray aging as decline are outcomes of a particular research orientation, driven by a value perspective that could be otherwise. If gerontologists view aging as decline, and are motivated "to help," then the search is on to document such decline. And if this is the assiduous aim of research, one may always find such evidence. In this sense, the aging population has been the 'victim of mis-measurement" (Allaire and Marsiske, 2002). Additionally, whether a pattern manifests decline and how significant this decline is are matters of interpretation. Even the way in which science is produced creates the subject under study, in this case, aging. For example, with a large sample size, statistically significant differences do not necessarily mean that there are substantial differences between two groups; for reaction time, the differences could be significant, but very slight indeed (one or two seconds, perhaps), with a high degree of overlap between the two groups. In addition, issues of sample selection, variable naming, context familiarity, and researcher conduct with the participants all play a role in producing results that affirm forms of decline with aging.

In selecting a sample to study, how a researcher chooses participants is critical. Often college students, who are easy to obtain as participants in research, are compared with older people in the population. This biases the results toward those who are already pre-selected for certain desired traits in terms of cognitive abilities, for example. College students are also more familiar with experimental contexts, and they are not overwhelmed with uncertainty when entering into a laboratory or other research settings; older people may have difficulties in accomplishing tasks in a research study in part because of the context in which they are performing. It is quite possible that they have never been in a psychology laboratory before. Last, it is hard to overemphasize the significance of variable naming in interpreting the outcomes of studies. Whether a researcher calls a variable "dementia detector" or "forgetfulness," for example, has consequences for how the research is interpreted. Variables do not "arrive" with names. The manner in which they are named is dependent upon the theoretical preferences of the researchers.

If nothing is demanded in the way we understand our world and self, what alternative can be generated to the common conception of age as decline? For us the answer is a vision of what we call positive aging. Specifically, we hope that our work can contribute to a vision of aging as a period of unparalleled development and enrichment (M. Gergen and K. J. Gergen, 2003). From a constructionist standpoint, the sense of the real and the good emerges from relationship. Thus, to establish an alternative to the traditional view requires a concatenation of voices. One form of giving voice is to develop resources in the media that are addressed to the general public and those who are professionally involved in working with older people. To achieve this end, we created the *Positive Aging Newsletter*, which is sent bimonthly and free of charge over the internet (www.positiveaging.net). The newsletter contains research summaries, news updates, book reviews, and other information and opinions. All the "voices" included in the newsletter challenge the common conceptions of aging as decline, and emphasize the various ways in which we may appreciate, embrace, and enjoy the fruits of this period of life (M. Gergen and K. J. Gergen, 2007). The newsletter goes out free of charge to almost 20,000 subscribers, and has stimulated volunteers to generate versions of the newsletter in French, German, Spanish, Italian and Chinese translations.

The success of the newsletter is, in part, related to the huge shift in the demographic constitution of populations in technologically advanced countries. To varying degrees, and as represented by the "baby boomers" in the USA, people aged over 55 are constituting larger and larger shares of the overall population. Because of changing economic patterns, begun in the 1960s, this group of people is the wealthiest and most educated cadre of older people in the history of the world, and they are challenging the stereotype of negative aging in various ways (Dychwald, 1999). They are eager for the transformation in stereotyping that our newsletter, among many other resources, provides.

In the remainder of this chapter we shall develop the following themes: first, we shall propose a broad conceptual framework for understanding the condition of positive aging. This framework, which emphasizes a *confluence* (or a flowing with) approach to understand change, will enable us to move beyond the traditional accounts of cause and effect that prevail in contemporary explanations of human action. Having established this account of positive aging, as a condition of confluence, we may then move directly to the potentials of the resilience metaphor. As we shall propose, resilience is achieved by engaging creatively in the construction and reconstruction of the confluence in which one lives. We shall illustrate the potentials of resilience in terms of collaborative attempts to generate positive reconstructions of otherwise debilitating circumstances.

Confluence and consequence

Within the Western cultural sphere, we inherit particular traditions of understanding people's actions. Most prominent within the social sciences is the narrative of *cause and effect*. As we understand it, people act in response to forces impinging on them. We believe that people can be "influenced," "educated," "rewarded," "threatened," or "forced" to change their behavior. In the social sciences we observe behavior we call aggressive, altruistic, or delinquent, and we ask how can we bring about more of one and less of another to improve the society. We pose questions such as the following: "What causes these behaviors?" What forces, influences, factors, or life situations bring them about? The question of cause then sets in motion mammoth programs of research. And in the area of gerontology, we conclude from such research that aging brings about changes in mental capacity, that helplessness causes depression, that marital accord increases the lifespan, and so on.

While having a measure of merit, the results of this linear form of explanation can also be paralyzing. We are invited by this tradition to see our actions as effects, the result of causal determinants lying outside our decision-making potentials. To view oneself as a mere effect is demeaning; one's agency is denied. Further, one is informed that there is little that can be done about the circumstances. If aging causes intellectual deficit, then "just get over it." If optimism brings about increased longevity, and one is a pessimist, then so much the worse for you. The dice have been cast.

On philosophical grounds, the presumption of cause and effect has long been criticized. One of these critiques contains the seeds of an alternative and potentially promising form of explanation. Specifically, one cannot define a "cause" without specifying an "effect"; and conversely, there are no "effects" until we can locate a "cause." If I wave my arm, and you point to a neural basis for this action, it is an effect; if you point to another's greeting that follows, then it is a cause. Cause and effect, then, are mutually defining. Now expand the case: you are walking by a park and see a man throw a ball into an open space before him. An aimless activity, you surmise, scarcely notable on a summer's day. Now, consider the same action when the ball is thrown to someone wearing a catcher's mitt. Suddenly the individual's action can be identified as "pitching." In effect, there is no pitching until there is catching, and no catching until there is pitching. The acts are mutually defining or constituting. We look further to see that there is a man with a bat, bags that form a diamond shape, men holding mitts in the field, and so on. At this point we might justifiably conclude that this is a "baseball game." Yet, following the earlier logic, each of these "independent" elements – the man with the bat, the bags, the men in the field – are not truly independent. They are all mutually defining. A man standing alone in the field wearing a mitt would not be playing baseball, nor would the bags constitute a game. Alone they would be virtually without meaning. It is when we bring all these elements into a mutually defining relationship that we can speak about "playing baseball." Let us then speak of the baseball game as a *confluence*, a form of life in this case that is constituted by an array of mutually defining "entities."

We may now apply this form of explanation to the condition of well-being in aging. Consider, for example, some of the familiar "causal agents" typically identified with such a condition: economic support, physical health, and a supportive social network (Argyle, 1999; Diener and Suh, 1999) If we consider them separately, we soon realize they are empty. The possession of money adds nothing to life without options for spending it; physical health owes its value importantly to the fact that there are significant activities in which one can engage; a supportive network of friends means little without the ability to relate with them. Each element within the confluence becomes what it is only in relationship to other elements. One may extend the analysis here by realizing that any "element" may also serve in more than one relationship. Most obviously, the availability of money may usefully contribute to many different conditions of positive confluence, such as living in a nice home, eating well, traveling, going to cultural events, playing golf, giving a gift to a university, supporting one's children, and so on. Similarly, the joy of a good, heart-to-heart conversation is welcomed in many times and places. A good conversation may occur with significant as well as banal activities – entering into a new business partnership, becoming engaged to be married, washing dishes or raking leaves; these conversations can positively transform the activities of which they are a part. A combination of otherwise unremarkable activities may be placed in combination in such a way that the outcome is joyous. A frosty night, a fire burning in the fireplace, a book, and a glass of wine together may bring about a nourishing evening, where none alone would suffice. No single component is sufficient; it is the combination that brings satisfaction. In this sense, aging well is not a matter of understanding cause-and-effect relationships, but recognizing that it is the work of a chef folding together a myriad of different ingredients.

One may inquire at this point into the origins of confluence. How are satisfying forms of confluence brought into existence? Here it is important to return to the social constructionist orientation with which we began. As proposed, all that we take to be real, valuable, rational, or otherwise meaningful owes its origins to a process of relationship. Thus, when we identify "components" of the confluence and their mutually defining potentials we are doing so as participants in a set of relationships. We single out "money" as a component of the confluence by virtue of a tradition of relationship; the value that money acquires in terms helping us "do what we want to do" is again a matter of socially derived definition. A baby has no idea that a dollar bill is a medium of exchange, and not a "chewable."

Positive aging and confluence

The confluence orientation helps us to expand on the vision of positive aging. Essentially, such a condition of life may be viewed as one in which the mutually defining components enable one to participate in a process of continuing enrichment and development. To elaborate and clarify, it may be helpful to sketch out several major proposals that attend this view:

1. From the standpoint of confluence, it first becomes clear that there are no particular features of life that, in themselves, necessarily make a contribution to (or detract from) positive aging. In this sense, factors like health and wealth do not necessarily "determine" one's sense of well-being. Whether an identifiable feature makes a contribution depends on how it is mixed within the existing confluence. Thus, for example,

economic wealth is not required for there to be a positive confluence, although various studies of well-being in old age suggest that it is often a strong contributor (Diener, Diener, and Diener, 1995). Fully enriching lives may be lived with modest financial resources as well. Artists of every age often find a great deal of satisfaction in their lives despite meager incomes. If one is living a life centered around gardening or fishing, a bank account of millions may be far less relevant to one's well-being than the availability of sun, rain, and calm weather.

Generally, research indicates that being of good health is important in order for people to ascribe to themselves many positive attributes and a sense of well-being. Many studies also find that making changes in one's lifestyle, such as quitting smoking, enhances one's health and sense of well-being (Franklin and Tate, 2009). At the same time, people often adjust so completely to changes in their physical health that they no longer focus on the changes in their daily lives. The sympathy people feel for those who are less fortunate than themselves is often misplaced, and this sense of "false empathy" creates a misunderstanding about the nature of any contribution to the confluence related to positive aging.

2. What it means to age positively is both culturally and historically contingent. Different cultures and subcultures may vary significantly in how they define the components of a positive confluence and how they fit with one another. The relational traditions in which one participates lay the groundwork for defining a positive confluence. Ethnic, religious, economic, and political traditions are important forms that may differentiate the ways in which positive aging is defined; it clearly has an impact on national differences in subjective well-being (Diener and Suh, (1999). In some agrarian cultures, having sufficient children to care for one in one's old age is sufficient for positive aging. Having a proper burial site is an important aspect for positive aging among the Balinese. At the same time, that we have lived a life within a set of traditions does not necessarily seal the future. Transformation of cultural traditions is always possible.

3. Because we participate in multiple relations over the course of our lives, we enter the latter third of life possessing enormous resources for achieving a positive confluence. We may not always be aware of these resources; many are latent and many remain untapped. Thus, from various relationships over a lifetime one might come to value religion, rock music, yoga, junk food, fine jewelry, the circus, Picasso, romantic comedies, soccer, friendly arguments, opera, wine, gardening, helping others, political participation, and so on. With strong cultural definitions about the nature of positive aging, and broad social expectancies about behavior "appropriate for the age," many of these resources may either recede

from consciousness or be dismissed as inappropriate. If a condition of positive aging is generally defined as one of peace and tranquility, the pleasures of rock music, competitive athletics, and riding roller coasters may be viewed as relics of a past life. But, of course, for some people, peace and tranquility are not desired endpoints, but distractions from the excitement and challenge that they may wish. In certain respects, the confluence approach to positive aging shares much in common with the convoy model of social support. In this model, the emphasis is on the diverse social relationships that people have over the life-course, and that are more or less influential, depending on other circumstances that are present (Antonucci, Birditt, and Akiyama, 2008).

4. The possibility for being part of a positive confluence is importantly dependent upon one's capacities for improvization. To illustrate, consider a couple who plan a picnic in the countryside. The day is beautiful, and a delicious meal is packed away in a basket. However, while ambling through the countryside, the sky turns gray, and soon they are threatened with rain. Their vision of a beautiful day is now in jeopardy. However, the couple spies a farmer's shed in the distance, and they arrive just as a downpour begins. Undaunted, they lay out their picnic on the floor of the shed, and as they listen to the rain overhead and enjoy what now seems a veritable banquet, they laugh and congratulate themselves on the success they have made of the day. This is the art of improvization, and, in our view, one that is essential in sustaining a condition of positive aging. Thus, one may inherit from longstanding traditions many resources for achieving a positive confluence. However, the match between traditional conceptions and the vicissitudes of everyday life is highly variable. There are deaths, divorces, births, marriages, accidents, volatile trends in economic conditions, changes in one's neighborhood, challenges to one's health, and so on. To sustain a condition of positive aging in a constantly changing ocean of contingencies requires imagination and innovation.

Resilience, reconstruction, and relationship

With the confluence orientation in place, we may explore the significant potentials of the resilience metaphor. Longstanding traditions of meaning-making provide the resources enabling people to create the sense of well-being in aging. However, it is the capacity to improvise that enables such patterns to be continuously reshaped as conditions of living change across time. At least one major threat to this process of reconstruction derives from what might be called "the concretization of the real." It is here that the traditions of what constitutes "the good life" are so fully solidified that the process of improvization is impeded. "Saving for retirement" is the most obvious example. We tend to view a certain level of retirement income as essential for positive aging. However, whether one's savings match the constantly changing conditions of the economy is variable. Due to shifts in the stock market, costs of living, or health care costs, one's savings may or may not be sufficient to maintain a condition that one continues to define as positive. Losses in physical health, close relationships, memory, and secure housing are also common challenges to the ease with which one may be resilient.

It is at this point that the reshaping of the confluence is required. One must be able to resist the traditional concretization of the good, and to generate alternatives that may restore the condition of positive aging. Herein lies the potential for revitalizing the confluence. There are not only the many and varied forms of fulfillment that we have known over a lifetime, but as well the many models to which we have been exposed. However, from a constructionist standpoint the greatest resource for resilience lies in the reconstructive potentials of dialogue. As we talk with one another, we share resources, make salient, long-forgotten resources, and garner support for wholly new amalgams. This strategy has gained importance in the last years as the market value of pensions and savings for retirement has dropped significantly.

The two of us have given many workshops on positive aging. To explore the potential contribution of dialogue to resilience, we have given small groups of participants the challenging task of locating or creating ways in which events that are commonly construed as age-related losses may be reconstructed. Among the topics these groups have been asked to address are declines in physical and mental abilities, chronic illnesses, retirement, lowered sexual interest, loss of income, diminished attractiveness in physical appearance, relocation, the empty nest, loss of friends or family through distance or death, and the increased proximity to personal death. In each case we have challenged the groups to locate the positive potentials of these events; we ask them: "Are there ways in which these conditions may be reconstructed in such a way that a sense of well-being may be restored?" We recognize that these are grave threats in many instances, and that this is no simple task for the groups to handle.

Yet we have been consistently amazed at the diversity of creative and emotionally stirring possibilities that emerge from these groups. As a preliminary example, the following is an extended account of how one participant narrated the onset of a chronic illness, namely diabetes:

At first I was shocked and dismayed that I had been diagnosed with Type II diabetes, at age 60, much as my mother had a few years before at 85. It shook my sense of who I was and created for me a vision my future – deprived for the rest of my life of the sweets and breads and wine that I loved. I was well-known for my famous vodka crust pies and my biscotti, and here I was sentenced to a life of deprivation and denial. So with a heavy heart, I went on a low carb diet; much to my surprise and pleasure, I lost about 20 pounds of fat I had accumulated over the previous 20 years. For the first time in many years, I was enjoying wearing size 6 clothes, and I began to revel in my new body, my new fashions. I even went to an exclusive hairdresser and acquired a new hairdo, replacing the salt-and-pepper hair for a layered blond look. The need for exercise was paramount, and my daily exercise regime became an invigorating and relaxing time of day for me, especially because I had the chance to listen to my favorite music on my i-pod while I was on the treadmill. Another thing I began to enjoy was taking my neighbor's dog for daily walks. It turned out that I was an incredibly skilled dog trainer, and I reveled in the tricks my Maxwell learned, as I plied him with "yummies." During the walks with Max, I met a lot of other dog owners, and made new friends. One of them offered me her summer place at the shore where I could go to birdwatch, another of my hobbies that I had neglected over the years. Finally, I became closer to my mother. We support each other, and keep each other on track in our testing, eating and taking pills. We are closer than we have been in a very long time. And it turns out that I can still drink wine, and treat myself to the occasional biscotti. My friends still love my pies.

In the sections below, we share in brief form some of the major pathways to resilience as developed within these groups.

Reduced income

Retirement typically brings less income, and one's savings may often dwindle as a result of inflation, stark market losses, and unanticipated crises in health or family matters. On one's own it is often difficult to reconstruct one's condition in such a way that it is positive in tenor. However, within the group situation numerous routes to resilience were generated. Among the prominent reconstructions:

1. More creativity and ingenuity are demanded, so that one can have the same pleasures at reduced cost. One can take pride in finding money saving ways to enjoy life.
2. Money does not buy happiness. The greatest rewards of life are found in relationships. The loss of income re-focuses one's life on what really matters.
3. Money brought with it a materialistic attitude toward life. Too many hours were absorbed with "getting and spending," as the poet said. Now there is openness to appreciating nature, music, art, and a spiritual life.
4. Without money we are not away from home so often. This gives us more quality time at home, in our neighborhood, and community.

5. Without a job, one can begin to remember other options in terms of career. The job one had was not necessarily the job one wanted. With some additional schooling, a new work life could be envisioned. Volunteering may be the avenue to a new work life.
6. Life becomes simpler, and there is a new tranquility.

Diminished attractiveness in physical appearance

Many people are troubled by the deterioration in their appearance with age. They feel young at heart and mind, but their bodily appearance seems to be dragging them into old age. One research study indicated that, on average, people aged from 70 to 104 years felt about 13 years younger than they were, regardless of age, but when they looked in the mirror, they reduced the discrepancy to 10. Women, particularly, were less satisfied with their mirror images than men (Kleinspehn-Ammerlahn, Kitter-Gruhn, and Smith, 2008). For many this means a loss in self-esteem, and a diminution in their aspirations for a social life. At least one result is the massive investment in plastic surgery and anti-aging pharmaceuticals. In Phoenix, Arizona, for example, a participant in our workshop said: "It's not a matter of 'if' one has plastic surgery, but when."

However, besides the option of "fighting it," people may generate other routes to resilience:

1. One need not accept the definition of "good appearance" with being young. Change is not deterioration. It is a new look.
2. A new definition of beauty may be developed. As many participants noted, they are no longer drawn by youthful beauty. It is often associated with naiveté and narcissism. Rather, they are far more compelled by their older peers, whose appearance suggests sophistication and a deeper wisdom about relationships. As some participants proposed, there are new standards of beauty now being developed by the media. They portray gray hair, for example, as lovely and sexy. Others reject the idea of beauty as an external appearance. As one participant put it: "We must nurture the beauty within, and that will resonate with those who are willing to discover it."
3. The meaning of an aging appearance may also be transformed. As one participant voiced: "I think we should be proud of how we look. Honor our wrinkles. We lived a long time to get them."
4. One may also find relief from the demands of appearance. As one participant put it: "For me it is rather a relief not to have to pay so much attention to how I look. It can take a lot of time and money to look great."

Declining physical and mental abilities

With increasing age, many people experience losses in various physical capacities (memory, dexterity, energy level, strength, etc.). These changes are often a matter of quiet frustration, and anxiety about the future. Within the group situation there are major resources for resilience:

1. We do not have to define these changes in ability as "losses." Over the lifetime we are always changing, and this is natural. We don't have to define some changes as gains and others as losses. Who has the right to impose such judgments?
2. We age within friendship and family groups, where everyone is changing. When we all share in the changes, we don't really pay attention to them. We may feel we suffer memory loss. But in a group of elderly people, we laugh about memory loss.
3. There is a challenge here to do more in the way of physical and mental exercise. We can renew our vigor, improve our stamina, and be proud of what we have achieved.
4. There is pleasure to be taken in being a "couch potato." As one participant in our workshops said: "After a life time of worrying about keeping myself fit for the job, and all the other responsibilities I have, it is a relief to relinquish the demands of being perfect."
5. Such losses are often minor, and rather than fretting over them, we are invited to see the broader perspective on life. Who cares if one can't recall every name, or read as fast, when there are such major challenges in the world in such matters as environment, religious conflict, and starvation?
6. The loss of physical abilities, they point out, can give rise to more frequent moments of tranquility, to a greater sense of personal skill as one finds ways to compensate for the deficit, and to the development of new and engaging hobbies or interests to replace the old.

Physical handicaps

In its extreme form, the loss of ability becomes a physical handicap – for example, an inability to hear, to see, or to walk. There is abundant evidence suggesting that once people get over the shock and dismay of having a physical limitation, for example, breaking one's neck and being unable to walk, they begin to focus their attentions on other matters. Thus, six months after sustaining a serious and perhaps permanent disability, their feelings of well-being are not so dissimilar to those who do not have such disabilities. Whether they are feeling up or down about the weather, their love lives, financial status, work, recreational activities, and so on, they are much like anyone else (Janoff-Bulman, 1992). At the same time, many of the forms of resilience generated in the case of diminished abilities are also found in groups discussing physical handicaps.

Some of our respondents found positive alternatives in physical handicaps:

1. There is a certain freedom from demands, and a new sense of tranquility that can often be found. A patient in a social services group in Sweden rejected further therapeutic aid, saying that he enjoyed being lazy and that a therapeutic obligation could interfere with his desire not to become a productive worker in his old age. (See Håkansson, 2009, for a further description of this case.)
2. One can become heroic in bearing up under the limitations of a physical handicap. That is, the handicap becomes an invitation to achieve at an outstanding level. Such narratives have long served as a cultural resource, from Demosthenes to Lance Armstrong. (Demosthenes suffered from a speech defect, and went on to become a significant orator in ancient Greece, and Lance Armstrong, a cancer survivor, became the famous cyclist who won the Tour de France.)
3. Emphasizing the significance of relationships in generating resilience: there are increasing numbers of organizations in society that attempt to redefine handicaps in other than terms of loss. For example, organizations of the deaf, the blind, and the autistic define such conditions simply as differences as opposed to deficits. And, as they explore, there are many ways in which such conditions are superior to "the normal." The people identified as part of the "Deaf Culture" consider their language and communication skills as superior to hearing people's abilities in many ways.
4. Work to recreate the community and society more generally so as to accommodate physical changes. In general, within the past 20 years, as a result of the national Disabilities Act, all communities and institutions are required to accommodate wheelchairs in terms of access and the use of all facilities. David Myers, a psychologist from the University of Michigan, has become highly involved in changing the sound systems in airports and public buildings, especially concert halls, to accommodate hearing deficits (Myers, 2000). He, himself, is nearly deaf. With changes in the public sphere, so-called deficits are erased in terms of many functions.

The "empty nest"

One of the most overwrought myths in the past 30 years, when the size of families has shrunk, is that "Mother" will become devastated and bereft after her children have flown the coop, and nested elsewhere. Although it is the case that losing one's functional value is a threat, the prevalence of women in the workplace has allowed the parenting function to lose its singular status as the most significant role in most women's lives. A few of the comments:

1. Given how busy life is anyway, having less housework and upkeep for children is a benefit not a curse.
2. Children are most loveable when they are no longer as dependent upon parents for sustenance and discipline.
3. Children actually don't leave home. They rely on it, either in theory or in fact, and the problem then is how to make room for them on re-entry. A very different relationship has to be developed so that tensions do not erupt when old patterns arise.
4. The empty nest allows for the "love birds" to reconnect. This later notion has been substantiated by research on the positive impact of the "empty nest" on marriage (Gorchoff, John, and Helson, 2008).

Approaching death

Death would appear to be a reality that resists reconstruction. Yet, when we take into account the views of death widely shared within various religions of the world, we do realize that death is not death is not death. We begin to see that the biological construction of death is only one, and to accept this definition is to strip the period of old age of its potentials. The loss of significant others is an increasingly frequent occurrence as people age. Studies of widowhood suggest that there are many ways of dealing with such losses, and no one developmental course is applicable. People do not necessarily adjust to their losses by giving up their bonds, but rather often seek to maintain their relationship to the dead person through "conversations" and other activities that are shaped by the preferences of the deceased spouse. Beyond simply coping and finding a way back to "normal," Wortman and Silver (1993) suggest that bereavement can be an opportunity for growth and development. Widows, for example, often report that they have acquired new skills and are more competent in dealing in the world after the loss of their husbands. There are many cases in which the death of a spouse may bring a sense of relief.

There is an old Italian saying: "Every woman deserves to be a widow for five years," suggesting that married life is a sacrifice for a woman. We share only a few of the resources for resilience developed by our groups:

1. There are good philosophic approaches to death, some from religion, others that view death as a normal part of the adventure of living. As one said: "Death can be the final adventure."
2. Death is a transition from a "vale of tears" to a place on unending joy. Life is just a brief interlude from eternity.
3. Most common is the view that awareness of death invites a deeper appreciation of day-to-day life. One pays more attention to the small details, sights, sounds, smells. One appreciates more fully one's friends and loved ones.
4. Death can be a peaceful event at the proper time; one may even prepare for it as one might write the final chapter of one's life story.
5. We live beyond death through our legacy with our children and our good deeds.
6. Without death, life would go on and on in a formless state. One needs the exclamation point of death.

As a general surmise, it may be concluded that when asking the right question, people can locate means of transforming otherwise dire circumstances into acceptable, nourishing, and even joyful alternatives. The most important wisdom for growing old well may lie in the art of joining with others in posing positive questions (Adams, 2004; M. Gergen and K. Gergen, 2006).

For some people there are limits to achieving resilience, especially when the loss is new. To be sure, with time many happily married people who are widowed find another partner, in some sense, in order to continue the lifestyle they once had. Often, when long caretaking has occurred, one may be glad for an end to overwhelming demands and responsibilities. The release of a loved one from suffering is also regarded as a blessing. In many circumstances, however, people gain resilience by integrating the remnants of the terminated relationship into their continuing activities (Hedtke and Winslade, 2004; Stroebe *et al.*, 1992).

Conclusion

In one sense the major message of this chapter adds new dimension to the old adage that aging is what we make it. As proposed, whatever happens to the body and to our behavior patterns over time has no intrinsic meaning; there is no condition that is necessarily good or bad. Whatever the meaning of our condition of life, it is generated within our relationships.

Within Western culture, there has been a strong tendency to view the latter third of life as one of necessary decline. As we propose, however, these same traditions can be mined for concepts and values that can transform the conception of aging. More specifically, with continuous construction and reconstruction of one's conditions, the latter years may become the most developmentally enriching period of life. To sustain this condition requires continuous improvization, as one's life conditions continue to change. There are numerous culturally defined losses that attend the aging process. At the same time, by drawing on the resources accumulated over the lifespan, and collaborating with one's cohort, these age-associated losses may be reconstructed and a positive confluence re-established. Herein lies a major route to resilience.

REFERENCES

Adams, M. (2004). *Change your questions: Change your life.* San Francisco, CA: Berrett-Koehler.

Allaire, J. C., and Marsiske, M. (2002). Well- and ill-defined measures of everyday cognition: Relationship to older adults' intellectual ability and functional status. *Psychology and Aging*, 17, 101–115.

Antonucci, T., Birditt, K. S, and Akiyama, H. (2008). Convoys of social relations: An interdisciplinary approach. In V. Bengston, M. Silverstein, N. Putney, and D. Gans, (eds.), *Handbook of theories of aging* (pp. 247–260). New York: Springer.

Argyle, M. (1999). Causes and correlate of happiness. In D. Kahneman, E. Diener, and N. Schwarz (eds.), *Well-being: The foundations of hedonic psychology* (pp. 353–373). New York: Russell Sage Foundation.

Diener, E., Diener, M., and Diener, C. (1995). Factors predicting the subjective wellbeing of nations. *Journal of Personality and Social Psychology*, 69, 851–864.

Diener, E., and Suh. E. (1999). National differences in subjective well-being. In D. Kahneman, E. Diener, and N. Schwarz (eds.), *Well-being: The foundations of hedonic psychology* (pp. 434–450). New York: Russell Sage Foundation.

Dychwald, K. (1999). *Age power: How the 21st century will be ruled by the new old.* New York: Penguin.

Foucault, M. (1979). *Discipline and punish: The birth of the prison.* New York: Random House.

Franklin, N. C., and Tate, C. A. (2009). Lifestyle and successful aging: An overview. *American Journal of Lifestyle Medicine*, 3, 6–11.

Gergen, K. J. (1994). *Realities and relationships.* Cambridge, MA: Harvard University Press.

(2009). *Relational being: Beyond self and community.* New York: Oxford University Press.

Gergen, K. J., and Gergen, M. (2000). The new aging: Self construction and social values. In K. W. Schaie (ed.), *Social structures and aging* (pp. 281–306). New York: Springer.

(2004). *Social construction: Entering the dialogue.* Chagrin Falls, OH: Taos Institute Publications.

Gergen, M., and Gergen, K. J. (2003). Positive aging: Living well as the best revenge. In J. Gubrium and J. Holstein (eds.), *Ways of aging* (pp. 203–224). New York: Blackwell.

(2005). Positive aging: Reconstructing the life course. In C. Goodheart and J. Worell (eds.), *Handbook of women and girls* (pp. 46–426). New York: Oxford University Press.

(2006). The prophetic power of positive questions. *The Career Planning and Adult Development Journal,* 22, 7–15.

(2007). Collaboration without end: The case of the Positive Aging Newsletter. In D. Gerhart and H. Anderson (eds.), *Collaborative therapy: Relationships and conversations that make a difference* (pp. 379–401). New York: Routledge.

Gorchoff, S. M., John, O. P, and Helson, R. (2008). Contextualizing change in marital satisfaction during middle age. *Psychological Science,* 19, 1194–2000.

Gubrium, J., and Holstein, J. (eds.) (2003). *Ways of aging.* New York: Blackwell.

Gubrium, J., Holstein, J. A, and Buckholdt, D. (1994). *Constructing the life course.* Dix Hills, NY: General Hall.

Håkansson, C. (2009). *Ordinary life therapy: Experiences from a systemic collaborative practice.* Chagrin Falls, OH: Taos Institute Publications.

Hazan, H. (1994). *Old age: Constructions and deconstructions.* Cambridge: Cambridge University Press.

Hedtke, L., and Winslade, J. (2004). *Remembering lives: Conversations with the dying and the bereaved.* Amityville, NY: Baywood Publishing.

Janoff-Bulman, R. (1992). *Shattered assumptions: Towards a new psychology of trauma.* New York: Free Press.

Kleinspehn-Ammerlahn, A., Kitter-Gruhn, D., and Smith, J. (2008). Self-perceptions of aging: Do subjective age and satisfaction with aging change during old age? *The Journals of Gerontology: Psychological Sciences,* 63B, P377–P385.

Levy, B. R., Slade, M. D., Kunkel, S. R, and Kasl, S. V. (2002). Longevity increased by positive self-perceptions of aging. *Journal of Personality and Social Psychology,* 83, 261–270.

Myers, D. (2000). *A quiet world: Living with hearing loss.* New Haven, CT: Yale University Press.

Stroebe, M., Gergen, K. J., Gergen, M., and Stroebe, W. (1992). Broken hearts or broken bonds: Love and death in historical perspective, *American Psychologist,* 47, 1205–1212.

Wortman, C., and Silver, R. (1993). Successful mastery of bereavement and widowhood: A life-course perspective. In P. Baltes and M. Baltes (eds.), *Successful aging: Perspectives from the behavioral sciences* (pp. 225–260). Cambridge: Cambridge University Press.

Index

Lightning Source UK Ltd.
Milton Keynes UK
UKOW05f2143260217

295343UK00022B/1301/P